"'R. C. Sproul,' someone said to me in the 1970s, 'is the finest communicator in the Reformed world.' Now, three decades later, his skills honed by long practice, his understanding deepened by years of prayer, meditation, and testing (as Martin Luther counseled), R. C. shares the fruit of what has become perhaps his greatest love: feeding and nourishing his own congregation at St. Andrew's from the Word of God and building them up in faith and fellowship and in Christian living and serving. The St. Andrew's Expositional Commentary will be welcomed throughout the world. It promises to have all R. C.'s hallmarks: clarity and liveliness, humor and pathos, always expressed in application to the mind, will, and affections. R. C.'s ability to focus on 'the big picture,' his genius of never saying too much, leaving his hearers satisfied yet wanting more, never making the Word dull, are all present in these expositions. They are his gift to the wider church. May they nourish God's people well and serve as models of the kind of ministry for which we continue to hunger."
—Sinclair B. Ferguson, Ligonier Ministries Teaching Fellow, Carnoustie, Scotland

"R. C. Sproul, well-known as a master theologian and extraordinary communicator, now shows that he is a powerful, insightful, helpful expository preacher. This collection of sermons is of great value for churches and Christians everywhere."
—W. Robert Godfrey, President, Westminster Seminary California

"I tell my students again and again, 'You need to buy good commentaries and do so with some discernment.' Among them there must be preacher's commentaries, for not all commentaries are the same. Some may tell you what the text means but provide little help in answering the question, 'How do I preach this text?' R. C. Sproul is a legend in our time. His preaching has held us in awe for half a century, and these pages represent the fruit of his latest exposition, coming as they do at the very peak of his abilities and insights. I am ecstatic at the prospect of reading the St. Andrew's Expositional Commentary series. It represents Reformed theology on fire, delivered from a pastor's heart in a vibrant congregation of our time. Essential reading."
—Derek W. H. Thomas, Senior Minister, First Presbyterian Church, Columbia, South Carolina

"R. C. Sproul is the premier theologian of our day, an extraordinary instrument in the hand of the Lord. Possessed with penetrating insight into the text of Scripture, Dr. Sproul is a gifted expositor and world-class teacher, endowed with a strategic grasp and command of the inspired Word. Since stepping into the pulpit of St. Andrew's and committing himself to the weekly discipline of biblical exposition, this noted preacher has demonstrated a rare ability to explicate and apply God's Word. I wholeheartedly recommend the St. Andrew's Expositional Commentary to all who long to know the truth better and experience it more deeply in a life-changing fashion. Here is an indispensable tool for digging deeper into God's Word. This is a must-read for every Christian."
—Steven J. Lawson, Founder and President, OnePassion Ministries, Dallas

"How exciting! Thousands of us have long been indebted to R. C. Sproul the teacher, and now, through the St. Andrew's Expositional Commentary, we are indebted to Sproul the preacher, whose sermons are thoroughly biblical, soundly doctrinal, warmly practical, and wonderfully readable. Sproul masterfully presents us with the 'big picture' of each pericope in a dignified yet conversational style that accentuates the glory of God and meets the real needs of sinful people like us. This series of volumes is an absolute must for every Reformed preacher and church member who yearns to grow in the grace and knowledge of Christ Jesus. I predict that Sproul's pulpit ministry in written form will do for Christians in the twenty-first century what Martyn Lloyd-Jones's sermonic commentaries did for us last century. *Tolle lege*, and buy these volumes for your friends."
—Joel R. Beeke, President, Puritan Reformed Theological Seminary, Grand Rapids, Michigan

ST. ANDREW'S EXPOSITIONAL COMMENTARY

JOHN

ST. ANDREW'S EXPOSITIONAL COMMENTARY

JOHN

R. C. SPROUL

ℝℝ *Reformation Trust*   A DIVISION OF LIGONIER MINISTRIES, ORLANDO, FL

John

© 2009 by R. C. Sproul

Published by Reformation Trust Publishing
A division of Ligonier Ministries
421 Ligonier Court, Sanford, FL 32771
Ligonier.org   ReformationTrust.com

Printed in Ann Arbor, Michigan
Sheridan Books, Inc.
September 2016
First edition, sixth printing

Cover design: Geoff Stevens
Interior design and typeset: Katherine Lloyd, The DESK

Unless otherwise indicated, all Scripture references are from the *New King James
Version*`. Copyright © 1982 by Thomas Nelson. Used by permission. All rights reserved.

Scripture references marked NIV are from the *Holy Bible, New International Version*`.
NIV`. Copyright © 1973, 1978, 1984 by Biblica, Inc.™. Used by permission of Zondervan.
All rights reserved worldwide. www.Zondervan.com

The "NIV" and "New International Version" trademarks are registered in the United
States Patent and Trademark Office by Biblica, Inc. Use of either trademark requires
the permission of Biblica, Inc.

Scripture quotations are from the ESV® Bible (The Holy Bible, English Standard
Version®), copyright © 2001 by Crossway, a publishing ministry of Good News
Publishers. Used by permission. All rights reserved.

All emphases in Scripture quotations have been added by the author.

Library of Congress Cataloging-in-Publication Data
Sproul, R. C. (Robert Charles), 1939-
John / R.C. Sproul.
    p. cm. -- (St. Andrew's expositional commentary)
    Includes bibliographical references and index.
    ISBN 978-1-56769-185-6
    1. Bible. N.T. John--Commentaries. I. Title.
    BS2615.53.S67 2009
    226.5'077--dc22
                            2009033886

To Sherrie,
A godly daughter who continues to
faithfully serve God and His kingdom.

CONTENTS

SERIES PREFACE

When God called me into full-time Christian ministry, he called me to the academy. I was trained and ordained to a ministry of teaching, and the majority of my adult life has been devoted to preparing young men for the Christian ministry and to trying to bridge the gap between seminary and Sunday school through various means under the aegis of Ligonier Ministries.

Then, in 1997, God did something I never anticipated: he placed me in the position of preaching weekly as a leader of a congregation of his people—St. Andrew's in Sanford, Florida. Over the past twelve years, as I have opened the Word of God on a weekly basis for these dear saints, I have come to love the task of the local minister. Though my role as a teacher continues, I am eternally grateful to God that he saw fit to place me in this new ministry, the ministry of a preacher.

Very early in my tenure with St. Andrew's, I determined that I should adopt the ancient Christian practice of *lectio continua*, "continuous expositions," in my preaching. This method of preaching verse-by-verse through books of the Bible (rather than choosing a new topic each week) has been attested throughout church history as the one approach that ensures believers hear the full counsel of God. Therefore, I began preaching lengthy series of messages at St. Andrew's, eventually working my way through several biblical books in a practice that continues to the present day.

Previously, I had taught through books of the Bible in various settings, including Sunday school classes, Bible studies, and audio and video teaching series for Ligonier Ministries. But now I found myself appealing not so much to the minds of my hearers as to both their minds and their hearts. I knew that I was responsible as a preacher to clearly explain God's Word *and* to show how we ought to live in light of it. I sought to fulfill both tasks as I ascended the St. Andrew's pulpit each week.

What you hold in your hand, then, is a written record of my preaching labors amid my beloved Sanford congregation. The dear saints who sit under my preaching encouraged me to give my sermons a broader hearing. To that end, the chapters that follow were adapted from a sermon series I preached at St. Andrew's.

Please be aware that this book is part of a broader series of books containing adaptations of my St. Andrew's sermons. The title of this series is *St. Andrew's Expositional Commentary*. As you can see, this is more than a convenient title—it is a description. This book, like all the others in the series, will *not* give you the fullest possible insight into each and every verse in this biblical book. Though I sought to at least touch on each verse, I focused on the key themes and ideas that comprised the "big picture" of each passage I covered. Therefore, I urge you to use this book as an overview and introduction, but if you desire to enhance your knowledge of this book of Scripture, you should turn to one or more of the many excellent exegetical commentaries (see my recommendations in the back).

I pray that you will be as blessed in reading this material as I was in preaching it.

—R. C. Sproul
Lake Mary, Florida
April 2009

PREFACE

When I was a sophomore in college, I signed up to take a course on the Gospel of John. Just before that course started, the professor who was to teach it became very ill and was forced to undergo major surgery. To replace him for that semester, the college summoned a man who was internationally known for his theological contributions. He was in his late eighties, but he came out of retirement to teach this course. Because I was receiving instruction from this man of international acclaim, at the end of that course I thought I knew everything there was to know about the Gospel of John.

Also while I was in college, when I took Greek, we translated from the Gospel of John for three years. Then I went to seminary and took three more years of Greek, and we translated the entire Gospel of John once more. So when I finished those courses, I was confident that I had a pretty good sense both of what was in the book and John's intended meaning.

However, when I spent nearly two years preaching through the Gospel of John from the pulpit of St. Andrew's in Sanford, Florida, I discovered that I knew nothing about this Gospel. I learned that until you begin to dig into a book for the purpose of preaching it each week, you don't really know it.

It is customary in New Testament studies to distinguish between the Gospel of John and the other three Gospels. The books of Matthew, Mark, and Luke are called the Synoptic Gospels for the simple reason that they give us synopses of the life of Jesus—overviews of His ministry on this earth. It's not as if John was not interested in giving us biographical details about the life of Jesus and samples of His teaching, but he proceeded in quite a different style. His is the most theological of the four Gospels in the New Testament, and he devoted almost two-thirds of his written account to the last week of Jesus' life. John, as it were, wanted to put a spotlight on the critically important redemptive-historical activity that Jesus performed during His stay on earth.

This means we find many unique features in John's Gospel that do not appear in the other records of Jesus' life. For instance, John's Gospel gives us the most extensive revelation from the lips of Jesus of the person and work of the Holy Spirit, the third person of the Trinity, information that is found in the upper room discourse that took place on Maundy Thursday, the day before Jesus' crucifixion.

It is my hope that as you read through the chapters of this book, which were adapted from my sermons at St. Andrew's, that you will discover the treasures of the Gospel of John as never before, just as I did. However, I am not referring here to mere facts about Palestine, about the Jews, or even about Jesus himself. My prayer is that you will grow in your knowledge of—and love for—the supreme treasure, Jesus the Redeemer, the One whom John the Baptist hailed as "The Lamb of God who takes away the sin of the world!" (1:29b).

1

THE PROLOGUE

John 1:1–18

In the beginning was the Word, and the Word was with God, and the Word was God. He was in the beginning with God. All things were made through Him, and without Him nothing was made that was made. In Him was life, and the life was the light of men. And the light shines in the darkness, and the darkness did not comprehend it. There was a man sent from God, whose name was John. This man came for a witness, to bear witness of the Light, that all through him might believe. He was not that Light, but was sent to bear witness of that Light. That was the true Light which gives light to every man coming into the world. He was in the world, and the world was made through Him, and the world did not know Him. He came to His own, and His own did not receive Him. But as many as received Him, to them He gave the right to become children of God, to those who believe in His name: who were born, not of blood, nor of the will of the flesh, nor of the will of man, but of God. And the Word became flesh and dwelt among us, and we beheld His glory, the glory as of the only begotten of the Father, full of grace and truth. John bore witness of Him and cried out, saying, "This was He of whom I said, 'He who comes after me is preferred before me, for He was before me.'" And of His fullness we have all received, and grace for grace. For the law

1

was given through Moses, but grace and truth came through Jesus Christ. No one has seen God at any time. The only begotten Son, who is in the bosom of the Father, He has declared Him.

The first eighteen verses of John's Gospel are commonly known as the prologue. No portion of the New Testament captured the imagination and the attention of the Christian intellectual community for the first three centuries more than this brief section of John's Gospel. In attempting to understand the person of Christ, the early church became virtually preoccupied with the high view of Christ that is expressed in the prologue. From this foundation, those early believers developed what was called the "*Logos* Christology*," or the understanding of Christ as **the Word**, who is introduced here in the opening words of John's Gospel.

We have to ask: Why does John begin his Gospel with this prologue? Why doesn't he simply start as Matthew and Luke do, by telling us about the circumstances of the conception of Jesus and His birth to a peasant girl? In a strikingly different approach, John begins his Gospel with Jesus already as an adult. The only material that precedes the launch of Jesus' ministry is this prologue of eighteen verses.

I believe the inclusion of the prologue has to do with John's overriding goal, throughout his Gospel, of making a case for the identity of Christ. John says later that he wrote what he did "that you may believe that Jesus is the Christ, the Son of God, and that believing you may have life in His name" (20:31). Simply put, John is not interested in being a detached observer and chronicler of the life of Jesus. He is trying to persuade his readers of the truth of Christ so that they might become His disciples. Therefore, before he enters into an overview of Jesus' life and ministry, he composes a quick look at Jesus' ultimate credentials.

In the prologue, John answers one of the main questions that we often ask when we meet people for the first time. We ask such questions as, "What's your name?" and "What do you do?" And, of course, we love to ask, "Where are you from?" Here in his prologue, John answers this question with respect to Jesus. John tells us where Jesus was from.

The New Testament uses many titles for Jesus. The one that occurs most frequently is *Christos*, or "Christ," which is the New Testament word for "Messiah." It is used so often that many people assume that it is Jesus' last name, that He is *named* Jesus Christ. Actually, His name is Jesus, but His title is Christ. Thus, "Jesus Christ" is an affirmation that Jesus is the Messiah. The

second-most-frequent title given to Jesus is "Lord," and this title is at the heart
of the earliest Christian creed: "Jesus is Lord." The next-most-used title, far
behind "Christ" and "Lord" in terms of its frequency of appearance in the
New Testament, is "Son of Man." This title is used roughly eighty times in
the New Testament, but even though it comes in third in usage by those who
wrote about Jesus, it was far and away Jesus' favorite self-designation. If we
were to ask Jesus, "Who are you?" He most likely would answer, "I am the
Son of Man."

When we hear Jesus call Himself the "Son of Man," we tend to see it as an
expression of His humility, for we understand Him to be identifying with our
humanity. This title does involve Jesus' identification and corporate solidarity
with our humanity, but that is not its primary emphasis. When Jesus called
Himself the Son of Man in front of Jewish people of the first century, they
understood that He was identifying Himself with that person who was defined
and described in the Old Testament book of Daniel as a heavenly being who
comes from the very throne of God on a mission to judge the world (Dan.
7:13ff.). So when Jesus called Himself the Son of Man, He was describing
Himself not only in terms of His activity but of His origin. He was telling
His hearers where He had come from.

Sometimes Jesus stated His origins very explicitly. For instance, He said on
one occasion, "I have come down from heaven, not to do My own will, but
the will of Him who sent Me" (John 6:38). Likewise, in a discussion about the
Jewish patriarch Abraham, Jesus said, "Most assuredly, I say to you, before
Abraham was, I AM." (John 8:58). The Jews immediately picked up stones to
put him to death because they understood His message—Jesus was equating
Himself with God, who had revealed Himself to Moses as "I AM WHO I
AM" (Ex. 3:14). Again, when He told a paralyzed man that his sins were
forgiven, He then healed the man so that, in His words, those who were there
would "know that the Son of Man has power on earth to forgive sins" (Matt.
9:6). These were not statements of humility. These were statements by which
Jesus openly declared that He had come from heaven. John's prologue was
intended to accomplish much the same goal—before John gave us his record
of the earthly visitation of Jesus, he told us where Jesus was from.

An Echo of Genesis

John begins by declaring that the Word was **in the beginning**, **was with
God**, and **was God** (v. 1). Here John echoes the opening words of the Old
Testament: "In the beginning God created the heavens and the earth." This
sentence in and of itself was enough to keep theologians busy for hundreds

of years because, on the one hand, the Word (Jesus) is distinguished *from* God, but from a different perspective, the Word is identified *with* God. This sentence, more than any other passage in Scripture, is foundational for the church's confession of the doctrine of the Trinity, the belief that God is one in three persons.

John goes on to write that **all things were made through Him** (v. 3). Jesus is now identified as the incarnation of that member of the Trinity for whom, by whom, and in whom all things were made. In this extraordinary statement, John says: "The One I'm going to tell you about, the One in whom there is life, the One in whom I want you to believe, is the One who created you in the first place. Nothing was made apart from Him."

As we make our way through John's Gospel, we will see two words appear again and again. Those words are *life* and *light*, and we encounter them here in the prologue. John says **in Him was life, and the life was the light of men** (v. 4). The Scriptures often use the antonyms of these words to describe the natural fallen condition of this world, speaking of it in terms of *death* and *darkness*. Recently, when I read this verse, which I have read countless times before, I was prompted to think back over my lifetime and rehearse the meaningful moments of my personal experience, and clearly the most defining moment in my life was my conversion to Christ. Sometimes people speak mockingly of those who are converted, saying they have "seen the light," but they're closer to the truth than they realize. For me, conversion was the point when "the lights went on"; I understood things I had not grasped before. I saw that there was life in Christ, that He gives eternal life. Conversely, of course, outside of Christ there may be biological life, but there is no ultimate life—there is only spiritual death.

Later in the prologue, John writes that **we beheld His glory, the glory as of the only begotten of the Father, full of grace and truth** (v. 14). John is surely speaking here of Jesus' transfiguration, that moment when, atop the mountain, His heavenly glory was made manifest and the three disciples accompanying Him were dazzled. At that time, Jesus' light was real and visible, but the light of truth that He brought was displayed throughout His ministry.

In the second century, when the Christian philosophers and apologists sought to define the Christian faith over against the pagan world and to answer the critics from Greek philosophy, Justin Martyr argued that geniuses such as Plato and Aristotle did not discover any great truths by their own power. Whatever light these pagan philosophers found was borrowed from the light that comes into the world. All light finds its origin in Jesus Christ, who is the fountain of all truth. That is the point John is making here.

In verses 6–8, John introduced John the Baptist: **There was a man sent from God, whose name was John. This man came for a witness, to bear witness of the light, that all through him might believe. He was not that Light, but was sent to bear witness of that Light**. John the Baptist was sent by God as Jesus' forerunner, to point Him out. We're told in verse 15 that John fulfilled his mission; he cried out, "This was He of whom I said, 'He who comes after me is preferred before me, for He was before me.'" Later, he pointed to Jesus with those stirring words, "Behold! The Lamb of God" (v. 29b).

The prologue also contains an awful word of judgment: **He was in the world, and the world was made through Him, and the world did not know Him. He came to His own, and His own did not receive Him** (vv. 10–11). Jesus Himself spoke of this rejection He experienced, saying, "This is the condemnation, that the light has come into the world, and men loved the darkness rather than light, because their deeds were evil" (3:19). Many years ago, I was interviewed by Dr. James Montgomery Boice for his radio program, and I had occasion to quote this verse. I attempted to quote the King James Version, which says, "Their deeds were evil," but instead I said, "Their eeds were deevil." That was the end of that interview, and as a result of it, even though it was long ago, I can hardly read that text without flinching. But we ought to flinch even when we read the words properly, for this verse tells us the world is exposed to the condemnation of God because people prefer the darkness to the light. They do not want to come to the light, Jesus Christ, because their evil deeds will be exposed.

Good News of Hope

But John's prologue also gives very good news: **But as many as received Him, to them He gave the right to become children of God, to those who believe in His name**" (v. 12). This is the good news of the gospel, the great hope that John wants his readers to know. John longs for them to believe in Jesus as the Christ.

I can't possibly know the state of the soul of anyone reading this book. We judge on outward appearances; only God can look at the heart. But if we go by the odds, the probabilities are extremely high that many of those reading this book do not know Christ and are still living in darkness, for the darkness covers their hearts and their souls, and they've never experienced the life that only He can give. It is my earnest prayer that as we look through the pages and the chapters of this Gospel, that God the Holy Spirit will make you see that light so clearly that you will be like those who did receive Jesus, to whom God gave the right to be called His children. My prayer is that through this Word, by which faith comes, you will come to know that light and that life. If you already have His life in you, and you already have seen the beauty of that life and have been rescued from darkness, I pray that you will move from light to light, from life to life, from faith to faith, and from grace to grace as we learn of Him.

2

WHO ARE YOU?

John 1:19–28

Now this is the testimony of John, when the Jews sent priests and Levites from Jerusalem to ask him, "Who are you?" He confessed, and did not deny, but confessed, "I am not the Christ." And they asked him, "What then? Are you Elijah?" He said, "I am not." "Are you the Prophet?" And he answered, "No." Then they said to him, "Who are you, that we may give an answer to those who sent us? What do you say about yourself?" He said: "I am 'The voice of one crying in the wilderness: "Make straight the way of the LORD,"' as the prophet Isaiah said." Now those who were sent were from the Pharisees. And they asked him, saying, "Why then do you baptize if you are not the Christ, nor Elijah, nor the Prophet?" John answered them, saying, "I baptize with water, but there stands One among you whom you do not know. It is He who, coming after me, is preferred before me, whose sandal strap I am not worthy to loose." These things were done in Bethabara beyond the Jordan, where John was baptizing.

Following his prologue (John 1:1–18), in which John sets forth the identity of Jesus, he moves on to a brief summation of the ministry and testimony of John the Baptist. I believe that John the Baptist is

7

one of the most neglected personages in all of sacred Scripture, but that was not the case in the first century. This man attracted enormous attention among the Jewish people during that time, and amazingly, the secular historians of the first century gave more information regarding John the Baptist than Jesus.

Why did John the Baptist attract such attention? I believe it had to do with the fact that while ancient Israel could boast a rich history of prophets sent from God, by John's day the office seemed to be just that—history. The prophetic ministry had ceased with the last canonical prophet of the Old Testament, Malachi, and for four hundred years there had been no word from God. Then, suddenly, the office of prophet was renewed with this strange and bizarre figure who came forth from the desert, the traditional meeting place between God and His prophets, to begin a radical prophetic ministry. In a very short time, John the Baptist's activity attracted widespread attention.

Cleansing for the Jews?

John's prophetic message was simple. "Repent," he cried, "for the kingdom of heaven is at hand!" (Matt. 3:2). John said that a crisis moment in history was at hand. The coming of the Messiah was not in the distant, unknown future; rather, He was at the door and would be coming in at any minute. Furthermore, His coming would be for the purpose of judgment: "His winnowing fan is in His hand, and He will thoroughly clean out His threshing floor, and gather the wheat into His barn; but the chaff He will burn with unquenchable fire" (Luke 3:17). Therefore, John declared, the people of Israel needed to get ready. With that, he called them to repent of their sins and submit to a ritual of cleansing—baptism.

It is important to understand that the ritual of proselyte baptism had arisen among the Jews during the intertestamental period, but it had been limited to Gentiles. It was not administered to Jews, only to non-Jews who converted to Judaism, for Gentiles were considered unclean and therefore needed to go through a purification rite—to take a bath, as it were—in order to be welcomed and received into the covenant community of Israel.

But John the Baptist, of course, directed his calls for repentance not to Gentiles but to Jews. He was saying to Israel: "The Messiah is about to arrive, but you're not ready for Him. *You*, the people of Israel, are unclean." Therefore, he called the Jews to submit to a ritual of cleansing that heretofore had been administered only to Gentiles.

Secondarily, we must understand that in proselyte baptism, the typical procedure was for the convert to baptize himself. He was not baptized by the

Levites or by the priests, who performed all the other purification rites in Israel. But John was actually baptizing, even though the baptistic ritual theretofore had been self-administered and even though John had no official status to perform any sort of cleansing ritual, since he was not a priest or Levite.

These "irregularities" soon came to the attention of the religious authorities in Jerusalem. You can imagine how upset they were. They asked themselves, "Who does this man think he is, to call us, the children of Abraham, to undergo a cleansing rite?" They wanted to know what was going on down there by the Jordan River. So they sent a delegation out to investigate and get more information about John and his activities. Their exchange with John is very important for our understanding of the entire Gospel of John.

When the priests and Levites came to John the Baptist, they wasted no time but asked, **"Who are you?"** (v. 19). According to the text, **he confessed, and did not deny, but confessed, "I am not the Christ"** (v. 20). Notice the awkward construction of that verse. It's even worse in the Greek; it's so convoluted, it's difficult to translate. Why did John choose to record the Baptist's response in this way?

When Martin Luther was brought before the Diet of Worms in the sixteenth century to be interrogated about his writings and his teaching, he was called to recant his views on justification. When he tried to explain his views, he was cut off in midsentence by his interrogators, who said, "Brother Martin, answer us directly, *non cornutum.*" The Latin phrase *non cornutum* literally means "without horns." Luther's interrogators were asking him to answer without any evasive techniques, without any craftiness. They wanted a straightforward response. So Luther said, "If you want an answer *non cornutum*, without horns, here it is: Unless I am convinced by sacred Scripture or by evident reason, I cannot recant," and so on. Luther spoke out clearly and unambiguously.

In this verse, John the apostle says that John the Baptist did the very same thing. When he writes that John the Baptist "confessed, and did not deny, but confessed," John utilizes the strongest possible method in the Greek to show how emphatic John the Baptist was in saying, "I am not the Christ." Those familiar with the Greek would have come away with no doubts as to John's denial that he was the Messiah. This verse took away all ambiguity.

Exploring the Possibilities

Having heard John deny that he was the Messiah, the priests and Levites of the Jewish delegation replied, **"What then?"** They were saying, "If you're not the Messiah, who *are* you?" Then they began to tick off various possibilities. First, they asked whether John was **Elijah**. Why did they ask this strange question? I noted above that the last canonical prophet in the Old Testament was Malachi, and in the last chapter of the book of Malachi, in the last paragraph of the book, the last prophecy in the entire Old Testament, Malachi recorded these words of God: "Behold, I will send you Elijah the prophet before the coming of the great and dreadful day of the LORD" (4:5). In other words, just before the four hundred years of divine silence commenced, God promised that the day of the Lord would come, but not until He first sent Elijah to announce it. That's why the Jewish people were waiting for the return of Elijah. Given this prophecy and this expectation, it is not surprising that the Jewish leaders, seeing John the Baptist behaving like Elijah, would come to him and ask, "Are you Elijah?"

John's reply, once again, was unambiguous: **"I am not"** (v. 21b). That reply creates a problem, because when Jesus spoke about John the Baptist to His disciples, He said, "If you are willing to receive it, he is Elijah who is to come" (Matt. 11:14). With that cryptic introduction—"If you are willing to receive it"—Jesus indicated that John *was* Elijah in a sense. That is, his ministry was the fulfillment of Malachi's prophecy, even though John the Baptist personally was not Elijah. This is borne out by what the angel told John's father; he said John would "go before [the Messiah] in the spirit and power of Elijah" (Luke 1:17). So while John was not Elijah reincarnated, his ministry was marked by a similar spirit and power. John was not lying when he said he was not Elijah.

Next, the priests and Levites asked, **"Are you the Prophet?"** (v. 21c). Notice that the question was not, "Are you *a* prophet?" Rather, it was, "Are you *the* Prophet?" Who did the delegates have in view? The book of Deuteronomy records that God told Moses: "I will raise up for [the Israelites] a Prophet like you from among their brethren, and will put My words in His mouth, and He shall speak to them all that I command Him" (Deut. 18:18). For centuries, the Jewish people had been waiting not just for the return of Elijah, but for the arrival of this special prophet who would be like Moses. We must not forget the uniqueness of Moses—he was not just a prophet, he was the mediator of the Old Testament. So a prophet like Moses would be a prophet who would mediate; He would be the mediator of the New Testament, the Messiah. For this reason, the Jewish leaders asked John: "Are you the Prophet? Are you the one like Moses we have been waiting for?" But once again John answered, **"No."**

You can almost sense the frustration the priests and Levites were feeling by this point. They asked: **"Who are you, that we may give an answer to those who sent us?"** (v. 22). John didn't keep them in suspense; he answered them. They had looked for his identity in the Old Testament books of Malachi and Deuteronomy, but John took them to another book, that of the prophet Isaiah.

I believe this choice of texts was significant. When Jesus began His public ministry after His temptation in the wilderness, He went to His hometown of Nazareth and went into the synagogue on the Sabbath day. While He was there, He was asked to read from the scroll for that day—which happened to be from the prophet Isaiah. So Jesus read from Isaiah 61:

"The Spirit of the LORD is upon Me,
Because he has anointed Me
To preach the gospel to the poor.
He has sent me to heal the brokenhearted,
To proclaim liberty to the captives
And recovery of sight to the blind,
To set at liberty those who are oppressed,
To proclaim the year of the LORD." (Luke 4:18-19)

After the reading, Jesus was invited, as the visiting rabbi, to give a sermon on the text. It was probably the shortest sermon ever. Jesus said, "Today this Scripture is fulfilled in your hearing" (Luke 4:21), and then He sat down. What was He saying? He was announcing, "I'm the One who has been anointed to be the Messiah."

John the Baptist did much the same to reveal his identity. He quoted from Isaiah 40: **"The voice of one crying in the wilderness: 'Prepare the way of the LORD,'" as the prophet Isaiah said** (v. 23). Isaiah declared that before the Messiah would come into the world, he would send His messenger, and the messenger would proclaim to the people: "Build a road! Knock down the hills. Dig a tunnel if necessary. Fill in the ditches. Make the road straight because it is going to be the highway for our King. Build the King's highway." God promised that someday the King's highway would be built, and the King would enter into the midst of His people. But by quoting this passage from Isaiah, John said: "That's who I am. I'm here to tell you to build the highway of the King."

John's Right to Baptize

The Jewish leaders' questions didn't stop once they knew John's identity. They remained troubled by the baptism issue, so they asked, **"Why then do you baptize if you are not the Christ, nor Elijah, nor the Prophet?"**

(v. 25). John replied: **"I baptize with water, but there stands One among you whom you do not know. It is He who, coming after me, is preferred before me, whose sandal strap I am not worthy to loose"** (vv. 26–27).

John's mention of Jesus' sandal strap was an idiom, an expression of the Jews. A disciple of a rabbi, such as Jesus' disciples, not only attended the lectures of the rabbi and learned the lessons that he taught, he took on the role of a servant. The disciple actually functioned as the personal slave of the rabbi and took care of all of his needs—making his housing arrangements, getting his food, and so forth. We see examples of this in the ministry of Jesus, such as the occasion when He sent His disciples into Jerusalem to make sure that a room was reserved where He could celebrate the Passover. But the one thing that differentiated a disciple in a rabbinical school from an actual bondslave was that the disciple was never required to take care of the shoes or the sandals of his teacher. A slave could be reduced to that humiliating task, but not a disciple. Therefore, when John said, "I'm not even worthy to unstrap His sandals," he was saying: "Don't look at me. I'm *lower* than a disciple. I'm even lower than a slave. I'm not even worthy to untie His shoes, to take off His sandals, to clean His feet. Don't look to me. Look to *Him*."

I believe John put this incident right at the beginning of his Gospel to help focus his readers' attention on the One whom John's Gospel announces. John is saying, through John the Baptist, "It's time to make straight the highway of our God."

Those of us who believe and trust in Christ are His disciples. But like John, we need to see that we are not worthy in and of ourselves to untie His shoes, for we have sinned against God and despised His just rule. Despite that, Jesus gave Himself for us, to redeem us from our sin. May we never cease to give thanks for such a great salvation.

3

THE LAMB OF GOD

John 1:29–51

The next day John saw Jesus coming toward him, and said, "Behold! The Lamb of God who takes away the sin of the world! This is He of whom I said, 'After me comes a Man who is preferred before me, for He was before me.' I did not know Him; but that He should be revealed to Israel, therefore I came baptizing with water." And John bore witness, saying, "I saw the Spirit descending from heaven like a dove, and He remained upon Him. I did not know Him, but He who sent me to baptize with water said to me, 'Upon whom you see the Spirit descending, and remaining on Him, this is He who baptizes with the Holy Spirit.' And I have seen and testified that this is the Son of God." Again, the next day, John stood with two of his disciples. And looking at Jesus as He walked, he said, "Behold the Lamb of God!" The two disciples heard him speak, and they followed Jesus. Then Jesus turned, and seeing them following, said to them, "What do you seek?" They said to Him, "Rabbi" (which is to say, when translated, Teacher), "where are You staying?" He said to them, "Come and see." They came and saw where He was staying, and remained with Him that day (now it was about the tenth hour). One of the two who heard John speak, and followed Him, was Andrew, Simon Peter's brother. He first found his own brother Simon, and said to him,

"We have found the Messiah" (which is translated, the Christ). And he brought him to Jesus. Now when Jesus looked at him, He said, "You are Simon the son of Jonah. You shall be called Cephas" (which is translated, A Stone). The following day Jesus wanted to go to Galilee, and He found Philip and said to him, "Follow Me." Now Philip was from Bethsaida, the city of Andrew and Peter. Philip found Nathanael and said to him, "We have found Him of whom Moses in the law, and also the prophets, wrote— Jesus of Nazareth, the son of Joseph." And Nathanael said to him, "Can anything good come out of Nazareth?" Philip said to him, "Come and see." Jesus saw Nathanael coming toward Him, and said of him, "Behold, an Israelite indeed, in whom is no deceit!" Nathanael said to Him, "How do You know me?" Jesus answered and said to him, "Before Philip called you, when you were under the fig tree, I saw you." Nathanael answered and said to Him, "Rabbi, You are the Son of God! You are the King of Israel!" Jesus answered and said to him, "Because I said to you, 'I saw you under the fig tree,' do you believe? You will see greater things than these." And He said to him, "Most assuredly, I say to you, hereafter you shall see heaven open, and the angels of God ascending and descending upon the Son of Man."

In Great Britain, it is always a momentous occasion when one of the citizens is elevated to a peerage or a knighthood and has the opportunity to come before the monarch to be recognized and honored. Britain has various ranks of hereditary peerage: duke, earl, viscount, baron, and so on. In addition, there are several orders of chivalry, including the Order of the Garter, the Order of the Thistle, and the Order of the Bath, all of which allow the honoree to carry the title "Sir" or "Dame." Many great men and women of the British Isles have carried a long list of titles.

However, I believe the most titled person in all of human history is Jesus of Nazareth. I remember attending an academic convocation at a theological seminary where the guest speaker was a distinguished New Testament scholar. These convocations are usually the occasion for the presentation of weighty academic papers. But on this occasion, the New Testament scholar did something that had never been done before in this institution. He went to the lectern and began a thirty-minute talk in which, without comment, he recited the titles of Christ that are found in the New Testament. He mentioned such titles as "the Christ," "the Son of God," "the Son of Man," "Lord," "the Consolation of Israel," "the Lion of Judah," "the Alpha and Omega," and many more. Then he sat down. There were enough scriptural titles that God the Father had been pleased to ascribe to His Son to fill a half-hour lecture period.

A Wealth of Titles

We need to look no further than the first chapter of John's Gospel to see this wealth of titles on display. We saw that, at the very beginning of the book, Jesus is introduced as the eternal "Word," who was with God and who was God. In the passage we are considering in this chapter, John the Baptist identifies Jesus by the title **Lamb of God** (v. 29). In verse 34, John the Baptist adds, **"I have seen and testified that this is the Son of God."** Verse 36 contains a second reference by the Baptist to Jesus as "the Lamb of God." In verse 38, some of the disciples of John address Jesus as **Rabbi**, a title that literally means "teacher." In verse 41, Andrew becomes the first to announce the messianic identity of Jesus when he finds his brother Peter and says to him, **"We have found the Messiah."** Dropping down to verse 49, we encounter Nathanael, who says to Jesus: **"Rabbi, You are the Son of God! You are the King of Israel!"** Finally, Jesus gives testimony about Himself at the end of the chapter, saying, **"I say to you, hereafter you shall see heaven open, and the angels of God ascending and descending upon the Son of Man"** (v. 51). So in this short literary span, we hear Jesus called "the Word," "the Lamb of God," "the Son of God," "Rabbi," "Messiah," "King of Israel," and "Son of Man."

In this chapter, I want to zero in on this significant title that John the Baptist twice used to refer to Jesus to announce His coming and appearance. The title is *Agnus Dei*, or "Lamb of God." This title is featured prominently in church history, in our art, in our music, and in the symbolism of Christ throughout Christendom. I'm sure it is not a new thing for you to hear that Jesus was called the "Lamb of God." But it might strike you as a bit strange to learn that there are only two books of the Bible wherein Christ is called the Lamb of God, and both of those books were written by the same man, the apostle John. We hear the title used here in the first chapter of the Gospel of John and again in the book of Revelation, which contains John's vision on the Isle of Patmos. In chapter 5 of that book, John records that he was told to await the coming of the Lion of Judah, but then he turned and beheld not the Lion but a Lamb that appeared to have been slain. The song of the angels incorporated that event:

"Worthy is the Lamb who was slain,
To receive power and riches and wisdom,
And strength and honor and glory and blessing!" (Rev. 5:12)

In this vision of the heavenly throne room of God, Jesus is honored as the Lamb of God.

The title "Lamb of God" has sparked a number of academic controversies. Some scholars point out that nowhere in the Old Testament do we find a lamb used in the expiation of sin. In the sin offerings in ancient Israel, bulls and goats were used in the sacrifice and the scapegoat was driven out into the wilderness, but lambs were not used. So these critics question the origin of the idea that Jesus is the Lamb of God who takes away sin. They conclude that the apostle John must have made up this idea and put it into the mouth of John the Baptist, since there's no Old Testament precedent for it.

Others respond that we do find lamb metaphors in the Old Testament, most notably in Isaiah 53, where God gave Isaiah the prophet the vision of the Suffering Servant. Isaiah writes that this Servant of God was "wounded for our transgressions" and "bruised for our iniquities (v. 5), and that God laid on him "the iniquity of us all" (v. 6). Significantly, Isaiah says the Servant was "led as a lamb to the slaughter, and as a sheep before its shearers is silent, so he opened not His mouth" (v. 7). In the metaphor of Isaiah 53, the Suffering Servant is compared to a lamb. However, He is not *called* the Lamb of God who takes away the sin of the world, so the critics of the apostle John still maintain that he invented this title.

Hearing these criticisms, I have to wonder whether it ever occurs to these critics that John the Baptist was himself a prophet and had as much authority to give a fresh revelation from the mind of God as Isaiah, Jeremiah, Ezekiel, Daniel or any other man sent as a prophet from God. The concept of Jesus as the Lamb of God is not a creation of the vivid imagination of the apostle John or a rhetorical flourish by John the Baptist; instead, it is *God's* designation for His Son.

Tracing the Theme of the Lamb

This idea of the Lamb of God is a strand that runs throughout the history of redemption. It can be traced all the way back to Genesis 22, when God called Abraham to go to Mount Moriah and offer his son Isaac as a sacrifice. Abraham, in obedience to God, was prepared to do just that, but at the last possible moment, after Abraham had tied Isaac to the altar and was preparing to plunge the knife into his heart, God stopped him, saying, "Do not lay your hand on the lad, or do anything to him; for now I know that you fear God, since you have not withheld your son, your only son, from Me" (v. 12). Then there was a ruckus behind Abraham, and he turned to see a ram that was caught in the thicket by its horns. God provided a lamb as a sacrificial substitute for Abraham's son. Of course, it is never stated in Genesis 22 that the ram Abraham caught and offered in the place of Isaac was an expiatory sacrifice. Nevertheless, it was a substitutionary sacrifice, and that is the idea that underlies the atonement of Christ. Jesus acts as our substitute, and God pours out His wrath on account of our sin onto Him instead of us. God, then, provides a Lamb of His own and accepts the life of that substitute.

Likewise, the Lamb of God is certainly prefigured in the Passover. When God prepared to bring His final plague on the Egyptians, the death of every firstborn male of the Egyptians, including the crown prince of the Pharaoh, He instructed His people Israel to slay lambs without blemish and to spread the blood on their doorposts. God promised to pass over all the houses where He saw the blood of the lambs on the doorposts (Ex. 12:3–13). Just as the blood of those lambs caused the people of Israel to be spared from God's wrath, the Lamb of God redeemed His people from the penalty that was due for their sin.

Given this imagery in Genesis 22, Exodus 12, and other passages throughout the Old Testament, it's foolish to say that the title "Lamb of God" is an invention of the apostle John. The words of John the Baptist were informed by his knowledge of the Old Testament, the sacred Scriptures of the Jews at the time of Christ.

Despite the abundant use of significant titles for Jesus in the first chapter of John—"Lamb of God," "Son of God," "Messiah," "Son of Man," and so forth—I don't believe that John the Baptist, Andrew, Nathanael, or any of the disciples had a comprehensive understanding of the meaning of these titles. John the Baptist, who here said, "Behold! The Lamb of God who takes away the sin of the world!" later was thrown into prison and sent messengers to Jesus, asking, "Are You the Coming One, or do we look for another?" (Luke 7:20). This question indicates that John had not fully understood the identity of Jesus, despite his dramatic testimony to Jesus' identity. The problem was that he had his own expectations. He expected that the Lamb of God would come and drive the Romans out, just as everybody else did. When he saw Jesus merely going about preaching, he became confused.

Jesus told John's messengers, "Go and tell John the things you have seen and heard: that the blind see, the lame walk, the lepers are cleansed, the deaf hear, the dead are raised, the poor have the gospel preached to them" (Luke 7:22). Jesus pointed to His miracles to confirm His identity for the doubting John. He also referenced the messianic prophecy in Isaiah 61:1–2a, which says:

> "The Spirit of the Lord GOD is upon Me,
> Because the LORD has anointed Me
> To preach good tidings to the poor;
> He has sent me to heal the brokenhearted,
> To proclaim liberty to the captives,
> And the opening of the prison to those who are bound;
> To proclaim the acceptable year of the LORD."

It was as if Jesus was saying: "John, if you had really studied your Bible, you wouldn't be asking whether I am the One who was to come. You don't have to look for another one. You had it right the first time. I *am* the Lamb of God."

Peter was likewise confused, even when he gave his great confession at Caesarea Philippi. In answer to Jesus' question as to whom the disciples thought Him to be, Peter said, "You are the Christ, the Son of the living God" (Matt. 16:16). Jesus affirmed that confession to be accurate and declared Peter "blessed" for understanding who He was. But immediately afterward, when Jesus told His disciples that He was bound to Jerusalem to suffer and die, Peter rebuked Him and said, "This shall not happen to You!" (16:22b). One minute Peter affirmed that Jesus was the Messiah, but the next minute he revealed that he didn't really understand all that it meant for Jesus to be the Messiah.

We, of course, are prone to the same confusion. Only when we look at the whole picture, taking into account the cross, the resurrection, the ascension, and the outpouring of the Spirit at the Day of Pentecost, do we begin to see the depths and the riches of all that God was communicating through the announcement of His messenger, who said, "Behold! The Lamb of God who takes away the sin of the world!"

4

THE WEDDING FEAST

John 2:1–11

On the third day there was a wedding in Cana of Galilee, and the mother of Jesus was there. Now both Jesus and His disciples were invited to the wedding. And when they ran out of wine, the mother of Jesus said to Him, "They have no wine." Jesus said to her, "Woman, what does your concern have to do with Me? My hour has not yet come." His mother said to the servants, "Whatever He says to you, do it." Now there were set there six waterpots of stone, according to the manner of purification of the Jews, containing twenty or thirty gallons apiece. Jesus said to them, "Fill the waterpots with water." And they filled them up to the brim. And He said to them, "Draw some out now, and take it to the master of the feast." And they took it. When the master of the feast had tasted the water that was made wine, and did not know where it came from (but the servants who had drawn the water knew), the master of the feast called the bridegroom. And he said to him, "Every man at the beginning sets out the good wine, and when the guests have well drunk, then the inferior. You have kept the good wine until now!" This beginning of signs Jesus did in Cana of Galilee, and manifested His glory; and His disciples believed in Him.

When the apostle John reports the miracles of Jesus, he habitually refers to them as "signs." For instance, in the passage we are considering in this chapter, he writes, **This beginning of signs Jesus did in Cana of Galilee** (v. 11a). The Greek word translated as "sign" here is *semeion*, which referred to a sign or token that distinguished a person or a thing from others. Thus, John is saying that Jesus did His miracles not for their own sake but to point the observer and the reader beyond them to something that was *signi*ficant—to Himself as the One who spoke the unvarnished word of truth. That is, the miracles represented God's accreditation that Jesus was sent from Him. But Jesus said that His signs pointed not only to His person, but to His work of bringing the kingdom of God.

It is important for us to understand all this as we focus on John's record of the very first sign that Jesus did. It was a sign that took place, surprisingly, at a wedding, and it seems almost profane in that it involved the transformation of water into wine for thirsty guests.

A Large, Lengthy Celebration

We're told that this wedding took place in Cana, and Jesus, His disciples, and His mother were invited. We can assume from this that the wedding involved people who were known to Jesus and to His family and friends. Based on what we're told about the water pots, it must have been a very large wedding. In the ancient world, it was customary for a wedding feast to last as long as a week. So this celebration probably was a large and lengthy event.

But in the midst of this celebration, something went wrong. The host, who was the bridegroom, ran out of wine. Maybe the groom had failed to make enough provision in the first place, possibly more people came than he expected, or maybe they drank more than he anticipated. In fact, the language in the text is a bit euphemistic. For whatever reason, the wine ran out. That represented two problems for the host. On the one hand, it was a massive embarrassment for the groom to run out of refreshments for the guests he had invited. Even worse, there is evidence that in the ancient Jewish world, if provisions such as this failed, the groom could face a lawsuit. That's how seriously hospitality was (and continues to be) treated in the Middle East. This was a truly scandalous moment.

Jesus' mother heard about the dilemma and, having compassion on the bridegroom, she immediately went to Jesus and said: "Jesus, they've run out of wine. Do something! Fix it!" He responded: **"Woman, what does your concern have to do with Me? My hour has not yet come"** (v. 4).

Three questions occur to me about Jesus' response to Mary's plea. First, why did He address her as "Woman"? In our day and age, this way of speaking sounds almost rude. However, in Jesus' time, "Woman" was a title of respect. It was like saying "Ma'am" or "Madam." It wasn't like a cab driver in New York saying, "Where to, Lady?" Remember, Jesus used this same word when He addressed Mary from the cross (19:26). Also, this was how Jesus addressed the woman at the well (John 4:21). It was a polite form of address in the Jewish culture of that time.

Second, what did Jesus mean when He asked, "What does your concern have to do with Me?" If you look at this passage in various translations of the Bible, you will see various arrangements of words. Even today, Greek scholars are not exactly sure how to translate this statement. Literally, Jesus said, "What is this to you to Me?" It's a strange and awkward construction, and the translators have to render it as best they can. But it seems clear that Jesus was saying to his mother, "Don't tell Me what to do in My earthly ministry." He was taking His directions from His heavenly Father. Ironically, however, after saying this to Mary, He proceeded to deal with the problem.

Third, why did Jesus make the enigmatic statement, "My hour has not yet come"? As we move through the Gospel of John, we will see Jesus referencing His coming hour again and again. Sometimes He referred to the hour of His passion, when He was to be given over to be crucified, but even those references went beyond the cross to the resurrection, and He talked about the hour in which the Father would manifest His glory. Mary knew, in a sense, that at some point Jesus' glory would be manifested. Jesus lived His whole life under the burden of that hour, the hour of death. So He said to His mother, "It's not time yet for Me to enter into My glory." In a sense, I think, He was gently rebuking her not to rush Him, because he had other things that He must do before His glory could be made manifest.

Following this mild rebuke, Mary said to the servants, **"Whatever He says to you, do it"** (v. 5). No one ever received better instructions from anybody in all of history than these servants received from the mother of Christ when she told them to follow Jesus' orders. That exhortation has application far beyond the immediate task those servants had to do.

An Unexpected Response

What would you expect Jesus to do in this situation? He had a perfect opportunity to chasten the people for overindulging in their wine. He could have stepped up and said, "You should not be abusing this gift that God gives to His people." But that's not what He did. Instead, He made more wine.

Verse 6 tells us, **Now there were set there six waterpots of stone,**

according to the manner of purification of the Jews, containing twenty or thirty gallons apiece. In the Mideast, water pots made from mud have been used for millennia and are still used today. They are earthen vessels. But the Jews also made jars and vessels out of stone for the simple reason that water contained in these pots would not become contaminated with bits of dirt. Every Jew who came to this large wedding celebration had to go through a purification rite before he could enter. If nothing else, he had to wash his hands and his feet when he arrived for the wedding feast. These jars were there for this purpose.

Jesus ordered the servants to **"fill the waterpots with water"** (v. 7a). When they were finished, He directed them to **"draw some out now, and take it to the master of the feast"** (v. 8). The master of the feast, an official who managed the feast for the bridegroom, tasted the water and immediately realized it was wine. But it wasn't ordinary wine—it was **"good wine"** (v. 10), the best the master had tasted so far at the feast. The master was amazed because hosts usually served good wine first and then resorted to cheaper stuff when people had largely had their fill and some were too drunk to notice the difference. Jesus not only had turned the water into wine, He had turned it into very good wine. Also, He had made a lot of it. Each of the six stone jars held twenty to thirty gallons of water, meaning Jesus potentially made 180 gallons of wine. Most commentators agree that this large amount is a sign of the abundance of God's grace.

Many of us have been taught that the Jews drank wine in the Old Testament era because the water was no good. Actually, the water was just fine. Wine was a special drink; it was reserved for special occasions. If the Jews had needed an alternative to water, they could have simply drunk the juice of the grapes. But the Old Testament Jew knew nothing of unfermented grape juice. Grapes were one of the two largest crops grown by the Old Testament Jews, the other being olives, which were raised for their oil. Vineyards were planted to produce grapes from which wine was made. The Jews saw wine as a gift of God. It was that which had the capacity to make the heart glad (Ps. 104:15). For these reasons, it seems impossible to deny that what Jesus created in those stone jars was fermented grape juice, or wine.

There is some important symbolism involved in Jesus' transformation of water into wine. At one point, Jesus took note of the different reactions of the Jewish leaders to His ministry and that of John the Baptist. We saw earlier that John had come in garb reminiscent of the Old Testament prophet Elijah, and that he lived in the wilderness and ate locusts and wild honey. There has been some speculation that John the Baptist may have taken the Nazirite vow, which would have required him to abstain from wine. Jesus said that John had come "neither eating bread nor drinking wine" (Luke 7:33). In short, John came in a spirit of austerity. But Jesus went to dinners with publicans and participated in feasts and other celebrations, such as the wedding in Cana; as Jesus put it, "The Son of Man has come eating and drinking" (Luke 7:34a). Much the same was true for the disciples of John and the disciples of Jesus. Jesus explained that it was appropriate for John and his followers to be in a mode of total abstinence because he carried out his ministry while the Bridegroom was not present, but Jesus *was* the Bridegroom, so it was appropriate for Him and His disciples to celebrate (Luke 5:34–35). The Bridegroom had come, so it was time for the party to start, and the use of wine was symbolic of that celebration.

Jesus also used wine as a symbol when He announced the coming of the kingdom. He said: "No one puts a piece from a new garment on an old one; otherwise the new makes a tear, and also the piece that was taken out of the new does not match the old. And no one puts new wine into old wineskins; or else the new wine will burst the wineskins and be spilled, and the wineskins will be ruined" (Luke 5:36–37). Jesus was telling the people that He represented a change from the order of the Old Testament, for He was bringing the new wine of the kingdom. In light of this teaching, Jesus' miracle of creating wine from water intended for Old Testament purification rites was especially significant.

Also, as John Calvin noted, wine was an important element of the Israelites' Passover feast, but at the Last Supper, Jesus gave the wine a new significance— He made it a symbol of His own life-giving blood. Thus, the redemption of Christ was foreshadowed in the very first miracle He performed.

Sources of Controversy

I must note that Jesus' transformation of water into wine has sparked controversy from two directions. One source of controversy was the liberals of the nineteenth century, who were allergic to anything supernatural and who especially wanted to de-supernaturalize the record of the ministry of Christ on earth. They denied that Jesus turned water into wine because they didn't believe in miracles and didn't believe that Jesus did any actual miracles. They explained what happened at Cana by theorizing that the master had been serving wine out of the water pots, and that when the water pots grew empty, the dregs of wine remained at the bottom. Thus, when the servants added water as Jesus ordered, the dregs gave the water a hint of the taste of wine, and the guests at the wedding celebration had already drunk so much wine that they didn't know the difference. In other words, Jesus simply engaged in a bit of trickery. In another manner of denying what the Bible says, my minister when I was growing up said, "Jesus told the servants to fill the pots and give the people water because, after all, water is the best wine." Isn't it interesting that this minister saw a miracle in the act of turning water into water? I think these examples show how many hoops the critics jump through to deny that Jesus really made wine.

Of course, some conservatives jump through just as many hoops because they're embarrassed by this biblical text that indicates Jesus made wine. Their premise is that drinking wine is a sin. Based on that premise and the premise that Jesus was sinless, they conclude that He couldn't or wouldn't have made wine.

Many people, particularly in the United States, have been raised in churches that taught strongly that Jesus never made wine or drank wine. They say that the Lord's Supper was based on "the fruit of the vine," which is a reference to grape juice. I've argued above that every Jew knew that the fruit of the vine was wine and that Jesus used wine when He instituted the Lord's Supper. However, if you have been taught all your life that Jesus made grape juice rather than wine, and if you are convinced that that was the case and that it would be a sin for your lips to touch wine, then for you to drink wine would be a sin. The apostle Paul, in Romans 14 and 1 Corinthians 8, taught that if someone is convinced that an action is sinful (even though it is not), he actually sins if he takes that action. It's not that the New Testament presents a relativistic ethic; it simply says that whatever is not of faith is sin (Rom. 14:23b). It is wrong to act against one's conscience, even if the action is not opposed to God's law.

For this reason, many churches, including the church where I serve, give the individual the option of wine or grape juice in the Lord's Supper. The outer ring of the communion tray holds cups of grape juice for those who are absolutely persuaded that one ought never to taste wine. As I noted above, I think the Bible is manifestly clear that our Lord made wine and drank wine, and I don't think there's a word in the Bible that teaches that it's sinful to drink wine. It's certainly sinful to get drunk, but the possibility of abuse does not require disuse. However, I recognize that some people are absolutely convinced that it's wrong, and I grant that they should not drink wine, because they believe it would be wrong.

Finally, John notes that by this miracle Jesus **manifested His glory; and His disciples believed in Him** (v. 11). His disciples came to faith in Him; they saw His significance. Jesus began His public ministry with a work that drew attention both to Him and to the new kingdom He was bringing to pass.

5

THE CLEANSING OF
THE TEMPLE

John 2:12–25

After this He went down to Capernaum, He, His mother, His brothers, and His disciples; and they did not stay there many days. Now the Passover of the Jews was at hand, and Jesus went up to Jerusalem. And He found in the temple those who sold oxen and sheep and doves, and the money changers doing business. When He had made a whip of cords, He drove them all out of the temple, with the sheep and the oxen, and poured out the changers' money and overturned the tables. And He said to those who sold doves, "Take these things away! Do not make My Father's house a house of merchandise!" Then His disciples remembered that it was written, "Zeal for Your house has eaten Me up." So the Jews answered and said to Him, "What sign do You show to us, since You do these things?" Jesus answered and said to them, "Destroy this temple, and in three days I will raise it up." Then the Jews said, "It has taken forty-six years to build this temple, and will You raise it up in three days?" But He was speaking of the temple of His body. Therefore, when He had risen from the dead, His disciples remembered that He had said this to them; and they believed the Scripture and the word which Jesus had said. Now when He was in

Jerusalem at the Passover, during the feast, many believed in His name when they saw the signs which He did. But Jesus did not commit Himself to them, because He knew all men, and had no need that anyone should testify of man, for He knew what was in man.

W e have seen that the apostle John approached the life of Jesus somewhat differently from the men who wrote the Synoptic Gospels (Matthew, Mark, and Luke). John's Gospel is more of a theological reflection than a strictly chronological or biographical portrait. This difference is quite apparent in the text we are considering in this chapter.

This text has been the focal point of much critical attention in biblical scholarship because John presents Jesus' cleansing of the temple as an event that happened very early in His ministry. According to John, following His first miracle in Cana, Jesus went to Capernaum, and then, a few days later, He went to Jerusalem for the feast of the Passover, which served as the occasion for His cleansing of the temple. By contrast, all three of the Synoptic Gospels present the cleansing of the temple as an event that happened in the last week of Jesus' life. So who has it right in terms of the actual historical chronology?

Some critics are quick to point out that the biblical writers were not always as concerned about chronology as we are; they sometimes arranged their material thematically or topically. These critics theorize that John may have taken an incident that occurred later and placed it at the early part of Jesus' ministry because he seems to be making contrasts in this section of his Gospel. We've already seen the contrast John made between the water and the wine, and now we see a contrast between the physical temple in Jerusalem and Jesus' body as the new temple.

I'm not satisfied with this explanation because John seems to take pains here to note precisely when this event took place in Jesus' ministry. So I think it *did* occur in the early part of his ministry, and I join many others in church history who believe that Jesus cleansed the temple *twice*.

That conclusion sometimes seems like special pleading to those who do not like duplication. I think, for example, of Rudolf Bultmann, the king of the negative critics in twentieth-century New Testament scholarship, who had no time for the theory that this event occurred twice. What I find ironic is that I've read several volumes of Bultmann's theology, and I find certain aspects of his teachings in almost every volume. This kind of repetition is a mark of a teacher. In fact, if you know anything about ministers, you know that they often give the same message more than one time.

So I don't think it's a stretch to assume that when Jesus came to this Passover celebration, the first one during His public ministry, that He was provoked to cleanse the temple by what He saw. He drove out the merchants, drove out the livestock, turned over the tables of the money changers, and so on. But I ask you, how long was it before those tables were upright once more and the money changers were back in business? Can we safely assume that when Jesus cleansed the temple on this occasion that that was the end of the problem? I don't think so. I believe it is perfectly consistent to conclude that when Jesus came to Jerusalem for the Passover right before His death, and when He saw the same things going on that He'd condemned three years earlier, that He took action to cleanse the temple again.

Legitimate Activities, Inappropriate Place

Let's look more closely at what our Lord did in this episode John recorded for us. We read in verses 13–14: **The Passover of the Jews was at hand, and Jesus went up to Jerusalem. And He found in the temple those who sold oxen and sheep and doves, and the money changers doing business.** The critical words in this verse are "in the temple"—the oxen, the sheep, the doves, and so forth were being bought and sold in the temple, and the money changers were practicing their trade there. If these activities had been going on outside the temple, there is every reason to believe that Jesus would have done nothing. But He took issue with the fact that these things were going on inside the temple precincts.

Why was the livestock there and why were the money changers there? The answer is simple. At the Passover, every pilgrim was required to sacrifice an animal. However, it was very difficult for the people who came to Jerusalem from the outer villages of Israel to bring their livestock with them. It was much easier for them to purchase the animals that were necessary for the sacrifices when they arrived in Jerusalem. The money changers were there because a temple tax had to be paid at this time, and the temple authorities were very particular about what kind of coinage was acceptable—the currency had to be minted from the purest silver that could be found. Unfortunately, there were numerous types of currency and coinage in Israel at this time, and some of them were very impure. Seeing a business opportunity, money changers had set up shop to exchange local currencies for the official currency for the tax. For this service, they received a commission, which, some say, may have been as high as twelve percent. Nevertheless, each of these activities was a service to the people who were coming to the temple.

Prior to this time, the booths for the sale of the animals and the exchanging of the money had been set up across the Kidron Valley, up on the slopes of the Mount of Olives, significantly removed from the temple complex. But by Jesus' time, for the sake of convenience, the outer court, the court of the Gentiles, had been transformed from a place of worship and prayer to a place of commerce. As noted above, it was this inappropriate location for these legitimate activities that so incensed Jesus. Thus, when He came into the house of God and saw that it was being used for something other than that for which it had been consecrated, He fashioned his whip and took action.

Some people look at this incident and see Jesus, in a fit of fury and rage, lashing people with His whip. Actually, the purpose of the whip was to drive the animals out of the temple complex. He then went over to the money changers and kicked over their tables, scattering the coins. It was probably a scene of incredible chaos.

In verse 17, John gives a hint as to why Jesus did what he did. He writes, **His disciples remembered that it was written, "Zeal for Your house has eaten Me up."** This is a quotation from Psalm 69, but that particular psalm is not usually considered to be a messianic psalm, a psalm that was prophetic about the coming Messiah. Instead, it is one of David's psalms, and David was talking, in the first instance, about himself. He wrote:

> Save me, O God!
> For the waters have come up to my neck.
> I sink in deep mire,
> Where there is no standing;
> I have come into deep waters,
> Where the floods overflow me.
> I am weary with my crying;
> My throat is dry;
> My eyes fail while I wait for my God.
>
> Those who hate me without a cause
> Are more than the hairs of my head;
> They are mighty who would destroy me,
> Being my enemies wrongfully;
> Though I have stolen nothing,
> I still must restore it.
>
> O God, You know my foolishness;
> And my sins are not hidden from You.

Let not those who wait for You, O Lord GOD of hosts, be ashamed
   because of me;
Let not those who seek You be confounded because of me, O God of
   Israel.
Because for Your sake I have borne reproach;
Shame has covered my face.
I have become a stranger to my brothers,
And an alien to my mother's children. (vv. 1–8)

David was clearly in deep distress as he wrote these words. But what was the reason for this distress? David gives the answer in verse 9: "Because zeal for Your house has eaten me up, and the reproaches of those who reproach You have fallen on me." David says: "Because I have proclaimed Your word, O God, I have become a reproach in my own family. Because of my zeal for Your house, a zeal that consumes me, a passion that eats me up, I'm despised." Seeing Jesus cleanse the temple, His disciples connected His zeal to the zeal David had expressed. They said, "David's greater Son has this in common with David." They saw in Jesus the same thing David experienced in his life—a zeal for the house of God.

Zeal for the Worship of God

But it wasn't simply zeal for the temple that motivated Jesus. It was zeal for the activity the temple was designed to accommodate—the worship of God. Imagine if you went to church on a Sunday morning and went into the sanctuary to pray, but you couldn't focus your thoughts because of the loud and persistent bleating of sheep and goats. That's what was going on in the temple. The sacred grounds that had been set apart for worship had become chaotic. Yes, people's needs were being met. I'm sure the temple authorities were saying, "We're just trying to be relevant; we're being seeker-sensitive for those who can't bring their lambs from home and who need their money exchanged." But in their efforts to make these procedures easy and convenient for the people, they had impacted the people's ability to worship.

At St. Andrew's, the church I serve, I delight to see the people chatting and fellowshiping before worship. But I strongly encourage the people in the congregation to become silent and prepare their hearts as the hour for worship approaches. Just before the service starts, we dim the lights and the strings begin to play the prelude. Those are signals for the people to turn from fellowshiping with one another to prepare to fellowship with God. As they do so, the sanctuary grows delightfully quiet, enabling us all to focus on worship. Simply put, noise is not conducive to worship.

The truth we need to grasp from this incident is one that has almost completely vanished from the landscape of contemporary Christianity—it is the truth that God is particular about how he is to be approached in the sanctuary. Jesus said to His contemporaries: "This is holy ground. This is a place for prayer. This is a place for adoration and for worship. Take your animals, take your produce, and go across the street. This is My Father's house. It is a serious thing to impede His worship."

In response to Jesus' actions, the Jews came to Him and said, **"What sign do You show us, since You do these things?"** (v. 18b). In other words: "Why should we listen to you? Give us some indication of your authority to declare improper what we have permitted." Jesus replied, **"Destroy this temple, and in three days I will raise it up"** (v. 19). The Jewish authorities did not understand what He meant by these words; they thought He was saying He could rebuild the literal temple in three days, and that seemed impossible since it had been under construction for forty-six years and still wasn't finished. His disciples were equally mystified; only after Jesus was raised from the dead on the third day did they make the connection. Therefore, John inserted some editorial help for his readers, explaining that Jesus was not talking about the literal temple but about His body.

The temple that was standing in Jesus' time was destroyed by the Romans in AD 70. Many evangelical Christians are waiting eagerly for the Jews to build a new temple, seeing that as a sign of the end of the age. They fail to understand that the temple already has been rebuilt. Christ is the temple, the locus of the living presence of God in the midst of His people, and the rebuilding of the temple took place on the day of His resurrection.

Like the Jewish leaders, people today constantly ask for signs. They say, "Show me a miracle and I will believe." Others say: "I read about Jesus' miracles in the Bible, but I wasn't there; I didn't see those things with my own eyes. I'm not going to believe in Christ until I see Him with my own eyes, hear Him with my own ears, or see a miracle done in His name today." These people need to consider what Paul said when he went to Athens and addressed the philosophers on Mars Hill. He said: "These times of ignorance God overlooked, but now commands all men everywhere to repent, because He has appointed a day on which He will judge the world in righteousness by the Man whom He has ordained. He has given assurance of this to all *by raising Him from the dead*" (Acts 17:30–31).

Here's what I get out of that. God says through Paul that the resurrection of Christ is the supreme sign, and that He will do it only once. God will not send Christ to die and be raised every week. By raising Christ from the grave, God established His church. Christ is the temple, and all men are commanded to come to Him in order to worship and serve the one true God.

As we continue this study of John's Gospel, we need to remember Jesus' zeal for the house of God and for the worship of God. Again and again throughout this book, we will see that worship is not something we are allowed to do as we please. Those who do so should fear that Christ will come with a whip of cords and drive them from His sanctuary.

6

REBIRTH

John 3:1–13

There was a man of the Pharisees named Nicodemus, a ruler of the Jews. This man came to Jesus by night and said to Him, "Rabbi, we know that You are a teacher come from God; for no one can do these signs that You do unless God is with him." Jesus answered and said to him, "Most assuredly, I say to you, unless one is born again, he cannot see the kingdom of God." Nicodemus said to Him, "How can a man be born when he is old? Can he enter a second time into his mother's womb and be born?" Jesus answered, "Most assuredly, I say to you, unless one is born of water and the Spirit, he cannot enter the kingdom of God. That which is born of the flesh is flesh, and that which is born of the Spirit is spirit. Do not marvel that I said to you, 'You must be born again.' The wind blows where it wishes, and you hear the sound of it, but cannot tell where it comes from and where it goes. So is everyone who is born of the Spirit." Nicodemus answered and said to Him, "How can these things be?" Jesus answered and said to him, "Are you the teacher of Israel, and do not know these things? Most assuredly, I say to you, We speak what We know and testify what We have seen, and you do not receive Our witness. If I have told you earthly things and you do not believe, how will you believe if I tell you heavenly things? No one has ascended to heaven but He who came down from heaven, that is, the Son of Man who is in heaven.

During my maiden reading of the New Testament when I was a new Christian, I was astonished that Nicodemus didn't understand what Jesus was saying. I said to myself: "I know *exactly* what Jesus is talking about because that's what has happened to me. I've experienced a new birth; I've come alive to the things of God. Why can't this teacher of the Jews understand it?"

The next year, as a college student, I signed up for a course on the Gospel of John. At the end of the course, the professor gave an examination that included a question on John 3. When I saw that question, I said to myself: "Oh boy! I know what this is all about!" To my surprise, I got a "C" on that paper. It was then that I found that I didn't really understand what Jesus was talking about.

To tell the truth, I still struggle with John 3 because there's so much to be found in it. I now believe it is one of the most difficult texts in all of the New Testament to deal with adequately.

I think it is important for us to see there is a carryover between the last verse of John 2 and the introduction of Chapter 3. Chapter 2 ends with these words: "But Jesus did not commit Himself to them, because He knew all men, and had no need that anyone should testify of man, for He knew what was in man" (vv. 24–25). There follows in John's narrative a series of encounters between Jesus and various people, such as Nicodemus, the woman at the well, and others. In these meetings, Jesus pierced the hearts of those with whom He spoke and indicated that He knew what was going on in their lives.

A Conversation with a Pharisee

Chapter 3 opens with Jesus' encounter with Nicodemus. It begins by saying, **Now there was a man of the Pharisees named Nicodemus, a ruler of the Jews** (v. 1). This brief introduction tells us that Nicodemus was a man of high authority in the religious leadership of Israel. He was a member of the Sanhedrin, the ruling body of the Jewish people. Not all of the Pharisees were elevated to membership in the Sanhedrin; those who served on this council were akin to senators in the present-day United States. Nicodemus was one of these.

Nicodemus was also skilled as a theologian—or at least he was supposed to be. In verse 10, Jesus reproached him because he was **"the teacher of**

Israel" and yet did not understand what Jesus was teaching him. Jesus implied that these were things Nicodemus should have understood from his study of the Jewish Scriptures, the Old Testament.

Nicodemus, we're told, **came to Jesus by night** (v. 2a). John doesn't tell us why he came at night; maybe he was too busy during the day or maybe, as many guess, he was embarrassed to be seen publicly with Jesus, who was gaining a negative reputation among the Pharisees and the rulers of the Jews. Perhaps Nicodemus was hoping the cover of darkness would enable him to have a clandestine meeting with Jesus so that he could interrogate Him in private.

Nicodemus addressed Jesus in words that seem respectful: **"Rabbi, we know that You are a teacher come from God; for no one can do these signs that You do unless God is with him" (v. 2b)**. Notice the words "we know." At this point, Nicodemus was not using the "imperial plural"; rather, he was speaking for himself and for at least some other members of the ruling body of the Jews. He was speaking from the perspective of collegiality. He said, in essence: "Jesus, we leaders can see that you're a bona fide teacher. You deserve the title 'Rabbi,' and we are prepared to welcome you into our club."

In this opening statement, Nicodemus asserted that he and his colleagues knew something about Jesus. What was it that they knew? "We know that You are a teacher come from God; for no one can do these signs that You do unless God is with him." This was not just a personal affirmation about the identity of Jesus—it was a theological affirmation, as well. But if Nicodemus were alive today, this conclusion that Jesus *must* be from God because of His signs (and notice that Nicodemus said "signs," indicating that Jesus had done other miracles besides changing water into wine at Cana) would place him in a minority of Christians. You see, most Christians believe that not just God can perform miracles, but that Satan can do so, too. Even some of Nicodemus' colleagues believed that, because they later charged Jesus with performing His miracles through the power of Satan (Luke 11:15). This was an unsound judgment; it was bad theology by the Pharisees and it is equally bad theology today.

One of the chief functions of miracles in the New Testament, according to the apostolic testimony, was to authenticate agents of revelation, such as the apostles. God attested that these people were speaking His Word by the wonders and the miracles they performed. Such authenticating miracles would have been completely useless if non-agents of revelation could have performed such works. If Satan had the ability to perform true miracles,

Nicodemus only could have said, "We know you are sent either from God or from the Devil."

It is true that the Bible warns us about "false christs and false prophets" who will perform "signs and wonders" (Mark 13:22). But Satan's so-called miracles are "lying wonders" (2 Thess. 2:9). Satan can perform incredibly clever tricks, but they are not true miracles; they are phony signs because Satan is not God. Satan cannot create something out of nothing; he cannot bring life out of death; he cannot do the things that only God can do. So Nicodemus was absolutely right when he declared, "No one can do these signs that You do unless God is with him." He wasn't confessing that Jesus was the Messiah or God incarnate, but he was sure that Jesus had been sent by God. We must grant that this first statement by Nicodemus was right theologically. On this point at least, Nicodemus was sound in his thinking.

Going to the Heart of the Matter

How did Jesus respond to this statement? Did He say, "I really appreciate that; I'm glad that you noticed and that you're welcoming Me into your club and giving Me this kind of affirmation"? No, Jesus didn't even so much as say, "Thank you very much." Remember, He knew what was in man (2:25) and He knew what was in Nicodemus. So in His characteristic way, He went straight to the heart of the issue. Jesus wasn't interested in diplomacy; He was interested in truth and in redemption. Therefore He said, **"Most assuredly, I say to you . . ."** (v. 3a). These words set the stage for what was to follow. Some translations render these words as "Truly, truly . . ." or "I tell you the truth . . . ." The translators are trying to get the flavor of what Jesus meant when He spoke these words, but it's difficult to do in English. The sense here is that Jesus was stressing the absolute certainty of the words He was about to utter. Jesus said, in effect, "Mark this carefully, Nicodemus—what I'm about to tell you is the unvarnished truth."

Here's that absolute truth: **"Unless one"**—anyone, any person—**"is born again, he cannot see the kingdom of God"** (v. 3b). When Jesus came on the scene in His earthly ministry, He came announcing the radical breakthrough of the kingdom of God (see Matt. 4:17; Mark 1:15). The kingdom of God refers, in the final analysis, to heaven, to the abode where the reign of God is made manifest. Only those who are members of the family of God, those who are members of the invisible church, those who are truly converted, those who are truly in Christ, will come into that kingdom; everyone else will miss it. We know this is so because of Jesus' use of the word *unless*. This word ought to get our attention when we see it in the New

Testament, because it signals a necessary condition, a *sine qua non*, something that has to happen before some desired consequence will follow. In this case, the necessary condition is the new birth, and the desired consequence is seeing the kingdom of God.

There's a question about what exactly Jesus meant in this verse. The word that is used here could be translated "born from above" rather than "born again." However, the significance and the meaning are the same either way. Clearly Jesus was acknowledging that everyone has a natural birth, a biological birth. But Jesus said that in addition to our natural birth, something more must happen before we can see the kingdom of God, and that is supernatural birth. Jesus said that in order for a person to participate in the kingdom of God, he or she must be born supernaturally.

In the mid-1970s, Charles Colson, an adviser to President Nixon who became embroiled in the Watergate scandal, was converted to Christ and wrote a book titled *Born Again*, which sold millions of copies. A few years later, President Carter revealed that he was a "born-again Christian." Suddenly, the words "born again" became part of the nomenclature of American culture. Many people began to call themselves "born-again Christians." That term, however, is a kind of stuttering, because "born-again Christian" is really a redundancy. It's like speaking about "an unmarried bachelor" or "a three-sided triangle." All bachelors are unmarried and all triangles have three sides. The simple reality is this: everyone who is truly a Christian is born again. There are no other kinds of Christians. There's no such thing as a non-born-again Christian or an unregenerate Christian. Yes, there are plenty of unregenerate church members and plenty of unregenerate people who profess to be Christians, but a person cannot be in Christ unless he or she is regenerate. By the same token, if you are regenerate, you are a Christian.

It is because of human weakness that people have to "stutter" like this to get their point across. Francis Schaeffer used to talk about "true truth." He was making the point that there are people who have a subjective view of truth, but he was talking about objective truth that corresponds to objective reality. Much the same kind of thing is going on when someone says, "I'm a born-again Christian." He means that he is a converted person. He is not just professing faith. He is saying that he is not just a member of a church. Rather, he is declaring that he has experienced a supernatural transformation of his soul and has been brought from the kingdom of darkness into the kingdom of light. That's what it means to be regenerate.

When Jesus declared that rebirth is necessary for anyone to see the kingdom of God, Nicodemus was flabbergasted. He replied: **"How can a man be**

born when he is old? Can he enter a second time into his mother's womb and be born?" (v. 4). Again, Nicodemus was not stupid or uneducated, yet he asked a question that was as crass as it could be. I don't believe he could have been more insulting to Jesus in his reply. "What are you talking about?" he asked "Are you suggesting that a man has to enter a second time into his mother's womb to be born? What a ridiculous idea that is."

Water and the Spirit

Jesus did not react to Nicodemus' insulting reply, but neither did he back down. He said: **"Most assuredly, I say to you, unless one is born of water and the Spirit, he cannot enter the kingdom of God"** (v. 5). With these words, Jesus expanded on His first statement. Here He declared that a person must be born "of water and the Spirit." Also, He talked about *entering* the kingdom rather than simply *seeing* it. Now He was talking about actually becoming a part of the kingdom of God. That can't happen, Jesus said, unless a person is born "of water and the Spirit."

I have struggled with this text for more than forty years, but I'm still not completely sure what it means. I know what Jesus meant by the reference to the Spirit; He was talking about being born from above, being born by the power of the Spirit. But I'm unsure what He meant by His reference to water. Some see this text as an oblique reference to baptism; they believe Jesus was saying, "You have to be baptized in water and regenerated by the Holy Spirit in order to come into My kingdom." But there was no reason for Jesus to expect a teacher of Israel to understand that. I think we have to look to the Old Testament use of the word *water* and the combination of the terms *water* and *Spirit* to understand what Jesus was getting at.

According to the Old Testament prophets, particularly Ezekiel, the people of God needed two things—they had to be purified and they had to be resurrected by the power of God. I may be wrong, but I think I hear this twofold emphasis in what Jesus said to Nicodemus. It was as if He said: "Nicodemus, everybody who is unregenerate is impure and spiritually dead, and as long as a person is impure and spiritually dead, he can never enter the kingdom of God. To enter the kingdom of God, a person must be purified and must be raised from spiritual death. He has to be cleansed and raised by the power of the Holy Spirit." In this, there is water for cleansing and the Spirit for new life. That's the way these images were used in Jewish conversation. Jesus knew He was talking to a teacher of the Jews, so I think this is what He was saying to Nicodemus. I could be wrong, but it's certainly true that no one who has not been purified by God and raised from spiritual death will ever enter the kingdom of God.

Jesus went on to say to Nicodemus, **"That which is born of the flesh is flesh, and that which is born of the Spirit is spirit"** (v. 6). No one is born a Christian. The flesh does not produce redemption. This was a common error the Jewish people made. They thought that because they were Jews, being descended from the Old Testament patriarch Abraham, that they were numbered among the people of God and would enter heaven. The Old Testament prophets and then the New Testament teachers had to show the people that this was not the case. Likewise, you may have been born to Christian parents, raised in a Christian home, and gone to a Christian school or a Christian college, but none of those things make you a Christian. All that your natural birth has given you is flesh, and flesh of that sort is powerless to enter the kingdom of God. That which is born of the Spirit is spirit. Unless you are born of the Spirit of the living God, whatever you do in your flesh will avail nothing toward entering the kingdom of God.

The Spirit and the Wind

Finally, Jesus said to Nicodemus: **"Do not marvel that I said to you, 'You must be born again.' The wind blows where it wishes, and you hear the sound of it, but cannot tell where it comes from and where it goes. So is everyone who is born of the Spirit"** (vv. 7–8). Jesus here made a play on the Greek word *pneuma*; it means the same thing as the Hebrew word *ruach*. It can mean "wind," "breath," or "spirit." He said, "You have to be born of the Spirit, and it's like the wind." In other words, the *pneuma* is like the *pneuma*. The wind, of course, blows wherever it wants, sometimes very powerfully, but we cannot see it. We can see only the consequences of it, the manifestation of its power, but we don't fully know where it's coming from or where it's going. Everyone who is born of the Spirit is somewhat like that, because spiritual rebirth is the work of God. Paul tells us this in Ephesians 2:4–5a, where he writes, "But God, who is rich in mercy, because of His great love with which He loved us, even when we were *dead* in trespasses, made us *alive* together with Christ." He is speaking here about regeneration, the act of giving new life. This is a supernatural work; it is done from above by the immediate power of God, and it's something only God can do. You cannot cause yourself to be reborn.

Nicodemus remained puzzled. **"How can these things be?"** he asked (v. 9). Jesus did not immediately answer that question. Instead, he chided Nicodemus for his ignorance. Jesus said to him, **"Are you the teacher of**

Israel, and do not know these things?" (v. 10). It was as if Jesus were saying: "You don't know this? How did you make it through graduate school? This is foundational biblical truth. This is not some mystery religion that I'm giving you, some esoteric truth that only the Gnostics know. I'm telling you something that any knowledgeable teacher of the Old Testament should have grasped a long time ago. Why don't you, the teacher of Israel, understand these things?" Jesus made clear to Nicodemus that the Old Testament books had pointed to Him and the atonement He would make for His people.

Jesus then went on to say: **"Most assuredly, I say to you, We speak what We know and testify what We have seen, and you do not receive Our witness. If I have told you earthly things and you do not believe, how will you believe if I tell you heavenly things? No one has ascended to heaven but He who came down from heaven, that is, the Son of Man who is in heaven"** (vv. 11–13). The main point Jesus was communicating with these words was that He had authority to speak about eternal truths, for He knew them and had seen them, having come from the presence of God in heaven. He said, in a sense: "Nicodemus, you're talking to the One who has come down from heaven. You are talking to the Son of Man in person, and you don't understand these basic truths that My Father has revealed in the Old Testament." Sadly, Nicodemus and his fellow religious leaders were rejecting His testimony.

In the next chapter, I will examine Jesus' response to Nicodemus' question, "How can these things be?" For now, it is enough for us to contemplate this shock that Jesus gave to Nicodemus, which, I'm afraid, is just as shocking to the twenty-first-century church—that there is an absolute requirement that must be met if a person is to enter God's kingdom. A person must be changed by God; the disposition of his heart, which by nature does not want to do God's bidding, must be altered by God the Holy Spirit. Man's natural tendency is to flee from the presence of God and to have no affection for the biblical Christ. Therefore, if you have in your heart today any affection for Christ at all, it is because God the Holy Spirit in His sweetness, in His power, in His mercy, and in His grace has been to the cemetery of your soul and has raised you from the dead. So you are now alive to the things of Christ and you rejoice in the kingdom into which He has brought you.

7

THE SON OF MAN
MUST BE LIFTED UP

John 3:14–21

"And as Moses lifted up the serpent in the wilderness, even so must the Son of Man be lifted up, that whoever believes in Him should not perish but have eternal life. For God so loved the world that He gave His only begotten Son, that whoever believes in Him should not perish but have everlasting life. For God did not send His Son into the world to condemn the world, but that the world through Him might be saved. He who believes in Him is not condemned; but he who does not believe is condemned already, because he has not believed in the name of the only begotten Son of God. And this is the condemnation, that the light has come into the world, and men loved darkness rather than light, because their deeds were evil. For everyone practicing evil hates the light and does not come to the light, lest his deeds should be exposed. But he who does the truth comes to the light, that his deeds may be clearly seen, that they have been done in God."

I n the previous chapter, we began looking at Jesus' dialogue with the Pharisee Nicodemus. As we saw, Jesus asserted that human beings must be "born again" in order to "see" and "enter" the kingdom of God. Nicodemus was baffled by Jesus' teaching and blurted out, "How can these things be?" (v. 9b). Jesus chided him for not understanding this teaching, even though he was a theologian. But Jesus also had compassion on Nicodemus and took time to explain the things of God to him.

As Jesus began to answer Nicodemus' question, He directed him back to the pages of the Old Testament. He said, **"As Moses lifted up the serpent in the wilderness, even so must the Son of Man be lifted up, that whoever believes in Him should not perish but have eternal life"** (vv. 14–15). Jesus was referring here to an event that took place during the ancient Israelites' wilderness experience. The book of Numbers tells us:

> Then they journeyed from Mount Hor by the Way to the Red Sea, to go around the land of Edom; and the soul of the people became very discouraged on the way. And the people spoke against God and against Moses: "Why have you brought us up out of Egypt to die in the wilderness? For there is no food and no water, and our soul loathes this worthless bread." So the LORD sent fiery serpents among the people, and they bit the people; and many of the people of Israel died. (Num. 21:4–6)

God delivered the people from slavery in Egypt, then provided for their physical needs supernaturally with manna from heaven, but as the journey to Canaan continued, the people became impatient and began to speak against God and Moses. They expressed their unhappiness about spending so much time in the desert and having nothing to eat except manna. This was nothing short of rebellion, and God responded by sending a plague on the people. This time the plague was not against the Egyptians, as God had done so memorably. This plague was against the Israelites. He sent an infestation of poisonous snakes, whose venom is described as being like fire. The snakes bit the people, and many of them died.

Have you ever contemplated this particular episode in redemptive history? I can think of few things that would be worse than being thrown into a pit full of vipers, any one of which could kill me with one bite. It would be like something out of an Indiana Jones movie. This horror was God's judgment against His people.

Thankfully, God's chastisement had its intended effect—repentance—so He prescribed a remedy:

Therefore the people came to Moses, and said, "We have sinned, for we have spoken against the LORD and against you; pray to the LORD that He take away the serpents from us." So Moses prayed for the people. Then the LORD said to Moses, "Make a fiery serpent, and set it on a pole; and it shall be that everyone who is bitten, when he looks at it, shall live." So Moses made a bronze serpent, and put it on a pole; and so it was, if a serpent had bitten anyone, when he looked at the bronze serpent, he lived. (Num. 21:7–9)

What is left unstated in this narrative is the number of people who died despite this remedy that God provided. Some of the people clearly repented, but the implication of the text is that some of those who were bitten looked at the bronze serpent while others did not. Even in their death agonies, in the throes of the terror and pain inflicted by these serpents, they would not trust God's prescribed course—even though the cure rate was one hundred percent.

We are told later in the Scriptures that King Hezekiah of Judah had to destroy this bronze serpent (2 Kings 18:4). It had been preserved for hundreds of years, but the people had turned it into an idol. God used it once as a symbol of His grace and mercy, and human nature being what it is, the people began to worship the bronze serpent, just like they had worshiped the golden calf at the base of Mount Sinai.

A Comparison for Nicodemus

What was Jesus' point in relating this story of the bronze serpent to Nicodemus? His intent was to make a comparison. After asking Nicodemus to recall this incident from the Old Testament, Jesus declared, "As Moses lifted up the serpent in the wilderness, even so must the Son of Man be lifted up" (v. 14).

A close examination of this verse reveals that Jesus used an expression here that carries more than one meaning. In Scripture, the expression "lifted up" usually means "to be exalted." For instance, when Isaiah had his vision of God exalted in His heavenly throne room, he wrote that he "saw the Lord . . . high and lifted up" (Isa. 6:1). Thus, when Jesus said, "As Moses lifted up the serpent . . . even so must the Son of Man be lifted up," it would make sense to understand Him to be saying, "I will be exalted." But when Jesus used the phrase "lifted up" here, He was speaking more directly to what had to happen for people to enter His kingdom—He must be lifted up on a cross; He must become the substitute serpent, if you will. He had to take on Himself the sting of death. He had to take on Himself the poison of sin on the cross. There's little doubt in the minds of the commentators that when Jesus spoke of being lifted up like the bronze serpent, He was referring primarily not to his exaltation but to His crucifixion.

Jesus then went on to say that He must be lifted up on the cross so "that whoever who believes in [the Son of Man] should . . . have eternal life" (v. 15). This statement parallels the situation of the Israelites in the wilderness. The people who had been bitten by the poisonous snakes were going to die, so God gave them a remedy to preserve them from certain destruction. Jesus told Nicodemus that we, too, are in this state; that apart from Christ, apart from the cross, we are as exposed to death and destruction as those people who had been bitten by deadly snakes. Looking to Jesus in His lifted-up state would effect a cure, just as looking to Moses' bronze serpent did, but the cure to be obtained by looking to Jesus would be deeper and better. Looking to Jesus would cure the problem of spiritual deadness wrought by sin, and it would do so for eternity.

The Most Distorted Verse?

Verse 16 of John 3 is surely the best-known verse in the New Testament. Many Bible versions put this verse in red to indicate that these words were spoken by Jesus. In my opinion, this verse should not be in red. I don't think Jesus said to Nicodemus, **"For God so loved the world that He gave His only begotten Son, that whoever believes in Him should not perish but have everlasting life."** It's difficult to tell where in this chapter Jesus' words end and John's editorial comments begin, but most commentators see John 3:16 as written by John, and I agree with that assessment. However, even if this is John speaking and not Jesus, this verse is not any less the Word of God or any less true, for John wrote under the inspiration of the Holy Spirit.

Not only is this undoubtedly the best-known verse in the New Testament, it's probably the most distorted verse, as well. Why? It is because people who love the apparent universality of this verse hate the undeniable particularity of it.

The verse begins by saying something about the love of God and the object of God's affection. God so loved . . . what? "The world." Now let me finish the verse for you according to the contemporary understanding: "God so loved the world that He gave His Son in order to save everyone in the world." Some people draw from this text a doctrine of universal salvation; they believe it teaches that God loves the world so much He saves everyone. But clearly that's not what the text says. On the other hand, those who are particularists and Arminians say that God loved the world enough to provide *a way* of salvation for everybody in it, but the verse doesn't say that either. Rather, John 3:16 says that God's love is so deep and so profound, He sent His only begotten Son.

Now let's look at what this verse doesn't mean. He did not love the world so much that He sent multiple saviors. Yet our culture tells us that if God were *really* loving, He would have provided avatars galore—He would have provided a smorgasbord of salvation options so that everyone could practice his or her own religion, and He would not have been so narrow-minded and exclusive as to require faith in Christ alone. Doesn't the Bible say that God loved "the world"? Yes, the Bible says that He loved the world. But how much did He love the world? He loved it enough to send His one and only Son.

Suppose there actually is a God in heaven, and suppose this God created the world and everything in it. Suppose that, in the process of making myriad species of birds, fish, and animals, He formed human beings in His image and gave them the most exalted position in all of creation. Suppose He said, "You will be holy, even as I am holy," and gave them only one command to obey—but fifteen minutes after He made them, these human beings revolted against Him by doing the very thing he had commanded them not to do. Suppose God then said, "I'm going to provide a way for you to escape My judgment," and He then called Abraham out of paganism, brought him to Himself, and said, "I'm going to make you the father of a great nation." Suppose that He blessed all the descendants of Abraham, expanded them into a whole nation, and said, "Through this nation I'm going to bless the whole world"—but this nation repeatedly turned against Him. Suppose God sent prophets to these people to tell them to come back to Him, just as an unfaithful spouse returns to his or her partner—but the people killed the prophets. Suppose God finally said, "I love you so much, even though you are a stiff-necked people, that I'm going to send My eternal, only begotten Son to you"—but the people rose up against His Son and crucified Him. Suppose that God loved the people enough in all of this that while they were in the very act of killing His Son, He transferred the sins of His people to His Son and said: "If you'll put your trust in Him, if you'll confess your sins and believe in Him, if you'll turn your gaze upon Jesus, you will not experience death. I'm going to give you eternal life with no pain, no tears, no evil, and no darkness." If God were to do all that, would you have the insolence to say to Him, "God, You haven't done enough for this world that hates You"?

Are you one who gets angry when he hears there is only one way to God? The question is not, "Why is there *only* one way?" but "Why is there *even* one way?" The answer to that question is that God loved the world enough to create a way. However, He didn't love the world enough to say that we can ignore the way He has provided. That would not be true love. We need to understand that our culture says, "If God provides only *one* way of salvation, He doesn't really love the world." Our culture does not perceive the depths of love that God has displayed by giving us Christ, whose name should not be mentioned in the same breath with those of Mohammed, Buddha, Confucius, or anyone else. God has one Son, who beheld the glory of the Father from all eternity, and yet, in the words of the Nicene Creed, "for us men and for our salvation, came down from heaven, . . . and was made man; and was crucified also for us under Pontius Pilate; . . . suffered and was buried."

Jesus Christ Came to Save

John goes on to say: **"For God did not send His Son into the world to condemn the world, but that the world through Him might be saved. He who believes in Him is not condemned"** (vv. 17–18a). John's meaning here could hardly be clearer. Jesus came into the world to save people. We are like those people writhing on the desert floor after being bitten by fiery serpents, but there is a remedy. Just as the Israelites could look to the uplifted bronze serpent and be saved, we can look to Christ. Those who look to Him will not perish in their sins and face eternal condemnation.

However, verse 18 continues with a terrifying alternative. As happens so often in Scripture, this alternative is signaled by the word *but*. John writes: **"But he who does not believe is condemned already, because he has not believed in the name of the only begotten Son of God"** (v. 18b). Those who look to Christ escape condemnation, but those who refuse to trust Him are as good as condemned already.

Sometimes we wonder why anyone would refuse to look to Christ and live. John has the answer: **"And this is the condemnation, that the light has come into the world, and men loved darkness rather than light, because their deeds were evil. For everyone practicing evil hates the light and does not come to the light, lest his deeds should be exposed. But he who does the truth comes to the light, that his deeds may be clearly seen, that they have been done in God"** (vv. 19–21). This is our natural state. We are in the darkness, so nothing terrifies us more than the appearance of light. But as we saw, Jesus is introduced as the light of the world in the very first chapter of this Gospel. This light shines into the darkness, but people love the darkness because their deeds are evil. That's our nature—we are children of darkness. It is against the nature of a child of darkness to come to the light because he knows the light represents exposure and humiliation.

Have you heard about the man who sent a letter to twenty-five men in his town? It said: "All has been exposed. Flee at once." In response, all twenty-five men left town. What would you do if you got a letter like that? Even as Christians, we still feel that tug at our heart that causes us to look for a place to hide in the darkness rather than seeking the light of Christ.

God said through John: "This is My condemnation. I sent the light, but you didn't want the light. But all who are of the light, who come to the light, who embrace the light, will not perish but have everlasting life." In a nutshell, that's the gospel Nicodemus heard from the lips of Jesus in the darkness of the night. It is the good news that snake-bitten people, people infected by a poison that goes to the depth of their souls, can look to the cross and find salvation.

8

JESUS AND
JOHN THE BAPTIST

John 3:22–36

After these things Jesus and His disciples came into the land of Judea, and there He remained with them and baptized. Now John also was baptizing in Aenon near Salim, because there was much water there. And they came and were baptized. For John had not yet been thrown into prison. Then there arose a dispute between some of John's disciples and the Jews about purification. And they came to John and said to him, "Rabbi, He who was with you beyond the Jordan, to whom you have testified—behold, He is baptizing, and all are coming to Him!" John answered and said, "A man can receive nothing unless it has been given to him from heaven. You yourselves bear me witness, that I said, 'I am not the Christ,' but, 'I have been sent before Him.' He who has the bride is the bridegroom; but the friend of the bridegroom, who stands and hears him, rejoices greatly because of the bridegroom's voice. Therefore this joy of mine is fulfilled. He must increase, but I must decrease. He who comes from above is above all; he who is of the earth is earthly and speaks of the earth. He who comes from heaven is above all. And what He has seen and heard, that He testifies; and no one receives His testimony. He who has received

His testimony has certified that God is true. For He whom God has sent speaks the words of God, for God does not give the Spirit by measure. The Father loves the Son, and has given all things into His hand. He who believes in the Son has everlasting life; and he who does not believe the Son shall not see life, but the wrath of God abides on him."

Through the early chapters of John's Gospel, we witness a series of incidents in which the new order Jesus was inaugurating was set in contrast with the old things, revealing the superiority of the new order to the old. We have seen the superiority of the wine Jesus made at Cana as compared with the waters of purification. We have seen that Christ promised that, when He was lifted up on the cross, He would provide a deeper, better cure than did the bronze serpent Moses made. Now, in this passage, we find a comparison of the ministries of John the Baptist and of Jesus.

We are told in verse 22 that after His discussion with Nicodemus, Jesus went into **the land of Judea** with His disciples. This is curious, for Jesus was already in Judea, in Jerusalem (see 2:13). Other biblical translations provide resolution to this problem by telling us that Jesus went "into the Judean countryside." In other words, He moved outside the city to a more rural area, expanding His Judean ministry. We also are told that Jesus **baptized** people during this time.

At this point, John's focus shifts from Jesus to John the Baptist. John the Baptist was still baptizing people with the help of a cadre of disciples. We have already seen that at least one of John's disciples had transferred his loyalty to Jesus—Andrew, Peter's brother (1:35–41). This was an altogether natural thing for Andrew to do, since John had pointed to Jesus as "the Lamb of God who takes away the sin of the world!" (1:29). Yet here in Chapter 3, we see that John still had disciples. These were followers who found it impossible to transfer their allegiance to Jesus. They were intensely loyal to John, and we see the depth of their loyalty as it became obvious to them that more people were going to Jesus to be baptized than were coming to their master. John the Baptist's disciples were gripped by envy as they saw the ministry they were involved with beginning to lose its popularity to another ministry.

This is something we all experience. We are assaulted by envy and covetousness, which cause us to want what others have. We must fight against these tendencies. We need to remember the remarkable words of the apostle Paul in Philippians 4:11: "I have learned in whatever state I am, to be content."

Finally, John's disciples came to him with their concerns. They addressed him as **"Rabbi,"** which was a term of respect, and said, **"He who was with you beyond the Jordan, to whom you have testified—behold, He is baptizing, and all are coming to him!"** (v. 26).

John's Unexpected Response

This statement of distress elicited no distress or envy on John's part. Not only was John not perturbed by the increasing attention being given to Jesus, he was pleased about it. His reply to his disciples is very instructive for us. He began by saying, **"A man can receive nothing unless it has been given to him from heaven"** (v. 27). In one sense, John was speaking here about the principle of vocation. What do we have that we haven't received? Every talent and ability that we have has been given to us from God, and we understand that we all have our own vocations. The term *vocation* comes from the Latin word that means "to call." God has called each one of us to the place where we are in this life. Sadly, we often slip into jealousy, envy, and backbiting, trying to advance our position at others' expense—tearing down our neighbors so that we can replace them in status or in exaltation. When we do that, we despise the gifts that God has distributed in His wisdom.

It was precisely because of his God-given vocation that John the Baptist was delighted to see Jesus' popularity growing and his own declining. He went on to say to his disciples, **"You yourselves bear me witness, that I said, 'I am not the Christ,' but, 'I have been sent before Him'"** (v. 28). From the start, John had declared that he was the voice crying in the wilderness, the herald of the kingdom of God. He was the forerunner of the King Himself, so he was thrilled to see the manifestation of the One whom the Father had sent as the Messiah. He had pointed to Jesus, and now his testimony to the Messiah was bearing fruit.

John added, **"He who has the bride is the bridegroom; but the friend of the bridegroom, who stands and hears him, rejoices greatly because of the bridegroom's voice. Therefore this joy of mine is fulfilled"** (v. 29). Perhaps John was thinking back to the Old Testament economy, where Israel sometimes was called the bride of God in anticipation of the New Testament references to the church as Christ's bride. John was saying: "I am not the Bridegroom. The bride isn't mine. The bride is His, but I'm the best man, and I get to go to the wedding feast and stand right next to the Bridegroom as He enters into the joy of this wedding." For John, that was an unspeakable privilege, a joy that was matchless and immeasurable. He didn't covet the bride, but he delighted to stand with the Bridegroom on the occasion of that wedding.

Then John gave one of the most famous statements that ever fell from his lips: **"He must increase, but I must decrease"** (v. 30). I want to point out just one small detail about this. John was not putting forth a strategy *he* had devised. He was not saying: "I think we can lighten up a little bit now. We pointed out the Messiah, we called attention to the Lamb of God, just as we were supposed to do. Now that He has emerged and is entering into His public ministry, I think we can pull back and relax." No, when John said, "He *must* increase," he was saying, "It is necessary." The increase of Christ was not an option. John had his marching orders from God. He was called to go before Christ, and once he had announced Christ, then John was to go into the background that Christ might emerge in the fullness of His leadership as the appointed Messiah. "It's necessary," John said. "It's not optional. This *has* to happen. It *has* to take place. I *have* to decrease. He *must* increase."

John plainly stated the reason for this necessity: **"He who comes from above is above all"** (v. 31a). There's a little play on words here. Jesus had not merely come from Nazareth. He hadn't just come out from Jerusalem and come along the Jordan River. His point of origin was heaven itself. He had come from above, and One from above must be above all.

For John the Baptist, the contrast between Jesus' origin and his own was plain: **"he who is of the earth is earthly and speaks of the earth"** (v. 31b). John obviously was speaking of himself here. He was saying, "I am a human being; I am of the earth." The greater point is that one who is of the earth cannot have preeminence over One who has come from heaven. So he said, **"He who comes from heaven is above all"** (v. 31c).

John then spoke of Jesus' own message: **"And what He has seen and heard, that He testifies"** (v. 32a). John was agreeing here with Jesus' testimony about Himself and His teaching, a testimony He stated plainly later in His ministry: "For I have not spoken on My own authority; but the Father who sent Me gave Me a command, what I should say and what I should speak" (John 12:49). Jesus had come from heaven with a message that was not of His own creation. He came with the words of God. He was the divinely appointed apostle of the Father who came to this planet to declare the very words of God Himself.

The Testimony of Jesus

John the Baptist then moved into a series of statements about the reaction to Jesus' testimony: **"and no one receives His testimony. He who has received His testimony has certified that God is true"** (v. 32b–33). First, John the Baptist declared that no one received what Jesus had to say.

This agrees with the words of the apostle John in the prologue to his Gospel: "The light shines in the darkness, and the darkness did not comprehend it. . . . He came to His own, and His own did not receive Him" (John 1:5, 11). But John the Baptist's next sentence seemed to contradict that, for he spoke of "he who *has* received His testimony. . . ." This affirmation that some received Jesus is also present in the prologue: "But as many as received Him, to them He gave the right to become children of God" (John 1:12a). There was certainly widespread opposition to Jesus, and the religious leaders of His time rejected Him almost universally. But amid that opposition there were those whose eyes and ears God opened to see and hear the truth of Jesus' words, and they received His teaching.

John continues: **"For He whom God has sent speaks the words of God, for God does not give the Spirit by measure"** (v. 34). When God anointed His Son as the Messiah, the Holy Spirit was not given to Him in a piecemeal or partial fashion. God the Father did not measure out a little dose of the Spirit to give to His Son; rather, He poured out the Spirit on the Son in immeasurable dimensions, enabling Him to speak God's words.

John concluded with a series of joyous affirmations: **"The Father loves the Son, and has given all things into His hand. He who believes in the Son has everlasting life; and he who does not believe the Son shall not see life, but the wrath of God abides on him"** (vv. 35–36). The whole of Scripture speaks to us of the love of God for His people, but so often we fix our attention on God's love for us that we forget that the ground of that love is the love that the Father has from eternity for His Son. Remember, we're not the natural children of God. We're the adopted children of God, and even our election must always be understood to be in the Son.

It is because of the Father's love for the Son that we can stand forgiven before the throne of God, delivered from wrath unto everlasting life. It is because of the love of the Father for the Son that we are invited to partake one day of the marriage feast of the Lamb. We are invited not simply as friends of the Bridegroom or as friends of the bride—we *are* the bride. Christ our Savior has set His love upon us and betrothed us to Himself. He who died for us will come again someday to receive us to Himself. Then we will rejoice with Him in the final increase of His exaltation.

9

THE WOMAN AT THE WELL, PART 1

John 4:1–15

Therefore, when the Lord knew that the Pharisees had heard that Jesus made and baptized more disciples than John (though Jesus Himself did not baptize, but His disciples), He left Judea and departed again to Galilee. But He needed to go through Samaria. So He came to a city of Samaria which is called Sychar, near the plot of ground that Jacob gave to his son Joseph. Now Jacob's well was there. Jesus therefore, being wearied from His journey, sat thus by the well. It was about the sixth hour. A woman of Samaria came to draw water. Jesus said to her, "Give Me a drink." For His disciples had gone away into the city to buy food. Then the woman of Samaria said to Him, "How is it that You, being a Jew, ask a drink from me, a Samaritan woman?" For Jews have no dealings with Samaritans. Jesus answered and said to her, "If you knew the gift of God, and who it is who says to you, 'Give Me a drink,' you would have asked Him, and He would have given you living water." The woman said to Him, "Sir, You have nothing to draw with, and the well is deep. Where then do You get that living water? Are You greater than our father Jacob, who gave us the well, and drank from it himself, as well as his sons and his livestock?" Jesus answered and said to her, "Whoever drinks of this water will thirst again, but whoever drinks of the water that I shall give him will never thirst. But the water that I shall give him will become in him a fountain of water springing up into everlasting life." The woman said to Him, "Sir, give me this water, that I may not thirst, nor come here to draw."

One of the reasons I love the Gospel of John is that it is filled with narrative accounts of encounters Jesus had with various people from all walks of life. We've already seen the extended conversation that He had with Nicodemus, who was not only a Jew but a ruler of the Jews, a member of the Sanhedrin. Now we get to eavesdrop on a conversation that Jesus had with a Samaritan; and not just a Samaritan but a female Samaritan; and not just a female Samaritan but a female Samaritan who obviously had a reputation for sexual immorality. All three of these aspects—that she was a Samaritan, that she was a woman, and that she was immoral—set her in a category radically different from Nicodemus, the thoroughly Jewish, male, and morally precise Pharisee.

The history of Samaria and the Samaritans can be traced to the division of the kingdom of Israel that occurred after the reign of David's son Solomon. When David became king of the Jewish people, he conquered Jerusalem and made it the nation's capital, and it was there that Solomon built the temple. But when Solomon's kingdom was divided into the northern kingdom, Israel, and the southern kingdom, Judah, those who were in the northern kingdom constructed Samaria as their capital city. When the northern kingdom was defeated by Assyria in 722 BC, many Jews were deported and pagan peoples were brought in. This mixture of Jews and Gentiles eventually became the people known as the Samaritans. Not surprisingly, this mixture also produced syncretistic religious practices. The Samaritans accepted only the first five books of the Old Testament, so they ignored the writings of the prophets and the Psalms. Specifically, they rejected anything that spoke of Jerusalem. Their central place of worship was Mount Gerizim, not the temple in Jerusalem, which, in Jesus' time, had been rebuilt by Herod.

Because the Samaritans rejected so much of the Word of God and because of their syncretistic practices, the Jews were very hostile toward them. So deep was this hostility that, in most instances, a Jew traveling from north to south or vice versa refused to pass through the territory of Samaria. Instead, he would take a roundabout route, crossing the Jordan River to the east and traveling the trans-Jordan highway.

A Divine Appointment

Not so for Jesus. John tells us that Jesus **left Judea and departed again to Galilee** (v. 3). But it seems He was in a hurry, for He decided against taking the roundabout route and instead went directly north into Samaria. John says He **needed to go through Samaria** (v. 4). It is unclear whether John meant it was necessary for Jesus to go through Samaria in order to reach His destination at the desired time or whether Jesus was aware of a divine appointment in Samaria. In light of what follows, the latter option seems likely.

We're told that Jesus **came to a city of Samaria which is called Sychar, near the plot of ground that Jacob gave to his son Joseph** (v. 5). When Jacob gave his patriarchal blessing to Joseph's sons, he mentioned this parcel of real estate (Gen. 48:22). This was a very important piece of land because **Jacob's well was there** (v. 6a). Nearly two thousand years after Jacob dug the well, it was still there to provide water for Jesus. That was a long, long time, so the well site was considered sacred by people who traced their roots back to the Old Testament patriarch. (As an aside, this well is still there today, right at the base of Mount Gerizim, and the water still flows freely. So that well has been meeting the needs of people for four thousand years.)

Jesus, **wearied from His journey, sat thus by the wall. It was about the sixth hour** (v. 6b). That means it was high noon. According to the Jewish method of keeping time, the hours started at 6 a.m., so "the sixth hour" was twelve o'clock. That was the hottest time of the day in this desert region. Jesus, in His humanity—and this is one of those marvelous texts that explore something of the reality of the human nature of Christ—was tired and thirsty.

John tells us that Jesus was alone because **His disciples had gone away into the city to buy food** (v. 8). You may think Jesus was acting a bit over-bearing by making His disciples fetch the groceries. However, this was normal because Jesus was the rabbi, and it was a rule in this kind of a peripatetic school that the students not only learned what the professor taught, they were expected to serve their master. The disciples took care of their rabbi's requirements—where he lodged, where the food came from, and so forth. Jesus, being a good rabbi and having good students, sent them into the city to get lunch and bring it to Him.

Jesus wasn't alone for long. **A woman of Samaria came to draw water** (v. 7). Ordinarily, the women of the village drew water early in the morning or after sunset, not in the heat of the day, and they would get a day's supply of water for drinking, for bathing, and for cleaning their utensils and clothes. Also, the women normally would come to the well as a group. That this woman came at noon and that she came alone tell us volumes about her social status in the community. She obviously was ostracized from the rest of the women. Being something of a pariah, she had to come by herself in the heat of the day to get her water.

Much to her surprise, the unknown man at the well said, **"Give Me a drink"** (v. 7b). Her surprised stemmed from the fact that Jesus was clearly a Jew, so she said, **"How is it that You, being a Jew, ask a drink from me, a Samaritan woman?"** Then John added, as background, **Jews have no dealings with Samaritans** (v. 9). The translation of the last part of this verse is a bad one; it's not true that the Jews had no dealings with the Samaritans. They had all kinds of dealings with the Samaritans. In fact, Jesus had sent the disciples into town for a business transaction, the purchase of food. What Jews were not allowed to do was to share eating utensils with Samaritans, particularly glasses or cups, because the Samaritans were considered to be unclean.

A Thought-Provoking Response

Jesus responded to the woman's question in a thought-provoking way, much as He did to Nicodemus' first comment (3:3). He said to the woman: **"If you knew the gift of God and who it is who says to you, 'Give me a drink,' you would have asked Him, and He would have given you living water"** (v. 10). In other words, Jesus said: "If you knew who I was, you wouldn't respond to My request by giving Me the history of the social problems between the Jews and the Samaritans. You would drop everything and would say to Me, 'Give Me a drink.'"

Like Nicodemus (3:4), the woman was puzzled by Jesus' words, so she asked for clarification: **"Sir, You have nothing to draw with, and the well is deep. Where then do you get that living water?"** (v. 11). It was the custom of travelers in the ancient world, when making a journey of several miles, to take along a goat-skinned bucket to retrieve water from wells or other sources, but Jesus obviously did not have one; it probably was with the disciples in town. The woman, in her confusion, pointed this out: "You don't have a bucket. You don't have anything to draw with. How are You going to give me something to drink? Not only that, this well is deep. Where are You going to get this living water?"

Then she asked a question that reflected the depth of her incredulity: **"Are You greater than our father Jacob, who gave us the well, and drank from it himself, as well as his sons and his livestock?"**

(v. 12). She could not believe that anyone who was greater than Jacob, the man who dug the well that had supplied water for two thousand years, could come along and talk to her.

Jesus answered: **"Whoever drinks of this water will thirst again, but whoever drinks of the water that I shall give him will never thirst. But the water that I shall give him will become in him a fountain of water springing up into everlasting life"** (vv. 13–14). In essence, Jesus told the woman: "I grant that Jacob was a great man, and he did a wonderful thing by giving you this well. It has stood the test of time for two thousand years. People come here every day to get their water. This isn't the first time you've been here to get water. If you drink from Jacob's well, you're going to have to come back tomorrow, because this water won't prevent you from thirsting again. But anyone who drinks the water I can give will never become thirsty again. Instead, it will become a fountain of water inside him springing up to eternal life."

When Jesus spoke of this water "springing up," He used a word that literally meant "leaping up." The picture He painted was of water so alive, so dynamic, so energetic, and powerful that it not only would assuage thirst for a moment, it would begin to pour up out of the soul of the person and continue to nurture him day after day, year after year. Obviously, Jesus was using the element of water as a metaphor to describe a spiritual reality, something that would meet not just a need of the moment but a need for all eternity.

Seeking the Gifts, Not the Giver

Can you imagine how thirsty this woman was? How empty her life was? How barren her soul was? I don't mean that she was passionately pursuing the things of God, hungering and thirsting after righteousness. That obviously wasn't the case. I'm speaking of spiritual bankruptcy.

It's very common to hear Christians say that their unbelieving friends are "seeking God" or "searching for God," but the Scriptures tell us that in our fallen condition, none of us ever seeks God (Rom. 3:11). The quest for God doesn't begin until conversion. Prior to our conversions, we run as fast and as relentlessly as we can away from God. So why do we hear it said that those who aren't Christians are seeking?

The best answer, I think, came from Thomas Aquinas. When Aquinas was asked why people seem to be seeking after God despite the Bible's affirmation that no one seeks for Him, Aquinas said such people are not actually seeking God. Instead, they are desperately seeking peace, seeking relief from their guilt, seeking something to fill the emptiness of their souls and their lives.

We know that the only thing that will satisfy that hunger and thirst within their souls is the living Christ, so we conclude that since they're seeking to have their thirst assuaged and their hunger satisfied, they must be seeking for God. Aquinas said that is not the case at all. People desperately search for the things that only God can give them while at the same time they are fleeing from Him.

Jesus knew all about this woman. He knew that her life was bankrupt. She had not stopped trying to find happiness. Five times she had married, and every time she had entered into a marriage she had thought: "This is the one that will make me happy. This is the one that will last." However, none of her marriages had lasted, and now she was living with somebody who was not her husband. Why was she doing that? Was it because she wanted to be sinful? No. She simply wanted to find happiness. She was lonely and empty. She was willing to grab at anything that might satisfy her thirst.

So when Jesus said, "Whoever drinks of this water will thirst again, but whoever drinks of the water that I shall give him will never thirst," the woman replied, **"Sir, give me this water, that I may not thirst, nor come here to draw"** (v. 15). Apparently the woman liked the idea of a kind of water that would permanently take away thirst. But it is the last part of this statement that I find most interesting: "nor come here to draw." The woman was particularly interested in a kind of water that would spare her from having to come to the well. It was as if she said: "I hate it every time I come here. I feel like I have a scarlet 'A' sewn on my clothing. I have to sneak past the eyes of every woman in the village. When I come here and sit at this place to get my water, I feel ashamed, embarrassed, and alone. If You have water like this, give it to me, and I'll never have to come back to this well again."

The woman was intrigued, but she wasn't yet ready to admit the emptiness of her soul. However, Jesus was not finished with her. In our next chapter, we will see how Jesus continued to interact with her to help her see her need of Him.

I am certain that among those who are now reading this book, there are some who have not yet tasted the sweetness of the living water of Christ Himself. There are people reading these words with heavy souls that are thirsty and empty. If you are in that category, we have looked at a woman with a soul as thirsty and empty as your own confronted by the only One who can fill that kind of void in your soul. I pray that you will hear the word of Christ to this woman, and that before you put your head on your pillow tonight that you will say to Him, "Give me a drink." He will certainly do it.

10

THE WOMAN AT THE WELL, PART 2

John 4:16–42

Jesus said to her, "Go, call your husband, and come here." The woman answered and said, "I have no husband." Jesus said to her, "You have well said, 'I have no husband,' for you have had five husbands, and the one whom you now have is not your husband; in that you spoke truly." The woman said to Him, "Sir, I perceive that You are a prophet. Our fathers worshiped on this mountain, and you Jews say that in Jerusalem is the place where one ought to worship." Jesus said to her, "Woman, believe Me, the hour is coming when you will neither on this mountain, nor in Jerusalem, worship the Father. You worship what you do not know; we know what we worship, for salvation is of the Jews. But the hour is coming, and now is, when the true worshipers will worship the Father in spirit and truth; for the Father is seeking such to worship Him. God is Spirit, and those who worship Him must worship in spirit and truth." The woman said to Him, "I know that Messiah is coming" (who is called Christ). "When He comes, He will tell us all things." Jesus said to her, "I who speak to you am He." At this point His disciples came, and they marveled that He talked with a woman; yet no one said, "What do you seek?" or, "Why are You talking with her?" The woman then left her waterpot, went her way into the city, said to the men, "Come, see a Man who told me all things that I ever did. Could this be the Christ?" Then they went out of the city and came to Him. In the meantime His disciples urged Him, saying, "Rabbi, eat." But He said to them, "I have food to eat of which you do not know." Therefore the disciples said to one another, "Has anyone brought Him anything to eat?" Jesus said to them, "My food is to do the will of Him who sent Me, and to finish His work. Do you not say, 'There are still four months and then comes the harvest'? Behold, I say to you, lift up your eyes and look at the fields, for they are already white for harvest! And he who reaps receives wages, and gathers fruit for eternal life, that both he who sows and he who reaps may rejoice together. For in this the saying is true: 'One sows and another reaps.' I sent you to reap for that which you have not labored; others have labored, and you have entered into their labors." And many of the Samaritans of that city believed in Him because of the word of the woman who testified, "He told me all that I ever did." So when the Samaritans had come to Him, they urged Him to stay with them; and He stayed there two days. And many more believed because of His own word. Then they said to the woman, "Now we believe, not because of what you said, for we ourselves have heard Him and we know that this is indeed the Christ, the Savior of the world."

In the previous chapter, we saw that Jesus, passing through Samaria, struck up a conversation with an immoral Samaritan woman. He sparked her interest by promising her "living water," but the woman wanted the water only for the temporal benefits it would provide—relief from having to tote water from the well and from having to come to the well alone and ostracized. Thus, when she asked Him for the water, Jesus continued to teach and confront her, zeroing in on the condition of her soul.

John tells us that Jesus said to the woman, **"Go, call your husband, and come here"** (v. 16). To this the woman replied, **"I have no husband"** (v. 17a). When the woman made this admission, Jesus gave her a shock. He said to her: **"You have well said, 'I have no husband,' for you have had five husbands, and the one whom you now have is not your husband; in that you spoke truly"** (vv. 17b–18). Think of the shock you would feel if a total stranger were to reveal a detailed knowledge of your past, particularly those parts of your past about which you are most ashamed. This is what happened to the Samaritan woman, and we can only imagine that she was astonished to find that Jesus had this knowledge of her. How did He know these things?

A Question to Change the Subject

The woman swiftly came to the conclusion that Jesus' knowledge of her past had come not from men but from God. She said, **"Sir, I perceive that You are a prophet"** (v. 19). That was a deduction on her part, but she was still shocked and troubled, so she tried to change the subject. Attempting to steer the conversation away from her private life, she asked a theological question, one that the Jews and Samaritans had been debating for many years. She said to Jesus, **"Our fathers worshiped on this mountain, and you Jews say that in Jerusalem is the place where one ought to worship"** (v. 20). She was asking about the proper place for the worship of God. The Jews had their temple in Jerusalem; Mount Zion was their holy place. The Samaritans, who rejected everything except the Pentateuch in the Old Testament, had their central sanctuary at Mount Gerizim. The woman may have had a real interest in the question, but she certainly hoped that this Jewish prophet would take the bait and forget His discomforting questions about her life.

Jesus replied, **"Woman, believe Me, the hour is coming when you will neither on this mountain, nor in Jerusalem, worship the Father"** (v. 21). Sometimes when we read this response, we almost get the idea that Jesus was saying, "It really doesn't matter whether you come to the Father according to the ways of the Samaritans or according to the ways of the Jews." We make that inference because Jesus said the hour was coming when the true worshipers would worship neither in Samaria nor in Jerusalem. Jesus pronounced the end of Mount Gerizim as the central sanctuary for Samaria and cryptically pronounced the end of Jerusalem as the central sanctuary for the Jews, anticipating its destruction in just a few years. Therefore, some say Jesus said it did not matter how one worshiped God. But those who make such an assertion are leaping to a premature conclusion. We need to consider all that Jesus said in this passage.

Jesus went on to make a comparison between Samaritans and Jews: **"You worship what you do not know; we know what we worship, for salvation is of the Jews"** (v. 22). With these words, Jesus declared that the Samaritan woman was an agnostic. The word *agnostic* comes from the Greek *agnosis*, with means "without knowledge." Jesus said that the Samaritans were worshiping without knowledge, but not so the Jews, whose worship was based on true knowledge of God through His self-revelation in the pages of Scripture.

Therefore, Jesus did not say that it did not matter whether one worshiped the Samaritan way or the Jewish way. On the contrary, one of those ways was wrong and one was right. The Jewish way was the correct one. That was the way God had ordained, for they were God's chosen people, and He had personally instructed them as to how to worship Him.

Principles for Worship

Jesus followed with an extremely important statement about worship: **"But the hour is coming, and now is, when the true worshipers will worship the Father in spirit and truth; for the Father is seeking such to worship Him. God is Spirit, and those who worship Him must worship in spirit and truth"** (vv. 23–24). I have several things to say about these verses.

First, Christians in the twenty-first century tend to have a woeful ignorance of the Old Testament. One of the most important problems that follows from an ignorance of the Old Testament is a profound ignorance of the character of God the Father. We somehow think that Christianity centers exclusively around Jesus. Obviously we are called to honor, exalt, and worship Christ, but we need to remember that Christ came in the first place to reconcile us to the Father. There is a certain sense in which the supreme focus of our worship on Sunday morning is to be the Father; that is why Jesus said here that "true worshipers will worship *the Father* in spirit and truth." Again, we worship the triune God: the Father, the Son, and the Holy Spirit, but we need to have the majesty of the Father, in all of His greatness, in our minds as we worship.

Second, this matter of worshiping the Father "in spirit and truth" is often misunderstood. What did Jesus mean by this? He was not saying that people are supposed to be Holy Spirit devotees and to worship God according to the Holy Spirit. We *are* supposed to do that, but that was not Jesus' intent here. Rather, He was calling us, in the first instance, to see that the worship we offer comes from the depths of our souls, from our inner spirits, from the very cores of our being.

When Mary sang her song of praise to God, her *Magnificat*, she cried out, "My soul magnifies the Lord, and my spirit has rejoiced in God my Savior" (Luke 1:46b–47). That's an example of true worship. But the Scriptures repeatedly give examples of the opposite of true worship. Jeremiah exposed such worship when the Lord sent him to the temple to declare, "Do not trust in these lying words, saying, 'The temple of the LORD, the temple of the LORD, the temple of the LORD are these'" (Jer. 7:4). He exhorted the people to take no pride in the temple because the temple would be destroyed, and he challenged them to go to Israel's former central sanctuary, Shiloh, which lay in ruins, to see what was ahead for the temple. Jeremiah, under the anointing of the Holy Spirit, told the people of Israel that their worship had become dead, outward, external formalism. They went through the motions, they recited the prayers, they sang the hymns, but their hearts weren't in it.

God doesn't want that kind of worship. That's dead religion. That's not authentic faith. We're to come to Him with hearts filled with a sense of awe, reverence, and adoration. The worship that we offer is to be a sacrifice of praise to His name.

Also, we are told, worship is to be according to truth. I don't think there's ever been a time in Christian history when the church has been exposed to more experimental worship than it is today, and so often the experiments are driven by polls that ask what people want on Sunday morning. Do they want sermons that will give them popular psychology? Do they want warm, fuzzy feelings as their felt needs are met? If so, the assumption goes, we need to tailor worship to meet those felt needs, because if we don't do that, our churches will be empty because people will be bored and will see church as irrelevant. But Jesus said that the Father wants people to worship Him according to what *He* wants.

The one worship service in the history of the world that was completely designed to minister to the felt needs of the people was the worship of the golden calf at the base of Mount Sinai (see Ex. 32). It was not an exercise in true worship but in idolatry. We have to keep a close watch on what we do in worship, asking ourselves: "Is this according to the truth of God? Is this God's teaching in His Word?" Our worship must be based on God's self-revelation in Scripture. He is truth and His Word is truth.

Jesus' Identity Revealed

Jesus' words about worship seemed to bring the Samaritan woman back to the subject at hand. She said: **"I know that Messiah is coming"** (who is called Christ). **"When He comes, He will tell us all things"** (v. 25). She went from affirming "You're a prophet" and asking unrelated questions to voicing thoughts about the Messiah. Then Jesus, who often was unwilling to reveal His messianic vocation, plainly stated His identity to this Samaritan woman: **"I who speak to you am He"** (v. 26).

When the woman heard these words, she was filled with excitement. She had come to the well to fill her water pot so she could meet her daily needs. But she was so excited by her conversation with Jesus, she left her water pot and hurried away. We have no record that she ever filled it. She couldn't wait to get into town, to go to that very city where she was a despised outcast, to tell of her experience.

I recently encountered a tremendous children's book by Max Lucado and brought it home for my grandchildren. The title is *If Only I Had a Green Nose*, and it's about a group of people who aren't satisfied with the way their creator made them; they want to be more "with it." There is a fellow in town named Willie-With-It who decrees what is "in," and he decrees that if the people really want to be "with it," they need to have green noses. But then the "with it" style changes. The next thing you know, they need to have yellow noses, so they have to get the green ones painted, but then the style changes again and red noses are in. It's one fad after another. Finally somebody says to Willie-With-It, "Who made you the thing-picker?" and that's how the story ends.

I sometimes wonder whether people look at me and say: "Who made you the preacher? What right do you have to stand up in the pulpit and tell people how to worship or what to do?" Actually, any Christian who has tried to bear witness to others has heard that charge: "Who do you think you are?" The greatest answer to that question that I've ever heard is the old answer, "I'm just one beggar telling other beggars where they can find bread." That's really all I am, and that's all any of us are.

That's what the Samaritan woman was. When she made it back to town, she said to the people there: **"Come, see a Man who told me all things that I ever did. Could this be the Christ?"** (v. 29). She didn't go to them and pronounce that she had suddenly become a righteous woman, a paragon of virtue, and issue a command that the community follow her. She simply told the people she had met the Messiah. She knew that she had been redeemed by that encounter, and she wanted everyone in town to know it. For the first time in her life, she was not an agnostic. She suddenly understood the things of God.

Because of this woman's witness, many of the Samaritans of Sychar believed in Jesus (v. 39). They asked Him to remain with them for a time, and He stayed two days. After that, the Samaritans could say that they believed not simply because of the woman's testimony, but because they had heard Jesus for themselves (v. 42).

In the midst of this story, Jesus' disciples returned and urged Him to eat

(v. 31). But He said, **"I have food to eat of which you do not know"** (v. 32). The disciples were confused by that statement and wondered whether someone else had brought Jesus food. So Jesus clarified His meaning; **"My food is to do the will of Him who sent Me, and to finish His work"** (v. 34). That's who Jesus is. His meat and His drink—His zeal, His passion—was to do everything that the Father sent Him to do. That included ministering to these people of Samaria, offering them the living water that wells up to eternal life.

11

THE NOBLEMAN'S SON

John 4:43-54

Now after the two days He departed from there and went to Galilee. For Jesus Himself testified that a prophet has no honor in his own country. So when He came to Galilee, the Galileans received Him, having seen all the things He did in Jerusalem at the feast; for they also had gone to the feast. So Jesus came again to Cana of Galilee where He had made the water wine. And there was a certain nobleman whose son was sick at Capernaum. When he heard that Jesus had come out of Judea into Galilee, he went to Him and implored Him to come down and heal his son, for he was at the point of death. Then Jesus said to him, "Unless you people see signs and wonders, you will by no means believe." The nobleman said to Him, "Sir, come down before my child dies!" Jesus said to him, "Go your way; your son lives." So the man believed the word that Jesus spoke to him, and he went his way. And as he was now going down, his servants met him and told him, saying, "Your son lives!" Then he inquired of them the hour when he got better. And they said to him, "Yesterday at the seventh hour the fever left him." So the father knew that it was at the same hour in which Jesus said to him, "Your son lives." And he himself believed, and his whole household. This again is the second sign Jesus did when He had come out of Judea into Galilee.

When I was in seminary, I had a classmate who had graduated from the Massachusetts Institute of Technology as the valedictorian of his class. He was the most brilliant young man I had ever met, with an IQ higher than 180. He had come to seminary embracing orthodox Christianity, but being deluged by higher criticism, he lost his confidence in the trustworthiness of the Bible.

One day during our senior year, as we talked, I mentioned to him that I still was persuaded of the divine inspiration of sacred Scripture. He said to me, "R. C., how can you believe that when the Bible is filled with contradictions?" I said to him, "Maybe I'm blind, but I haven't noticed that the Bible is filled with contradictions." He said, "Well, they're all over the place." I replied: "I'd like you to do me a favor. Let's plan to meet back here tomorrow at this same time. When we meet, I'd like you to give me a list of fifty contradictions that you find in Scripture. With all the criticisms you've heard around here in the last three years, and given your statement that the Bible, which is a big book, is filled with contradictions, it shouldn't be difficult to come up with fifty." He agreed to the challenge.

The next day, he showed up for our meeting bleary-eyed and unkempt. He confessed that he had been up all night searching the Scriptures to list the contradictions. Plus, he had enlisted the help of other skeptics in this task. But as hard as they had searched, they had been able to come up with only thirty of them. However, I assured him thirty was plenty. I said: "That's enough to persuade me that the Bible is not the inspired Word of God—if they are genuine contradictions. So let's look at them."

One by one, we examined these alleged contradictions in sacred Scripture. My classmate, having been a student of philosophy, was aware of the laws of logic, and together we subjected all of these difficult passages in Scripture to the tests to see whether they had in fact violated the law of contradiction. Not merely to my satisfaction, but to his, we were able to resolve every single one of those alleged contradictions.

When we finished, he said, "Look at all the gymnastics that you had to go through to prove that these texts technically did not violate the law of contradiction." I said: "That's right, we went through those gymnastics so that we could exonerate God's Word from the slander that it's filled with contradictions. That's what we've had to do. The fact that there are tensions, discrepancies, and difficult-to-harmonize passages in a book this thick shouldn't surprise anyone. But to say there are actual contradictions is a serious charge." With that, we parted as friends on the issue.

Where Was Jesus' Homeland?

I mention that experience for this reason: in the text we are examining in this chapter, we encounter one of the passages that critics like to point out to show that the Bible is "filled" with contradictions. John writes: **Now after the two days He departed from there and went to Galilee. For Jesus Himself testified that a prophet has no honor in His own country** (vv. 43–44). Then, in the very next verse, John writes, **So when He came to Galilee, the Galileans received Him** (v. 45a). In fact, the force of the text here is that the Galileans welcomed Him. But wait, we just read that a prophet has no honor in his own country. Jesus came back to His homeland after visiting Judea and received an enormously warm welcome, according to John. So the critics look at that and say: "See, the Bible says that a prophet's not without honor except in his own country. But when Jesus comes to His own country, He receives all kinds of honor."

What do we do with that? Scholars go through gymnastics to reconcile those two lines. But before I join the gym, let me say that it would surprise me if John actually contradicted himself, and to do it in consecutive sentences would indicate incredible stupidity. So before I leap to the conclusion that the apostle fell into a contradiction here, let's see if there are any alternatives.

Many scholars believe that John is saying that Jesus left Judea to go to Galilee because He had encountered serious hostility from the officials in Jerusalem. In short, the people of Judea were not honoring Him, so He decided to go to a place that would be more conducive to His public ministry, namely Galilee. They point out that Jesus was born in Bethlehem, which is in Judea, so there's no contradiction whatsoever. Jesus received no honor in His homeland—Judea.

The only problem with that view is that the New Testament consistently speaks of Jesus' place of origin as Nazareth in Galilee, despite the fact that He was born in Bethlehem in Judea. Nazareth was where He grew up. That was His home and where He was known. So it's a little iffy to say that Jesus was going to Galilee because He had received no honor in Judea, His homeland.

If we take the position that Galilee was Jesus' homeland, we have to reconcile and resolve the tension between these verses. This may seem like an insignificant detail in this text, but there's something that is important for us to understand, not only for this text, but for everything that comes after in the Gospel of John.

We don't know in what sense or nuance John quoted Jesus' statement about a prophet not being without honor except in his home country. We don't have the advantage of listening to the tone of voice of the people quoted in the Bible when they spoke. Neither can we see their facial expressions or their gestures. Rarely do we get an editorial comment that tells us Jesus spoke in a loud voice or something along those lines. So sometimes the text statements, if read in their bare content, seem to mean one thing, but if we understand that they were said in irony or sarcasm, they seem to yield a completely different significance.

Just for the sake of argument, let's suppose that Galilee was Jesus' homeland. Let's also suppose that when John wrote that the people came out and welcomed Jesus, that John was using sarcasm. The support for this view comes from what follows—the people often welcomed Jesus when they happened to be looking for signs and wonders, but they gave Him no real honor as the Messiah. Unlike the Samaritans, who embraced Him as the Messiah and asked Him to stay with them, the Galileans (and the Judeans, for that matter) never gave Him the honor that was due to Him.

Sought for His Power and Gifts

We see an example of this in the passage before us. A nobleman came to Jesus, seeking Him out for His power and His gifts. This was not an isolated incident in Jesus' ministry; in fact, it continues to happen in our day. People rush to hear the gospel for what they can get out of it. I've talked with people who have gone to faith healers even though they had no desire to learn the things of God. They say, "Look, when you have a disease that's chronic or incurable, you'll try anything." There were people like that in Jesus' day, people who were desperate with their afflictions, and when the word got around that He was a miraculous healer, these people unabashedly sought Him out. They pursued Him for the benefit they could derive from Him without any sense of repentance for their sins, without any intent to bow to Him as Lord, and without any willingness to receive Him as the Savior

John writes, **So Jesus came again to Cana of Galilee where He had made the water wine** (v. 46a). That miracle, Jesus' first sign, had created quite a stir, and now his reputation has gotten around the community. The result: **And there was a certain nobleman whose son was sick at Capernaum. When he heard that Jesus had come out of Judea into Galilee, he went to Him and implored Him to come down and heal his son, for he was at the point of death** (v. 46b–47).

The nobleman was a man of wealth and status; he obviously had the means to bring in the best physicians to treat his son's serious illness. But nothing had availed, and he had grown desperate. It so happened that he heard about the miracle at the wedding feast of Cana. Maybe he didn't believe it (unless he was there), but he had a need, a need that was so pressing it was consuming his life. So he went to Jesus and implored Him, "Please come with me!" He thought, "Maybe if I can get this miracle worker to come to my house, He can save the life of my son." So he begged Jesus to go home with him.

Jesus did not grant the request. You would think if Jesus really cared, that when He saw the man in absolute agony about the life of his son, he would have said: "I'll go to your home and help you." However, I think Jesus recognized that the man came to Him out of an earthly need, one that had nothing to do with a desire for salvation. So Jesus said, **"Unless you people see signs and wonders, you will by no means believe"** (v. 48).

That was a stern rebuke, but Jesus sometimes issued such reproofs. Later, He rebuked two disciples who were on the way to Emmaus, lost in skepticism and despair after His death in Jerusalem, and said to them, "O foolish ones, and slow of heart to believe in all that the prophets have spoken!" (Luke 24:25). Then, "beginning at Moses and all the Prophets" (24:27a), Jesus went through the Old Testament and showed them that had they believed the Scriptures, they would not have needed the resurrection to attest His truth. We're like those people. We have calluses on our hearts. It's as if we're not going to believe or trust ourselves to Christ unless we see Him work wonders with our eyes. There's a lot of that skepticism in the world today.

Something in the Way Jesus Spoke

The nobleman did not waste time arguing the point with Jesus. He said, **"Sir, come down before my child dies!"** (v. 49). It is as if he was saying: "I don't want to get involved in discussions about theology. Please come. I need you. That's all I ask." But Jesus steadfastly refused to go. Instead He said, **"Go your way; your son lives"** (v. 50a).

I would love to know how Jesus said that. I don't think He said it this way: "Get out of here, your son's OK." I believe it was more like this: "Go your way. Your son is fine. I'm not going with you, but it's all right." There must have been something in how He said it that elicited trust from this man, who just seconds before had been in a panic, begging Jesus, insisting that Jesus come with him. I say that because of the man's response: **So the man believed the word that Jesus spoke to him, and he went his way** (v. 50).

This nobleman, in the midst of his desperation, heard the promise of Christ and believed it. He trusted the word of Christ. He didn't say, "I'll just go see if that's true." He didn't grab Jesus by the hand and physically drag Him to his house. Rather, he grew calm, he stopped pleading, and he departed. His trust was well placed: **And as he was now going down, his servants met him and told him, saying, "Your son lives!"** (v. 51).

Now, if I had been that man, I think my first reaction would have been to leap in the air, to shout with joy, or to exclaim "That's fantastic!" Instead, the nobleman asked his servants a question: **Then he inquired of them the hour when he got better. And they said to him, "Yesterday at the seventh hour the fever left him." So the father knew that it was at the same hour in which Jesus said to him, "Your son lives"** (vv. 52–53a).

With that, **he himself believed, and his whole household** (v. 53b). The nobleman took the next step. He enjoyed the tremendous benefit that he had received from Jesus, but in that act of mercy and compassion, the man came to understood who Jesus was, and he believed in Him. John's words in this text point to something far beyond mere trust in Jesus for a miracle. This nobleman came to possess nothing less than saving faith.

John declared that he wrote his Gospel "that you may believe that Jesus is the Christ, the Son of God, and that believing you may have life in His name" (20:31). The healing of the nobleman's son is just one more glimpse of the person of Christ, the person who, by His command, by His very word, brings life out of death, safety out of danger, healing out of disease, salvation out of lostness. This is our Jesus, in whom we believe. This is why we're called Christians.

12

THE POOL OF BETHESDA

John 5:1–15

After this there was a feast of the Jews, and Jesus went up to Jerusalem. Now there is in Jerusalem by the Sheep Gate a pool, which is called in Hebrew, Bethesda, having five porches. In these lay a great multitude of sick people, blind, lame, paralyzed, waiting for the moving of the water. For an angel went down at a certain time into the pool and stirred up the water; then whoever stepped in first, after the stirring of the water, was made well of whatever disease he had. Now a certain man was there who had an infirmity thirty-eight years. When Jesus saw him lying there, and knew that he already had been in that condition a long time, He said to him, "Do you want to be made well?" The sick man answered Him, "Sir, I have no man to put me into the pool when the water is stirred up; but while I am coming, another steps down before me." Jesus said to him, "Rise, take up your bed and walk." And immediately the man was made well, took up his bed, and walked. And that day was the Sabbath. The Jews therefore said to him who was cured, "It is the Sabbath; it is not lawful for you to carry your bed." He answered them, "He who made me well said to me, 'Take up your bed and walk.'" Then they asked him, "Who is the Man who said to you, 'Take up your bed and walk'?" But the one who was healed did not know who it was, for Jesus had withdrawn, a multitude being in that place. Afterward Jesus found him in the temple, and said to him, "See, you have been made well. Sin no more, lest a worse thing come upon you." The man departed and told the Jews that it was Jesus who had made him well.

I mentioned in Chapter 1 that the Gospel of John is different from the other three Gospels, Matthew, Mark, and Luke. These books are called the Synoptic Gospels because they each provide a biographical synopsis of the life and ministry of Jesus. Even though John, like the other Gospel writers, recorded many events and teachings of Jesus, it was not his goal to provide a complete synopsis of the Lord's life and work. About two-thirds of the material in the Gospel of John covers the last week of Jesus' life. John's Gospel is more of a theological reflection on Jesus' life, an overview of the redemptive-historical acts that Jesus performed during His stay on earth.

In our study thus far, John has presented a series of encounters between Jesus and other people—Nicodemus, the Samaritan woman, the nobleman whose son was ill. As Chapter 5 opens, Jesus has yet another encounter, this time with a man who has an infirmity. But the mood and the editorial structure of the beginning of this chapter show us that John's focus is not on the sick man himself. Rather, John is introducing the winds of hostility that are starting to blow from the hierarchy of the Jewish establishment against Jesus. Here we begin to get some insight as to why so much fury broke out against Christ from the Jewish leaders of His day.

An Unusual Phenomenon

Chapter 5 begins with this introductory statement: **After this there was a feast of the Jews, and Jesus went up to Jerusalem** (v. 1). Quite often in the book of John, we see Jesus attending one of the various Jewish feasts. Almost always, when John sets the stage for an event that took place during a Jewish feast, he tells us which feast it was. In this case, however, he does not. There has been much speculation about this, but no one really knows which feast Jesus went to Jerusalem to observe on this occasion.

John continues, **Now there is in Jerusalem by the Sheep Gate a pool, which is called in Hebrew, Bethesda, having five porches** (v. 2). The Sheep Gate was in the northern section of Jerusalem, and there were actually two pools there, side by side, and they were surrounded by five columns. These columns supported a covering that provided shelter beside these pools. People who had illnesses and maladies came and waited under the shelter to take advantage of a rather unusual and fascinating phenomenon. John writes, **In these [porches] lay a great multitude of sick people, blind, lame, paralyzed, waiting for the moving of the water. For an angel went down at a certain time into the pool and stirred up the water; then whoever stepped in first, after the stirring of the water, was made well of whatever disease he had** (vv. 3–4).

This is the only instance in sacred Scripture where we find any indication that there was a pool in Jerusalem where an angel came periodically, stirred up the water, and gave miraculous healing to the first person who managed to get down into the water. How are we to understand this strange account?

Let me preface what I'm about to say with some background about the manuscripts of the biblical books. We don't possess the original manuscripts; they have been lost. What the church possesses are hundreds, and in some cases, thousands of copies that were made in the earliest days. Through the science of textual criticism, scholars try to reconstruct what was in the original documents. Thanks to the great number of copies and the precision of textual criticism, we have a high degree of confidence that the biblical manuscripts as we now have them are very close to the originals. However, occasionally we find manuscripts differing as to what was in the original text, and this is one of those instances—some of the best texts of the Gospel of John do not include verse 4. Therefore, it's very possible that this statement about an angel stirring up the water and healing the first person who stepped into the pool may have been a textual gloss that reflected more of the superstition of the people in and around the pool of Bethesda than the actual truth of God.

But if the stirring of the water and the healings were not caused by an angel, what was happening? We know these pools in Jerusalem were occasionally fed by artesian wells. The wells would start to flow and the pools would be stirred with an influx of water with special characteristics—something like the hot springs people visit even today for therapeutic reasons. That may have been what was happening at Bethesda, and the people, not knowing the science of artesian wells, simply believed that the stirring of the water was due to the presence of an angel.

A Thirty-Eight-Year Malady

We're told, **Now a certain man was there who had an infirmity thirty-eight years** (v. 5). This man certainly believed in the healing powers of the waters; he was convinced that if he could get in the water first he would be cured. For thirty-eight years he suffered from what seems to have been a kind of paralysis, and that malady was what prevented him from getting into the pool first—he could not move quickly enough when the waters were stirred.

Jesus saw the man lying there and knew that he had been in that condition a long time. His first words to the man, therefore, seem curious: **"Do you want to be made well?"** (v. 6b). If Jesus knew the man had been ill for thirty-eight years, and if He understood that the man was at the pool trying to get into the water, why did He ask the man whether he *wanted* to be healed?

It's possible that this man had become satisfied in his state of inertia, having learned to depend on others to tend to his needs. In that case, Jesus' question likely was intended to warn him that being healed would bring radical life changes. There would be no more handouts, no more assistance. Instead, he would have to be productive. He would have to function in a society where he had been unable to be productive for thirty-eight years.

One day years ago, when I was working at a gym in the East Liberty section of Pittsburgh, I left work and headed home after dark. Just as I was walking past a jewelry store, a man rushed out the door with the owner right behind him hollering, "Stop, thief!" The thief ran into me and almost knocked me to the ground. At that point, I reacted instinctively—I grabbed the man and said, "Hold it!" I half expected him to pull out a gun and shoot me, but he only looked at me and said, "I give up." Soon the police came and took him to jail.

The next day, I saw one of the police officers whom I knew and asked him about the man and his curious behavior. He said: "Oh, we know him. We can put him in jail for six months, but the day he gets out he'll go do something like this." It turned out that the man committed crimes in hopes of getting caught because he wasn't able to survive outside of jail. He was used to living behind bars, where he had a bed every night and three meals a day. There are people like that, who are satisfied in their paralyzed condition and who are threatened by life to such a degree that they don't want to have to deal with the vagaries of human existence.

In response to Jesus' question, the man said, **"Sir, I have no man to put me into the pool when the water is stirred up; but while I am coming, another steps down before me"** (v. 7). Evidently the man was hoping Jesus would help him get into the water at the appropriate time. But Jesus had other plans. He said, **"Rise, take up your bed and walk"** (v. 8). The "bed" he was lying on was probably a mat made of reeds that he could roll up. Hearing Jesus' command, the man obeyed—literally.

Immediately the man was made well, took up his bed, and he walked (v. 9a).

Then came the ominous signal of trouble: **And that day was the Sabbath. The Jews therefore said to him who was cured, "It is the Sabbath; it is not lawful for you to carry your bed"** (vv. 9b–10). Now, I ask you—where in the Word of God does it say it is unlawful for a person who has been healed of paralysis to carry his bed? You know the answer to that question: nowhere. But the rabbis, in their historical interpretation of the law, had enumerated thirty-nine specific types of work that were illegal on the Sabbath day, and the thirty-ninth rule of Sabbath observance—the very last one in the list—was the prohibition against carrying something from one place to another. As a result of that human rule, the Jews reacted very negatively when they saw this man—a man who had been lying paralyzed for thirty-eight years—walking and carrying his bed. Instead of responding to the miracle of his healing with joy and praise to God, they said, "Why are you carrying your bed?" How wicked and deceitful is the human heart. The Jews were so caught up in the rules they had added to the law of God that they were more concerned with this man's disobedience to rabbinic tradition than with rejoicing and glorifying God for the man's astonishing deliverance from suffering.

An Unwilling Witness

When we studied Jesus' encounter with the Samaritan woman, we saw that when Jesus revealed Himself to her, she ran into town and told everyone that she had just met the Messiah. She couldn't wait to bear witness to the greatness of Jesus. How about this fellow? When the Pharisees chided him for carrying his bed on the Sabbath, what did he say? **He answered them, "He who made me well said to me, 'Take up your bed and walk'"** (v. 11). In essence, the man was saying: "It wasn't my idea. Somebody came along and told me to pick up my bed and walk for the first time in thirty-eight years, so what was I supposed to do? I only did what He told me to do. If you have a problem with that, go talk to Him."

When do we first read this kind of thinking in the Bible? "The woman whom You gave to be with me, she gave me of the tree, and I ate" (Gen. 3:12). Nothing had changed since the fall of Adam in the Garden of Eden. Instead of rejoicing and defending the glory of the One who had delivered him from his malady, the healed man simply passed the buck, saying, "This fellow who healed me told me to carry my bed." When the Jewish leaders pressed him to name his healer, he could not do so. This man needed to ponder Jesus' words in Luke 12:8–9: "Whoever confesses Me before men, him the Son of Man also will confess before the angels of God. But he who denies Me before men will be denied before the angels of God."

There was an occasion when the army of Alexander the Great was engaged in a very serious battle, and in the course of the battle, one of the soldiers fled the scene. He was a coward. After the battle, the coward was apprehended and brought to Alexander's tent. As the man stood trembling before his general, Alexander looked at him and said, "Why did you run?" The soldier said, "I was afraid." Alexander said: "So I see. What is your name?" The soldier mumbled his answer so that Alexander couldn't hear him, so the great warrior said: "Speak up. What is your name?" The young soldier looked at him and said, "My name is Alexander." Alexander the Great replied, "Either change your behavior or change your name."

If you are embarrassed by Jesus and you're afraid to confess Him before men, either change your behavior or cease to call yourself a Christian.

The story doesn't end there, of course: **Afterward Jesus found him in the temple, and said to him, "See, you have been made well. Sin no more, lest a worse thing come upon you"** (v. 14). There are many passages in John's Gospel and elsewhere where we are warned against concluding that a particular calamity is a direct result of a specific sin. That doesn't mean we should conclude that calamity is *never* a result of sin. When Jesus mentioned the deaths of eighteen people in the collapse of the tower of Siloam, He noted, "Unless you repent you will all likewise perish" (Luke 13:1–5). So He said to this man, "Stop your sinful lifestyle lest a worse thing befall you."

Jesus had already healed this man of a thirty-eight-year malady. Here He gave him an excellent piece of advice. How did the man repay these kindnesses from Jesus? **The man departed and told the Jews that it was Jesus who had made him well** (v. 15).

What a marked contrast there was between this man and so many others who encountered the living Christ. Most of them, having felt Jesus' touch, having received blessings from His hand, would have crawled over glass to bear witness to Him as their Lord. But this man, who received the physical blessing of healing, apparently never went past the physical to saving faith.

How easy it is for us to be faithful to Christ when we receive some benefit from His hand. Likewise, how difficult it can be for us to remain faithful when we do not receive what we want. We need to remind ourselves that if God never blessed us another moment for the rest of our lives, we would have no reason under heaven to do anything but glorify Him, adore Him, and be grateful to Him for the blessings we already have experienced. If He abandoned us tonight (which He certainly will not do), we would have no excuse to do anything but serve Him until we draw our final breaths. Let us learn from this man how *not* to receive the blessings of Christ.

13

THE SON OF THE FATHER

John 5:16–30

For this reason the Jews persecuted Jesus, and sought to kill Him, because He had done these things on the Sabbath. But Jesus answered them, "My Father has been working until now, and I have been working." Therefore the Jews sought all the more to kill Him, because He not only broke the Sabbath, but also said that God was His Father, making Himself equal with God. Then Jesus answered and said to them, "Most assuredly, I say to you, the Son can do nothing of Himself, but what He sees the Father do; for whatever He does, the Son also does in like manner. For the Father loves the Son, and shows Him all things that He Himself does; and He will show Him greater works than these, that you may marvel. For as the Father raises the dead and gives life to them, even so the Son gives life to whom He will. For the Father judges no one, but has committed all judgment to the Son, that all should honor the Son just as they honor the Father. He who does not honor the Son does not honor the Father who sent Him. Most assuredly, I say to you, he who hears My word and believes in Him who sent Me has everlasting life, and shall not come into judgment, but has passed from death into life. Most assuredly, I say to you, the hour is coming, and now is, when the dead will hear the voice of the Son of God; and those who hear will live. For as the Father has life in

Himself, so He has granted the Son to have life in Himself, and has given Him authority to execute judgment also, because He is the Son of Man. Do not marvel at this; for the hour is coming in which all who are in the graves will hear His voice and come forth—those who have done good, to the resurrection of life, and those who have done evil, to the resurrection of condemnation. I can of Myself do nothing. As I hear, I judge; and My judgment is righteous, because I do not seek My own will but the will of the Father who sent Me.

For this reason the Jews persecuted Jesus, and sought to kill Him, because He had done these things on the Sabbath (v. 16). In this verse, John refers to the events we studied in the previous chapter—Jesus' healing of a paralytic on the Sabbath and His command to the healed man to "Rise, take up your bed and walk" (v. 8). We saw that the Jewish leaders, blind to the wonder of the miracle Jesus had performed, were incensed that He had violated their man-made command against a specific form of labor on the Sabbath. As I noted, this was the beginning of the storm winds of opposition against Jesus from the Jewish leadership.

How did Jesus respond to this opposition, which was so hate-filled that it constituted a physical threat to His life? **Jesus answered them, "My Father has been working until now, and I have been working"** (v. 17). This is an astonishing declaration. There are many New Testament records of conversations between Jesus and the authorities, instances when questions were raised to Christ and He then gave a response, but this one is unique. Most of our English Bible translations begin this verse with the words "Jesus said" or "Jesus answered," but hidden behind the English is the fact that the verb translated as "answered" is exceedingly rare. It is found only in the context of trials and courtrooms, when a formal defense is given against charges that are made. So John is telling us that Jesus was not simply answering a question. He was giving His legal defense before the authorities who were accusing Him of things they deemed worthy of death.

A Brilliant Defense

What was the defense that Christ presented for telling the paralyzed man that it was OK to carry his bed on the Sabbath day? It was brief but astonishing. He said, "My Father has been working until now, and I have been working." You may wonder what is so interesting about that simple statement. Jesus was reminding the Jewish authorities that Sabbath rest was built into creation because God created all things in six days, then rested on the seventh day. That set the pattern for man to work six days and then rest every seventh day. But Jesus showed these theologians, who should have known this already, that when the Bible says that God rested on the seventh day, it doesn't mean that God ceased being active.

The deists believed that God was the great watchmaker. In their view, God formed the universe, established its laws, and fixed the gears and machinations of the machine, much as a watchmaker builds a watch. He then wound up the mechanism and stepped out of the picture, allowing the clock to run on its own. That is not the biblical view of God or of creation. The very word "create" in the first chapter of Genesis is the English translation of the Hebrew word *bara*, which implies sustained action. God did not simply create the universe and then step out of the picture. God created all things and continues to sustain them. He didn't just bring the world into existence, but He continues to preserve it and maintain it. That's why there is still a world. If God stopped working for one instant, the whole universe would be annihilated, because in Him we live and move and have our being (Acts 17:28). Without God upholding the universe from moment to moment, nothing could continue to be.

But that's not the way we think today. We've been overwhelmed with a naturalistic view of science that tells us nature operates under its own steam, by its own power. It may be indebted to God for its origin, but once things were started, God was no longer needed. This naturalistic view of the universe has even pervaded the church. How many times have we heard this question: "Where was God on September 11, 2001?"? The assumption behind the question is that God was off somewhere taking a nap, uninvolved with human events.

When Jesus said "My Father has been working until now, and I have been working," He was saying that the naturalistic understanding of the universe is wrong. He was denying that God is some nebulous power who merely started the ball rolling. Instead, He was affirming that God is the omnipotent Lord who governs everything that He makes from moment to moment.

A few years ago, I had an interesting encounter on a train. At dinnertime, I was seated with strangers; I was next to an elderly woman, and there was a young woman seated across from us. When I sat down, the young woman was excitedly telling the older woman that she had recently come home after two years of training in a camp that indoctrinated her into New Age philosophy. She said to the older woman: "Do you know what I learned? I learned that I am God." I didn't say anything; I was trying to mind my own business.

However, the young woman kept glancing over to see my reaction. Finally, she looked at me and said, "What do you think?" I said: "Well, this is a new experience for me. This is the first time in my life that I've been able to sit across a table, visibly, from the Almighty." She laughed when I said that, but then I looked at her and said, "You don't *really* believe that you're God, do you?" She laughed again and said, "Well, no, not really." I thank God that in thirty seconds we were able to undo her two years of indoctrination. But, of course, she was only one of the many who are buying into this absurd notion because we have lost an understanding of who God is.

That's why this verse is so important—it teaches us so much about the nature of God and of Christ. Though the work of creation was completed at the end of the sixth day, God's involvement with His creation didn't stop. In fact, Jesus said, it continues even until now.

Using the Jews' Own Law

There was something subtle in this statement from Jesus. The Jewish rabbis also had a theory about God's work. They granted that God continued to labor after He finished creation, but the question with which they wrestled was this: "Is it acceptable for God to work on the Sabbath?" The rabbis had formulated reasons why it was acceptable and legal for God to work on the Sabbath day.

In the previous chapter, I mentioned that the rabbis had composed thirty-nine laws that defined which work was acceptable and which was not on the Sabbath day. We saw that the final law prohibited the Jews from moving their possessions from one place to another. But how about God? Was he free to move His possessions on the Sabbath day?

The hymn "Holy God, We Praise Your Name," includes this stanza:

Holy God, we praise your name;
Lord of all, we bow before you;
All on earth your scepter claim,
All in heav'n above adore you.
Infinite your vast domain,
Everlasting is your reign.

Did you notice the affirmation that God's domain is infinite? That's a biblical truth, and the rabbis understood it. So they taught that God was exempt from their thirty-ninth law. People, being finite, were not allowed to move anything from one domain to another on the Sabbath, but since God is infinite and His domain is infinite, He rises above that restriction. The rabbis therefore said that whatever God does on the Sabbath day always takes place within the confines of His personal domain. That's theological casuistry at its finest.

Jesus used this teaching as the basis of His defense. He argued: "My Father works even on the Sabbath day. So do I. Since it is permissible for Him to do it, and since God is My Father, therefore I'm allowed to do it. If you argue with what I'm doing on the Sabbath day, you're arguing with God." In short, Jesus claimed to be God.

The issue of working on the Sabbath was a regular flashpoint for disagreement between Jesus and the authorities. On another occasion He said, "The Sabbath was made for man, and not man for the Sabbath. Therefore the Son of Man is also Lord of the Sabbath" (Mark 2:27–28). Here Jesus was even more straightforward. When He spoke these words, everyone understood what He was saying. Everyone knew that God created the Sabbath, so only God could be Lord over the Sabbath. Jesus was clearly claiming to be God.

What follows this declaration by Jesus is not surprising: **Therefore the Jews sought all the more to kill Him, because He not only broke the Sabbath, but He also said that God was His Father, making Himself equal with God** (v. 18). Jesus' rationale for His Sabbath conduct infuriated the Jewish leaders even more.

The Son and the Father

Now we come to the heart of our text for this chapter, a very difficult passage: **"Most assuredly, I say to you, the Son can do nothing of Himself, but what He sees the Father do; for whatever He does, the Son also does in like manner. For the Father loves the Son, and shows Him all things that He Himself does; and He will show Him greater works than these, that you may marvel. For as the Father raises the dead and gives life to them, even so the Son gives life to whom He will. For the Father judges no one, but has committed all judgment to the Son, that all should honor the Son just as they honor the Father. He who does not honor the Son does not honor the Father who sent Him"** (vv. 19–23).

Do you know the meaning of the word *Trinity*? In all likelihood, most of those reading this book are familiar with this word and its meaning in theology. But what if I were to ask you to distinguish between the "ontological Trinity" and the "economic Trinity"? If I said, "Please describe for me the difference between the ontological Trinity and the economic Trinity," could you do it? The distinction is very important.

Ontology is the study of being. When we talk about the ontological Trinity, or as some theologians term it, the "immanent Trinity," we are referring to the Trinity in itself, without regard to God's works of creation and redemption. In the Trinity, there are three persons—the Father, the Son, and the Holy Spirit—who together are one being. The ontological structure of the Trinity is a unity (Deut. 6:4). When we speak of the economic Trinity, on the other hand, we are dealing with the activity of God and the roles of the three persons with regard to creation and redemption.

In terms of the ontological Trinity, the three persons are distinguished by what the Westminster Larger Catechism calls "their personal properties" (WLC 9). It then goes on to define these personal properties: "It is proper to the Father to beget the Son, and to the Son to be begotten of the Father, and to the Holy Ghost to proceed from the Father and the Son from all eternity" (WLC 10). With regard to the economic Trinity, we distinguish among the three persons of the Godhead in terms of their roles in creation and redemption. It is the Father who sends the Son into the world for our redemption. It is the Son who acquires our redemption for us. It is the Spirit who applies that redemption to us. We do not have three gods. We have one God in three persons, and the three persons are distinguished in the economy of redemption in terms of what They do.

In orthodox Christianity, we say that the Son is equal to the Father in power, in glory, and in being. This discussion rests heavily on John 1:1, where we read, "In the beginning was the Word, and the Word was with God, and the Word was God." This verse indicates that the Father and the Word (the Son) are different and are one. In one sense, the Son and the Father are identical. In another sense, They are distinguished. From all eternity, within the ontological Trinity, the Father begets the Son, and the Son is begotten of the Father. From all eternity, God also freely decrees the salvation of yet to be created human beings in what theologians refer to as the "covenant of redemption." This covenant of redemption among the Persons of the Trinity is the eternal foundation for the work of the three Persons in the history of redemption. From all eternity the Father agrees to send the Son, and the Son is willingly sent. The Son doesn't send the Father; the Father sends the Son. So even though the Father and the Son are equal in power, glory, and being, and even though there is no eternal subordination within the ontological Trinity, nevertheless there is a subordination of the Son to the Father in the economy of redemption.

That is what Jesus said here. He declared: "I don't do anything on My own. I do what the Father tells Me to do. I do what the Father sent Me to do.

I watch the Father, and I do what the Father does. The Father is preeminent. The Father is the One to whom I am obedient and subordinate." He even affirmed that He could not do anything of Himself, only what He saw the Father do. Out of His love for the Son, the Father showed Him all the things that He Himself did. Then Jesus stated that the Father would show Him even greater things, so they should expect His works to become greater. In this context, Jesus specifically mentioned the raising of the dead.

Judgment Committed to the Son

Jesus said, **"The Father judges no one"** (v. 22a). Please do not read this verse and conclude that there is no judgment. Jesus did not say that. He went on to explain that the Father **"has committed all judgment to the Son"** (v. 22b). The Father doesn't judge because He has delegated the task of judging the world to the Son.

Sobering words follow. Jesus declared that the Father delegated the task of judging to the Son so that **"all should honor the Son just as they honor the Father. He who does not honor the Son does not honor the Father who sent Him"** (v. 23). Western culture tells people they can believe in anything they want to believe in, that we all worship the same God, that we can come to God by any means we choose, and that we can reject Jesus and still have the Father. No, we cannot honor the Father without honoring the Son, and the Father has appointed a day when He will judge the world by the One whom He has appointed to be the Judge, who is Christ (Acts 17:31). So those who do not honor Christ fail to honor the Judge whom God has appointed.

It is difficult for me to believe what Jesus said to the Jewish leaders. He was on trial, as it were, but He said to them: "You're talking to the judge. You're talking to the Lord of the Sabbath. You're talking to the One before whom you will stand in judgment. You're talking to the One to whom the Father has given the power of life in Himself. If you won't honor Me, you cannot honor the Father."

This is merely the beginning of Jesus' defense; it goes on not just for a few more verses but a few more chapters, and it's heavy going. It will take us into deep theological waters, but those deep theological waters are at the very heart of the faith of the Christian church, and it's because of these things that we come together to worship Him and to honor Him.

14

WITNESSES TO CHRIST

John 5:31–47

"If I bear witness of Myself, My witness is not true. There is another who bears witness of Me, and I know that the witness which He witnesses of Me is true. You have sent to John, and he has borne witness to the truth. Yet I do not receive testimony from man, but I say these things that you may be saved. He was the burning and shining lamp, and you were willing for a time to rejoice in his light. But I have a greater witness than John's; for the works which the Father has given Me to finish—the very works that I do—bear witness of Me, that the Father has sent Me. And the Father Himself, who sent Me, has testified of Me. You have neither heard His voice at any time, nor seen His form. But you do not have His word abiding in you, because whom He sent, Him you do not believe. You search the Scriptures, for in them you think you have eternal life; and these are they which testify of Me. But you are not willing to come to Me that you may have life. I do not receive honor from men. But I know you, that you do not have the love of God in you. I have come in My Father's name, and you do not receive Me; if another comes in his own name, him you will receive. How can you believe, who receive honor from one another, and do not seek the honor that comes from the only God? Do not think that I shall accuse you to the Father; there is one who accuses you—Moses,

in whom you trust. For if you believed Moses, you would believe Me; for
he wrote about Me. But if you do not believe his writings, how will you
believe My words?"

When a witness is sworn in during a trial, certain words customarily
are used. The witness is asked, "Do you promise to tell the truth,
the whole truth, and nothing but the truth, so help you God?"
By swearing an oath before God, the witness promises that his testimony will
be true and not an exercise in perjury.

In the Old Testament, when capital crimes were committed, the suspects
were tried at the city gate in the presence of the judges of the land. Before
the death penalty could be given, at least two eyewitnesses to the crime had
to give testimony, and their testimony had to agree completely. The idea of
giving a true, accurate witness in a law court was so important to Israel that
when God fashioned the constitution of His people, He included among the
top ten laws a prohibition against bearing false witness. The law also included
strong sanctions against anyone who delivered a false witness in a capital crime.
That person would himself be subject to the death penalty. So great care was
taken about how the truth was to be discerned in the context of a trial.

I recite that background because the section of John's Gospel that is before
us in this chapter has to do with accusations being brought against Jesus
by the officials of the Jewish community. We already have seen that Jesus
was charged with violating the Sabbath law for healing a paralytic and then
ordering the man to pick up his bed and to walk with it. Because Jesus stood
accused of violating the law of God in regard to the Sabbath, the language
of this text is bathed in the "legalese" of the Jewish community of the first
century. We need to understand that lest we get confused or misled by some
of the statements we read.

In fact, the first statement is striking. Jesus said, **"If I bear witness of
Myself, My witness is not true"** (v. 31). How many times in Scripture did
Jesus make pronouncements about His mission, His work, and His identity?
He did it over and over again, but here He said, "If I bear witness of Myself,
My witness is not true." Was He telling us, then, not to believe Him when He
declared who He was or what His mission was? No, He was speaking here in
the legal context. He said that His testimony was not legally valid in a trial
setting unless it was verified or corroborated by other sources.

I recently had to sign some documents for the bank. There was a place for
me to write my name at the bottom of one official document, and then there

was a line for the signature of someone who was a witness to my signature. Now suppose I had written my name on the left, and then I also signed my name on the line that was reserved for a witness. That wouldn't have worked; I couldn't legally bear witness to my own action. I needed someone else to confirm that I was the one who had signed on the first line. It was impossible for me to prove by signing on the second line that I had actually signed on the first line.

That's what Jesus meant when He said, "If I bear witness of Myself, My witness is not true." His witness to Himself would not have been valid in the courtroom.

However, Jesus was not without corroborating witnesses. As He defended Himself against the accusations of the Jewish leaders, He "called" four witnesses who could support His testimony. Let's look at these four.

Witness No. 1: John the Baptist

Jesus began by saying, **"There is another who bears witness of Me, and I know that the witness which He witnesses of Me is true"** (v. 32). It appears that Jesus was speaking here of God Himself, about whose witness He had more to say later. But He quickly moved on to a witness who was familiar to His hearers. He said: **"You have sent to John, and he has born witness to the truth. Yet I do not receive testimony from man, but I say these things that you may be saved. He was the burning and shining lamp, and you were willing for a time to rejoice in his light"** (vv. 33–35).

Earlier I made the point that at the time Jesus uttered these words, John the Baptist was more famous than Jesus. John had created a national stir when he appeared, coming out of the wilderness and baptizing people in the Jordan River, for he represented the restoration of the office of the Old Testament prophet after God had been silent in Israel for four hundred years. Every Jew in Israel had heard of John the Baptist, and before his life was taken by the whim of Herod the Tetrarch, he was extremely popular. Jesus described him as a "burning and shining lamp." John was a light that brought not only illumination but intense heat. He was a lamp before the people, and Jesus reminded the leaders of Israel, "There was a time when you basked in the light of John."

In Chapter 1, when we looked at the prologue of John's Gospel, we saw that the apostle declared that John the Baptist "came for a witness, to bear witness of the Light, that all through him might believe. He was not that Light, but was sent to bear witness of that Light" (1:7–8). Given that this was John the Baptist's task, it is not surprising that Jesus here called John as His first witness. Jesus was saying in the context of the trial: "My primary witness in this world was John the Baptist. He bore witness to Me. He announced Me before you. He's the one who said, 'Behold! The Lamb of God who takes away the sin of the world.' But you didn't believe him, even though for a time you basked in the glory of his light."

Witness No. 2: Miracles

John, however, was not Jesus' only witness: **"But I have a greater witness than John's; for the works which the Father has given Me to finish—the very works that I do—bear witness of Me, that the Father has sent Me. And the Father Himself, who sent Me, has testified of Me"** (vv. 36–37a). Jesus here used an argument that was understood in His day but which seems to go over our heads today—the purpose of miracles. Many people today look at the biblical miracles and say, "The miracles in the Bible prove the existence of God." No, they don't. The existence of God is established before a single miracle takes place. For a miracle to be recognized as a miracle presupposes the existence of God, because a miracle, technically and correctly defined, is a work that only God can do, such as bringing something out of nothing or bringing life out of death. For this reason, I plead with you not to fall into thinking that Satan can do actual miracles. He can perform tricks, but he can't do what God can do.

So rather than proving the existence of God, the biblical miracles serve to authenticate the messenger sent from God. When we looked at Jesus' conversation with Nicodemus in Chapter 6, we saw that Nicodemus came to Jesus by night and said, "Rabbi, we know that you are a teacher come from God; for no one can do these signs that You do unless God is with him" (John 3:2). That was sound reasoning. Nicodemus understood that Jesus' ability to do miracles meant that God was endorsing Him.

This is why we need to be very careful about accepting so-called miracles in our day. There are people in the world who claim to perform miracles, but they are theological charlatans of the worst kind. If they really are doing miracles, their writings ought to be included in the New Testament, because their miracles mean that God is authenticating them as agents of revelation. However, we know God is doing nothing of the sort because their teachings disagree with the New Testament. On this basis, we have to question their miracles.

So Jesus appealed to his miracles as a *corroborative witness* to His identity. He said: "The Father bears witness to Me by giving Me the power to perform the miracles that you have seen. If you won't believe My words, believe Me for My works. My works ought to be enough to prove to you that I am sent by the Father" (cf. 10:37–38). He did not say, "By doing My works, I am proving that I am the Son of God." No, He said that the works He was doing showed that God was authenticating His identity.

Witness No. 3: The Father

Jesus continued, **"You have neither heard His voice at any time, nor seen His form. But you do not have His word abiding in you, because whom He sent, Him you do not believe"** (vv. 37b–38). These people obviously had not been present at Jesus' baptism, because on that occasion the voice of God was audible. When the dove came upon Jesus, the voice of God was heard from heaven, saying, "This is My beloved Son, in whom I am well pleased" (Matt. 3:17). The Father also gave audible testimony to His Son at Jesus' transfiguration (Matt. 17:5). On each of these occasions, the Father called attention to the identity of Jesus as His Son.

I'm sure you've seen the popular bumper sticker that says, "God said it; I believe it; that settles it." How arrogant is that? We need a new bumper sticker, one that says: "God says it; that settles it." It doesn't matter whether I believe it. It's settled long before my assent. If God Almighty opens His holy mouth and declares something, we don't need another witness. It's over. It's settled.

Witness No. 4: The Scriptures

So far, we have seen that Jesus cited John the Baptist, His miracles, and even the audible voice of the Father Himself as witnesses to His identity. He then cited a fourth witness—the Scriptures. He said, **"You search the Scriptures, for in them you think you have eternal life; and these are they which testify of Me"** (v. 39). It is worthwhile to remember that Jesus was speaking here not to liberals, not to secularists, but to card-carrying fundamentalists, people who wouldn't have thought about going to church without carrying their Bibles. It was as if Jesus said: "You have Bible study every week. You don't just have a fifteen-minute daily devotional, but you search the Scriptures. You are disciplined students of the Scriptures, because you think that in studying the Scriptures you have eternal life. Yes, the Scriptures do lead to eternal life. But they do so by leading people to Me. The Scriptures point to Me. How can you read these Scriptures and not believe in Me?"

The problem was simple: **"You are not willing to come to Me that you may have life"** (v. 40). The Jewish leaders read the Scriptures, which spoke of Jesus, but they were unwilling to heed the testimony of the Scriptures and come to Him for life.

Several years ago, I received an invitation to lecture at a college on the existence of God. The invitation came from a campus group called the Atheist Club. I went to Romans 1 and talked about how God has manifestly, clearly, and without ambiguity revealed Himself to every creature, and that this knowledge gets through to every person; as much as we fight and kick against it, we can't extinguish that light. And so we are left, according to the apostle, without excuse. Our problem is not that we don't know that God exists. Our problem is that we refuse to acknowledge the God whom we know to be true.

Jesus continued, **"I do not receive honor from men. But I know you, that you do not have the love of God in you. I have come in My Father's name, and you do not receive Me; if another comes in his own name, him you will receive"** (vv. 41–43).

Someone once asked me, "How can you get a person who is famous and busy to make time in his schedule to come and speak for an event?" I said: "Give him an honor. Promise him an honorary degree, a great big monument, or a plaque, and invite him to come for the presentation." Human beings love to be honored, and Jesus understood this. But Jesus refused to seek honor from men. Compared with every other human being who has ever lived or ever will live, Jesus is most deserving of honor. Yet the Jewish leaders would not give Him that honor.

Finally Jesus said: **"Do not think that I shall accuse you to the Father; there is one who accuses you—Moses, in whom you trust. For if you believed Moses, you would believe Me; for he wrote about Me"** (vv. 45–46). This is an extremely controversial text. Proponents of higher critical theories about the Bible deny that Moses wrote anything. They say that the Pentateuch was compiled over many centuries by various editors and redactors, and that Moses had nothing to do with writing it. That view, of course, provoked a crisis in biblical scholarship, not only with the credibility of Moses but with the credibility of Jesus. It requires some amazing linguistic gymnastics to get around this text, where our Lord said Moses wrote about Him. The critics have to say that Jesus was wrong in what He taught about earthly things, for He couldn't possibly have known that Moses didn't write the Pentateuch. So we have a whole generation of scholars who don't believe

Jesus concerning earthly things but claim to believe Him concerning heavenly things, the very thing that Jesus Himself announced as foolishness.

So Jesus here affirmed the authorship of the Pentateuch by the hand of Moses, and He turned that on His critics. He said: "You call yourselves the disciples of Moses. You trust in the teaching of Moses. You exalt the Torah. But you don't really believe it because Moses was writing about Me. Don't you understand that when he described the tabernacle, he was describing Me? Don't you understand that when Moses said in Deuteronomy that there would come another Prophet like him, he was referring to Me? If you don't believe Moses' teachings, how are you going to believe Mine?"

So when the question of Jesus' identity came up, four witnesses came forth—John the Baptist, the miracles of Jesus, the audible testimony of the Father, and the testimony of sacred Scripture through the authorship of Moses. If that's not enough to convince people, what is?

A Fifth Witness?

What's the end of this? I don't think the last of this is heard until we go to the book of Acts, to the account of Paul's address to the philosophers at Mars Hill in Athens. Paul declared, "Truly, these times of ignorance God overlooked, but now commands all men everywhere to repent" (Acts 17:30). Paul cited a change in historical circumstances. He said: "There was a time when God was forbearing with your pagan religion and with your ignorance. God was merciful. He was patient. He put up with this for a long time. But now He commands you to repent." How different Paul's approach was from modern techniques of evangelism. The one essential of modern evangelism is the invitation. But the apostle did not say, "But now God invites all men to repent." Why? Because you can decline an invitation with impunity, but you cannot refuse God's command to repent with impunity.

Paul went on to say that God commands repentance "because He has appointed a day on which He will judge the world in righteousness by the Man whom He has ordained. He has given assurance of this to all by raising Him from the dead" (Acts 17:31). Paul brought up the resurrection of Christ. Do we want more testimony or evidence than that? We're not going to get it. God said: "I've made it clear to the whole world that this is My only begotten Son, and the days of patience and forbearance are over. Now I command you all to come to Him because I'm going to judge the whole world through Him, and I have already proven Him to be the judge by raising Him from the dead." The resurrection was the final witness to Jesus' identity.

15

FEEDING THE
FIVE THOUSAND

John 6:1–15

⚬⚬⚬⚬⚬⚬

After these things Jesus went over the Sea of Galilee, which is the Sea of Tiberias. Then a great multitude followed Him, because they saw His signs which He performed on those who were diseased. And Jesus went up on the mountain, and there He sat with His disciples. Now the Passover, a feast of the Jews, was near. Then Jesus lifted up His eyes, and seeing a great multitude coming toward Him, He said to Philip, "Where shall we buy bread, that these may eat?" But this He said to test him, for He Himself knew what He would do. Philip answered Him, "Two hundred denarii worth of bread is not sufficient for them, that every one of them may have a little." One of His disciples, Andrew, Simon Peter's brother, said to Him, "There is a lad here who has five barley loaves and two small fish, but what are they among so many?" Then Jesus said, "Make the people sit down." Now there was much grass in the place. So the men sat down, in number about five thousand. And Jesus took the loaves, and when He had given thanks He distributed them to the disciples, and the disciples to those sitting down; and likewise of the fish, as much as they wanted. So when they were filled, He said to His disciples, "Gather up the fragments that remain, so that nothing is lost." Therefore they gathered them up, and filled twelve baskets with the fragments of the five barley loaves which were left over by those who had eaten. Then those men, when they had seen the sign that Jesus did, said, "This is truly the Prophet who is to come into the world." Therefore when Jesus perceived that they were about to come and take Him by force to make Him king, He departed again to the mountain by Himself alone.

W e have come now to the sixth chapter of John, which is one of the most important chapters of the entire Gospel. It begins with an account of the only miracle of Jesus that is reported in all four of the Gospels. It is the miracle of the feeding of the five thousand.

Many of the events John records took place in Judea, but on this occasion Jesus was ministering in Galilee, which was in the northern part of Israel. In fact, Jesus was beside **the Sea of Galilee** (v. 1), that large lake that was also known as the Lake of Gennesaret (Luke 5:1) and, in the Old Testament, the Sea of Chinnereth or Kinnereth (Num. 34:11). The lake gained yet another name early in the first century, when Herod Antipas dedicated a city on its shores to the reigning emperor of the time, Tiberius Caesar, and so John makes reference to **the Sea of Tiberius** (v. 1).

As John sets the scene, he mentions that **a great multitude** (v. 2a) was following Jesus because they had seen those **signs which He had performed on those who were diseased** (v. 2b). So far, John has reported only one miracle of healing in Galilee, the healing of the nobleman's son (4:46–54), but this passage seems to indicate Jesus had done other such signs. John also notes that the **Passover** was near (v. 4a). As I mentioned in an earlier chapter, John frequently goes out of his way to connect the events he records in his Gospel with the feast of the Jews that was being celebrated at the time. In this case, his mention of the Passover is very significant, as we shall see.

Jesus, we're told, **went up on the mountain, and there He sat with His disciples** (v. 3). From that vantage point, he could see the tremendous multitude that was following him. A huge throng of people pressed up toward Him, and presumably Jesus instructed them for quite some time, till they grew hungry. Unfortunately, there was not nearly enough food on hand, and other accounts of this event tell us there was nowhere nearby to purchase any (Mark 6:35–36).

Seeing the crowd and their need, He asked one of His disciples, Philip, **"Where shall we buy bread, that these may eat?"** (v. 5b). This is one of those times when the Scriptures tell us that Jesus put one of His disciples to the test. There was a serious logistical problem, similar to that which the steward faced at the wedding in Cana, when the wine ran low and Jesus performed His first miracle (2:1–12). Jesus **knew what He would do**, but as a test, he asked Philip for ideas as to how the people could be fed (v. 6).

Listen to Philip's great response of faith: **"Two hundred denarii worth of bread is not sufficient for them, that every one of them may have a little"** (v. 7). A denarius was the standard daily wage for a laborer in Israel at this time, so Philip was saying, "Eight months' salary of a normal employee won't be enough money to buy food so that each person assembled here can get just a little taste." Philip, who had been present for Jesus' other miracles, couldn't see past the logistical difficulties. His response to Jesus amounted to this: "It's going to cost more than two hundred denarii in order to feed this mass of humanity. I have no idea where we're going to get that kind of money." So Philip flunked Jesus' test.

Then another disciple came into the picture, Andrew, who was Peter's brother. He said to Jesus, **"There is a lad here who has five barley loaves and two small fish"** (v. 9a). Now if Andrew had stopped right there, we would be excited about this projection of faith. As Jesus looked around for provisions for the multitude, Andrew said, "I asked around and I found one little boy who brought five barley loaves and a couple of fish." If he had said no more, we could assume he was indicating that he believed Jesus could take these loaves and fishes and make more than enough for everybody. But he went on to say, **"What are they among so many?"** (v. 9b). His faith was no greater than Philip's.

Fascinating Details

Andrew's words contain one interesting detail that none of the other Gospel writers provide. Andrew said the boy had barley loaves. Why is that significant? Some commentators say this tidbit of information draws attention to a miracle that was performed by Elisha in the Old Testament. Elisha multiplied twenty barley loaves into enough bread to feed one hundred men (2 Kings 4:42–44). Whether that miracle was in John's mind or not is pure speculation, but one thing that is beyond dispute is that the boy was carrying the lowest quality of bread available to people at the time. Only those who lived in poverty, for the most part, ate bread made from barley.

It is also important to note that the boy was not carrying large loaves of bread and large fish. These barley loaves were small cakes, similar in size to Twinkies, if you will. The fish were small fish that were used to give some flavor to the barley cakes, like sardines or smoked herring or something of that size. The boy had enough food only for his own lunch. The provisions were even more meager than we would assume just by reading the words of the text.

Then Jesus said, "Make the people sit down" (v. 10a). Here another detail surfaces: **there was much grass in the place** (v. 10b). This squares with John's statement that this event happened near the time of Passover, which occurs in the spring. There would not have been such abundant grass if this incident had occurred later in the year. This miracle occurred on what today is known as the Golan Heights. When summer comes, the heat burns away the grass on these slopes and leaves scorched earth. But that had not yet occurred; the grass was still abundant, and so Jesus had the people sit down.

Now we come to perhaps the most astounding detail in this passage. John writes, **So the men sat down, in number about five thousand** (v. 10c). John does not say there were five thousand *people*. Rather, he reports five thousand *men*, not counting the women and children. When women and children are factored in, estimates of the total size of this crowd range from ten thousand to fifteen thousand people. It is remarkable that such a large crowd would gather to hear a teacher in this time and place, but the size of the crowd is even more remarkable when considered in light of the miracle that was to follow.

John continues, **And Jesus took the loaves, and when He had given thanks He distributed them to the disciples, and the disciples to those sitting down; and likewise of the fish, as much as they wanted. So when they were filled, He said to His disciples, "Gather up the fragments that remain, so that nothing is lost." Therefore they gathered them up, and filled twelve baskets with the fragments of the five barley loaves which were left over by those who had eaten** (vv. 11–13).

Jesus not only multiplied the five barley loaves and the two fish to feed fifteen thousand people, He fed them to their fullest satisfaction—they were able to eat "as much as they wanted." After the feast, there were twelve baskets of leftovers. Some think that the number twelve represents the twelve tribes of Israel and the complete way in which their covenant God met their needs. It is difficult to say whether such symbolism is intended. Certainly this is the God of providence at work, the God who provides for His people. Also, this incident certainly echoes Israel's wilderness experience in the Old Testament, when God's people were nurtured daily by the bread from heaven that appeared as manna.

One of the beautiful aspects of the structure of John's Gospel, as we will see in the coming chapters, is that the feeding of the five thousand sets the stage for Jesus' teaching that He is the bread of life and the bread of heaven. John will show that God miraculously meets the needs of His people through His Son, the One who multiplies the loaves and the fishes.

Struggling with the Miraculous

John unambiguously proclaims that the feeding of the five thousand men with five loaves and two fish was a miracle. Accounts such as this vex higher critics of Scripture, who are hostile to purported miracles. In the nineteenth century, there developed an academic school, the religious-historical school, that sought to reinterpret and revise the biblical record to strip it of all supernatural elements and reduce it to accounts of natural events centered around a Man who distinguished Himself as a great ethical teacher, namely, Jesus of Nazareth.

I was exposed to this kind of antipathy when I was growing up. The minister of the church where my family worshiped when I was a child was described by the dean of one seminary as "an unreconstructed nineteenth-century liberal," and that's the viewpoint I was exposed to in Sunday school.

I'll never forget how our minister dealt with this story of the feeding of the five thousand. "Here's how it really happened," he said. He then explained that this crowd of thousands of people included many who had had the foresight to pack lunches for themselves. But there were also those who had neglected to make provision for a long day on the mountain. Therefore, when this huge assembly came together and it was time to eat, there were "haves" and "have-nots." So Jesus found a little boy who was willing to share his lunch with others, and using this little boy as an example, Jesus persuaded those who had brought provisions to share with those who had none. Thus, the miracle was an ethical miracle.

Other interpretations are even less sanguine. One of the scholars of the nineteenth century, trying to understand what really happened there, came up with this scenario: prior to the event, Jesus and His disciples had found a nearby cave in which they had stored a huge cache of bread and fish. When it came time to feed the people, Jesus had His disciples line up, forming a bucket brigade of sorts from the cave. As Jesus stood at the mouth of the cave, the disciples clandestinely passed bread and fish to Him, and He then pulled the food out of His sleeve until He had fed all of the people. If that's what actually happened, that was the most prodigious magical act in the history of the world. This is the extent to which biblical critics will go to remove the miraculous from Scripture.

This same unwillingness to accept the biblical accounts at face value results in antipathy toward biblical statements that are not even miraculous but merely extraordinary. For instance, according to the account of David's battle with Goliath (1 Sam. 17), Goliath was a giant who was nine feet nine inches tall. Critical scholars declare that Goliath could not have been that tall and that the biblical account is exaggerated. They find it impossible to believe that a young boy, without armor, came out and hurled a stone at the giant's head, knocked him down, and then cut off his head. The critics read that and say, "See, the Bible is filled with fairy tales."

I recently read an article about the Dead Sea Scrolls. Much of the information in the scrolls has been kept secret for decades, but now it's being revealed. According to this article, one of the texts of the Dead Sea Scrolls has an account of the confrontation between David and Goliath. This account, which dates from more than one hundred years before Christ and about a thousand years before the Masoretic Text, which is the surviving Hebrew text that we have for Old Testament records, has a different description for Goliath's size. Instead of describing him as nine feet nine, this ancient text reportedly describes Goliath as six feet nine. Now that's a figure you can believe. Nine feet nine makes Shaquille O'Neal seem like a shrimp by comparison, but a man standing six feet nine is not unheard of.

It might disturb you to learn that there is a discrepancy between two ancient texts, but one of the most common forms of discrepancies in the copies of the ancient manuscripts involves numbers. As meticulous and as careful as the scribes were, even they made mistakes in copying from time to time, such as you or I do when we incorrectly write down someone's telephone number or address. It is easy to make a mistake with a number.

So if that text from the Dead Sea Scrolls is correct, Goliath was only six feet nine. He has just shrunk by three feet, a yard. A little problem I have with that is that Saul, who was the commander in chief and king of the Israelite forces that Goliath challenged, was himself "head and shoulders" above everybody else in the community (1 Sam. 9:2). If Saul was six feet three or six feet four, his cowardice was all the worse if it was caused by a soldier who was only four or five inches taller than he.

I remember watching a television documentary about twentieth-century giants. These were men whose growth had run amok. Two of the men who were profiled were over nine feet tall. Most of these men lived until their early twenties and then died of medical complications, but they are modern proof that men sometimes grow to extraordinary heights.

I have no problem with the Bible's teaching that Goliath was nine feet nine. Maybe there is a textual variant that makes him six feet nine. Either way, I'm comfortable with it, and I don't have to try to find a way to escape the sober teaching and declaration of Holy Scripture. The same is true for the account of the feeding of the five thousand. Every gospel writer in the New Testament attests that Jesus miraculously fed this huge multitude, and this miracle revealed that He was sent from the One who provides our daily bread.

The Wrong Kind of King

In conclusion, we must not miss the reaction of the crowd that witnessed this miracle of Christ. In the first instance, they said, **"This is truly the Prophet who is to come into the world"** (v. 14b). They concluded that Jesus was the Prophet like Moses, whom Moses himself had foretold (Deut. 18:15). But then we read in verse 15, **Therefore when Jesus perceived that they were about to come and take Him by force to make Him king, He departed again to the mountain by Himself.** Apparently the people had seen something in Jesus that caused them to attempt to crown Him on the spot.

However, Jesus would have none of it. Just as He refused Satan's offer to make Him ruler of the world (Matt. 4:8–9), He rejected this human attempt to crown Him and left the scene. Why did He do this? Was He not the anointed King of kings? Was He not the King of the Jews? Why did He leave?

Here's another reason why John may have mentioned that this incident took place near the time of the Passover. Remember that at this time in Jewish history, when the people of Israel were under Roman occupation, the Passover was not just an exciting and important religious festival, it was the supreme celebration of national pride. Americans' celebration of the Fourth of July is not worthy to be compared to the Jews' experience of Passover, when they reaffirmed their hope that God would deliver them from the tyranny of Rome. So while this frenzy was going on, stoking the people's hopes for someone to deliver them from the yoke of Roman tyranny, the perfect political candidate appeared on the scene. He even provided that which wins political votes everywhere—a chicken in every pot, or a loaf and a fish in every lunch. It doesn't get any better than that. The people said, "This is the kind of king we want—one that will care for us from the cradle to the grave." But Jesus read their hearts, and He knew that the kind of king they were looking for had nothing to do with the kind of kingdom He had come to inaugurate. They were looking for the kingdom of man; He came to bring the kingdom of God. It was His mission to provide His people with so much more than bread and fishes.

As I noted earlier, the spiritual import of this event will be central to the discourse that follows. For now, let us celebrate the providence of God, remembering that the word *providence* points to the One who provides—Christ. He is the bread of heaven. He is the One who more than duplicates the manna that is spread in the wilderness. He is our King, who gives us all that we need and more.

16

BREAD FROM HEAVEN

John 6:16–34

Now when evening came, His disciples went down to the sea, got into the boat, and went over the sea toward Capernaum. And it was already dark, and Jesus had not come to them. Then the sea arose because a great wind was blowing. So when they had rowed about three or four miles, they saw Jesus walking on the sea and drawing near the boat; and they were afraid. But He said to them, "It is I; do not be afraid." Then they willingly received Him into the boat, and immediately the boat was at the land where they were going. On the following day, when the people who were standing on the other side of the sea saw that there was no other boat there, except that one which His disciples had entered, and that Jesus had not entered the boat with His disciples, but His disciples had gone away alone— however, other boats came from Tiberias, near the place where they ate bread after the Lord had given thanks— when the people therefore saw that Jesus was not there, nor His disciples, they also got into boats and came to Capernaum, seeking Jesus. And when they found Him on the other side of the sea, they said to Him, "Rabbi, when did You come here?" Jesus answered them and said, "Most assuredly, I say to you, you seek Me, not because you saw the signs, but because you ate of the loaves and were filled. Do not labor for the food which perishes, but for the food which endures to everlasting life, which the Son of Man will give you, because God the Father has set His seal on Him." Then they said to Him, "What shall we do, that we may work the works of God?" Jesus answered and said to them, "This is the work of God, that you believe in Him whom He sent." Therefore they said to Him, "What sign will You perform then, that we may see it and believe You? What work will You do? Our fathers ate the manna in the desert; as it is written, 'He gave them bread from heaven to eat.'" Then Jesus said to them, "Most assuredly, I say to you, Moses did not give you the bread from heaven, but My Father gives you the true bread from heaven. For the bread of God is He who comes down from heaven and gives life to the world." Then they said to Him, "Lord, give us this bread always."

In the previous chapter, we examined the apostle John's record of Jesus' miracle of feeding the five thousand. We saw that the end result of that incident was that the people were about to take Jesus by force to make Him king, not because they recognized Him as their rightful Lord and Master but because He had done a wonderful sign and filled their bellies. But Jesus was not willing to be crowned on that basis, so He sought solitude in the hills by the Sea of Galilee.

John introduces the next incident in his Gospel with foreboding words: **Now when evening came, His disciples went down to the sea, got into the boat, and went over the sea toward Capernaum. And it was already dark, and Jesus had not come to them. Then the sea arose because a great wind was blowing. So when they had rowed about three or four miles, they saw Jesus walking on the sea and drawing near the boat; and they were afraid** (vv. 16–19).

John tells us that as the day was waning, Jesus' disciples went down to the Sea of Galilee and got into their boat to row back to Capernaum, but Jesus remained behind. Soon darkness fell and the wind kicked up. There were professional fishermen among the disciples, seasoned veterans of this lake, but they were able to make little or no progress toward their destination.

In ancient Jewish writings, the image of the sea often carries negative connotations. Especially in Hebrew poetry, the sea represents that which is ominous, chaotic, and destructive. Part of the reason for this antipathy was that, because of the rocky coastline of Palestine, the Jews never developed a sea trade. As a result, they were unfamiliar with the sea. It is true that there was extensive fishing on the Sea of Galilee, and the apostle John was a fisherman there before he was called to follow Christ. But even the Sea of Galilee, though it is an inland lake, is subject to violent storms. It sits six hundred feet below sea level, and it is situated, as it were, in a wind tunnel—gales blow off the Mediterranean and through the mountains, stirring up the lake without warning. During the storm recorded in this passage, even an experienced fisherman such as John could become alarmed, and we can only imagine how fearful the landsmen among the disciples were.

A Deeper Fear

Then something happened that heightened the disciples' fears exponentially. They saw Jesus approaching them without the benefit of a boat. He was walking in the darkness over the chaotic, frothing sea. John tells us in the prologue of his Gospel that "In the beginning was the Word, and the Word was with God, and the Word was God" (John 1:1). Christ was God in the flesh, but His divine nature was masked and hidden by that veil of humanity. Sometimes, however, His divine nature showed through. There were moments when Jesus' deity burst through the veil and became obvious and manifest to anyone who was watching. That's what happened on this occasion; cloaked in mortality and veiled in humanity, Jesus did what no human being could possibly do. He strode across the sea, and the waters supported Him.

Think for a moment how you would feel if you were in that boat with the waves crashing against the gunwales and the oars straining to bring inches of progress. You would be nervous because of the storm, but then you would look up and see the Master walking across the sea toward you. Suddenly it would hit you that Jesus could do this because He is the One who made the sea and ruled the sea. The One who is very human is also very divine. How would you react? You would react just like the disciples did. Instead of feeling relieved and saying, "I'm glad to see you," you would be terrified. Any human being would feel that way while watching Jesus walk across an angry sea without sinking. But Jesus said to the disciples in their terror, **"It is I; do not be afraid"** (v. 20).

Several years ago, I did a study of the "I am" sayings of Jesus, all taken from the Gospel of John. These are those famous statements wherein Jesus declares such things as, "I am the way, the truth, and the life" (14:6), "I am the vine, you are the branches" (15:5), "I am the good shepherd" (10:11, 14), "I am the door" (10:9), "I am the bread of life" (6:48), as well as others. In all of these sayings, Jesus prefaced descriptions of His office by a strange combination of Greek words, *ego eimi*. The word *ego* in Greek means "I am." We get the word *ego* from it. But the word *eimi* also means "I am." If you put them together, *ego eimi* literally means "I am, I am," as if one were stuttering. In order to understand what Jesus was doing, we need to look at the Greek translation of the Old Testament, where we see that the ineffable name of God, Yahweh, was translated into the Greek language by this same strange construction, *ego eimi*, which can be translated "I AM WHO I AM" (Ex. 3:14). Therefore, almost every commentator recognizes that when Jesus said, "I am the door," "I am the bread of life," and other "I am" sayings, He was using the divine name for Himself.

However, when scholars enumerate the "I am" sayings in the Gospel of John, they don't include Jesus' statement here: "It is I; do not be afraid." I'm not sure why, because it's exactly the same structure, *ego eimi*. Jesus said to His disciples, "Don't be afraid. It is I AM WHO I AM."

Whether the next sentence communicates a second miracle is debated. After Jesus announced Himself in this manner, the disciples **willingly received Him into the boat, and immediately the boat was at the land where they were going** (v. 21). This suggests that when He got into the boat, that was the end of the sea's resistance to the efforts of His disciples to gain headway into the wind. By His mere presence, the boat immediately came safely to the other shore.

There's an illustration here. I don't want to be maudlin, but this is the way our lives are. This story is not a parable; it is a historical narrative. However, it certainly illustrates what happens when Jesus comes into our lives. Life is a time of pulling against the oars, against resistance, trying to get somewhere. However, we're not getting anywhere and we're about to be engulfed. But as soon as Jesus gets in the boat, we're home free. That's what happens when Christ comes into the lives of His people. He doesn't take away all difficulties and make our lives beds of ease, but He gets us through the darkness. He gets us through the violence. He carries us through the storm.

"How Did You Get Here?"

This miracle of walking on the water was directly witnessed only by Jesus' disciples. But that doesn't mean it was undetected by the clamoring multitude. John tells us: **On the following day, when the people who were standing on the other side of the sea saw that there was no other boat there, except that one which His disciples had entered, and that Jesus had not entered the boat with His disciples, but His disciples had gone away alone—however, other boats came from Tiberias, near the place where they ate bread after the Lord had given thanks—when the people therefore saw that Jesus was not there, nor His disciples, they also got into boats and came to Capernaum, seeking Jesus. And when they found Him on the**

other side of the sea, they said to Him, "Rabbi, when did You come here?" (vv. 22–25).

With this question, the people essentially asked Jesus, "*How* did you get here?" Jesus doesn't give the answer I wish He had given. When the people asked, "How did you get here?" I would have loved to have heard Him reply, "I walked," just to watch their reaction. But that's not what He did. He knew what was on their minds and what they were looking for, so He ignored their question and said to them, **"Most assuredly, I say to you, you seek Me, not because you saw the signs, but because you ate of the loaves and were filled"** (v. 26).

It is true that they sought Him because they saw the signs. But Jesus said that they hadn't seen the *significance* of the signs. He told them: "You saw the miracle, you enjoyed the benefit of the miracle, and so you've been chasing after Me to make Me your King because I filled your bellies. But will you want Me to be your King when you see the baptism with which I am baptized? You want to enter into the feast, but do you want to enter into My sufferings? Do you want to pick up your cross and follow Me?" Jesus gave a warning to these fair-weather fans.

Then He said, **"Do not labor for the food which perishes, but for the food which endures to everlasting life, which the Son of Man will give you, because God the Father has set His seal on Him"** (v. 27). I often have the opportunity to speak with people who are dissatisfied about the direction of their lives. When I speak with such a person and we discuss his or her job, I usually ask: "Is that your vocation? Is that what you want to do?" Many times the person says, "Well, no, I'm just trying to put food on the table." How empty life can seem when our labor is done simply so that we can put food on the table. Don't get me wrong—sometimes it is necessary to do that because we have the responsibility to feed our families, and if we can't get work anywhere else, we need to take on work that may not be part of our vocations to make sure we get food on the table. But that is frustrating, because that food perishes. We set the table one night and eat the dinner, but the next day we have to set the table again, and we have to get more food because every helping that we enjoy perishes. Jesus said: "Don't spend your life pursuing that sort of thing. Don't spend your life pursuing that which has no ultimate significance."

I think about this every day. I see my friends who aren't Christians get up in the morning, get dressed, go to work, and go through the anguish and the struggles that life brings each day, and I think, "Why are they doing this?" It usually happens that such people wake up one day, discover that they're sixty or seventy years old, and they say: "Why did I do that? Is that all there is?"

Thankfully, that's not all there is. There is much more than the food that perishes. Jesus said: "Seek that which is eternal. Invest in that which doesn't perish. Store up for yourselves treasures in heaven where there are no moths, no rust, and no thieves that come in to steal it."

A Sealed Promise

Have you ever asked yourself what you are doing with your life? Do you wonder why you live the way you are living? Do you think about what you're trying to accomplish? Do you know what you have to gain? Have you not heard that he who gains the whole world and loses his own soul has no profit (Matt. 16:26)? "Do not labor for the food which perishes, but for the food which endures to everlasting life, which the Son of Man will give you." Why? Because God the Father has set His seal on Him.

Each time we have a baptism, I mention that baptism is not magic and that it doesn't convert anybody, but it is God's sign and seal of His promise of redemption for all who believe. Some people ask, "What good is that?"

In the old Robin Hood movies, there was usually a scene in which the king would send his henchmen to the town square to nail up a "wanted" poster announcing a reward of five hundred ducats or some such figure for the capture of the bandit. At the bottom of the edict there was usually a wax impression that bore the image of the royal signet ring. That impression authenticated that the announcement came not from the village blacksmith, the tanner, or the tinker. The impression was the seal of the king; it indicated that the edict carried royal authority. Therefore, the promise was sure.

That is what Jesus was saying about eternal bread, the bread that doesn't perish. He said: "I, the Son of Man, will give you this bread because the Father has put His seal on Me. He has authenticated, by these miracles, that I have come from Him, and I speak nothing on My own authority, but He has given to Me all authority in heaven and on earth, and I have the authority now to give eternal life to you." Jesus is authorized to give bread that comes from heaven, and His promise is utterly sure for all who believe in Him.

17

BREAD OF LIFE

John 6:35–51

And Jesus said to them, "I am the bread of life. He who comes to Me shall never hunger, and he who believes in Me shall never thirst. But I said to you that you have seen Me and yet do not believe. All that the Father gives Me will come to Me, and the one who comes to Me I will by no means cast out. For I have come down from heaven, not to do My own will, but the will of Him who sent Me. This is the will of the Father who sent Me, that of all He has given Me I should lose nothing, but should raise it up at the last day. And this is the will of Him who sent Me, that everyone who sees the Son and believes in Him may have everlasting life; and I will raise him up at the last day." The Jews then complained about Him, because He said, "I am the bread which came down from heaven." And they said, "Is not this Jesus, the son of Joseph, whose father and mother we know? How is it then that He says, 'I have come down from heaven'?" Jesus therefore answered and said to them, "Do not murmur among yourselves. No one can come to Me unless the Father who sent Me draws him; and I will raise him up at the last day. It is written in the prophets, 'And they shall all be taught by God.' Therefore everyone who has heard and learned from the Father comes to Me. Not that anyone has seen the Father, except He who is from God; He has seen the Father. Most assuredly, I say to you, he who believes in Me has everlasting life. I am the bread of life. Your fathers ate the manna in the wilderness, and are dead. This is the bread which comes down from heaven, that one may eat of it and not die. I am the living bread which came down from heaven. If anyone eats of this bread, he will live forever; and the bread that I shall give is My flesh, which I shall give for the life of the world."

Years ago, I received a letter from a woman who said she had subscribed for many years to *Tabletalk*, the devotional magazine published by Ligonier Ministries, and had been reading diligently through the daily devotions. However, she was writing to cancel her subscription. The devotions that year were based on a commentary on Paul's letter to the Romans written by the late James Montgomery Boice. The woman went on to say in her letter that she had read several *Tabletalk* devotions covering the doctrine of predestination, and she said, "I will no longer read this magazine because I don't believe in predestination." I was sorry to hear she was cancelling her subscription, but I was glad she didn't say she would no longer read Paul's letter to the Romans.

That woman's response to the doctrine of predestination is not unusual, I'm sorry to say. Some people get very exercised about it and refuse to have anything to do with it, while others who struggle with it go the second mile and search the Scriptures to learn whether it is a biblical doctrine. I myself struggled with the doctrine of predestination when I was a young Christian. Even now, I struggle with certain things that are plainly taught in the Word of God. To combat this tendency in my life, when I was in seminary I kept a card on my desk that said, "You are responsible to believe and to teach what the Bible teaches, not what you would like for it to teach." I realize that when there's something in the Word of God that I don't like, the problem is not with the Word of God, it's with me.

I say this by way of preface to the very difficult and profound text we are considering in this chapter, a text that always sends chills up and down the spines of those who love the doctrines of grace. This text includes Jesus' pronouncement that He descended to this world from heaven. Just as manna, which perished, came from heaven, so the living bread descended from the Father's presence. However, not all of those who rushed to listen to Jesus after seeing His miracles, particularly the feeding of the five thousand, were pleased by the content of this discourse. As we will see in the next chapter, many of those who had been following Jesus and had claimed to be His disciples turned back when they heard this speech, which is so manifestly predestinarian, and walked no more with Him.

The Bread of Life

Following the somewhat hasty request of the people in verse 34, "Lord, give us this bread always," Jesus replied, **"I am the bread of life. He who comes to Me shall never hunger, and he who believes in Me shall never thirst"** (v. 35). In this, the first of His seven "I am" sayings in the Gospel of John, Jesus made clear that the bread of heaven was not physical bread; rather, it was Jesus Himself. Those who would cease to hunger and thirst needed to come to Him and believe in Him. But Jesus went on to remind the people, **"But I said to you that you have seen Me and yet do not believe"** (v. 36). The people had been exposed to Jesus, they had sat under His teaching, and they had seen His miracles, but they had not yet believed. Why? Simply put, they lacked the ability.

Verse 37 is a crucial text. Jesus said, **"All that the Father gives Me will come to Me, and the one who comes to Me I will by no means cast out."** If we could understand the import of this single verse of Scripture, all of the theological battles of the ages over election, divine sovereignty, and human responsibility would vanish. Jesus spoke here about those who come to Him, respond to Him, receive Him, embrace Him, and place their trust in Him—and about how they are motivated to do that.

With these words, Jesus taught those who were gathered, including His disciples, that there are a number of people whom the Father has determined will come to the Son. They are gifts of the Father to the Son. We will return to this topic when we get into the upper room discourse and the great High Priestly Prayer of Jesus, wherein Jesus prayed for those whom the Father had given Him and rejoiced that none whom the Father had given Him would ever be lost.

The deepest theological question that I can think of, the one for which I have no adequate answer, is the question, "Why me?" My students come to me with all kinds of conundrums from theology, but they rarely ask, "Why did God save me?" It sometimes seems as if we're thinking: "Why *wouldn't* He save me?" Yes, we have little aphorisms such as, "There, but for the grace of God, go I." Do we really believe that? Are we really amazed by the measure of grace God has poured out on us? Can we say with John, "Behold what manner of love the Father has bestowed on us, that we should be called children of God!" (1 John 3:1). I cannot give a single reason under heaven why God would save me other than, as the prophet Isaiah said, that the Suffering

Servant of Israel should see the travail of His soul and be satisfied—that God has determined to honor His Son by giving Him adopted brothers and sisters (Isa. 53:11).

In the final analysis, the only reason I am a Christian is that the Father wants to honor the Son. From all eternity, He determined that the Son's work would not be in vain and that He would be the firstborn of many brethren. Therefore, He determined not just to make salvation possible and then step back and cross His fingers, hoping that somebody would take advantage of the ministry of Jesus. No, God the Father, from all eternity, determined to make salvation *certain* for those whom He had determined to give to His Son.

The Rock of Offense

So our Lord said, "All that the Father gives Me will come to Me." That's the rock of offense, the stone over which we trip, for that verse suggests that God never intended to save everyone.

A few years ago, my doctor said to me, "R. C., I struggle with limited atonement, with the idea that God did not intend to save everybody. How should I handle that?" I said: "Well, let me ask you a question. When you prescribe a medication for me, do you cross your fingers and hope it will have some healing impact on my life, or do you have a reasonable degree of confidence that the medication you prescribe will actually effect what you intend it to effect?" She said, "It's the latter." I said: "Good. But still, even though you're highly educated and you're a doctor, you're still mortal. You're finite. You don't have omniscience. You don't know for sure that the medication you prescribe will do what you want it to do. I may be in that small number of people who have a violent reaction to that medication, and you don't know that in advance. Nevertheless, you prescribe it with great hope."

Then I said: "But let's think about God. Do you think that when God planned His way of salvation that He just threw some medication out there and hoped that some people would take advantage of it and be healed? Or did He know the effect that it was going to have, since He had sovereignly determined that there were people who were going to be healed by the medicine of His grace, to honor His Son?" She said, "I never thought about it that way."

The vast majority of Christians today are what we call semi-Pelagian in their theology. They read the statement of Jesus this way: "All who come to Me the Father will give to Me." That's Arminianism. We come; we decide. Then the Father recognizes our decision and makes us gifts to His Son. But that's not the way Jesus taught it. Jesus said, "The ones whom the Father has given to Me will come to Me—every one of them."

We must not overlook the final part of this statement: ". . . the one who comes to Me I will by no means cast out." Jesus said: "All whom the Father gives Me will come to Me, and when they come to Me they will never be sent out; they will never be separated from Me. They are Mine forever." Jesus wasn't teaching only the doctrine of unconditional election or irresistible grace. Here He was setting forth the doctrine of the perseverance of the saints, or the preservation of the saints. Those who are truly saved will continue in that condition, for Jesus will not let them fall away. In his first epistle, John writes, "They went out from us, but they were not of us; for if they had been of us, they would have continued with us" (1 John 2:19). What is John saying? Speaking of some church members who had left the fellowship, he asserts, "If you truly have it, you never lose it; and if you lose it, you never truly had it." In short, those who are saved cannot be separated from the Savior.

The Essential Condition

Then Jesus expounded this theme even further: **"For I have come down from heaven, not to do My own will, but the will of Him who sent Me. This is the will of the Father who sent Me, that of all He has given Me I should lose nothing, but should raise it up at the last day. And this is the will of Him who sent Me, that everyone who sees the Son and believes in Him may have everlasting life; and I will raise him up at the last day"** (vv. 38–40). It is God's will that those whom He has given to the Son—whom the Bible over and over again describes as the elect, or those who are called and chosen by God—should not be lost but have everlasting life.

It was at this point that Jesus' hearers complained. Puzzled, they asked: **"Is not this Jesus, the son of Joseph, whose father and mother we know? How is it then that He says, 'I have come down from heaven'?"** (v. 42). Notice that they were wrestling with His statement about His origins and apparently had not heard His dramatic words about salvation. Because He was familiar to them, they had difficulty getting past His statement that He had come from heaven.

Jesus responded with a stern admonition: **"Do not murmur among yourselves"** (v. 43b). Then He gave a statement that both reiterated what He had already said about salvation and expanded upon it: **"No one can come to Me unless the Father who sent Me draws him; and I will raise him up at the last day"** (v. 44).

This astonishing pronouncement is what is called a universal negative proposition. Jesus began with the words "No one," which meant "No person" without exception. He then added the word "can." This word has to do with ability, but since Jesus had already made clear that He was talking about something "no one" is able to do, He was speaking of an inability. He was about to declare that there was something no one was capable of doing. What was it? "Come to me." In short, Jesus said no one, no human being, was capable of coming to Him. All people are infected with a moral inability as a result of their fallen condition.

That doesn't mean no one ever *will* come to Jesus. It can happen, but Jesus' next word, "unless," indicated a necessary condition, a *sine qua non*, something that must take place before the desired result can happen. What is this necessary condition? ". . . the Father who sent Me draws him." Jesus said, "No one has the power or the ability to come to Me unless the Father draws Him."

The understanding of this verse in the Protestant church has been largely colored by semi-Pelagianism, specifically the word *draw*. When we talk about drawing people, we tend to think of flies and honey, of trying to woo, entice, or persuade. But the Greek word translated here as "draws" actually means "to compel." So why isn't that word used in our English Bibles? It is for the same reason people walked away when they heard Jesus give this teaching originally—the translators don't like it. Jesus simply wasn't saying, "No one will come to Me unless the Father woos them to Me." No, His meaning was much stronger. He used the same Greek word that is used in the book of Acts when Paul was seized and dragged out of the temple at Jerusalem (Acts 21:30). We can be sure those angry Jews did not try to woo Paul to come with them.

I once took part in a public debate with the head of the New Testament department at a Midwestern seminary. We were debating the doctrine of election, and we eventually came to this text. I pointed out to him that the Greek word translated as "draws" actually means "compel," not "entice" or "woo." In response, he quoted an obscure text from the secular literature of ancient Greece wherein the same Greek word was used to speak of drawing water out of a well. He said, "Now, Dr. Sproul, when you get water out of a well, do you compel it or drag it out of the well?" Everyone in the audience roared, so I said: "Well, you've got me there. I didn't even know that text existed in classical Greek. But let me ask you, how *do* you get water out of a well? Do you stand up there and look down and say, 'Here, water, water, water'? Do you woo it up? Of course not. The water is inert. You have to go get it. It's not able, unless the well is an artesian well, to come up out of there for you."

Jesus said that we are so corrupt, that our hearts have been so hardened toward the things of God, that we cannot respond to God and come to Him on our own. This is exactly what He told Nicodemus when He said, "Unless one is born again, he cannot see the kingdom of God" (John 3:3). Here is another universal negative proposition with a necessary condition—the new birth. Jesus said: "You can't even see the kingdom of God unless God the Holy Spirit changes your heart of stone into a heart of flesh." In our natural state, we are completely unwilling and morally incapable of coming to Christ. If the Father wants us to come to Christ, He must effectually draw us to His beloved Son.

If you are a Christian, that's exactly what He did for you. He brought you to the bread of life, to the bread who came down from heaven. Please don't despise the marvelous work of grace God has done in your soul. Please don't take credit for what God has so mercifully done for you by working in you, by removing the blinders from your eyes and the wax from your ears, by giving you the capacity to hear the Word of God and to see the sweetness and the loveliness of the Savior. Consider anew the wonderful news that the Father has given you to His Son and has drawn you to Him.

18

HARD SAYINGS

John 6:52–71

The Jews therefore quarreled among themselves, saying, "How can this Man give us His flesh to eat?" Then Jesus said to them, "Most assuredly, I say to you, unless you eat the flesh of the Son of Man and drink His blood, you have no life in you. Whoever eats My flesh and drinks My blood has eternal life, and I will raise him up at the last day. For My flesh is food indeed, and My blood is drink indeed. He who eats My flesh and drinks My blood abides in Me, and I in him. As the living Father sent Me, and I live because of the Father, so he who feeds on Me will live because of Me. This is the bread which came down from heaven—not as your fathers ate the manna, and are dead. He who eats this bread will live forever." These things He said in the synagogue as He taught in Capernaum. Therefore many of His disciples, when they heard this, said, "This is a hard saying; who can understand it?" When Jesus knew in Himself that His disciples complained about this, He said to them, "Does this offend you? What then if you should see the Son of Man ascend where He was before? It is the Spirit who gives life; the flesh profits nothing. The words that I speak to you are spirit, and they are life. But there are some of you who do not believe." For Jesus knew from the beginning who they were who did not believe, and who would betray Him. And He said, "Therefore I have said to you that no one can come to Me unless it has been granted to him by My Father." From that time many of His disciples went back and walked with Him no more. Then Jesus said to the twelve, "Do you also want to go away?" But Simon Peter answered Him, "Lord, to whom shall we go? You have the words of eternal life. Also we have come to believe and know that You are the Christ, the Son of the living God." Jesus answered them, "Did I not choose you, the twelve, and one of you is a devil?" He spoke of Judas Iscariot, the son of Simon, for it was he who would betray Him, being one of the twelve.

F rom time to time in the Scriptures we encounter what theologians call "hard sayings." This term is employed for two reasons. On the one hand, such sayings are difficult for us to penetrate in our understanding, so they are hard in that sense. On the other hand, such sayings seem harsh to our ears; that is, they are difficult to accept. But because we encounter these hard sayings so frequently in Scripture, and because many of them come to us from the lips of Jesus, we need to approach them with a posture of humility, that we may be instructed by our Lord.

This discourse of Jesus in John 6, which we've spent three chapters studying so far and which we will complete in this chapter, provoked many of Jesus' hearers to leave His company. Throughout this study of John, we have noted that the crowds that came to hear Jesus' teaching or to witness His miracles exhibited a certain fickleness. But after this discourse, those who walked away from Him were His disciples. We don't know exactly how many disciples Jesus had before this discourse, but afterward it appears He was left only with the Twelve, one of whom, Jesus said, was **"a devil"** (v. 70). So by the end of John 6, the ranks of those who received the teaching of Christ had dwindled to eleven.

I must say that many so-called disciples of Christ today exhibit this same fickleness—they profess allegiance and loyalty to Jesus until they hear Him teach certain things they don't like. I pray you will not be so inclined to walk away as we wrestle with the hard sayings in this passage.

A Dispute over "Flesh"

We saw in the previous chapter that Jesus described Himself as "the bread of life" (vv. 35, 48). Building on that metaphor, He said: "I am the living bread which came down from heaven. If anyone eats of this bread, he will live forever; and the bread that I shall give is My flesh, which I shall give for the life of the world" (v. 51). This statement provoked further confusion and controversy: **The Jews therefore quarreled among themselves, saying, "How can this Man give us His flesh to eat?"** (v. 52). Jesus, aware of their struggle with His words, then went on to give the hard saying that particularly troubled His disciples on this occasion: **"Most assuredly, I say to you, unless you eat the flesh of the Son of Man and drink His blood, you have no life in you. Whoever eats My flesh and drinks My blood has eternal life, and I will raise him up at the last day. For My flesh is food indeed, and My blood is drink indeed. He who eats My flesh and drinks My blood abides in Me, and I in him. As the living Father sent Me, and I live because of the Father, so he who feeds on Me will live because of Me. This is the bread which came down from heaven—not as your fathers ate the manna, and are dead. He who eats this bread will live forever"** (vv. 53–58).

Did you notice the recurrence of that little word *unless* early in this discourse? In the previous chapter, we saw that this word introduces a *sine qua non*, a necessary condition that must occur before some desired consequence or effect can take place. Here, the condition Jesus set forth was eating His flesh and drinking His blood, and He assured His hearers that if they did not do these things, "you have no life in you" (v. 53). They might have biological life, but they wouldn't have the life Christ came to give to His people, those given to Him by the Father. Just to reinforce the point, Jesus restated it in the form of a promise: "Whoever eats My flesh and drinks My blood has eternal life, and I will raise Him up at the last day" (v. 54). He went on to say His flesh and blood were "food indeed" and "drink indeed" (v. 55); that those who eat His flesh and drink His blood abide in Him and He in them (v. 56); and that, unlike the manna the Israelites ate in the desert, Jesus' flesh and blood would give eternal life (v. 58).

When Jesus had finished speaking, John tells us: **Therefore many of His disciples, when they heard this, said, "This is a hard saying; who can understand it?"** (v. 60). I want you to notice two things here. First, John employs the word *therefore*. This tells us the disciples' reaction was provoked by the preceding words. Second, the disciples actually made a good point and asked a good question. This certainly *is* a hard saying and it *is* hard to understand. I'm not even sure I understand it. If you consult all the commentaries and the scholars of church history as you seek to understand this discourse, you'll find a divided house.

Many biblical scholars through the ages have thought that Jesus was giving a discourse on the meaning of the Lord's Supper and was saying that unless a person partakes of the real body and blood of Christ in the sacrament of Holy Communion, he cannot be redeemed. I don't agree with that position. This is one of the few occasions when the majority of scholars hold the position that I hold, though I'm less than dogmatic about it. I believe that Jesus is speaking here not about the Lord's Supper but about the same subject He addressed in His conversation with the Samaritan woman (John 4:1–26), when He talked about the living water that He would give. In short, I believe Jesus was making the point that He is the giver of supernatural life, the living Redeemer who had been sent by the living God to impart eternal life to all who put their trust in Him. Furthermore, He was calling for a deep commitment. He told His disciples: "You have to come into Me, be united to Me, feast upon Me—not just have a casual relationship to Me." He was calling His followers to a wholehearted pursuit of union with Him—a union without which there is no spiritual life.

To put it another way, Jesus declared that religion won't do it. Church attendance won't do it. Good works in and of themselves won't do it. The only thing that gets us into the kingdom of God, by which we participate in the gift of eternal life, is union with Christ Jesus. To emphasize this, our Lord said, "You have to take all of Me, as if you were ingesting Me."

No Offense Given

That's a hard saying. The disciples certainly found it to be so, and Jesus knew they found it to be so. Therefore, John writes, **When Jesus knew in Himself that His disciples complained about this, He said to them, "Does this offend you?"** (v. 61). There's an important distinction in Christian ethics that we all need to master, and that is the difference between an offense given and an offense taken. Many times we take offense at things people do or say when no offense was given. We simply don't like what was done or said. We may feel insulted when no one has insulted us. That kind of thing happens in the church all the time. We are sometimes too easily offended by things that should not offend us. We are commanded as Christians not to give offense, not to violate people, not to do harm to other people. But sometimes we can do exactly the right thing and people take offense anyway.

No one ever spoke more perfectly or inoffensively than our Lord did in this encounter with His own disciples, but they took offense. Jesus noticed that, so he said, "Does this offend you?" Notice, however, that He did not apologize; He had nothing for which to apologize. Instead, He asked a probing question:

"What then if you should see the Son of Man ascend where He was before?" (v. 62). In other words, "What if you see Me clothed in glory, rising up to heaven, surrounded by the angels, going in My glory. Will that offend you?" The answer, of course, is that they would not be offended by the sight of His ascension but delighted. Jesus told them that there might be many things He would say that would offend them, but those "offenses" would all be forgotten when they saw His perfection made manifest before their eyes. In short, Jesus sought to restore their perspective.

Jesus went on to tell His wavering disciples some other vital things. First, He said, **"It is the Spirit who gives life; the flesh profits nothing"** (v. 63a). It is important to see that when Jesus mentioned "the flesh" here, He was not talking about His own flesh, of which He had spoken repeatedly in the previous verses. Rather, He was talking here about *our* flesh, the fallen human nature. This is a major motif throughout the Bible, and we already have encountered it in John, when we studied Jesus' discourse with Nicodemus. If you remember, He told Nicodemus that unless a person is born of water and the Spirit, he cannot enter the kingdom of God (3:5). He went on to say, "That which is born of the flesh is flesh, and that which is born of the Spirit is spirit" (3:6). He told Nicodemus that the flesh cannot produce spiritual fruit. In our natural, fallen condition, we cannot do the things of God. We have no strength for spiritual things and no inclination toward the things of heaven until God, by His Holy Spirit, changes the disposition of our hearts and raises us from that state of pure flesh, which the Bible says is spiritual death.

This was what engaged Martin Luther in his debate with Desiderius Erasmus of Rotterdam. Erasmus had written his *Diatribe* against Luther and Luther's doctrine of predestination because Erasmus held on to the idea that there remains in the soul of fallen man a little island of righteousness by which we can choose to come to God or to reject Him. Luther, picking up on Jesus' words here in chapter 6, "the flesh profits nothing," said to Erasmus, "That 'nothing' is not a little something."

If you are resting on the strength of your righteousness, you've missed what our Lord taught here. In your flesh dwells no good thing (Rom. 7:18a); your flesh cannot get you into the kingdom of God. It is the Spirit who brings life, who raises us from spiritual death.

Words of Life

Jesus then said, **"The words that I speak to you are spirit, and they are life"** (v. 63b). How does the Spirit make us alive? He does it through the Word of God. The Spirit comes with the Word. He uses the Word to pierce our hearts, to change the disposition of our souls. It was by the Word of God that the universe was brought out of nothing. It is at the Word of God that you and I are rescued from spiritual nothingness and made alive to the things of God.

I love to hear the Word of God read aloud. One of the most difficult pastoral tasks I've ever had came very early in my ministry. I was teaching at a college in Massachusetts, and a man closely connected to the school became sick unto death. I used to go to Massachusetts General Hospital every day and sit by his bed and watch him die a day at a time. Finally we came down to the last few hours of his life, and there was very little I could do to comfort him other than put some ice on his parched lips, wipe the sweat from his forehead, and read to him from the Word of God. But that is what he most wanted because of the comfort the Scriptures provided. That's how I want to die—listening to the Word of God, because that Word is life.

Finally, Jesus became very blunt with His hearers: **"But there are some of you who do not believe. . . . Therefore I have said to you that no one can come to Me unless it has been granted to him by My Father"** (vv. 64–65). There's that doctrine of predestination again. Jesus knew that some of His disciples were not believers, and here He made it clear to them that they could not believe unless God took action. That was the final straw for some of them: **From that time many of His disciples went back and walked with Him no more** (v. 66).

Jesus watched this exodus of false disciples, all of those who had taken offense at His teaching. Then He turned to the Twelve and, much like Caesar in his dying moment said, "*Et tu, Brute?*" Jesus said, **"Do you also want to go away?"** (v. 67). That sparked Peter's great confession of faith: **"Lord, to whom shall we go? You have the words of eternal life. Also we have come to believe and know that You are the Christ, the Son of the living God"** (vv. 68–69). Peter didn't deny that Jesus' sayings were hard, but he also acknowledged that Jesus' words were words of life. The Twelve had nowhere else to go.

Are you ever tempted to leave? I certainly have been, many times, and I don't know how many times these words of Peter have echoed through my mind. Where can I go? Should I go to Mohammed and join the *jihad*? I'm not going to find words of eternal life there. I won't find them with Immanuel Kant or Jean-Paul Sartre. I won't find them in the lyrics of contemporary music. If I want the words of eternal life, there's only one place I can go to get them—to the One who gave His life that we might live.

19

UNBELIEF

John 7:1–13

After these things Jesus walked in Galilee; for He did not want to walk in Judea, because the Jews sought to kill Him. Now the Jews' Feast of Tabernacles was at hand. His brothers therefore said to Him, "Depart from here and go into Judea, that Your disciples also may see the works that You are doing. For no one does anything in secret while he himself seeks to be known openly. If You do these things, show Yourself to the world." For even His brothers did not believe in Him. Then Jesus said to them, "My time has not yet come, but your time is always ready. The world cannot hate you, but it hates Me because I testify of it that its works are evil. You go up to this feast. I am not yet going up to this feast, for My time has not yet fully come." When He had said these things to them, He remained in Galilee. But when His brothers had gone up, then He also went up to the feast, not openly, but as it were in secret. Then the Jews sought Him at the feast, and said, "Where is He?" And there was much complaining among the people concerning Him. Some said, "He is good"; others said, "No, on the contrary, He deceives the people." However, no one spoke openly of Him for fear of the Jews.

One of the principles I teach my seminary students is to try to find the drama in Scripture. I say to them, "When you come to a text of Scripture, before you decide what to preach, look for the drama, because in every passage of the Bible that God the Holy Spirit inspires, there is drama." I have to confess, however, that when I preached John 7:1–13 at St. Andrew's, I struggled to find the drama. This passage seems almost like a travelogue, a record of where Jesus was going to go. Would He stay in Galilee or would He go to Judea for the feast? However, as I continued to read over this text and reflect on it, I began to see this as one of the most troubling texts I have ever found in the New Testament. I came to feel that way because of one small sentence that is really just a parenthetical comment added by John. That sentence is found in verse 5: **For even His brothers did not believe in Him.**

We have already seen that at this juncture of Jesus' ministry, many of His disciples had departed and walked with Him no more, having found the bread of life discourse to contain a "hard saying" (6:60). With this passage, we learn more about Jesus' isolation and loneliness. From a certain perspective, this seems like a low point in Jesus' ministry.

There are those who argue that Mary was a virgin perpetually and that she had no more children after she gave birth to Jesus, but this text and others clearly teach that Jesus had younger brothers (Matt. 13:55; Mark 6:3). One of them was James the Just. He was the author of the epistle of James in the New Testament. The New Testament shows that James and Jesus' other brothers were believers shortly after the resurrection and ascension (Acts 1:14), and James eventually became a "pillar" of the church (Gal. 2:9) and presided over the council of Jerusalem (Acts 15).

But even by the time of the events recorded in John 7, which happened relatively late in Jesus' ministry, His brothers still had not believed. They had grown up with Him and had followed His ministry, likely witnessing many of His miracles, but they had not yet come to faith in Him.

Avoiding the Jewish Leaders

John tells us that after the discourse recorded in John 6 and the departure of many of His disciples, **Jesus walked in Galilee; for He did not want to walk in Judea, because the Jews sought to kill Him** (v. 1). Jesus knew that the Jews in Judea, in the area of Jerusalem, were plotting to take His life (see 5:16, 18), so He stayed in the north, in Galilee. But the time came for the Jewish **Feast of Tabernacles**, a seven-day celebration of God's provision for His people during their wilderness wandering, as well as a festival to commemorate the completion of the harvest. All Jews, from all parts of the nation, were required to make the pilgrimage to Jerusalem to celebrate. Therefore, it was Jesus' duty under the law to go to Jerusalem for the feast. So His brothers came to him and said: **"Depart from here and go into Judea, that your disciples also may see the works that You are doing. For no one does anything in secret while he himself seeks to be known openly"** (vv. 3–4).

It seems as if Jesus' brothers were His self-appointed campaign managers. Their advice was all about gaining attention: "You're never going to get anywhere up here in Galilee. If You want to be King, if You want to be the Messiah, You're going to have to go down to Jerusalem and do Your works down there, not hide Your lamp under a bushel. Do You want a public ministry? Do You want public acclamation? Then You can't operate in the obscurity of Galilee. You must go to the capital city."

When we studied the record of Jesus' first miracle, the turning of water into wine at the wedding feast of Cana (John 2:1–11), we saw that in the midst of the embarrassment of the host, Jesus' mother came to Him and said: "The wine is gone and the steward is embarrassed. You need to do something." Jesus had to rebuke His own mother: "Woman, what does your concern have to do with Me? My hour has not yet come" (2:4). Jesus reacted in much the same way when His brothers suggested He go to Judea: **"My time has not yet come, but your time is always ready. The world cannot hate you, but it hates Me because I testify of it that its works are evil. You go up to this feast. I am not yet going up to this feast, for My time has not yet fully come"** (vv. 6–8). In other words, Jesus said: "I'll determine when I go to Jerusalem. You men go ahead. My hour has not yet come."

However, just as Jesus first rebuked His mother and then went on to perform the miracle of making wine, here, after rebuking His brothers and implying that He would not go to the feast, He then *did* go: **He also went up to the Feast, not openly, but as it were in secret** (v. 10).

John then explains why Jesus went secretly. The Jewish authorities were keeping a sharp lookout for Him at the feast: **Then the Jews sought Him at the feast, and said, "Where is He?"** (v. 11). Even though Jesus wasn't there, He was the talk of the feast: **And there was much complaining among the people concerning Him. Some said, "He is good"; others said, "No, on the contrary, He deceives the people"** (v. 12). However, all this talk about Jesus was clandestine, because the Jewish leaders' antipathy to Jesus was known: **No one spoke openly of Him for fear of the Jews** (v. 13). Clearly the Jewish leaders' hostility to Jesus had not grown less intense while He was in Galilee.

In the next chapter, we'll see how events unfolded at the feast. However, I want to focus on verse 5 and spend a bit more time considering the unbelief of Jesus' brothers.

Seeking Deliverance

John tells us that even though Jesus' brothers were imploring Him to go down to Jerusalem that He might make Himself known there, they were not believers. In a very real sense, they did the same thing the other disciples had done. They were following Jesus for what He could provide. In this case, I believe their specific hope was that He would deliver them from the oppressive yoke of Roman bondage. If that is the case, their understanding of His mission was deeply distorted. They didn't know who He really was. They did not believe in Him in a saving way because their expectations of Him were not at all in accordance with what He was about. They saw Him as a secular deliverer, and the sooner He went to Jerusalem and took on the establishment, the better.

Let me tell you why I find this text so troubling. These were people who had been with Jesus during His earthly ministry, watching Him day after day. In fact, they were His blood brothers and they had grown up with Him. They thought they knew Him. They thought they were on His team. However, they had their own agenda for Him. They were rooting for Him to go to Jerusalem to manifest His power. This tells us they were still unbelievers, outside the kingdom of God.

It sometimes happens that a person comes to me with urgent questions about the state of his or her soul, and says: "R. C., how can I know that I am saved? How can I know that my profession of faith is genuine?" In response, I ask three simple questions. First, I'll ask, "Do you love Christ perfectly?" The person always says no, because if he did love Christ perfectly, he wouldn't sin at all. Second, I ask, "Do you love Christ as much as you ought to love Him?" If the answer to the first question was no, the answer to the second question has to be no also because we ought to love him perfectly. Third, I'll ask the most important question: "Do you love Him at all?" Usually the person will say: "Well, yes, I do. I have affection for Christ." Then I say: "That's wonderful. But remember, in your natural state, in your fallen human condition, you have no capacity whatsoever to have affection for Jesus. If you have any real affection in your heart for Jesus, that's proof positive that you are a converted person. So you can enjoy the assurance of your salvation."

In most cases, I have to add one major qualifier to those questions. I have to ask, "Do you love the *biblical* Christ?" The qualifier is necessary because people are prone to declare their belief in a Jesus who has nothing to do with the Man depicted in the biblical record.

When I was in graduate school, an important theological work was issued by a radical, critical theologian. It was titled *Jesus Means Freedom*. In this book, the author argued that we cannot know anything about the historical Jesus; He may not have existed, for all we know. But the name *Jesus* has become a symbol of human liberation from any form of oppression. So if you believe in the liberation of people from political oppression, racial oppression, or even sexual oppression, then you believe in Jesus.

We saw this kind of redefinition in the nineteenth century, when the liberal critics declared that Jesus was a great ethical teacher, but nothing more. Likewise, with the advent of existential theology, it was said, "Jesus is a great existential example." But the Jesus who is the symbol of liberation, the Jesus who is merely a great ethical teacher, or the Jesus who is the existential paradigm is not the real Jesus, the biblical Jesus.

Believing in the Real Jesus

If we could have asked Jesus' brothers, "Do you believe in your brother?" they would have said: "Of course we believe in Him. Why else would we want Him to go to Jerusalem and make Himself known? We want the people to know about Him. We want to see His ministry grow and expand. Just like John the Baptist, we want Him to increase." Nevertheless, the Word of God says Jesus' brothers were unbelievers. That is why we have to ask ourselves, "Is the Jesus we believe in the real Jesus?"

We disappoint Jesus when we expect things of Him that are not part of *His* agenda. We become like His unbelieving brothers, who looked to Him only for what they could get, for worldly power and worldly success. We are confronted today with the prosperity gospel, the "name it and claim it" faith, which preaches that we may come to Jesus with any expectation and, like magic, Jesus will meet it. No, the only thing I can guarantee He'll give you is forgiveness, reconciliation with the Father, and eternal life. I can't imagine what else we could ask from Him.

I think doctrine, truth, and biblical ethics are vitally important. But Christianity is all about Jesus. We have to understand the real Jesus, the Jesus whom we know through the pages of Scripture. Whatever ideas of Jesus you may have, if they don't correspond to the biblical portrait of Jesus we are discovering as we progress through John, I urge you to put them aside and believe on the Jesus who comes to us in His Word. We need the real Jesus.

20

CHRIST THE SCHOLAR

John 7:14–31

Now about the middle of the feast Jesus went up into the temple and taught. And the Jews marveled, saying, "How does this Man know letters, having never studied?" Jesus answered them and said, "My doctrine is not Mine, but His who sent Me. If anyone wills to do His will, he shall know concerning the doctrine, whether it is from God or whether I speak on My own authority. He who speaks from himself seeks his own glory; but He who seeks the glory of the One who sent Him is true, and no unrighteousness is in Him. Did not Moses give you the law, yet none of you keeps the law? Why do you seek to kill Me?" The people answered and said, "You have a demon. Who is seeking to kill You?" Jesus answered and said to them, "I did one work, and you all marvel. Moses therefore gave you circumcision (not that it is from Moses, but from the fathers), and you circumcise a man on the Sabbath. If a man receives circumcision on the Sabbath, so that the law of Moses should not be broken, are you angry with Me because I made a man completely well on the Sabbath? Do not judge according to appearance, but judge with righteous judgment." Now some of them from Jerusalem said, "Is this not He whom they seek to kill? But look! He speaks boldly, and they say nothing to Him. Do the rulers know indeed that this is truly the Christ? However, we know where this Man is from; but when the Christ comes, no one knows where He is from." Then Jesus cried out, as He taught in the temple, saying, "You both know Me, and you know where I am from; and I have not come of Myself, but He who sent Me is true, whom you do not know. But I know Him, for I am from Him, and He sent Me." Therefore they sought to take Him; but no one laid a hand on Him, because His hour had not yet come. And many of the people believed in Him, and said, "When the Christ comes, will He do more signs than these which this Man has done?"

W hen I was a child, my favorite grade in elementary school was the third grade. A lot of that had to do with Mrs. MacGraw, who was the best teacher I had; plus, third grade was fun. But there was a little cloud of fear that hung over us when we were in third grade. We would hear the testimony from the fourth-graders: "Just you wait. In fourth grade, school really gets hard, because you have to learn geography and history and much more difficult multiplication tables." We third-graders trembled when we heard this testimony. In time, however, I entered fourth grade, and somehow, by the grace of God, I made it through.

Then history repeated itself. As we progressed through the grades, we heard, in fear and trembling, of that huge leap in difficulty that awaited us when we moved from junior high school to senior high school, where the homework assignments would be so much more plenteous and we'd have to study arcane sciences such as physics and chemistry. But again, through God's grace, I made it through high school and actually got into college. In those days, it was customary for colleges to flunk out fifty percent of a freshman class. Thankfully, I was converted in my first semester and made an "A" in Bible, which kept me from flunking out.

After college, I went on to seminary, which brought a whole new level of difficulty. But probably the biggest academic adjustment in my life occurred when I enrolled in doctoral studies in the Netherlands. I had no idea how rigorous the academic discipline at that level would be. But as I completed my academic work, I realized that there were many of us who had been educated well beyond our intelligence. That is a problem with upper levels of education—once we get through them, we have a tendency to think we actually know far more than we do, and we have a tendency to tilt the nose a bit and look down at those who have not gone through such rigorous train-ing. We put a lot of focus on people's degrees and wonder whether their credentials are really credible.

Challenging the Credentials

No man's credentials were ever more seriously challenged by the established academic community than were those of Jesus of Nazareth. We read in John 7:15 that when Jesus went up to Jerusalem and taught in the temple, **the Jews marveled, saying, "How does this Man know letters, having never studied?"** The Pharisees, the scribes, and the doctors of the law who had studied under Gamaliel, Hillel, or one of the other rabbinic traditions looked askance at Jesus, asking where His sheepskin could be found. "Who did You study under, Mr. Jesus? How many credit hours in theology do You have? As far as we know, You don't even have a baccalaureate degree, and do You, then, come into the temple and presume to teach us?" Of course, this was the same Jesus who, when He was twelve years old, had shown Himself to be a child prodigy and absolutely amazed the scholars in the temple with the depth of His understanding of the things of theology. So where *did* He get His education?

Jesus answered the question forthrightly. He said, **"My doctrine is not Mine, but His who sent Me. If anyone wills to do His will, he shall know concerning the doctrine, whether it is from God or whether I speak on My own authority. He who speaks from himself seeks his own glory; but He who seeks the glory of the One who sent Him is true, and no unrighteousness is in Him"** (vv. 16–18). In other words, Jesus said His doctrine was not His invention. It came from another source.

If I were to ask a group of Christians today, "Where did Jesus get the knowledge He displayed when He taught in the temple?" I suspect many would give the answer that is prevalent among evangelicals today: "Well, He's God!" The logic is that, since Jesus is God, He has all knowledge, so He never had a need to go to school or study under anyone else. He is the source and fountain of all truth.

Let me respond to that answer with another question: "When Jesus was lying in the manger during His nativity, did He know that the world is round?" If someone asked me that question, my answer would be basically no. As a baby, Jesus did not know the world is round, at least touching His human nature.

The human Jesus had to grow in His knowledge and understanding of the things of God. The human nature of Jesus did not come equipped with the divine attribute of omniscience, and when we let ourselves think that the human nature of Christ possessed these divine characteristics, we slip into a very serious and ancient heresy by which the divine nature swallows up the human nature. We must remember to recognize the limits of Jesus' knowledge.

Another example of those limits is found in Mark 13:32. When the disciples asked Jesus about the day and the hour of His return, He said, "Of that day and hour no one knows, not even the angels in heaven, nor the Son, but only the Father." In that response to His disciples, Jesus Himself clearly put a limit on His knowledge about the future.

The greatest minds of church history have been baffled when trying to understand how Jesus could not know the time of His return. Thomas Aquinas, for example, who arguably was the most brilliant theologian of all time, stumbled in attempting to answer that question. Aquinas scratched his head and said: "Jesus *had* to know the day and the hour. He was God incarnate. There was a perfect unity between the human nature and the divine nature, so how could it have been possible that Jesus did not know this?" So Aquinas developed what he called his "accommodation theory." He said, in essence: "Jesus really *did* know, but the knowledge was too holy, too high, too wonderful to talk about. Jesus didn't want to go into a lengthy explanation as to why He couldn't reveal the day and the hour at that point, so He simply told His disciples He didn't know."

That's a nice way out, except that if Jesus knew the answer and said He didn't, he told a lie. It might have been just a fib, but even that would have been enough to tarnish His perfection and make Him a lamb with a blemish, and therefore incapable of being our Savior. So I prefer not to go into all these gymnastics to explain why Jesus said there was something He didn't know and simply take our Lord at His word.

When Jesus said there was something He didn't know, He obviously was speaking of His human nature. Historically, the church has embraced the dual nature of Christ, that He is *vera homo, vera Deus*—truly man and truly God, one person with two natures. If we are to have a correct understanding of Jesus, we have to understand that His divine nature has all of the attributes of deity while the human nature has all of the limitations of humanity.

We can distinguish the two natures of Christ, but we cannot separate them. Let me illustrate what I mean. We all know that a human being is made up of a body and a soul. Therefore, I can distinguish your two natures—your physical side and your non-physical side—without doing you any damage. However, if I separate your body from your soul, I kill you. So there's a big difference between a distinction and a separation.

When Jesus was hungry, that was a manifestation of His human nature, not of His divine nature. When He perspired, that was a manifestation of His human nature, not of His divine nature. Likewise, when He said, "I don't know," that was a manifestation of His human nature, not His divine nature.

At this point, you might ask, "If that is true, why is it that throughout the Bible, and even in John's Gospel, we see Jesus manifesting supernatural knowledge?" For instance, at the beginning of His public ministry, He told Nathanael everything about him, even though He'd never met Nathanael (1:47–49). Likewise, He knew the sordid past of the Samaritan woman (4:17–18). He read what was in people's minds; He knew what people were going to say before they said it. Jesus gave many such evidences of supernatural knowledge. Where did that come from? It came from the communication of the divine nature to the human nature.

Not Omniscient but Infallible

There were things that Jesus didn't know, but whatever He taught was impeccable, because He never taught on the basis of His own human insight. So the Christian church has understood for centuries that, touching His human nature, Jesus is not omniscient, but He is infallible, because if He teaches something that isn't true, then He's held accountable.

Here's an example: the biggest argument that the Bible is the inspired Word of God is that Jesus said it is. The critics say: "He wasn't omniscient, so it's OK if He made a mistake when He taught His disciples that the Bible was the Word of God and that Moses wrote of Him in the Pentateuch and so forth. We can't hold Him responsible to know things He couldn't possibly know." Oh, yes, we can. Suppose a teacher walks into your classroom and says, "I won't say anything in here by my own authority, but everything that I am going to teach you comes from God Himself." If you found that teacher making an error, what would you think about his claim of teaching only what God had given him? Or suppose I went into the pulpit and said, "Ladies and gentlemen, this morning when you listen to me preach, I want you to be aware that what you will hear is the plain, unadulterated, unvarnished truth, because I am the truth." If you were in the congregation, you would need to be concerned, because we are warned in Scripture that those who teach are never to claim more knowledge than they actually have. Therefore, when Jesus declared that the Scriptures are the Word of God, if He was wrong, He transgressed His own principles for teaching, and thereby disqualified Himself as our Savior.

This debate between Jesus and the Jewish authorities was about credentials. The Jewish leaders asked, "Where did You get Your degree?" Jesus replied: "I brought it with Me from heaven. I don't teach anything on My own, but My doctrine comes from the Father. If you want the truth, if you want knowledge, if you care about theology, you should believe every word that I tell you because the only words I give you are from Him. If you want to do the will of God, you should hear My voice and listen to Me."

On the occasion of Jesus' transfiguration, the Father spoke audibly about His Son: "This is My beloved Son. Hear Him!" (Luke 9:35). The Father Himself attested to the authority of the teaching of Jesus, that His doctrine was true and, as Jesus claimed here, there was no mixture of unrighteousness in it.

John then tells us that Jesus said, **"Did not Moses give you the law, yet none of you keeps the law? Why do you seek to kill me?"** (v. 19). The people replied, **"You have a demon. Who is seeking to kill You?"** (v. 20a). What did that mean? They were saying: "You must be out of your mind. You must be demon-possessed. No one is trying to kill You." They denied their hostile intentions, but Jesus' accusation that they failed to keep the law only increased their anger.

Jesus then turned the table on His enemies: **"I did one work, and you all marvel. Moses therefore gave you circumcision (not that it is from Moses, but from the fathers), and you circumcise a man on the Sabbath. If a man receives circumcision on the Sabbath, so that the law of Moses should not be broken, are you angry with Me because I made a man completely well on the Sabbath? Do not judge according to appearance, but judge with righteous judgment"** (vv. 21b–24). In other words: "You question My credentials while you hide behind the law of Moses. You tell Me that you are disciples of Moses and students of the law. Well, where did circumcision come from? It didn't come from Moses; it came from the patriarchs before Moses. It came from Abraham, Isaac, and Jacob. So Moses didn't invent circumcision."

Why did Jesus bring this up? The law of Moses required that every infant boy be circumcised exactly eight days after birth (Lev. 12:3). But what if the day of circumcision fell on the Sabbath? Did Moses require that it be postponed? No, not only did the law of Moses allow circumcision on the Sabbath day, it required circumcision on the Sabbath day. If the law of Moses required that the sign of a person's wellness be given on the Sabbath day, how could the Jewish leaders object when Jesus healed a man completely on the Sabbath day? This was classic *ad hominem* argumentation, not in the abusive sense but in the logical sense. Jesus took the foolishness of His critics to its logical conclusion and showed that He was not the One who was violating Moses, they were. In so doing, He showed that despite their great knowledge and their academic credentials, they remained ignorant of the things of God.

Christian education is in tough times. We've seen numerous seminaries slip into radical liberalism, denying the central tenets of the Christian faith. We've seen Christian colleges, one after another, deny Christianity altogether. Why does that happen? I once read an essay by an Anglican scholar that was titled, fittingly, "The Treason of the Intellectual." Many Christians, unfortunately, have fled from serious study of the things of God because they can't trust their teachers anymore; the intellectual leadership of the body of Christ has committed treason. Of course, there's nothing really new about that. It was the intellectual community of Jesus' day that was most antagonistic toward Him, because when perfect knowledge manifests itself, when perfect truth appears, that which is muddled or blemished is exposed.

The Debate over Jesus

Despite Jesus' exposure of their hypocrisy, the Jewish leaders hesitated to take action against Him; they were fearful of the public reaction (Luke 22:2). That only sparked the people's questions: **Now some of them from Jerusalem said, "Is this not He whom they seek to kill? But look! He speaks boldly, and they say nothing to Him. Do the rulers know indeed that this is truly the Christ?"** (v. 25–26). The leaders' inaction caused the people to openly speculate that Jesus was the Messiah.

There was only one problem—Jesus' origins were known: **"However, we know where this Man is from; but when the Christ comes, no one knows where He is from"** (v. 27). The people knew Jesus was from Galilee, whereas the Messiah was to be a native of Bethlehem or, according to some traditions, of unknown origin. Jesus didn't seem to fit the criteria.

To this, Jesus replied, **"You both know me, and you know where I am from; and I have not come of Myself, but He who sent Me is true, whom you do not know. But I know Him, for I am from Him, and He sent me"** (vv. 28–29). Neither Bethlehem nor Galilee was Jesus' ultimate point of origin; He had come from the Father. The people needed to consider His teaching and His miracles rather than His family tree.

In essence, Jesus said: "Do you want to give Me a doctoral examination in theology, the most rigorous test Gamaliel has ever thought of? Give Me the test. I know the Father, and not just from a distance—I'm from Him. He sent Me." Do you hear the warning? "If you won't hear the One whom God sent, whom will you hear?"

We desperately need to hear this warning today. When we hear Jesus teach from the pages of sacred Scripture, our response, like Samuel of old, should be, "Speak, for Your servant hears" (1 Sam. 3:10b).

21

WHO IS THIS MAN?

John 7:32–8:1

The Pharisees heard the crowd murmuring these things concerning Him, and the Pharisees and the chief priests sent officers to take Him. Then Jesus said to them, "I shall be with you a little while longer, and then I go to Him who sent Me. You will seek Me and not find Me, and where I am you cannot come." Then the Jews said among themselves, "Where does He intend to go that we shall not find Him? Does He intend to go to the Dispersion among the Greeks and teach the Greeks? What is this thing that He said, 'You will seek Me and not find Me, and where I am you cannot come'?" On the last day, that great day of the feast, Jesus stood and cried out, saying, "If anyone thirsts, let him come to Me and drink. He who believes in Me, as the Scripture has said, out of his heart will flow rivers of living water." But this He spoke concerning the Spirit, whom those believing in Him would receive; for the Holy Spirit was not yet given, because Jesus was not yet glorified. Therefore many from the crowd, when they heard this saying, said, "Truly this is the Prophet." Others said, "This is the Christ." But some said, "Will the Christ come out of Galilee? Has not the Scripture said that the Christ comes from the seed of David and from the town of Bethlehem, where David was?" So there was a division among the people because of Him. Now some of them wanted to take Him, but no one laid hands on Him. Then the officers came to the chief priests and Pharisees, who said to them, "Why have you not brought Him?" The officers answered, "No man ever spoke like this Man!" Then the Pharisees answered them, "Are you also deceived? Have any of the rulers or the Pharisees believed in Him? But this crowd that does not know the law is accursed." Nicodemus (he who came to Jesus by night, being one of them) said to them, "Does our law judge a man before it hears him and knows what he is doing?" They answered and said to him, "Are you also from Galilee? Search and look, for no prophet has arisen out of Galilee." And everyone went to his own house. But Jesus went to the Mount of Olives.

T hroughout John 7, the apostle records various events surrounding a trip by Jesus from Galilee up to Jerusalem to celebrate the Jewish Feast of Tabernacles. As we saw earlier, this feast commemorated God's provision for the Israelite people during their sojourn in the wilderness after their exodus from Egypt. Specifically, the feast reminded the people of two benefits their forefathers received from God during that time. One was the manna from heaven. It is no coincidence that Jesus mentioned the manna when He called Himself the "bread of life" (6:48–51). The other benefit was the water that came forth from the rock (Num. 20:2–13). This provision was celebrated during the Feast of Tabernacles with a ceremony that involved the pouring out of water that was carried to the temple in golden vessels. This was the highlight of the feast. In the passage before us in this chapter, John tells us that Jesus used this observance to speak again about the "living water" He had come to offer.

Our passage begins with an ominous announcement. The authorities in Jerusalem, the members of the Sanhedrin, hearing many in the crowds openly speculating that Jesus was the Messiah (vv. 25–27, 31–32) and seeing that many were believing in Him (v. 31), wrote a formal commission for Jesus' arrest and sent the temple officers to apprehend Him and bring Him back for trial with a view toward execution (v. 32). As we have already noted, Jesus told His brothers that "My time has not yet fully come" (v. 8b). However, the Pharisees were convinced that His time *had* come. They had heard all they wanted to hear from Jesus, so they acted decisively—they issued the arrest warrant and dispatched the officers.

In conjunction with the arrival of these officers, Jesus spoke publicly and said: **"I shall be with you a little while longer, and then I go to Him**

who sent Me. You will seek Me and not find Me, and where I am you cannot come" (vv. 33–34). The people who heard these words had no idea what Jesus was talking about; His remarks were cryptic. He said, "I'm going somewhere; you won't be able to find Me and you won't be able to follow Me there." The Jews said among themselves, **"Where does He intend to go that we shall not find Him? Does He intend to go to the Dispersion among the Greeks and teach the Greeks?"** (v. 35). They speculated that perhaps Jesus was going to leave Judea to live among Jews who dwelt beyond the borders of Israel. These were the Jews of the *Diaspora*, or the Dispersion—the Greek-speaking Jews. This was the best guess the people could formulate. "Is He going to leave the nation?" they asked. "Is He going to go out into the hinterlands, where those Greek-speaking people are?"

The rest of the New Testament makes it abundantly clear what Jesus was talking about, particularly the later chapters of this very Gospel. Jesus spoke about His departure from earth by way of His ascension. I am convinced that the most neglected dimension of the life of Jesus in the church today is His ascension. Without the ascension, both the cross and the resurrection are meaningless. The climax of Jesus' earthly ministry came when He ascended to heaven and sat down at the right hand of God. This was His investiture, His coronation, when the Father crowned Him as King of kings and Lord of lords. It was at that moment that Jesus' glory was restored to Him in His heavenly kingdom.

An Offer of "Living Water"

The narrative breaks at this point. John leaves hanging the people's discussion about Jesus' enigmatic statement and the attempt of the temple officers to arrest Him in order to skip to an event that happened on the last day of the feast. We are told: **On the last day, that great day of the feast, Jesus stood and cried out, saying . . .** (v. 37a). I want you to imagine the scene. Great crowds were gathered in Jerusalem for the sacred ceremony of the outpouring of the water, by which the people remembered the water that came from the rock in the wilderness. Suddenly, Jesus came into the midst of them and began to shout. In short order, everyone stopped what he was doing and turned to listen to Jesus' words, because they were very provocative. He said: **"If anyone thirsts let him come to Me and drink. He who believes in Me, as the Scripture has said, out of his heart will flow rivers of living water"** (vv. 37b–38).

Jesus had spoken about His provision of living water in private conversation with the woman of Samaria. Here, however, He shouted an invitation to the masses to come to Him and drink. What did He mean? John tells us: **But this He spoke concerning the Spirit, whom those believing in Him would receive; for the Holy Spirit was not yet given, because Jesus was not yet glorified** (v. 39).

Through the pages of the Old Testament, the Holy Spirit appears frequently. It was the Holy Spirit who anointed the prophets, anointed the priests, and anointed the king. It was the Holy Spirit who changed the hearts of unbelievers in the Old Testament and made them the people of God. As it is today, so it was then—there was no regeneration, no salvation, apart from the operation and ministry of the Holy Spirit. The Spirit was present in the Old Testament, but the anointing of the Spirit for power was limited to a few individuals, such as Moses, Samson, or Elijah.

During Israel's wilderness wanderings, Moses once became so distressed over the complaints of the people that he asked God to take his life (Num. 11:15). In response, God told Moses to bring seventy elders to the tabernacle, where God would take from the Spirit that was upon Moses and distribute it to the elders so that they might help Moses bear the burden of ministry. When the Spirit came upon these men, they prophesied. However, two men, Eldad and Medad, had remained in the camp, but they too began to prophesy. Moses' assistant, Joshua, was very upset, and he said to Moses, "Moses, my lord, forbid them" (11:28b). Moses replied: "Are you zealous for my sake? Oh, that all the LORD's people were prophets and that the LORD would put His Spirit upon them!" (11:29).

That cry of Moses became a prophecy on the lips of Joel, who spoke the word of the Lord, saying, "And it shall come to pass afterward that I will pour out My Spirit on all flesh; your sons and your daughters shall prophesy, your old men shall dream dreams, your young men shall see visions" (Joel 2:28). This great outpouring of the Spirit came at the Day of Pentecost, when all heaven broke loose and the Spirit descended on the church (Acts 2). With the Spirit's coming, that which Martin Luther called the priesthood of all believers became a reality—every member of the community of faith was endowed by the Holy Spirit, empowered from on high to participate in the ministry of Christ's kingdom. If you are a Christian, you have received the Holy Spirit. You are an anointed person, fit to be used of God for the furtherance of the kingdom of Christ.

Jesus invited the people gathered in Jerusalem to come to Him for salvation and the outpouring of the Holy Spirit. That great outpouring of the Spirit was still a future hope during Jesus' ministry. In fact, John makes it clear here that the Spirit was not to be poured out till the Messiah entered His glory.

The Spirit would not come on the church until He was lifted up, until He had returned to the Father. Then the Father and the Son together would send the Holy Spirit into the world to apply the work of the Son. Today, that is the chief ministry of the Holy Spirit—to take the work of the Son and bring it to fruition in us.

Differences of Opinion

John writes: **Therefore many from the crowd, when they heard this saying, said, "Truly this is the Prophet." Others said, "This is the Christ." But some said, "Will the Christ come out of Galilee? Has not the Scripture said that the Christ comes from the seed of David and from the town of Bethlehem, where David was?"** (vv. 40–42). The people said: "We all know from where the Christ is going to come. We've read the Old Testament. We've read Micah. Christ is to come from Bethlehem, from Judea, from the city of David." These people had no idea that Jesus had been born in Bethlehem; all they knew was that He had come to them from Galilee. So the people scratched their heads. Was Jesus the Prophet Moses had prophesied (Deut. 18:15)? Was He the Messiah? John writes: **So there was a division among the people because of Him. Now some of them wanted to take Him, but no one laid hands on Him** (vv. 43–44). Some people believed He ought to be locked away as a blasphemer, but they took no action, perhaps because the contingent of believers in the crowd was so numerous.

Meanwhile, where were the temple officers? They had been sent to arrest Jesus, but when they came to the temple and came forward to grab Him, Jesus spoke: "If anyone thirsts, let him come to Me and drink." Soon the people around him were speculating: "Is this the Prophet? Is this the Christ?" So the officers went back to the authorities without Him. Not surprisingly, that caused some consternation among the Jewish leaders. They asked, **"Why have you not brought Him?"** (v. 45b). To that, the officers gave a simple answer: **"No man ever spoke like this Man!"** (v. 46). They had heard the authority in Jesus' teaching and had found themselves unable to act against Him.

The Pharisees were beside themselves. They asked: **"Are you also deceived? Have any of the rulers or the Pharisees believed in Him? But this crowd that does not know the law is accursed"** (vv. 47–49). I do not believe there has ever been a more arrogant bunch in all of history than the Pharisees. First, they accused the officers of being deceived, of falling under Jesus' rhetorical spell. Then they implied that the officers ought to follow the example of the rulers themselves in their disbelief. Finally, they denigrated the crowds of faithful Jews who were hearing and responding to Jesus. The rabbinic tradition used the term *amhorets*, or "ignoramus," to refer to the uneducated masses, the people who didn't have sophisticated learning. That's essentially what the rulers said about the crowds listening to Jesus— they were ignorant of the law of God, which, the Pharisees believed, clearly showed that Jesus could not be the Messiah, and in that ignorance the people were falling into condemnation by exalting a mere man.

Then one of their own stepped forward and said, **"Does our law judge a man before it hears him and knows what he is doing?"** (v. 51). This piercing question came from Nicodemus, who had come to visit Jesus by night (John 3). He was saying: "Excuse me. Is this the way we operate with our law? Will we condemn this Man without even hearing Him, without investigating, without examining the evidence?" Nicodemus argued that if the Pharisees wanted to use the law to judge Jesus, they ought to follow the law in doing so.

The Pharisees' hatred for Jesus quickly turned on Nicodemus at that moment: **"Are you also from Galilee? Search and look, for no prophet has arisen out of Galilee"** (v. 52). What invective this is. The Pharisees' contempt for Galilee as a backwater of ignorance is clearly seen in the insult they hurled at Nicodemus. In short, they accused him of acting as ignorantly as a Jew from Galilee. In their minds, the case was closed—no prophet had ever come from Galilee, so no prophet ever *could* come from Galilee. The limitations they were willing to impose on God were astounding.

In the end, the moment passed and the officers were not sent back to arrest Jesus on the spot. The feast concluded and **everyone went to his own house** (v. 53), while **Jesus went to the Mount of Olives** (8:1). But the storm clouds were rising, and Jesus could see how events were about to unfold that would take Him out of this world and back to His Father.

22

THE WOMAN CAUGHT
IN ADULTERY

John 8:2–11

Now early in the morning He came again into the temple, and all the people came to Him; and He sat down and taught them. Then the scribes and Pharisees brought to Him a woman caught in adultery. And when they had set her in the midst, they said to Him, "Teacher, this woman was caught in adultery, in the very act. Now Moses, in the law, commanded us that such should be stoned. But what do You say?" This they said, testing Him, that they might have something of which to accuse Him. But Jesus stooped down and wrote on the ground with His finger, as though He did not hear. So when they continued asking Him, He raised Himself up and said to them, "He who is without sin among you, let him throw a stone at her first." And again He stooped down and wrote on the ground. Then those who heard it, being convicted by their conscience, went out one by one, beginning with the oldest even to the last. And Jesus was left alone, and the woman standing in the midst. When Jesus had raised Himself up and saw no one but the woman, He said to her, "Woman, where are those accusers of yours? Has no one condemned you?" She said, "No one, Lord." And Jesus said to her, "Neither do I condemn you; go and sin no more."

The passage we are considering in this chapter may not appear in your version of the Gospel of John. Alternatively, it may be in a footnote or it may be included somewhere else in your Bible. On the other hand, the version I am quoting from in this book, *The New King James Version*, includes this passage in the text of John 8. These different treatments of this text stem from the fact that it is not included in all of the early Greek manuscripts of this Gospel.

In biblical scholarship, we distinguish between two types of criticism directed toward the Bible. The first is called "higher criticism," which focuses on the content of the Bible itself. This is a task with which I am not greatly enamored. In addition, there is "lower criticism" or "textual criticism," which is a very exact science by which efforts are made to reconstruct the original text of Scripture as accurately as possible. The oldest parchment that we have of any portion of the New Testament is a fragment believed to be from the first century; that is the closest thing we have to what may be an original portion of Scripture. The so-called Rylands fragment is a very small portion of the Gospel of John. But when John wrote this Gospel, no one stashed it away in a museum to preserve it for future generations. Like the letters of Paul, James, Peter, John, and Jude, John's Gospel was intended to be circulated throughout the Christian community. It became the task of people within the church to make copies of those original documents.

The church has confessed her faith historically in the inspiration of the Bible, the teaching that the original writers of the text of Scripture were so superintended by God the Holy Spirit that the writings they produced were nothing less than the Word of God. But the church has not taken the position that each and every copyist received the same divine superintendence; that is, we restrict inspiration to what is called the *autographa*, the original manuscripts of the Bible.

The science of textual criticism weighs and evaluates thousands of extant copies of the New Testament. There are different families, different schools of these copies, and some of those families are considered to be more accurate than others. But the copies don't always agree at every detail. With respect to the main substance of Scripture, more than ninety-nine percent is in agreement in all of the families of the copies; it is in less than one percent of the texts in the Bible that variant readings are found. No major doctrine of the Christian church is affected by those variant readings.

The text that is perhaps the most interesting in this whole story is the one before us in this chapter. Frankly, the best manuscripts from antiquity do not include this story in the Gospel of John. The overwhelming consensus of textual critics is that it was not part of the original Gospel of John, at least not this portion of John. At the same time, the overwhelming consensus is that this account is authentic, it's apostolic, and it should be contained in any edition of the New Testament. Whether it belongs here in John's Gospel, in Luke's Gospel (where some ancient manuscripts place it), or somewhere else is a question I leave for the ages. But I believe it is nothing less than the very Word of God, so I will treat it as such in this chapter.

As an aside, let me say that I hope you are not disturbed to learn that there are copy errors in the early manuscripts of the books in our Bible. Some people hear that and say, "We don't have the originals, so how can we say that the Bible is the Word of God?" That's like saying that if someone put a bomb in the National Institute of Standards and Technology in Washington and blew up our official yardstick, there wouldn't be enough accurate yardsticks and copies to allow us to reconstruct what a yard is. Of course we would be able to reconstruct it, and we could do so with infinitesimal variation. The same holds true for the text of Scripture.

An Adulteress Apprehended

This disputed text certainly appears in an appropriate place in John's Gospel, because it displays the same kind of antipathy toward Jesus by the scribes and Pharisees that we have been seeing in recent chapters. The text opens innocently enough: we are told that following the events of the previous day, the final day of the Feast of Tabernacles, and after spending the night on the Mount of Olives, **early in the morning He came again into the temple, and all the people came to Him; and He sat down and taught them** (v. 2). All was calm and serene. Jesus taught in the temple and the people listened to Him. But this peaceful scene was soon interrupted by a group of **scribes and Pharisees** (v. 3a).

Sometimes we tend to think of the scribes and the Pharisees as one and the same, but they were not. The scribes were the Jewish theologians. They were sometimes called "lawyers" because they were the experts in interpreting the Old Testament law. In other words, "scribe" was a career. By contrast, the Pharisees constituted a party, a movement of conservative religious practice. The term *Pharisee* means "separated one." During the intertestamental period, many of the people moved away from zealous obedience to the law of God, so a group of people committed to spiritual, moral, and theological reform banded together in an effort to purify the Jewish community. They committed themselves to zealous and passionate pursuit of obedience to the law, and so they were called "the separated ones," or Pharisees. They were the Puritans of ancient Israel. But not all Pharisees were scribes. Likewise, not all scribes were members of the party of the Pharisees.

John tells us that these scribes and Pharisees **brought to Him a woman caught in adultery. And when they had set her in the midst, they said to Him, "Teacher, this woman was caught in adultery, in the very act. Now Moses, in the law, commanded us that such should be stoned. But what do You say?"** (vv. 3–5).

The law of Moses did indeed outlaw adultery, which was defined as sexual relations between two people, at least one of whom was married to a different person. The penalty for adultery was execution of both people, though stoning was not specified (Deut. 22:22). However, under Jewish law, if a man or woman was engaged but not yet married, and if either of them was unfaithful with another partner, that was also considered adultery, and the specific mode of execution in such a case was stoning (Deut. 22:24). Perhaps the scribes' and Pharisees' mention of the penalty of stoning indicates that this woman was not yet married but was engaged when she was unfaithful.

A Missing Adulterer

I see one major unanswered question in this text. The Jewish leaders said this woman had been caught in adultery, "in the very act." But if that was so, where was her partner? According to the law, if the woman was engaged to someone else, her adulterous partner was subject to stoning, too. Had he fled for his life? Had he escaped? Was this woman a victim of sexual bias by the scribes and Pharisees? Had they simply singled out the feminine partner as the guilty party in this crime? Or is it possible that the man was someone of such importance that the scribes and Pharisees did not want to get him in trouble? We don't know, but the question begs to be asked.

In any case, the scribes and Pharisees did not bring this woman to Jesus because they were zealous on this particular morning to uphold the law against adultery. They didn't bring her because they were scandalized by her behavior and wanted Jesus to clean up Jerusalem. John is clear about their motive: they were **testing Him, that they might have something of which to accuse Him** (v. 6a). This woman was being used by the scribes and the Pharisees in order to trap Jesus. Can you imagine someone who was truly zealous for the things of God using a person in this kind of a situation to destroy the Son of God? Yet that's exactly what was going on. The scribes and Pharisees hoped to induce Jesus to take a stand against the law, giving them "something of which to accuse Him."

To whom were they going to make their accusations? We need to remember that Israel was under Roman occupation at this time. The Romans permitted significant self-rule in the nations they conquered, but they did not allow vassal nations to exercise the death penalty in capital cases. If someone was to be put to death for a crime in a Roman province, it had to be done through the Roman judicial system. That's why Jesus was sentenced by Pontius Pilate and not by Caiaphas. The people, who followed Jesus, hated the Roman occupation, so the sly scribes and Pharisees laid a clever trap for Jesus. If Jesus were to say, "Stone the woman," they would run to the Roman headquarters and say, "This teacher is advocating that we exercise capital punishment without going through the Roman system." That way they would get Jesus in trouble with the Romans. But if He were to say, "Don't stone her," they would run back to the Sanhedrin and say, "This Jesus is a heretic because He denies the law of Moses." No matter how Jesus answered the question, He would be in serious trouble.

What did Jesus do? He did an incredible thing: **But Jesus stooped down and wrote on the ground with his finger, as though He did not hear** (v. 6b). This is the only mention in Scripture of Jesus writing anything. We know that He was literate, but He didn't write an autobiography, epistles, or treatises in theology or religion. When He chose to write on this occasion, He wrote like a quarterback in a sandlot football game, drawing the play in the dirt. The burning question is, what did He write?

Guilty Accusers Exposed

We have to be careful about speculation. As John Calvin said in his commentary on Romans, when God closes His holy mouth, we should desist from inquiry. But scholars have speculated through the ages about what was going on with this particular action by Jesus. Some say that Jesus made a strong allusion to the law of God, which was said to have been written on the stone tablets "with the finger of God" (Ex. 31:18). Others say He symbolically reminded the scribes and Pharisees of the warning in Jeremiah 17:13: "O LORD, the hope of Israel, all who forsake You shall be ashamed. Those who depart from Me shall be written in the earth, because they have forsaken the LORD, the fountain of living waters." Some see a reference to a practice in Roman courts—before a judge gave his verdict, he would write it down and then announce it. Still others speculate that Jesus was doodling just to gather some time.

My favorite theory is linked with Jesus' eventual answer to the scribes and Pharisees: **"He who is without sin among you, let him throw a stone at her first"** (v. 7b), after which He resumed writing. My guess is that He looked at one of the accusers and wrote, "embezzler." He then let the man see what He had written, after which the man cleared his throat and slunk away. He then continued by writing "murderer," after which the murderer left. Or perhaps He was more direct. When He said, "He who is without sin among you, let him throw a stone at her first," He may have been thinking of Deuteronomy 17:6–7, which reads: "Whoever is deserving of death shall be put to death on the testimony of two or three witnesses; he shall not be put to death on the testimony of one witness. The hands of the witnesses shall be the first against him to put him to death, and afterward the hands of all the people. So you shall put away the evil from among you." In short, if you accused someone of a capital offense, you had to be on hand to throw the first stones. You had to participate in the execution. Perhaps, then, Jesus used His writing to reveal to the scribes and Pharisees that He knew of instances of the same sin, adultery, in their lives.

When Jesus said, "He who is without sin among you, let him throw a stone at her first," He was not destroying the whole judicial system of the law of God. He was speaking to people who were hypocritically bloodthirsty in their desire to shame and punish a person who had fallen. In other words, they had no concept of the grace of God. It is not wrong to punish criminals for their crimes. But it is wrong to convene a kangaroo court, drag a person before such a court, and add insult to her injury. So I believe Jesus was dealing with the manifest hypocrisy of these who were judging this woman.

Notice that Jesus did not hedge between the Jewish law and the Roman law. He sided with Moses. He gave His verdict—the woman was guilty and should be stoned. But He then examined the executioners and found them lacking. Only He met the qualifications that He Himself had given for carrying out the execution.

John tells us that after Jesus spoke these words, **again He stooped down and wrote on the ground. Then those who heard it, being convicted by their conscience, went out one by one, beginning with the oldest even to the last. And Jesus was left alone, and the woman standing in the midst** (vv. 8–9). The scribes and Pharisees all got the message and quickly went away.

Then, **when Jesus had raised Himself up and saw no one but**

the woman, He said to her, "Woman, where are those accusers of yours? Has no one condemned you?" She said, "No one, Lord" (vv. 10–11a). Here we find the only words spoken by the accused woman in this passage. It is significant that she called Jesus "Lord." The Greek word used there is *kurios*. This word has a wide range of possible meanings. She may have been simply saying, "No one, sir," because the lowest form of *kurios* is the polite form of address for a man. Or, by the grace of God, her eyes may have been opened to understand that she was in the presence of her redeeming Lord.

In response, we might expect Jesus to say, "Well, I'm still here." He did not do that. Jesus said to her the sweetest words that any human being could ever hear from His lips: **"Neither do I condemn you"** (v. 11b). If you can't relate to those words, then your heart has been hardened, because each one of us comes to God like this woman, guilty, ashamed, naked, and exposed. But Christ clothes us with the cloak of His righteousness, covering our nakedness and shame, and says to us, "Neither do I condemn you."

Then what? Now that grace had abounded, should sin abound still more (Rom. 6:1)? No. Jesus said to the woman, **"go and sin no more"** (v. 11c). In other words: "Don't do this anymore. Be done with this kind of life. Go now in your forgiveness, and sin no more." Those who are forgiven should gladly put aside their sinful ways and walk in newness of life.

23

JESUS' SELF-WITNESS

John 8:12–30

Then Jesus spoke to them again, saying, "I am the light of the world. He who follows Me shall not walk in darkness, but have the light of life." The Pharisees therefore said to Him, "You bear witness of Yourself; Your witness is not true." Jesus answered and said to them, "Even if I bear witness of Myself, My witness is true, for I know where I came from and where I am going; but you do not know where I come from and where I am going. You judge according to the flesh; I judge no one. And yet if I do judge, My judgment is true; for I am not alone, but I am with the Father who sent Me. It is also written in your law that the testimony of two men is true. I am One who bears witness of Myself, and the Father who sent Me bears witness of Me." Then they said to Him, "Where is Your Father?" Jesus answered, "You know neither Me nor My Father. If you had known Me, you would have known My Father also." These words Jesus spoke in the treasury, as He taught in the temple; and no one laid hands on Him, for His hour had not yet come. Then Jesus said to them again, "I am going away, and you will seek Me, and will die in your sin. Where I go you cannot come." So the Jews said, "Will He kill Himself, because He says, 'Where I go you cannot come'?" And He said to them, "You are from beneath; I am from above. You are of this world; I am not

of this world. Therefore I said to you that you will die in your sins; for
if you do not believe that I am He, you will die in your sins." Then they
said to Him, "Who are You?" And Jesus said to them, "Just what I have
been saying to you from the beginning. I have many things to say and to
judge concerning you, but He who sent Me is true; and I speak to the
world those things which I heard from Him." They did not understand
that He spoke to them of the Father. Then Jesus said to them, "When
you lift up the Son of Man, then you will know that I am He, and that I
do nothing of Myself; but as My Father taught Me, I speak these things.
And He who sent Me is with Me. The Father has not left Me alone, for
I always do those things that please Him." As He spoke these words,
many believed in Him.

As I noted in an earlier chapter, one distinctive feature of John's Gospel
is that it contains seven "I Am" statements by Jesus. We already have
seen that Jesus referred to Himself as "the bread of life" (6:35, 48).
At the opening of this passage, we encounter a second "I Am" saying; Jesus
said: **"I am the light of the world. He who follows Me shall not
walk in darkness, but have the light of life"** (v. 12). John touched on
this theme of Jesus as light in the very prologue of his Gospel (1:7–9). The
idea is that Jesus brought illumination and understanding of truth when He
came into the world.

The Pharisees were quick to find fault with this statement by Jesus. They
said, **"You bear witness of Yourself; Your witness is not true"**
(v. 13). The first part of this statement was obvious—Jesus *was* speaking about
Himself. This was not John the Baptist or someone else declaring that Jesus
was the light; Jesus Himself made this affirmation. The second part of this
statement is more difficult to understand. Under Jewish law, when testimony
was given in the law court, a suspect could be convicted only on the basis
of the testimony of at least two witnesses, whose testimony naturally had to
agree. In other words, any witness had to have corroboration. Thus, when
they heard Jesus say "I am the light of the world"—again using that strange
Greek construction *ego eimi*, which literally means "I am, I am" and which
can be translated "I AM WHO I AM," the great name that God claimed for
Himself in the Old Testament (Ex. 3:14)—the Pharisees said: "You're saying
that by Yourself. Therefore, Your witness is not true." They were discounting
Jesus' testimony about Himself on the ground that there was no corroborating
witness. But they went a step further and, instead of merely declaring Jesus'

testimony inadmissible, they declared it false. They accused the One who is the very incarnation of truth of being a false witness.

There is an irony here. The Greek word translated as "witness" in this verse is *marturia*, from which we get the English word *martyr*. This word, which indicates one who loses his life for a cause, comes from the Greek word for "witness" because there was such a close relationship between the martyrs of the early church and their witness to the truth claims of Jesus. They bore witness to Christ by giving their lives; their testimony was emphatic because it involved their own blood. The irony is this: the first martyr of the Christian church was Christ Himself, and in His martyrdom He bore supreme witness to the truth of the things that He was speaking even here.

It terrifies me to think of anyone standing before Christ and saying, "Your testimony is false." If somebody says that my testimony is false, that's one thing; to hear testimony from Jesus Himself and to declare that testimony false is quite another. Yet, that's what every unbeliever in this world says to Jesus, because the spirit of unbelief accuses Christ of being a false witness.

Defending His Testimony

How did Jesus respond to this charge? He stated a number of reasons why His testimony was sure. First, He said: **"Even if I bear witness of Myself, My witness is true, for I know where I came from and where I am going; but you do not know where I come from and where I am going"** (v. 14). He said His testimony was based on firsthand knowledge of heaven, for He had come from there and was going back there. The Pharisees did not even know the simplest fact about Him—where He actually was from.

Second, Jesus said, **"You judge according to the flesh. I judge no one"** (v. 15). Jesus did not say here that He would not serve as a judge over all men; other passages in Scripture show that He will (Matt. 25:31ff; Rom. 2:16; 14:10; Rev. 19:11). Rather, He said, "You judge according to the flesh; I judge no one that way." Jesus judges from the perspective of that place from which He had come—heaven.

Third, Jesus said, **"And yet if I do judge, My judgment is true; for I am not alone, but I am with the Father who sent Me. It is also written in your law that the testimony of two men is true. I am One who bears witness of Myself, and the Father who sent Me bears witness of Me"** (vv. 16–18). Jesus' bottom-line argument was that He *did* have corroboration. Not only did He bear witness of Himself, the Father bore witness of Him.

When we read this passage, we know, in light of the rest of Scripture, that when Jesus referred to His Father who sent Him that He was referring to the first person of the Trinity, His heavenly Father. But if we put ourselves into the shoes of the people who heard Jesus make this affirmation, we can imagine their confusion when He said, "My Father sent Me here and My Father backs up My witness." They must have wondered whether He was talking about His earthly father, Joseph.

When I was a child, I had a friend, Eric, who lived up the street. He got in more fights than anybody in the community—and he lost every one. Every time he lost a fight, he went away crying and said, "I'm going to get my cousin, and my cousin will come and beat you up." Eric never actually sent his cousin back to deal with those of us who topped him in various playground fights, but wouldn't you know, a few years ago I met a fellow who had the same last name, and I said, "You're not related to Eric, are you?" He said, "That's my cousin." I was afraid he was going to say, "I've been looking for you for many years."

Plenty of boys claim that they're going to get their big brothers when bullying occurs. Sometimes they threaten to bring their dads. Such threats are appeals to "higher powers," as it were, to others who have greater resources of strength or authority. In a sense, Jesus did this; He told the Pharisees that a "higher power" than Himself stood behind His words.

Knowing the Father and the Son

Of course, the full effect of Jesus' words was lost on the Pharisees because they did not understand about whom Jesus was talking. I imagine the Pharisees wondered who this Father was who had so much authority that He sent Jesus to say what He said and who was going to back up that testimony. They had no idea that He was speaking of His heavenly Father. Therefore, they asked Him, **"Where is Your Father?"** (v. 19a). Likewise, later in the conversation, John tells us that **They did not understand that He spoke to them of the Father** (v. 27).

Actually, at least one of them understood. When Nicodemus came to Jesus at night, he said, "Rabbi, we know that You are a teacher come from God; for no one can do these signs that You do unless God is with him" (3:2). Nicodemus understood the function of miracles. I mentioned in Chapter 14 that I hear people say that the miracles of the New Testament prove the existence of God, but they do not. God demonstrates His existence long before a single miracle is ever performed by anyone. The function of miracles is not to prove the existence of God but to demonstrate and authenticate a messenger of God.

That's why Jesus said, "Believe Me that I am in the Father and the Father in Me, or else believe Me for the sake of the works themselves" (John 14:11). Jesus' miracles manifested that God was with Him, and all of the Pharisees should have seen that.

Jesus went on to make a statement that deserves our close attention. He said: **"You know neither Me nor My Father. If you had known Me, you would have known My Father also"** (v. 19b). Later on, as we will see, He turned this statement around when the Jewish leaders claimed to be children of God. He said, "If God were your Father, you would love Me, for I proceeded forth and came from God" (8:42a). There are millions, if not billions, of people in this world who claim to know God as their Father yet reject the Son. You cannot know God the Father and repudiate the Son, and you cannot know the Son and repudiate the Father, because Their testimony is one. The Father bears witness to the Son and the Son bears witness to the Father.

John writes, **These words Jesus spoke in the treasury, as He taught in the temple; and no one laid hands on Him, for His hour had not yet come** (v. 20). The treasury was an area in the temple where there stood thirteen receptacles, each shaped in the form of a *shofar*, a ram's horn, and each dedicated to a different need or concern. Into these receptacles the worshiping Jews could deposit alms that would be used to alleviate suffering in the community. It is sad that it was in this place where the donations were given that the greatest gift that God has given us was attacked.

Significant Moments in Time

This verse also contains the third instance in John's Gospel of the strange, foreboding comment that Jesus' hour had not yet come (see 2:4; 7:30). In the mid-twentieth century, Oscar Cullman, a Swiss New Testament scholar, wrote a book titled *Christ and Time*. In it, Cullman analyzes in great detail the "time" words that we find in sacred Scripture. He notes that whereas the English language has one word for "time," the Greek language has two. There's the word *chronos*. This Greek word had to do with the moment-by-moment passage of time. A clock or a wristwatch is a chronometer, a device that measures *chronos*. That's one way in which the Bible speaks of time—in terms of chronological sequence.

But there's another word for time in the Greek, *kyros*. The word *kyros* refers to a specific moment in time. We have something close to it in English, but not exactly. We distinguish between the words *historical* and *historic*. Someone might say, "Such-and-such was a historical moment," but every moment is a historical moment. However, when we speak about a "historic moment," we speak of a moment of great significance. Something like this is in view when the word *kyros* is used.

Throughout Scripture, we encounter many such moments, what we may call *kyrotic* moments. A *kyrotic* moment is a moment in time that is so pregnant with meaning that it defines all of time. The exodus is a *kyrotic* moment. The birth of Christ is a *kyrotic* moment. The cross is a *kyrotic* moment. Likewise, when Jesus referred to "My hour," He talked about a *kyrotic* moment. Sometimes He spoke of the hour of glory, the hour of exultation, His finest hour. At other times He spoke of the darkest moment of His life, the hour of His grand passion, of His suffering and death. But in every case, He spoke of a moment of overwhelming significance.

Jesus addressed the first of these *kyrotic* moments when He said: **"I am going away, and you will seek Me, and will die in your sin. Where I go you cannot come"** (v. 21). Jesus spoke here not of His ascension but of His death on the cross. We know this because of what Jesus said later in this conversation: **"When you lift up the son of Man . . ."** (v. 28). The Jews, not knowing that the cross lay ahead, were confused: **"Will He kill Himself, because He says, 'Where I go you cannot come'?"** (v. 22). He could have answered, "No, you're going to do it for Me."

Notice the terrifying words Jesus spoke to the Pharisees in verse 21: "you . . . will die in your sin." He returned to this subject as the conversation continued: **"You are from beneath; I am from above. You are of this world; I am not of this world. Therefore I said to you that you will die in your sins; for if you do not believe that I am He, you will die in your sins"** (vv. 23–24).

The Bible speaks of two ways of dying. The people of God, the saints of the Old and New Testaments, die in faith, and their deaths are precious in the sight of God (Ps. 116:15). All of those who die in faith enter that place God has prepared for His people from the foundation of the world. The only other way one can die is to die in one's sins. The Bible makes it clear that we're all sinners, but when the Bible speaks of being in sin or in faith, it is talking about the state of our souls before God. A person who has no faith, the unconverted person, remains in sin, and the worst calamity that could ever befall a human being is to die in that state. But for those who die in faith, there will be eternal blessing.

John tells us that **many believed in Him** (v. 30b) as He taught these things. I pray that many will believe as they read the Gospel of John and study it with the help of this book.

24

ABRAHAM AND FREEDOM

John 8:31–59

Then Jesus said to those Jews who believed Him, "If you abide in My word, you are My disciples indeed. And you shall know the truth, and the truth shall make you free." They answered Him, "We are Abraham's descendants, and have never been in bondage to anyone. How can You say, 'You will be made free'?" Jesus answered them, "Most assuredly, I say to you, whoever commits sin is a slave of sin. And a slave does not abide in the house forever, but a son abides forever. Therefore if the Son makes you free, you shall be free indeed. I know that you are Abraham's descendants, but you seek to kill Me, because My word has no place in you. I speak what I have seen with My Father, and you do what you have seen with your father." They answered and said to Him, "Abraham is our father." Jesus said to them, "If you were Abraham's children, you would do the works of Abraham. But now you seek to kill Me, a Man who has told you the truth which I heard from God. Abraham did not do this. You do the deeds of your father." Then they said to Him, "We were not born of fornication; we have one Father—God." Jesus said to them, "If God were your Father, you would love Me, for I proceeded forth and came from God; nor have I come of Myself, but He sent Me. Why do you not understand My speech? Because you are not able to listen to My word. You are of your father the devil, and the desires of your father you want to do. He was a murderer from the beginning, and does not stand in the truth, because there is no truth in him. When he speaks a lie, he speaks from his own resources, for he is a liar and the father of it. But because I tell the truth, you do not believe Me. Which of you convicts Me of sin? And if I tell the truth, why do you not believe Me? He who is of God hears God's words; therefore you do not hear, because you are not of God." Then the Jews answered and said to Him, "Do we not say rightly that You are a Samaritan and have a demon?" Jesus answered, "I do not have a demon; but I honor My Father, and you dishonor Me. And I do not seek My own glory; there is One who seeks and judges. Most assuredly, I say to you, if anyone keeps My word he shall never see death." Then the Jews said to Him, "Now we know that You have a demon! Abraham is dead, and the prophets; and You say, 'If anyone keeps My word he shall never taste death.' Are You greater than our father Abraham, who is dead? And the prophets are dead. Who do You make Yourself out to be?" Jesus answered, "If I honor Myself, My honor is nothing. It is My Father who honors Me, of whom you say that He is your God. Yet you have not known Him, but I know Him. And if I say, 'I do not know Him,' I shall be a liar like you; but I do know Him and keep His word. Your father Abraham rejoiced to see My day, and he saw *it* and was glad." Then the Jews said to Him, "You are not yet fifty years old, and have You seen Abraham?" Jesus said to them, "Most assuredly, I say to you, before Abraham was, I AM." Then they took up stones to throw at Him; but Jesus hid Himself and went out of the temple, going through the midst of them, and so passed by.

I f you have watched any of the debates between the presidential candidates in recent years, you know that the art of debate is at a low ebb. That which we call a debate is more often a series of "sound bites" strung together to score points. There is very little exchange of ideas and thoughts that leads to deeper understanding on the part of the hearers. This is regrettable, for a true debate can yield many benefits. Sometimes debates generate more heat than light, but at other times, important distinctions and clarifications are made so that we can get to the heart of a matter.

In the passage before us in this chapter, we are privileged to see Jesus Himself engaging in debate with His adversaries. Some very important insights for our understanding as Christians come out of this debate, so we need to give close attention to the key points that Jesus makes here.

Abiding in Jesus' Word

In the previous chapter, we saw that John wrote, "As He spoke these words, many believed in Him" (v. 30). The passage we are examining in this chapter begins with Jesus' words to these new believers: **"If you abide in My word, you are My disciples indeed. And you shall know the truth, and the truth shall make you free"** (vv. 31-32).

There is probably enough truth packed into these verses to warrant a separate book, but I need to be much more succinct. The first thing I want us to see is that Jesus made a distinction between those who are indeed His disciples and those who are not His disciples. The necessary condition that He announced is that of abiding, or remaining, in His Word.

We already have seen an example of followers of Jesus who did not abide in His Word. When Jesus gave His discourse on the bread of life (recorded in John 6), He spoke to the people about their natural inability to come to Him apart from the work of the Father (6:65). When they heard that, many of those disciples who had walked with Him in the earlier periods of His ministry walked with Him no more (6:66). They had been "believers"—not believers in the New Testament sense of those who possess saving faith, but believers in the ordinary sense of those who agreed with the things they heard from the lips of this itinerant rabbi. They believed what Jesus taught up to a certain point. However, once He got to the crux of the matter, they demurred. Their discipleship was temporary, and therefore it was not genuine.

It is important that we understand the difference between saving faith, which is the *possession* of the true believer, and the mere *profession* of faith. Many people mistakenly think that they enter into the kingdom of God simply by making a profession of faith. They say, "But preacher, I went to an evangelistic meeting, I raised my hand, I answered the altar call, I prayed the sinner's prayer, I signed the card—doesn't that make me a Christian?" The only answer I can give is "Maybe." It's not the profession that gets you into the kingdom. It's the possession. We must possess what we profess.

That's what Jesus said here. The test He put before these people was the test of staying power. Jesus said, "Not everyone who *says* to Me, 'Lord, Lord,' shall enter the kingdom of heaven" (Matt. 7:21a). On the other hand: "If you abide in My word, you are My disciples indeed. And you shall know the truth, and the truth shall make you free" (vv. 31-32). Do you see the series of links here? Remaining makes you a disciple; by remaining, you know the truth; and by remaining and knowing the truth, you are set free. With these words Jesus encouraged those who had responded to Him to stay with Him.

While Jesus' previous comments were directed to "those Jews who believed Him," the response came from the Pharisees: **"We are Abraham's descendants, and have never been in bondage to anyone. How can You say, 'You will be made free'?"** (v. 33). The Pharisees were furious with Jesus for suggesting that they were in some kind of bondage and needed liberation. They indignantly said to Him: "We're Abraham's descendants. We haven't been in bondage to anyone. I can show You my birth certificate. I can tell You which Israelite tribe I am a member of. I grew up in the covenant community. My father was a descendant of Abraham; my mother was a descendant of Abraham; my grandfather was a descendant of Abraham." So it went. The Pharisees counted on their biological lineage, on their family tree, to get them into the kingdom.

This kind of argument sounds alien to us, but it should not. Do you know how many times I've heard people say: "Of course I'm a Christian. I was born a Christian. My father was a Christian; my mother was a Christian; my grandfather was a Christian. I come from a long line of Christians." We can make the same kind of argument as the Pharisees. Unfortunately, no one is born a Christian. No one has ever entered the kingdom of God because of biology. As we have seen, "Unless one is born again, he cannot see the kingdom of God" (3:3). A physical birth, no matter how significant the lineage in human terms, is not enough.

Bondage and True Freedom

Jesus gave a powerful statement in response to the Pharisees' challenge: **"Most assuredly, I say to you, whoever commits sin is a slave of sin. And a slave does not abide in the house forever, but a son abides forever. Therefore if the Son makes you free, you shall be free indeed"** (vv. 34–36).

Imagine that you went to church one Sunday morning and the guest preacher was Jesus. Then imagine that He stayed after the worship service and spent some time answering questions. If you were to ask Him a question and He were to preface His answer with the words "Most assuredly," you would know He wasn't just giving an opinion. The answer to your question would not be an off-the-cuff, casual remark. You would know that you were hearing words of great importance. When Jesus says "Most assuredly," as He does in verse 34, we need to listen carefully.

Jesus' first words were designed to show the Pharisees the error of their understanding. They were taking Jesus to mean some sort of actual bondage, something akin to slavery. "No," Jesus said, "I'm not talking about slavery to the Romans or to some master to whom you are sworn as an indentured servant. I'm talking about slavery to sin."

I am frequently asked questions about the issue of free will. People ask, "Don't we have free will?" I warn people all the time to be careful how they understand the concept of free will, because if there's any idea from the secular culture that has permeated Christianity, it is the idea that we are born with wills that are ethically neutral and indifferent. In all likelihood, you have been taught from the day you went to kindergarten that you have a free will.

The church has labored the point, with its greatest thinkers throughout history, that when God made Adam and Eve, He endowed them with a faculty of choosing. They were free moral agents. They were responsible for their actions, and they had the moral power to choose what they wanted to do apart from external coercion. Theologians have showed that even after the fall, that power of making choices remained intact. Fallen human beings are not robots or puppets. They still have minds that think, wills that make choices, and hearts that have affections. So they think they're free.

But Jesus says we are not really free. We are like slaves on a galley. We still have minds, wills, and hearts, but the chains of our slavery limit our choices. When Jesus describes the natural human condition, He says: "By nature you're slaves. You're slaves to your own wicked desires, your own wicked impulses. Nobody else is forcing you to commit the sins you commit; you sin because you're a slave to sin." The pagan believes that his will is unaffected by the fall, but Christianity teaches that by nature we have sinful and corrupt natures that keep us in moral bondage.

Jesus went on to say: **"I know that you are Abraham's descendants, but you seek to kill Me, because My word has no place in you. I speak what I have seen with My Father, and you do what you have seen with your father"** (vv. 37–38). Later in this conversation, Jesus said, **"Your father Abraham rejoiced to see My day"** (v. 56a). Jesus said, "You might be Abraham's children, but you are not conducting yourselves as Abraham did." To this the Pharisees insisted, **"Abraham *is* our father"** (v. 39a). Jesus replied, **"If you were Abraham's children, you would do the works of Abraham"** (v. 39b). Jesus defined sonship not in terms of biology but in terms of obedience.

The Pharisees then employed a new tactic: **"We were not born of fornication; we have one Father—God"** (v. 41b). It is possible the Pharisees were making a slanderous comment about Jesus' parentage, denigrating His claim that God was His Father by implying that He didn't even have a legitimate human father, and staking their own claim to be sons of the Father. But

Jesus would have none of it: **"If God were your Father, you would love Me, for I proceeded forth and came from God; nor have I come of myself, but He sent Me"** (v. 42). Jesus was essentially making the same point He made in verse 39—sonship is shown by obedience. Jesus put it very simply later in His ministry: "If you love Me, keep My commandments" (John 14:15). True sons of God show their love for Him by obeying His Son, not by persecuting His Son.

Then Jesus cut to the crux of the matter: **"Why do you not understand My speech? Because you are not able to listen to My word"** (v. 43). Far from abiding in Jesus' Word, the Pharisees could not even listen to it. Here is unshakeable proof that they were not born again but were still lost in their sins.

This is the point that the great Augustine labored his entire life and his ministry. He argued that the fall left man morally impotent. Fallen man does not come to the Word of God because he has no taste for the things of God. By nature the things of God are foreign to him. He doesn't want God in his thinking. He refuses to have anything to do with Him. He has no desire for the things of God. By nature his desires are only wicked continually. That's why God has to change the disposition of a person's heart before he will ever respond to the Word of Christ. The Spirit has to set him free.

Doing the Devil's Desires

Jesus then said, **"You are of your father the devil, and the desires of your father you want to do"** (v. 44a). Here we learn what is meant by spiritual bondage, by bondage to sin. Notice how Jesus described it. He did not say, "You do the works of the Devil," so that they could maybe appear on judgment day and say: "Lord, I'm sorry, but the Devil made me do it. What could I do? He's more powerful than I am." Instead, Jesus said, "You do the *works* of the Devil because you want to do the *desires* of the Devil." By nature we are Satan's willing slaves, volunteers in the kingdom of darkness. By nature we love the darkness rather than the light because we want to do the desires of Satan. That's what sin is. Sin is not simply making bad choices or mistakes. Sin is having the desire in our hearts to do the will of the enemy of God. Paul made this very point to the Ephesians: "And you He made alive, who were dead in trespasses and sins, in which you once walked according to the course of this world, according to the prince of the power of the air, the spirit who now works in the sons of disobedience, among whom we also once conducted ourselves in the lusts of our flesh, fulfilling the desires of the flesh and of the mind, and were by nature children of wrath, just as the others"

(Eph. 2:1–3). This is a picture of the bondage from which Jesus delivered us; a bondage of desiring to carry out Satan's wishes.

Jesus spelled out some of Satan's wishes: **"He was a murderer from the beginning and does not stand in the truth, because there is no truth in him. When he speaks a lie, he speaks from his own resources, for he is a liar and the father of it"** (v. 44b). Satan is a murderer, and the Pharisees desired to kill Jesus. Satan does not stand in truth, but lies. His resources for dishonesty, falsehood, and perversion are almost inexhaustible. Because they were so given over to falsehood, the Pharisees could not receive what Jesus said: **"Because I tell the truth, you do not believe Me"** (v. 45).

Do you see the two points Jesus has made to the Pharisees? He said: "Don't tell Me you're children of Abraham, because if you were children of Abraham, you would do the things that Abraham loved; but you hate the things that Abraham loved. And don't claim to be children of God, because if you were children of God, you would love the things of God; but you hate the things of God."

This kind of teaching comes like a freight train against the basic beliefs of American culture. We're told that God has many faces and that we can choose to believe in Mohammed, Buddha, Confucius, or any of those avatars, as well as Jesus. In fact, it doesn't matter what we believe, just as long as we're sincere. Not so, according to Jesus. If we reject Christ, we reject the Father. We cannot have the Father and not have the Son, and we cannot have the Son and not have the Father, because the Father sent the Son.

Jesus said: **"He who is of God hears God's words; therefore you do not hear, because you are not of God"** (v. 47). Every time I stand in the pulpit of St. Andrew's to read Scripture on Sunday morning, I conclude the reading with the same words: "He who has ears to hear, let him hear" (see Mark 4:9). That's not an empty ritual. I take very seriously the truth that the Word of God that we read and proclaim will fall on deaf ears unless God Himself attends that Word by the Holy Spirit and opens the ears of those who hear it. There is no greater gift we could ever receive from God than to have our ears opened, to have the scales taken from our eyes, to have our stony hearts softened so that they become beating, pulsating, responding hearts of love as we hear the Word of God.

Jesus continued in His debate with the Pharisees. They accused Him of being a **Samaritan** and of having a **demon** (v. 48). Jesus denied those charges and affirmed, **"If anyone keeps My word he shall never see death"** (v. 51b). The Pharisees declared He could not possibly be greater than

Abraham or the **prophets** (v. 53). Jesus replied that **"Abraham rejoiced to see My day, and he saw it and was glad"** (v. 56). Then, when the incredulous Pharisees asked how Jesus could possibly have seen Abraham, Jesus said, **"Most assuredly, I say to you, before Abraham was, I AM"** (v. 58). Notice that Jesus didn't say, "Before Abraham was, I was." Here as perhaps nowhere else in Scripture Jesus claimed for Himself equality with the Father by clearly using the divine name that God revealed to Moses (Ex. 3:14). Jesus identified Himself as eternal deity, declaring that He was alive as the second person of the Trinity before Abraham was born. The Pharisees did not miss the import of what He said; they picked up **stones** to execute Him on the spot. But Jesus, whose hour still had not come, **hid Himself** from them and **went out of the temple** (v. 59).

Disciples of Christ abide in His Word. Those who abide in His Word know the truth and are free. By contrast, the unregenerate are in bondage to sin and desire to do Satan's wishes. These stark contrasts emerge from this debate between Jesus and the Pharisees. Where do you stand? Are you abiding in God's Word and growing in the truth? Or are you in bondage to do Satan's wishes? Abide in God's Word that you might be free indeed.

25

THE MAN BORN BLIND, PART 1

John 9:1–12

Now as Jesus passed by, He saw a man who was blind from birth. And His disciples asked Him, saying, "Rabbi, who sinned, this man or his parents, that he was born blind?" Jesus answered, "Neither this man nor his parents sinned, but that the works of God should be revealed in him. I must work the works of Him who sent Me while it is day; the night is coming when no one can work. As long as I am in the world, I am the light of the world." When He had said these things, He spat on the ground and made clay with the saliva; and He anointed the eyes of the blind man with the clay. And He said to him, "Go, wash in the pool of Siloam" (which is translated, Sent). So he went and washed, and came back seeing. Therefore the neighbors and those who previously had seen that he was blind said, "Is not this he who sat and begged?" Some said, "This is he." Others said, "He is like him." He said, "I am he." Therefore they said to him, "How were your eyes opened?" He answered and said, "A Man called Jesus made clay and anointed my eyes and said to me, 'Go to the pool of Siloam and wash.' So I went and washed, and I received sight." Then they said to him, "Where is He?" He said, "I do not know."

arly in Chapter 5 of John's Gospel, we read the account of Jesus'
healing of a lame man at the pool of Bethesda. That miracle sparked
great hostility toward Jesus from the Jewish authorities. As we begin
to consider John 9, we find history repeating itself. Jesus performed another
miraculous healing, this time of a man who had been born blind. Just like
the earlier miracle, this healing left the authorities incensed. In this chapter
we will focus on the miracle, while the next chapter will deal more with the
ensuing controversy.

John's account begins with a theological question from Jesus' disciples,
probably the kind of question they asked Him all the time as they journeyed
about and He taught them. John writes, **Now as Jesus passed by, He
saw a man who was blind from birth** (v. 1). John does not explain
how Jesus knew that the man had been blind all his life, but it seems that
the fact was mentioned in the conversation with His disciples, for they were
intrigued and asked, **"Rabbi, who sinned, this man or his parents,
that he was born blind?" Jesus answered, "Neither this man nor
his parents sinned, but that the works of God should be revealed
in him"** (vv. 2–3).

The disciples were curious about the providential reason for the man's
affliction, and they saw two possible options: either his sin was to blame or
his parents' sin. Thus, the disciples fell into a logical fallacy called the fallacy
of the false dilemma or the either/or fallacy. This happens when people say,
"It's either this or it's that," when in fact there may be a *tertium quid*, a "third
option." There are certain issues that can be reduced, justly, to either/or terms.
For instance, God either exists or He doesn't; there is no middle ground. But
if I say, "Let's paint the house either red or blue," I am ignoring a host of
other color options that could be selected. We are not thinking clearly when
we reduce options to two when there are actually more than that.

So Jesus' first concern in His response was to correct the disciples' logical
fallacy, which He did with one word: "neither." In other words, there was
another option they had failed to consider.

Sin and Suffering

Jesus also had to correct a false assumption in the disciples' question, the
assumption that sin on the part of the blind man himself or his parents was
responsible for the blindness this man had endured throughout his life. This
assumption was based on a deeper assumption—the idea that *all* affliction,
pain, or suffering is divine punishment for sin.

This idea is addressed throughout the book of Job. Job's friends come to the conclusion that Job is the worst sinner in the land because he is the most grievously afflicted person in the land. Their logic is this: there has to be some kind of ratio between the degree of a person's suffering and the degree of his sin. The book of Job was written to refute this falsehood by showing that Job's suffering had nothing to do with sin on his part.

However, we should not be too quick to dismiss the disciples' question as utterly stupid. We need to remember that on many occasions in the history of God's people and in the biblical record, personal afflictions *were* visited upon individuals because of sin.

My father was scrupulous about the principle of tithing. In fact, as a lay preacher, he would frequently preach in the Methodist Church about the biblical obligation of tithing. Because of that conviction on his part, when I was a boy, if I was given an allowance of fifty cents, the first nickel had to go in the collection plate. When my allowance was raised to a dollar, it was a matter of discipline in our house that a dime of that dollar had to go into the collection plate. My father not only taught us the principle of tithing, he also insisted, and rightly I believe, that the tithe should come off the top, not out of what was left after we had indulged ourselves with our money.

Even though I wasn't a Christian at that time, the discipline of tithing became so ingrained in me that when I did become a Christian, I didn't have to adjust. Many people become used to living without tithing, and when they become Christians, they find it difficult to be obedient in this area. It can be difficult to adjust one's financial priorities to permit tithing.

In the forty-ninth year of my father's life, a friend of his who owned an automobile dealership was on the brink of bankruptcy, and since my father was a corporate bankruptcy accountant, he agreed to help this man with his problem. During that year, my father gave to his friend—gave, not lent—the sum of ten thousand dollars to help him in his business. Fifty years ago, ten thousand dollars was a tidy sum of money, but my father gave that amount to his friend who needed it. However, my father's business was suffering because of all the time he was working to help this friend and his income was not what it was normally, so for the first time in his life, he didn't tithe that year.

Early in the next year, he suffered the first of three debilitating strokes that ultimately took his life. He could hardly speak, but I remember him saying to me, "Son, I'm convinced that God has afflicted me because I failed to tithe." He went to his grave believing that. I didn't believe it, because I knew how scrupulous he had been over his whole life, and I thought, "Surely God would not do that to my father just because he had one bad year and didn't give the full tithe."

I was absolutely wrong. God *can* and *does* visit people with afflictions when they disobey Him. Throughout biblical history, when people violated the law of God, God visited them with judgment. What happened to the baby born of David and Bathsheba? The judgment of God came on the child; God took the baby's life as judgment on David and Bathsheba (2 Sam. 12:15–23). How about Moses' sister Miriam, who protested against Moses' marriage and rebelled against his leadership? God, we are told, visited her with leprosy (Num. 12:1–10). That is, a physical affliction came on her as a direct result of her sin. So there are times when God disciplines His people by affliction. We simply cannot say that sin and affliction are *never* linked.

Other Factors behind Suffering

On the other hand, we can never rush to the conclusion that every affliction is directly a result of God's judgment on sin. Scripture also shows us that other factors may be the reason for affliction. Clearly, Jesus' suffering occurred because of the sin of the world, but not because of sin on His part. Also, God allows suffering to come into our lives to refine us, as it were, to teach us how to be more and more dependent on Him, to the end that we are sanctified and molded through those difficult tribulations. The New Testament abounds with teachings that warn us against making the assumption that when we suffer, it is because of a specific sin.

In general terms, had there never been any sin in the world, there never would have been pain or death. In heaven, there will be no more sin, and not coincidentally, there will be no pain or death. So there is an overarching relationship between the reality of sin in this world and the reality of pain, but we err when we reduce that to a one-to-one relationship in individual people's lives.

Years ago, a friend of mine stayed with us and took classes while I was teaching at a local college. This young man, whose name was Harvey, was a victim of cerebral palsy; there was nothing wrong with his mind, but his body was profoundly afflicted. One day he came to me and asked to talk to me privately, and he poured out his heart. He said that he had some friends at his college who were convinced of the power of faith healing. They had laid hands on him for his healing, but he hadn't been healed. So they had told him it was because he didn't have enough faith. They tried it again, but he still wasn't healed. Then they told him to claim his healing in advance; they said he needed to have the faith of a blind man who could say "I believe I have vision" while everything was black. Well, my friend tried that and still was not healed. His friends then said, "The problem must be that there is some secret sin in your life." So he confessed all his sin and they laid hands on him again, but still he had cerebral palsy. Finally they came to the ultimate explanation. They said, "Well, Harvey, you must be demon possessed," and they tried to exorcise the demon of cerebral palsy out of his body.

When Harvey came to me, he asked me in tears, "R. C., do you think I'm demon possessed?" I prayed for him and thanked God for the incredible, brilliant testimony of his life in faithfulness to the things of God, for the triumph over sickness and disease he had manifested so many times. I said in that prayer, "Lord, I thank You that You have given this man such a sweetness of disposition and such a profound faith in You." When I finished praying, he looked at me, and his smile went from ear to ear. He said to me, "Do you know what you said in your prayer?" I said, "What's that, Harvey?" He said: "You called me a man. That's the first time anybody has ever called me a man."

I have no idea why Harvey has cerebral palsy, and he doesn't either. But it doesn't matter. God gave him the greatest gift He could give any person, and Harvey was happy with that until people with a distorted view of the relationship between suffering and sin tried to take away the joy of his salvation.

Afflicted to be Healed

It was with this same kind of assumption that the disciples came to Jesus and asked, "Whose fault was it—this man's or his parents'—that he was born blind?" Jesus said, "Neither this man nor his parents sinned." Jesus was not saying that the man born blind and his parents were sinless. Rather, He was saying to His disciples, "His affliction is not a direct result of his sin or the sin of his parents." Instead, there was another reason for his blindness: "That the works of God should be revealed in him." In other words, Jesus was saying that, in the providence of God, this man had been afflicted with blindness so that God might someday heal him and thereby receive glory.

How many years did that man grope in the darkness, asking: "Why me, God? Everybody else can see, but I can't see anything. My whole life I have listened to people talk about what they're seeing, and I can only imagine. I don't even have any memories to aid me in my imagination because I've never seen anything. Why me?" Imagine the frustration, the torment. Year after year he dealt with this affliction. He had no idea that one day the Son of God would come to him and heal him. But that was the plan of God for his life from all eternity.

Only God knows why we go through the things that we go through, but the promise of God is that He brings good out of everything that befalls us

(Rom. 8:28) and uses the worst pain, the worst suffering, the most confusing events in our lives to bring about, ultimately, His glory. The blind man's life is a concrete example of suffering that went on and on for year after year until it finally resulted in glory. That's why the apostle Paul wrote, "For I consider that the sufferings of this present time are not worthy to be compared with the glory which shall be revealed in us" (Rom. 8:18). If the blind man had remained sightless for eighty years or ninety years, what would that have been compared with eternity in the presence of the glory of God?

By God's grace, however, the blind man didn't have to wait to go to heaven to see the face of Christ. Jesus said to His disciples, **"I must work the works of Him who sent Me while it is day; the night is coming when no one can work. As long as I am in the world, I am the light of the world"** (vv. 4–5). With these words, Jesus revealed his strong sense of mission—He had tasks to do during the limited time of His sojourn on earth, and healing this blind man obviously was one of them. As He had already said, He was the light of the world, and He must shine that light until the time came for Him to return to his Father.

John then tells us: **When He had said these things, He spat on the ground and made clay with the saliva; and He anointed the eyes of the blind man with the clay. And He said to him, "Go, wash in the pool of Siloam"** (which is translated, Sent). **So he went and washed, and came back seeing** (vv. 6–7).

There is a striking difference between the methodology Jesus used for this miracle and that of some of His other miracles. For instance, at the wedding feast of Cana, He didn't mix various ingredients with the water in the purification jars in order to produce the wine. As we'll see later, when He went to the tomb of Lazarus and raised him from the dead, He didn't administer mouth-to-mouth resuscitation to the corpse or rub some balm on Lazarus' forehead. He just stood outside the tomb and commanded Lazarus to come out. In those miracles we see the "immediate" power of God, that power by which God works without means.

But sometimes God brings His results to pass through means. When God parted the Red Sea for the children of Israel, Moses didn't just stand there and say, "Separate, O sea!" Rather, God brought a great wind that drove back the waters to permit the exodus to happen. Likewise, Jesus used the means of spit and dirt to heal this blind man's eyes. He didn't need to do it that way. There was no chemical in the Palestinian clay that could bring sight to blind people. That wasn't the point. Jesus was giving an object lesson. For reasons we don't know, He dramatized this healing. It was almost as if He were saying:

"Not everyone who was born from the clay got everything right the first time around. Some people are born from the dust with birth defects, and this man was one of them. Let's go back to the clay." That's pure speculation on my part. But then He took the clay, put it on the man's eyes, and sent him to the pool of Siloam, saying, "Go, wash in the pool." We're told that the man obeyed and came back seeing.

The One He Most Desired to See

What do you suppose was going through this man's mind? The biblical writers are often masters of understatement. John simply writes that the man went, did what Jesus said to do, and came back seeing. But we need to remember that he was seeing things for the first time in his life. He saw the light. He saw people. He saw all the things that he had only heard about throughout those many years of blindness.

Soon, however, there was one person he wanted to see above all others—Jesus, his healer. So he went back. Jesus wasn't there, but the residents of the area and those who knew the man caught sight of him: **Therefore the neighbors and those who previously had seen that he was blind said, "Is not this he who sat and begged?" Some said, "This is he." Others said, "He is like him." He said, "I am he"** (vv. 8–9). Some were saying, "Wait just a minute, isn't this the fellow who is always out here begging, the blind man?" Others could not believe that lifetime blindness could be overcome. They said, "No, no, it can't be him—it's just someone who looks like the man that we're used to seeing groping in the darkness." Finally the man himself, in his joy, settled the argument: "I am he. It's true. I have been healed."

Naturally, they were curious about what had happened: **Therefore they said to him, "How were your eyes opened?" He answered and said, "A Man called Jesus made clay and anointed my eyes and said to me, 'Go to the pool of Siloam and wash.' So I went and washed, and I received sight"** (vv. 10–11). I'm sure you've heard the famous Latin phrase attributed to Julius Caesar, "*Veni, vidi, vici,*" which means "I came, I saw, I conquered." This man's motto might have been, "I went, I washed, I see." But he fully acknowledged that it was all at the behest of and by the power of Jesus.

The people then asked where Jesus was. The man did not know; of course, he didn't even know what Jesus looked like. But the moment would come soon when he would behold Him.

Jesus opened the physical eyes of this blind man. As we will see, through this miracle, He also opened this man's spiritual eyes. The Bible uses the metaphor of blindness again and again for people who have never perceived the truth of Christ. The eyes of their hearts are blind until God the Holy Spirit, without the help of spit and clay, opens them. When He does, they not only perceive the light of day, they see the light of the world. John said in his prologue, "We beheld His glory" (1:14). All those whose spiritual eyes have been opened may say the same. Are you among them?

26

THE MAN BORN BLIND, PART 2

John 9:13–41

❦

They brought him who formerly was blind to the Pharisees. Now it was a Sabbath when Jesus made the clay and opened his eyes. Then the Pharisees also asked him again how he had received his sight. He said to them, "He put clay on my eyes, and I washed, and I see." Therefore some of the Pharisees said, "This Man is not from God, because He does not keep the Sabbath." Others said, "How can a man who is a sinner do such signs?" And there was a division among them. They said to the blind man again, "What do you say about Him because He opened your eyes?" He said, "He is a prophet." But the Jews did not believe concerning him, that he had been blind and received his sight, until they called the parents of him who had received his sight. And they asked them, saying, "Is this your son, who you say was born blind? How then does he now see?" His parents answered them and said, "We know that this is our son, and that he was born blind; but by what means he now sees we do not know, or who opened his eyes we do not know. He is of age; ask him. He will speak for himself." His parents said these things because they feared the Jews, for the Jews had agreed already that if anyone confessed that He was Christ, he would be put out of the synagogue. Therefore his parents said, "He is of age; ask him." So they again called the man who was blind, and said to him, "Give God the glory! We know that this Man is a sinner." He answered and said, "Whether He is a sinner or not I do not know. One thing I know: that though I was blind, now I see." Then they said to him again, "What did He do to you? How did He open your eyes?" He answered them, "I told you already, and you did not listen. Why do you want to hear it again? Do you also want to become His disciples?" Then they reviled him and said, "You are His disciple, but we are Moses' disciples. We know that God spoke to Moses; as for this fellow, we do not know where He is from." The man answered and said to them, "Why, this is a marvelous thing, that you do not know where He is from; yet He has opened my eyes! Now we know that God does not hear sinners; but if anyone is a worshiper of God and does His will, He hears him. Since the world began it has been unheard of that anyone opened the eyes of one who was born blind. If this Man were not from God, He could do nothing." They answered and said to him, "You were completely born in sins, and are you teaching us?" And they cast him out. Jesus heard that they had cast him out; and when He had found him, He said to him, "Do you believe in the Son of God?" He answered and said, "Who is He, Lord, that I may believe in Him?" And Jesus said to him, "You have both seen Him and it is He who is talking with you." Then he said, "Lord, I believe!" And he worshiped Him. And Jesus said, "For judgment I have come into this world, that those who do not see may see, and that those who see may be made blind." Then some of the Pharisees who were with Him heard these words, and said to Him, "Are we blind also?" Jesus said to them, "If you were blind, you would have no sin; but now you say, 'We see.' Therefore your sin remains."

I n most instances, when Jesus performed miracles during His earthly ministry, there were widely varying reactions. As a general rule, some believed in Him and glorified God when they saw His signs, others refused to accept that the miracles substantiated His claim to be the Son of God, and still others questioned the veracity of the miracles themselves. Jesus' healing of the man born blind was no exception in terms of the reactions it caused.

This portion of John's account of this miracle and its aftermath begins with these words: **They brought him who formerly was blind to the Pharisees. Now it was a Sabbath when Jesus made the clay and opened his eyes. Then the Pharisees also asked him again how he**

had received his sight. He said to them, "He put clay on my eyes, and I washed, and I see" (vv. 13–15). For reasons that are not clear, the man's neighbors and acquaintances, upon finding him healed of his blindness, decided to take him to the Pharisees. The Pharisees questioned him about what had happened to him, just as the people had, and he gave them the same answer. But John gives us one new detail in these verses that is of crucial importance—the miracle had happened on a Sabbath. An earlier miracle, the healing of the crippled man at the pool of Bethesda, also took place on a Sabbath (5:8–9), and that, too, had raised the ire of the Jewish authorities (5:10, 16). The same thing occurred here.

John continues: **Therefore some of the Pharisees said, "This Man is not from God, because He does not keep the Sabbath." Others said, "How can a man who is a sinner do such signs?" And there was a division among them** (v. 16). There was nothing in the law of God against anything Jesus had done for the man born blind. But as I noted earlier, the Jews had enumerated thirty-nine specific types of work that were illegal on the Sabbath day. One of the Sabbath prohibitions set forth by the Pharisees was the kneading of dough to make bread. It may be that the Pharisees concluded that Jesus had violated the Sabbath prohibitions by mixing spittle and dust, then presumably kneaded it to make clay. If so, they were accusing Jesus of violating the Sabbath law because He made clay. Never mind the reason for which He made it; never mind that the Sabbath was made for man and not man for the Sabbath (Mark 2:27); never mind that the Lord of the Sabbath declares that it is lawful to do good on the Sabbath. If these people had been the people of God, they would have been throwing their yarmulkes in the air and praising God for the manifestation of His mercy in the healing of this poor beset man. Instead, they quibbled over their own technicalities and accused Jesus of breaking the Sabbath. Of course, if He was a Sabbath breaker, He was a sinner, and therefore could not have been sent from God.

But that opinion was not unanimous. Others raised an excellent question: "How can a man who is a sinner do such signs?" This group seems to have had a good grasp of the purpose of miracles as we have defined it—to authenticate agents of revelation. This faction therefore spoke out against the other Pharisees, saying: "Wait a minute! If this man is a sinner, he wouldn't be able to do these things." They understood that miracles were divine attestations.

So there was a division among the Pharisees. In their confusion, they decided to ask the healed man for his opinion about Jesus: **They said to the blind man again, "What do you say about Him because He opened**

your eyes?" He said, "He is a prophet" (v. 17). Notice that he did not say, "He is the Son of God." He hadn't come to that full realization yet, but like the woman of Sychar (4:19), he was convinced that Jesus was a prophet. He, too, seems to have had a good grasp of the significance of miracles, that they designate true agents of revelation, such as prophets.

Man-Fearing Parents

At this point, some of the Pharisees must have realized that the whole case hinged on one question: Was he or wasn't he really blind? To get at the answer, they summoned the man's parents: **But the Jews did not believe concerning him, that he had been blind and received his sight, until they called the parents of him who had received his sight. And they asked them, saying, "Is this your son, who you say was born blind? How then does he now see?" His parents answered them and said, "We know that this is our son, and that he was born blind; but by what means he now sees we do not know, or who opened his eyes we do not know. He is of age; ask him. He will speak for himself." His parents said these things because they feared the Jews, for the Jews had agreed already that if anyone confessed that He was Christ, he would be put out of the synagogue. Therefore his parents said, "He is of age; ask him"** (vv. 18–23).

The Pharisees asked the healed man's parents two simple questions: "Is this your son?" and "How can he now see?" A third question is implied: "Is it true he was born blind?" The parents affirmed that the man was their son and that he had been born blind, but as to how he had come to see, they professed not to know. This is an incredible manifestation of corruption. How many years had these people agonized over the sightless condition of their son? He was their own flesh and blood. What a crushing blow it is to bring a child into the world and discover that the child cannot see, and that there's no hope that the child ever will see. Put yourself in the place of a parent who brings such a child into the world and imagine helping that child grope through the darkness year after year. Then imagine that, one afternoon after that child has grown to adulthood, the child walks into your house and says, "Mother, Father, I can see!" You'd want to crawl over glass to thank the One who made this possible. But not these parents. They professed ignorance and told the Pharisees to ask their son, for he was old enough to answer for himself.

John does not leave us to guess why these parents were so reticent to speak of their son's healer. The Pharisees, he writes, had issued an edict that anyone who confessed that Jesus was the Messiah would be excommunicated from the synagogue. That was a serious threat, and the parents feared that crediting Jesus with the miracle of their son's healing might well be judged as a confession of faith in Jesus as the Messiah.

We are like this man and woman. God works in our lives and gives us blessings that we cannot possibly describe, but when the heat is turned on, we are quick to disassociate ourselves from Him. I pray that each of you, if and when you are called upon to profess your faith in Christ before hostile people, will have the integrity and the courage to do it.

"One Thing I Know"

Having heard the healed man's parents, the Pharisees turned back to him: **So they again called the man who was blind, and said to him, "Give God the glory! We know that this Man is a sinner." He answered and said, "Whether He is a sinner or not I do not know. One thing I know: that though I was blind, now I see"** (vv. 24–25). This statement, "Give God the glory!" seems positive until we read the remainder of the sentence, in which the Pharisees revealed that they had concluded that Jesus was a sinner and therefore could not have performed the miracle. They were saying that the man should give glory to God, not to Jesus. The man was straightforward with them, saying: "I don't know whether He's a sinner. I don't even know Him. All I know is this: once I was blind and now I see."

With these simple words, the man bore witness to Christ. He testified about the redemptive work of Christ. However, he did not preach the gospel. What am I getting at? In the evangelical Christian community, we sometimes employ language that is not always sound or biblical. You've heard the lingo. It goes something like this: "I plan to become an evangelist so I can bear witness to Christ." Or sometimes we say, "I had a chance to witness the other day," meaning, "I shared the gospel with someone." We tend to use the terms *evangelism* and *witnessing* interchangeably, but they are not synonymous. Any time I call attention to the person and work of Christ, I am bearing witness to Christ. But that is not the same thing as preaching the gospel.

More than thirty years ago, I learned the evangelism technique taught by Evangelism Explosion, and I trained more than 250 people in that program and led them through evangelism efforts in Ohio. One of the finest aspects of that program is that everyone who goes through it must write out and memorize his or her testimony. Your testimony is your story of how you became a Christian. I think it's very important that Christians are able to articulate to other people how and why they became believers. We all should have a prepared testimony, and we should be willing to share it at the drop of a hat.

But we shouldn't confuse our personal testimonies with the gospel. Sharing our personal testimonies is not evangelism. It's merely pre-evangelism, sort of a warm-up for evangelism. Our testimonies may or may not be significant or meaningful to those with whom we are speaking. There are lots of folks who can relate to my story; they say, "Yeah, I know what he's talking about because I used to live like that too." But not everyone can relate to my story. In any case, the gospel is not what happened to R. C. Sproul. God makes no promise that He will use my story as His power unto salvation. The gospel is not about me. The gospel is about Jesus. It is the proclamation of the person and work of Christ, and of how a person can appropriate the benefits of the work of Christ by faith alone.

We see this from our passage in John's Gospel. The healed man could say, "I once was blind, but now I see," and that was a wonderful testimony. But it was not the gospel. The man could not tell the Pharisees about Jesus' saving work and about how they could be delivered from their sins by faith in Him. So we need to learn not only our testimonies but the concrete elements and content of the biblical gospel. Evangelism takes place when the evangel is proclaimed and announced to people—that is the gospel.

Thankfully, the healed man did not remain ignorant of the gospel. The Pharisees continued to press him to explain his healing, trying to get him to discount Jesus' role. But he stood his ground and continued to assert that Jesus' miracles proved him to be a prophet. He declared: **"Since the world began it has been unheard of that anyone opened the eyes of one who was born blind. If this Man were not from God, He could do nothing"** (vv. 32–33). Finally, their wrath boiling over, the Pharisees **cast him out** of the synagogue (v. 34).

But Jesus sought him out and found him, and a wonderful exchange ensued: **Jesus heard that they had cast him out; and when He had found him, He said to him, "Do you believe in the Son of God?" He answered and said, "Who is He, Lord, that I may believe in Him?" And Jesus said to him, "You have both seen Him and it is He who is talking with you." Then he said, "Lord, I believe!" And he worshiped Him** (vv. 35–38). Jesus revealed Himself to the man, and he went from seeing Jesus as a prophet to seeing Him as the Messiah. He professed faith in Christ and worshiped Him.

It is good to have a testimony. It is good to acknowledge that Jesus was a prophet, that He taught marvelous things, and that He did great works. But these things are not enough. As John writes later in his Gospel, "These are written that you may believe that Jesus is the Christ, the Son of God, and that believing you may have life in His name" (20:31). *This* is the gospel. Believe these things and have life.

27

THE GOOD SHEPHERD
DISCOURSE

John 10:1–21

"Most assuredly, I say to you, he who does not enter the sheepfold by
the door, but climbs up some other way, the same is a thief and a robber.
But he who enters by the door is the shepherd of the sheep. To him the
doorkeeper opens, and the sheep hear his voice; and he calls his own sheep
by name and leads them out. And when he brings out his own sheep, he
goes before them; and the sheep follow him, for they know his voice. Yet
they will by no means follow a stranger, but will flee from him, for they
do not know the voice of strangers." Jesus used this illustration, but they
did not understand the things which He spoke to them. Then Jesus said
to them again, "Most assuredly, I say to you, I am the door of the sheep.
All who ever came before Me are thieves and robbers, but the sheep did
not hear them. I am the door. If anyone enters by Me, he will be saved,
and will go in and out and find pasture. The thief does not come except
to steal, and to kill, and to destroy. I have come that they may have life,
and that they may have it more abundantly. I am the good shepherd. The
good shepherd gives His life for the sheep. But a hireling, he who is not
the shepherd, one who does not own the sheep, sees the wolf coming and

leaves the sheep and flees; and the wolf catches the sheep and scatters them. The hireling flees because he is a hireling and does not care about the sheep. I am the good shepherd; and I know My sheep, and am known by My own. As the Father knows Me, even so I know the Father; and I lay down My life for the sheep. And other sheep I have which are not of this fold; them also I must bring, and they will hear My voice; and there will be one flock and one shepherd. Therefore My Father loves Me, because I lay down My life that I may take it again. No one takes it from Me, but I lay it down of Myself. I have power to lay it down, and I have power to take it again. This command I have received from My Father." Therefore there was a division again among the Jews because of these sayings. And many of them said, "He has a demon and is mad. Why do you listen to Him?" Others said, "These are not the words of one who has a demon. Can a demon open the eyes of the blind?"

At the conclusion of John's account of Jesus' healing of the man born blind (John 9), two radically different responses were apparent. The healed man first came to the conclusion that Jesus was a prophet, but by the end of the narrative he recognized that Jesus was not only a prophet but the Son of God, and he bowed in worship before Him. It's significant for our understanding of the person of Christ that Jesus accepted worship from him, which no mere prophet or apostle would dare to do in the economy of the kingdom of God. When the people of Lystra sought to worship Paul and Barnabas, the two missionaries rebuked them (Acts 14:8–18). But Jesus did not reprimand the man who had been blind.

By contrast, Jesus had no compliments for the Pharisees, for they refused to believe after seeing the miracle. Jesus said to them, "If you were blind, you would have no sin; but now you say, 'We see.' Therefore your sin remains" (9:41). The Pharisees were not ready to worship Jesus because they could not even admit they were sinners.

The Shepherd and His Sheep

At that point, Jesus began a lengthy discourse focusing on Himself as the Shepherd and on His care for the sheep as their Savior. John's account of this discourse commences with the opening of Chapter 10.

Jesus said: **"Most assuredly, I say to you, he who does not enter the sheepfold by the door, but climbs up some other way, the same is a thief and a robber. But he who enters by the door is the shepherd**

of the sheep. To him the doorkeeper opens, and the sheep hear his voice; and he calls his own sheep by name and leads them out" (vv. 1–3). Jesus began with contrasts, and the first contrast was between the one who enters the door of the sheepfold and those who climb over the fences and try to sneak into the sheepfold by some other way. Those who try to sneak in are thieves and robbers, Jesus said, but the shepherd uses the door.

Some biblical commentators look at this text and say that when Jesus spoke of thieves and robbers, He referred to false messiahs or to the Devil. I don't think so; this comment is far more pointed than that. Remember, this comment came right on the heels of a very heated discussion between Jesus and the Pharisees about the man born blind. This is the context here. Jesus addressed those whom God had called to be the shepherds over His flock, the clergy of His day, who had so recently cast the healed man out of the synagogue, rejecting a sheep in the flock of God. Jesus called these clergy, the Pharisees, thieves and robbers.

Jesus drew this illustration from the sheep industry of the day. The way sheep were cared for in ancient Israel was very different from the way they are handled today. In those days, there was one large, central pen, or sheepfold, in a given community, and at the end of the day people brought their small individual flocks and led them into the big sheepfold. With their combined resources, they paid a gatekeeper, and it was his job to stay with the sheep during the night.

In the morning, the gatekeeper opened the gate to those who were truly shepherds, whose sheep were enclosed in the sheepfold. The shepherds entered by the door, for they had every right to do so—the sheep were theirs and the gatekeeper was their paid servant. When a shepherd entered the sheepfold, the sheep of all the local flocks were mixed, but he began to call, and his sheep recognized his voice and came to him. In fact, a good shepherd was so intimately involved with the care and the nurture of his sheep that he had names for them, and he would call them by name. His sheep followed him out because they knew him.

Jesus used this particular illustration over and over again to speak about His relationship to those whom the Father had given Him, to those who are believers. The illustration teaches us that Christ knows the believer and the believer knows Him, recognizes His voice, and follows Him. This two-way knowledge is absolutely essential. Jesus gave a dreadful warning about this at the end of the Sermon on the Mount when He said: "Many will say to Me in that day, 'Lord, Lord, have we not prophesied in Your name, cast out demons in Your name, and done many wonders in Your name?' And then I will declare to them, 'I never knew you; depart from Me, you who practice lawlessness!'" (Matt. 7:22–23). He said, "You are not My sheep if you don't know Me and I don't know you."

Obviously, in terms of the illustration, the gatekeeper, who opens the door of the sheepfold to the shepherd, represents the Father, who opens the gates of heaven to Christ and lets Him bring his sheep into the safety of the fold.

My friend John Guest once preached on this text, and he noted that one of the church's strongest hymns in the past was "The Ninety and Nine," which described the mission of the good shepherd. Do you recall the words of that hymn? The first stanza goes like this:

"There were ninety and nine that safely lay
In the shelter of the fold.
But one was out on the hills away,
Far off from the gates of gold.
Away on the mountains wild and bare.
Away from the tender Shepherd's care.
Away from the tender Shepherd's care."

The remainder of the hymn celebrates the pursuit of the Good Shepherd, who goes over land and sea to find His one lost sheep and bring him in. But John Guest went on to say that this hymn is no longer a fit theme song for the contemporary church. Instead, he suggested "Little Bo-Peep Has Lost Her Sheep," because our attitude seems to be, "Leave them alone, and they'll come home, wagging their tails behind them." Of course, in our culture, few people believe that anyone is actually lost, but the biblical view is that our Lord is the Shepherd who seeks and saves those who are lost.

Jesus continued: **"And when he brings out his own sheep, he goes before them; and the sheep follow him, for they know his voice. Yet they will by no means follow a stranger, but will flee from him, for they do not know the voice of strangers." Jesus used this illustration, but they did not understand the things which He spoke to them** (vv. 4–6). There is another major difference in the way sheep were tended in the past and the way they are tended today. Today, sheep are herded, usually by dogs that drive them and keep them going where the shepherd wants them to go. However, in ancient Israel, sheep were led. The shepherd went ahead of them, and where the shepherd went, the sheep followed. They didn't simply roam all over; they followed the shepherd. The shepherd was their leader, and if one sheep began to stray, the shepherd would simply call it. The sheep knew his voice and followed him, but they did not follow a stranger.

The Door of the Sheepfold

Then Jesus changed the analogy. He said: **"Most assuredly, I say to you, I am the door of the sheep. All who ever came before Me are thieves and robbers, but the sheep did not hear them. I am the door. If anyone enters by Me, he will be saved, and will go in and out and find pasture. The thief does not come except to steal, and to kill, and to destroy. I have come that they may have life, and that they may have it more abundantly"** (vv. 7–10). Here we find yet another of the seven "I am" sayings of Jesus in the Gospel of John: "I am the door." First Jesus said He was the Shepherd to whom the gatekeeper opened the door. Here He said, "I'm not only the Shepherd who leads the sheep in and out of the sheepfold, I am the door." His meaning becomes clear in the following words: it is through Him that salvation is found. Those who come to Him find access to life and sustenance. Others have promised these things, but they were thieves, intent only on stealing, killing, and destroying. In other words, they wanted to profit from the sheep and then dispose of them. Jesus came not to steal but to give, and His gift is abundant life. No one goes into the sheepfold except through Him.

Jesus continued: **"I am the good shepherd. The good shepherd gives His life for the sheep. But a hireling, he who is not the shepherd, one who does not own the sheep, sees the wolf coming and leaves the sheep and flees; and the wolf catches the sheep and scatters them. The hireling flees because he is a hireling and does not care about the sheep. I am the good shepherd; and I know My sheep, and am known by My own. As the Father knows Me, even so I know the Father; and I lay down My life for the sheep"** (vv. 11–15). Yet another of Jesus' "I am" sayings appears here: "I am the good shepherd." Here, Jesus contrasted Himself not with the thief and the robber, but with the hireling. Sometimes people took care of their own sheep, but sometimes, if they were too busy with other things, they hired others to look after their sheep. But since tending the sheep was just a job for the hireling, the sheep usually did not receive the same kind of tender care they received from their true shepherd. When the master of a flock is tending his own sheep and a wolf threatens, he stands in the gap and uses his rod to beat off the attack. If necessary, he lays down his life for his sheep, for they are his. Not so with a hireling. He doesn't own the sheep, so if he sees a wolf coming, he flees.

He thinks: "My life is worth more to me than these sheep. Let the wolves have them."

I tell my congregation that they are God's sheep. I don't own them. They don't belong to me; Christ is their shepherd. The best they can hope from me is that I'll be a good hireling, but that is all I can ever be—a hireling. Therefore I tell them that they should not look to me but to Christ, who is their Good Shepherd, the One who will never desert them.

Verse 16 is probably one of the most misinterpreted verses in the Bible: **"And other sheep I have which are not of this fold; them also I must bring, and they will hear My voice; and there will be one flock and one shepherd."** I've heard this text cited to prove that Jesus, after His ministry on earth, went to Mars, Venus, or some other galaxy and continued His mission of redemption, seeking out sheep elsewhere in the cosmos. That's not what He was talking about at all. He was simply saying that He had sheep that were not members of the house of Israel. He was talking about the expansion of the gospel beyond the borders of Israel to the world of the Gentiles. He was prophesying that He would bring from the Gentiles those whom the Father had given to Him, and there would be one sheepfold—Jew and Gentile—in the church that the Good Shepherd would build.

A Voluntary Sacrifice

Wrapping up this portion of His discourse, Jesus said: **"Therefore My Father loves Me, because I lay down My life that I may take it again. No one takes it from Me, but I lay it down of Myself. I have power to lay it down, and I have power to take it again. This command I have received from My Father"** (vv. 17–18). Jesus warned those who already were busily plotting His death, telling them: "You can't take My life from Me. I give My life for My sheep, but you have no power over Me unless I give it to you." On the night of His arrest, when one of Jesus' disciples drew a sword to fight for His freedom, Jesus said: "Put your sword in its place, for all who take the sword will perish by the sword. Or do you think that I cannot now pray to My Father and He will provide Me with more than twelve legions of angels? How then could the Scriptures be fulfilled, that it must happen thus?" (Matt. 26:52–54). At any moment Jesus could have stopped His execution. He could have prayed to His Father, and just as a myriad of angels surrounded Elisha in the Old Testament (2 Kings 6:17), they could have come to Calvary, brought Jesus down from the cross, and slain all of His enemies. But the Father had given the Son a cup to drink. The cross was the Father's command; it happened in fulfillment of the Scriptures.

It is important for us to remember that the death of Christ, His perfect sacrifice for us, was voluntary. Pilate had no power over Him. Caiaphas had no power over Him. Annas had no power over Him. The Roman emperor had no power over Him. He laid down His life for His sheep, to save His sheep from something far worse than wolves, thieves, or robbers—the judgment of God.

At a low point in the life of the nation of Israel, God sent the prophet Ezekiel to announce these words to the people:

> And the word of the LORD came to me, saying, "Son of man, prophesy against the shepherds of Israel, prophesy and say to them, 'Thus says the Lord GOD to the shepherds: "Woe to the shepherds of Israel who feed themselves! Should not the shepherds feed the flocks? You eat the fat and clothe yourselves with the wool; you slaughter the fatlings, but you do not feed the flock. The weak you have not strengthened, nor have you healed those who were sick, nor bound up the broken, nor brought back what was driven away, nor sought what was lost; but with force and cruelty you have ruled them. So they were scattered because there was no shepherd."'" (Ezek. 34:1–5a)

When God looked at the corruption of His people, He laid the responsibility at the feet of the priests and of the clergy, who had been charged by God to feed the flock.

Now fast forward to the end of John's Gospel, to the post-resurrection discussion between Jesus and Peter, who was filled with remorse for having denied his Lord:

> So when they had eaten breakfast, Jesus said to Simon Peter, "Simon, *son* of Jonah, do you love Me more than these?"
>
> He said to Him, "Yes, Lord; You know that I love You."
>
> He said to him, "Feed My lambs."
>
> He said to him again a second time, "Simon, *son* of Jonah, do you love Me?"
>
> He said to Him, "Yes, Lord; You know that I love You."
>
> He said to him, "Tend My sheep."
>
> He said to him the third time, "Simon, *son* of Jonah, do you love Me?" Peter was grieved because He said to him the third time, "Do you love Me?"
>
> And he said to Him, "Lord, You know all things; You know that I love You."
>
> Jesus said to him, "Feed My sheep." (John 21:15–17)

The leaders of Israel failed to shepherd the flock. The Pharisees failed to shepherd the flock. Like them, the leaders of the church are called to be shepherds, but we too often fail to shepherd the people of God. Therefore, let us keep our eyes on the Good Shepherd, who laid down His life for us, for we are the sheep of His pasture.

28

THE SON OF GOD

John 10:22–42

Now it was the Feast of Dedication in Jerusalem, and it was winter. And Jesus walked in the temple, in Solomon's porch. Then the Jews surrounded Him and said to Him, "How long do You keep us in doubt? If You are the Christ, tell us plainly." Jesus answered them, "I told you, and you do not believe. The works that I do in My Father's name, they bear witness of Me. But you do not believe, because you are not of My sheep, as I said to you. My sheep hear My voice, and I know them, and they follow Me. And I give them eternal life, and they shall never perish; neither shall anyone snatch them out of My hand. My Father, who has given them to Me, is greater than all; and no one is able to snatch them out of My Father's hand. I and My Father are one." Then the Jews took up stones again to stone Him. Jesus answered them, "Many good works I have shown you from My Father. For which of those works do you stone Me?" The Jews answered Him, saying, "For a good work we do not stone You, but for blasphemy, and because You, being a Man, make Yourself God." Jesus answered them, "Is it not written in your law, 'I said, "You are gods"'? If He called them gods, to whom the word of God came (and the Scripture cannot be broken), do you say of Him whom the Father sanctified and sent into the world, 'You are blaspheming,' because I said, 'I am the Son of God'? If I do not do the works of My Father, do not believe Me; but if I do, though you do not believe Me, believe the works, that you may know and believe that the Father is in Me, and I in Him." Therefore they sought again to seize Him, but He escaped out of their hand. And He went away again beyond the Jordan to the place where John was baptizing at first, and there He stayed. Then many came to Him and said, "John performed no sign, but all the things that John spoke about this Man were true." And many believed in Him there.

After the Good Shepherd discourse in the first half of John 10, there is an apparent gap of time before John resumes his narrative during the Feast of Dedication. I noted earlier that John is prone to tell us the occasion when certain things took place, and often Jesus' encounters with the Jewish authorities occurred when He was in Jerusalem for one of the traditional feast days of the Jews, such as the Passover or the Feast of Tabernacles. But where in the Old Testament do we find mention of the Feast of Dedication? We don't, because this feast arose during the intertestamental period as a celebration of the victory of the Maccabees over the Seleucids in the second century BC. It became known as the Feast of Dedication and later the Feast of Lights, which is celebrated to this day as Hanukkah during the same period when we celebrate Christmas.

Jesus had come again to Jerusalem for the feast and was walking one day in Solomon's porch, a colonnade alongside the temple. There the Jewish leaders surrounded Him and demanded: **"How long do You keep us in doubt? If You are the Christ, tell us plainly"** (v. 24).

When I read this question that was put to Jesus, I am reminded of a similar circumstance that occurred in sixteenth-century Germany at the Diet of Worms, where Martin Luther was put on trial for his life before the princes of the church and Charles V, the Holy Roman emperor at the time. There at the Diet, the authorities placed on a table copies of all the books Luther had written, and his interrogator demanded that he recant his writings. Luther responded by saying: "Which writings? I have written many things. Surely you're not indicating that everything that I have written is heretical." He wanted the Roman Catholic authorities to specify exactly which of his works were regarded as heretical. But his interrogator would have none of it and asked Luther to answer "without horns," that is, simply and directly. That same kind of demand was made of Jesus at the Feast of Dedication:

"No more evasions, no more ambiguities. Speak to us 'without horns.' Tell us plainly, are you the Messiah?"

Jesus was not being evasive to escape personal consequences. Throughout His public ministry, He was careful about using the term *Messiah* to describe His role. He revealed who He was privately, to His disciples or to the woman at the well, for example. But when the public became too vocal in proclaiming Him to be the Messiah, He resisted. He had a good reason for that—they didn't understand what it meant for Him to be the Messiah. The popular view was that the Messiah would come as a warrior and drive the hated Romans out of the land. But Jesus understood that the office of Messiah was merged in the Old Testament with the office of the "Servant of the Lord," of whom Isaiah writes in the latter part of his book—that one who is called the "Suffering Servant of Israel." The people had no concept of a Messiah who would suffer and die. So Jesus was very guarded about the use of that title, particularly as the cross drew nearer.

A Message Already Conveyed

Let's listen to how He handled it in this instance. They said, "If You are the Christ, tell us plainly." **Jesus answered them, "I told you, and you do not believe. The works that I do in My Father's name, they bear witness of Me. But you do not believe, because you are not of My sheep, as I said to you. My sheep hear My voice, and I know them, and they follow Me. And I give them eternal life, and they shall never perish; neither shall anyone snatch them out of My hand. My Father, who has given them to Me, is greater than all; and no one is able to snatch them out of My Father's hand. I and My Father are one"** (vv. 25–30).

First, I want us to see that Jesus declared that He had told the Jews who He was, but they had not believed Him. How had He told them? By His works, His miracles, which plainly showed that He was God in the flesh. But the Jews could not understand the significance of His miracles because they were not of His sheep. It had not been granted to them by the Father to come to Jesus (6:65).

Second, notice that Jesus openly declared that there is a unity between Him and the Father. This text has been ripped from its context time and again in church history. In the fourth century, Arius used this verse to argue that Jesus was one with the Father only in the sense that they agreed on the same mission. In other words, the Father and the Son thought alike; they embraced the same ethic. But Arius denied that Jesus was God. Jesus, he said, did not share in the being of God or the essence of God, only the agenda of God. In our day, Jehovah's Witnesses and Mormons interpret this text the same way; they hold that it cannot be interpreted as an expression of deity for Jesus.

To get at the true meaning of Jesus' words here, we must consider them within their context—both the immediate context and the broader context of the whole book, and even that of the whole Bible. We know that since the very first chapter of this Gospel, John has been laboring the point of the deity of Christ; he began by saying that in the beginning, Christ "was with God" and "was God" (1:1). We see this purpose fulfilled again in this passage. Jesus said of His sheep, "I give them eternal life" (v. 28a). No creature has the power or the authority to give eternal life, but Jesus claimed to have that power and authority. Unmistakably, He claimed to be God.

He went on to say that His sheep "shall never perish; neither shall anyone snatch them out of My hand" (v. 28b). Many Christians wrestle with fears that they might lose their salvation. They wonder, "Can we really say, 'Once in grace, always in grace'?" We respond by saying, "If you have it, you never lose it; if you 'lose' it, you never had it," because that's what the New Testament teaches. We believe in the perseverance of the saints and the security of every believer, but not because we have an inflated view of our ability to persevere in the Christian life. If it were left to us, we would all fall away from the faith and perish. But Jesus promised here that He will keep all of His sheep secure; no one can rip them away from Him.

Here is a very simple illustration of this biblical concept. A strong father is walking with his three-year-old son beside a dangerous railroad track. There are two ways the father can protect the son. He can reach out his hand and say to the little boy, "Now listen, son, hold on tightly to my hand, because if you let go you could fall onto the tracks and be killed." Or the father can say, "Son, give me your hand," and he takes the boy's hand and holds on to him. Thus, the father holds on to the son rather than the son holding on to the father. Which is the surer method?

Jesus said no one can snatch His sheep out of His hand. We are secure, not because we hold tightly to Jesus, but because He holds tightly to us. Jesus said: "Every one of My sheep is going to have eternal life. They will never perish—I'm going to see to it. I give them eternal life, and nobody will snatch them out of My hand." This is a tremendous promise that affords great comfort, but it is a promise only God could make.

Jesus then repeated the promise with a twist. He said, "No one is able to snatch them out of *My Father's hand*" (v. 29b). Are the sheep held in the Son's hand or the Father's hand? The answer is simple—both. Jesus went on to say, "I and My Father are one" (v. 30). The Son and the Father are one in essence, with the Holy Spirit included as well. The preservation of the saints is the work of the triune God.

Who Is the Blasphemer?

Hearing these words, "I and My Father are one," the Jewish authorities began to grab stones to execute Jesus on the spot (v. 31). They heard Jesus' words. They understood He had just claimed that He was God, and they were convinced that He had blasphemed, for He was so clearly a man. It seems that Jesus had answered them *too* clearly this time.

John writes: **Jesus answered them, "Many good works I have shown you from My Father. For which of those works do you stone Me?" The Jews answered him saying, "For a good work we do not stone You, but for blasphemy, and because You, being a Man, make Yourself God"** (vv. 32–33). Why did Jesus bring up His works again? I believe this was an ironic question. Jesus' miracles had already well attested that He was from God and should have mitigated against any charge of blasphemy. But the Jewish authorities gave no credence to the miracles or to Jesus' claim to be God. They could admit no evidence except that which they beheld with their eyes—that Jesus was a man, and therefore could not be God.

They said, "We're stoning You for blasphemy because You, being a man, make Yourself God." How ironic it is that exactly the opposite had happened. As I noted above, John tells us in the very first verse of his Gospel that Jesus "was with God, and . . . was God." A little later he notes, "The Word became flesh and dwelt among us" (1:14a). The eternal second person of the Trinity, who from all eternity was very God of very God, became man. He took upon Himself a human nature. God *made Himself* man. But the Jewish authorities accused Jesus of being a man who *made Himself* God (or represented Himself as God). They got it completely backward.

Jesus' reply is difficult to understand. **Jesus answered them, "Is it not written in your law, 'I said, "You are gods"'? If He called them gods, to whom the word of God came (and the Scripture cannot be broken), do you say of Him whom the Father sanctified and sent into the world, 'You are blaspheming,' because I said, 'I am the Son of God'?"** (vv. 34–36). It almost sounds as if Jesus was trying to take advantage of a Jewish technical loophole here. He said: "You're accusing me of blasphemy because I call myself God. Aren't you familiar with the verse in the Old Testament where human beings are called 'gods'?" The verse Jesus cited is Psalm 82:6. In all probability, it was a reference to human judges, who carried out a divine function, dispensing justice. In popular nomenclature, they were called gods. So Jesus was appealing to historical precedent. He was saying: "In the Old Testament, some human beings were called gods and nobody picked up stones to kill them for blasphemy. Why are you ready to stone Me?"

By citing this verse, which gave evidence that some mere mortals were called gods, Jesus was not implying that He was a mere mortal too. That's not the way the argument was going. This is a "lesser to the greater" argument. Basically Jesus was saying to His adversaries, "If it was OK in Old Testament times for people who were mere mortals to be called gods, how much more legitimate is it for one who is God incarnate to be called God?"

Notice what He said about His identity: "Do you say of Him whom the Father sanctified and sent into the world, 'You are blaspheming,' because I said, 'I am the Son of God'?" Jesus was saying: "I am the One whom the Father set apart for this task of coming to the world to save My sheep. Do you think it is blasphemy for Me to say that God set Me apart for this? If God gave Me this holy mission and this holy task, if God sent Me into the world to perform the works that I've done before your very eyes, to accuse Me of blasphemy is the worst of all kinds of blasphemies." Of course, if God had not set Jesus apart and sent Him into the world, and He had then stood up and said, "I am the Son of God, I give everyone eternal life," with no corroborating miracles, that would have been blasphemy. But there was nothing in the thinking of His adversaries to even allow for the possibility of the incarnation of God.

In our day, the great stumbling block for the pagan is the resurrection. But in the first century, the great stumbling block for the enemies of the Christian faith was the incarnation—the idea that God would take upon Himself a human nature. That was the scandal to the first-century mind, and those who fought it and denied it were not His sheep. They were the wolves that wanted to destroy the sheep and the Shepherd together.

Jesus' View of Scripture

I do not want to pass over a brief parenthetical comment Jesus made in this passage: **"The Scripture cannot be broken"** (v. 35b). I'm often asked why I have such a high view of sacred Scripture. It's very simple. Let's assume the Bible is only basically reliable, not inspired, but simply a decent historical record from history. Let's further assume we go through it with a fine-tooth comb and get rid of all the passages that we think are not historical and just keep the ones that are undisputed among the critics. After all that, in that little piece of Scripture that would be left, we would find that Jesus of Nazareth taught that the Bible is more than generally reliable. Now if there's enough evidence to come to the conclusion that Jesus was a prophet, then what do we do with His prophetic teaching about the nature of Scripture? He tells us that Scripture is much more than basically reliable. It cannot be broken.

I've heard it said that the days of Billy Graham-style evangelism are over. No longer can a minister stand up in a pulpit and hold up this book and say, "The Bible says . . . ." We're too sophisticated for that, because we believe that our increase in knowledge and critical understanding has smashed the authority of Scripture into smithereens. But Jesus disagreed. He said Scripture cannot be broken.

Jesus went on to say, **"If I do not do the works of My Father, do not believe Me; but if I do, though you do not believe Me, believe the works, that you may know and believe that the Father is in Me, and I in Him"** (vv. 37–38). Jesus' challenge to the Jewish leaders was to consider His words in the light of His works. As we have discussed again and again throughout this study, miracles are intended by God to corroborate divine revelation. The Pharisees and their cohorts needed to see that the wonderful miracles Jesus was doing proved that He was who He said He was.

There was another attempt to seize Jesus at that point, but He escaped and left Jerusalem. John writes that He **went away again beyond the Jordan to the place where John was baptizing at first, and there He stayed** (v. 40). This is the only hint we get as to where Jesus went after He departed from Jerusalem in the midst of the hostility and the threats of the Jewish authorities. Some commentators think He went a day's journey across the Jordan. Others believe that He went farther north. In any case, the location is significant for our understanding of the events that unfolded soon afterward, as recorded in John 11—the death and resurrection of Lazarus.

As we go forward, keep Jesus' words from this passage, "I and My Father are one," in mind. Later, in His High Priestly Prayer, we will see Jesus praying that His disciples may be one even as He and the Father are one. Most people take that to mean organizational unity, doctrinal unity, and so forth. But Jesus spoke in His High Priestly Prayer in the same manner He spoke here. You and I may totally disagree on certain doctrines, but if you and I are both Christians, then I am in Christ and you are in Christ, and Christ is in me and Christ is in you. We don't have to have an ecumenical meeting to be one in Christ. We are one with Him and with one another.

29

THE DEATH OF LAZARUS

John 11:1–27

Now a certain man was sick, Lazarus of Bethany, the town of Mary and her sister Martha. It was that Mary who anointed the Lord with fragrant oil and wiped His feet with her hair, whose brother Lazarus was sick. Therefore the sisters sent to Him, saying, "Lord, behold, he whom You love is sick." When Jesus heard that, He said, "This sickness is not unto death, but for the glory of God, that the Son of God may be glorified through it." Now Jesus loved Martha and her sister and Lazarus. So, when He heard that he was sick, He stayed two more days in the place where He was. Then after this He said to the disciples, "Let us go to Judea again." The disciples said to Him, "Rabbi, lately the Jews sought to stone You, and are You going there again?" Jesus answered, "Are there not twelve hours in the day? If anyone walks in the day, he does not stumble, because he sees the light of this world. But if one walks in the night, he stumbles, because the light is not in him." These things He said, and after that He said to them, "Our friend Lazarus sleeps, but I go that I may wake him up." Then His disciples said, "Lord, if he sleeps he will get well." However, Jesus spoke of his death, but they thought that He was speaking about taking rest in sleep. Then Jesus said to them plainly, "Lazarus is dead. And I am glad for your sakes that I was not there, that you may believe. Nevertheless let

us go to him." Then Thomas, who is called the Twin, said to his fellow
disciples, "Let us also go, that we may die with Him." So when Jesus came,
He found that he had already been in the tomb four days. Now Bethany
was near Jerusalem, about two miles away. And many of the Jews had
joined the women around Martha and Mary, to comfort them concerning
their brother. Now Martha, as soon as she heard that Jesus was coming,
went and met Him, but Mary was sitting in the house. Now Martha said
to Jesus, "Lord, if You had been here, my brother would not have died.
But even now I know that whatever You ask of God, God will give You."
Jesus said to her, "Your brother will rise again." Martha said to Him, "I
know that he will rise again in the resurrection at the last day." Jesus said
to her, "I am the resurrection and the life. He who believes in Me, though
he may die, he shall live. And whoever lives and believes in Me shall never
die. Do you believe this?" She said to Him, "Yes, Lord, I believe that You
are the Christ, the Son of God, who is to come into the world."

Jesus left Jerusalem for an unspecified location after nearly being stoned by
the Jewish leaders during the Feast of Dedication. While He was there,
He received a message. John writes: **Now a certain man was sick,
Lazarus of Bethany, the town of Mary and her sister Martha. It
was that Mary who anointed the Lord with fragrant oil and wiped
His feet with her hair, whose brother Lazarus was sick. Therefore
the sisters sent to Him, saying, "Lord, behold, he whom You love
is sick." When Jesus heard that, He said, "This sickness is not
unto death, but for the glory of God, that the Son of God may be
glorified through it"** (vv. 1–4).

Mary, Martha, and Lazarus were three adult siblings who lived together in
Bethany, a village just outside Jerusalem. Mary is noted in history for anointing
Jesus' feet with expensive oil and wiping them with her hair (John 12:1–3).
Apparently Jesus knew this family well and loved them greatly. It seems also
that they were disciples of Jesus who supported His ministry. Therefore, it is
not surprising that the sisters summoned Jesus when Lazarus fell ill. They had
seen others healed and hoped Jesus would do the same for their brother.

When Jesus received this message, He did not immediately set out for
Bethany. Instead, He said, "This sickness is not unto death, but for the glory
of God, that the Son of God may be glorified through it." He said that the
purpose of this illness that had befallen Lazarus was not to terminate his life

in this world, but he had been visited with this affliction for the glory of God, that the glory of the Son of God would be made manifest through it.

It's important that we understand the meaning of Jesus' words here. In the early days of the Christian church, debate raged over the deity of Christ. There were those who resisted the concept of the deity of Christ because they believed that glorifying Jesus would detract from the glory of God the Father. They were not speaking of the glorification of Christ that occurs when we praise Him, but glorification in the sense of the revelation of the greatness and majesty of His person. But the point of the New Testament teaching both here and in the Epistles is that the Father is glorified through the glory of His Son. So as Christ is revealed as the Son of God and exalted, God the Father is glorified also. So in the glorification of Christ comes the glorification of the Father. It was with this idea in mind that Jesus said to His disciples: "Let's not worry about this. Lazarus is not sick unto death, but this is for My glory and for the glory of God."

Curious Statements and Actions

Then we read a most curious statement: **"Now Jesus loved Martha and her sister and Lazarus. So, when He heard that he was sick, He stayed two more days in the place where He was"** (vv. 5–6). If Jesus loved Martha, Mary, and Lazarus, why did He linger instead of going to His sick friend? His action almost seems heartless. But as we will see, there was a very good reason for Jesus to delay—so that God might be glorified to the utmost.

Finally, at the end of the two days, Jesus took action: **Then after this He said to the disciples, "Let us go to Judea again"** (v. 7). This directive provoked something of a crisis among the disciples. They hastily reminded Him that the Jews had been on the verge of stoning Him during His last visit to Jerusalem; to go there was to risk His life (v. 8). Jesus replied, first cryptically, then more plainly. He said: **"Are there not twelve hours in the day? If anyone walks in the day, he does not stumble, because he sees the light of this world. But if one walks in the night, he stumbles, because the light is not in him." These things He said, and after that He said to them, "Our friend Lazarus sleeps, but I go that I may wake him up"** (vv. 9–11). He was telling them that just as a typical day in their agrarian culture had a number of hours of daylight in which work could be done, He had a set amount of time in which to accomplish the deeds given Him by His Father. In other words: "The night of My soul has not yet come. I still have work to do. The day is not finished. And My ministry to Lazarus is part of that work."

Jesus' statement that "Lazarus sleeps," by which He meant that Lazarus had died, is unusual because that euphemism for death is almost never found in biblical language. Not surprisingly, therefore, the disciples missed Jesus' meaning: **Then His disciples said, "Lord, if he sleeps he will get well"** (v. 12). They took Jesus' announcement that Lazarus was sleeping as evidence that he must be convalescing. But John makes plain that Jesus was telling them that Lazarus had died (v. 13), and then Jesus Himself said it straightforwardly: **"Lazarus is dead"** (v. 14).

However, Jesus then added another astounding statement. Immediately after saying "Lazarus is dead," He added, **"And I am glad for your sakes that I was not there, that you may believe. Nevertheless let us go to him"** (v. 15). Gladness isn't the usual response to the death of a friend, but Jesus stated that the reason for His gladness had to do with the disciples. Because of Lazarus' death, and because of what He knew He was going to do, the disciples would see His power made manifest and would be strengthened in their faith in Him. In this way, God would bring good out of the agony of Lazarus' death.

These words from Jesus were not quite enough to reassure at least one of Jesus' disciples—Thomas. He said with resignation, **"Let us also go, that we may die with Him"** (v. 16). Thomas was sure that returning to Judea was a fatal mistake for Jesus, and probably for all of Jesus' disciples, too.

John then writes, **So when Jesus came, He found that he had already been in the tomb four days** (v. 17). The fact that Lazarus had been buried for four days may seem like an insignificant detail, but it helps us get at the reason for Jesus' delay in going to Bethany. Among the rabbinic teachings in Jesus' day was the idea that when a person died, the person's spirit hovered over the body for three days, and if, somehow, the body was resuscitated, the spirit returned to it. But according to the rabbinic tradition, the spirit departed after three days and the body was beyond all hope of resuscitation at that point. In light of this teaching, it seems likely that Jesus wanted to get to Bethany after the three days had passed so that, once He had raised Lazarus from the grave, the Jewish authorities could not say Lazarus' spirit had been lingering and his body had merely been resuscitated. By delaying His return, Jesus let enough time pass to make it absolutely certain that the raising of Lazarus was completely against nature and could not be seen as anything other than a miracle.

Accusation or Affirmation?

When Jesus drew near to Bethany, word of His coming was passed to the sisters, and Martha went out to meet him (v. 20). Martha said, **"Lord if You had been here, my brother would not have died. But even now I know that whatever You ask of God, God will give You"** (vv. 21–22). How should we interpret this? This is one of those times when we wish we could hear the tones and inflections of voice that were used by the speaker. This might have been an accusation: "Some friend You are! Why do You think we sent a message to You? If only You had been here, this wouldn't have happened." But I prefer to think this was a triumphant statement of confidence in Christ: "Lord, we know that had You been here, You would have healed Lazarus." I think Martha's following statement lends credence to that interpretation. She said: "Lord, even now I know that whatever You ask of God, God will do it. Even though Lazarus died, Jesus, my confidence in You remains, and I know that You're in such harmony with God that this has to be of God."

Jesus said, **"Your brother will rise again"** (v. 23). Martha didn't understand—or perhaps she didn't dare to hope that what He said might happen. She said, **"I know that he will rise again in the resurrection at the last day"** (v. 24). The question of a resurrection at the end of history was hotly debated in Jesus' time; the Pharisees believed there would be a resurrection, but the Sadducees did not. Martha apparently was with the Pharisees on this question; she was persuaded of the future resurrection of the people of God. So when Jesus said, "Your brother will rise again," she confessed her faith that he would be raised at the last day. But that wasn't what Jesus was speaking about.

Jesus then said to her: **"I am the resurrection and the life"** (v. 25a). This is the fifth of the seven "I am" sayings of Jesus in the Gospel of John. Jesus was saying: "I hold the keys of life and of death. I am the foundation, the power of life itself, and I have the power to raise dead people from the grave. I don't just teach the resurrection, I *am* the resurrection. I am the very power of God unto life."

Jesus then added a pair of comments that are somewhat curious: **"He who believes in Me, though he may die, he shall live. And whoever lives and believes in Me shall never die. Do you believe this?"** (vv. 25b–26). First He said, "He who believes in Me, though he may die, he shall live." In other words, if a person meets the precondition of believing on Jesus, he will live—even if he dies. Then He said something even stronger: "Whoever lives and believes in Me shall never die. Do you believe this?"

The day before I preached on this passage at St. Andrew's, the space shuttle Columbia disintegrated over Texas while heading for a landing here in Central Florida. All seven astronauts aboard were killed. I watched television coverage of the tragedy for hour after hour that day, but the same picture was shown over and over again. It was the image of the spacecraft disintegrating and leaving a trail of smoke in the air. I couldn't help thinking what a catastrophe this was for the families of the people who had been instantly destroyed, but I also thought that if there were believers among those crew members, just as quickly as they died, they were in heaven. If they were believers, they could not die. Yes, they died biologically, but biological death doesn't disturb the continuity of living, personal existence for God's people in the slightest. This is what Jesus said. Once a person believes in Christ, the life of Christ is poured into the soul of that person, and that life is eternal. Everyone who is in Christ has already begun to experience eternal life. We're never going to die. We may go through the transition of physical death, but that death cannot destroy the life that Christ has given to us.

In answer to Jesus' question, "Do you believe this?" Martha said, **"Yes, Lord, I believe that You are the Christ, the Son of God, who is to come into the world"** (v. 27). I don't think there is a greater confession of faith anywhere in Scripture than this confession that Martha made in the midst of her sorrow. She had seen Jesus' miracles and heard His authoritative teaching, and she had believed He was who He said He was.

Jesus is the resurrection and the life for all of His people. If you believe in Him, you will never die. Like Martha, do you believe this?

30

THE RAISING OF LAZARUS

John 11:28–44

And when she had said these things, she went her way and secretly called Mary her sister, saying, "The Teacher has come and is calling for you." As soon as she heard that, she arose quickly and came to Him. Now Jesus had not yet come into the town, but was in the place where Martha met Him. Then the Jews who were with her in the house, and comforting her, when they saw that Mary rose up quickly and went out, followed her, saying, "She is going to the tomb to weep there." Then, when Mary came where Jesus was, and saw Him, she fell down at His feet, saying to Him, "Lord, if You had been here, my brother would not have died." Therefore, when Jesus saw her weeping, and the Jews who came with her weeping, He groaned in the spirit and was troubled. And He said, "Where have you laid him?" They said to Him, "Lord, come and see." Jesus wept. Then the Jews said, "See how He loved him!" And some of them said, "Could not this Man, who opened the eyes of the blind, also have kept this man from dying?" Then Jesus, again groaning in Himself, came to the tomb. It was a cave, and a stone lay against it. Jesus said, "Take away the stone." Martha, the sister of him who was dead, said to Him, "Lord, by this time there is a stench, for he has been dead four days." Jesus said to her, "Did I not say to you that if you would believe you would see the glory of God?" Then they took away the stone from the place where the dead man was lying. And Jesus lifted up His eyes and said, "Father, I thank You that You have heard Me. And I know that You always hear Me, but because of the people who are standing by I said this, that they may believe that You sent Me." Now when He had said these things, He cried with a loud voice, "Lazarus, come forth!" And he who had died came out bound hand and foot with graveclothes, and his face was wrapped with a cloth. Jesus said to them, "Loose him, and let him go."

Back in the 1960s, Vesta and I had the privilege of living in the Boston area for a couple of years. This was during the heyday of the Boston Celtics, when the team seemed to have an annual date in the NBA Championship behind players like John Havlicek, Bill Russell, and K. C. Jones. There was a player for the Celtics of that era whom you almost never hear about anymore, a player who was one of the best shooters on the team. His name was Sam Jones, and he was known for getting his shot off faster than anybody else in the league. In fact, he was so fast, when someone would pass him the ball, he'd make his jump shot—swish!—and they would say, "Too late." So he was known as Sam "Too Late" Jones, which was a compliment to him.

In the passage before us, it is said to Jesus, "Lord, you're too late," and it is not meant as a compliment. When Jesus came to Bethany in response to the summons of Mary and Martha, it seemed He was too late to see His friend Lazarus or to be of help in any way—Lazarus had already been in the tomb for four days. As we see in the passage before us, many in Bethany certainly thought He was too late. But they were thinking only in terms of healing. Christ is never too late.

The Comfort of Friends

In the previous chapter, we examined the discussion between Jesus and Martha in which Jesus affirmed that He was "the resurrection and the life" (v. 25) and Martha declared her belief that Jesus was the Messiah, the Son of God (v. 27). Then, at the request of Jesus, Martha went to call Mary and said, **"The Teacher has come and is calling for you"** (v. 28). Mary immediately got up and left her house to go see Jesus (v. 29), who was waiting for her somewhere just outside the village (v. 30).

John tells us earlier in this narrative that "many of the Jews" had come to comfort Mary and Martha after Lazarus' death (v. 19). When these people saw Mary suddenly leave the house, they said, **"She is going to the tomb to weep there"** (v. 31b). Desiring to comfort her, they followed.

Scripture says, "The heart of the wise is in the house of mourning, but the heart of fools is in the house of mirth" (Eccl. 7:4). I believe there is something sacred, something holy, about people coming together to bring human comfort to those who have lost loved ones. But it's hard to do, isn't it? When we go to a funeral home or to visit someone who has just lost a loved one, we feel nervous because we want to think of some profound way to express our sympathy. What do we say?

My father was an invalid for three years before he died. He sat in his chair all day long, completely alone. I became rather bitter about that as a boy. I asked my mother: "Why is it that none of Dad's friends ever come to visit him? He was always the first one in their homes when trouble arose." My mother said: "Son, they're too embarrassed to see your father like this because they don't know how to handle it. They don't know what to say."

The truth is, it doesn't really matter what we say in such instances; in fact, we don't have to say anything. Just by going, touching the bereaved person, squeezing his or her hand, or putting an arm around him or her, we show love and concern. That is a profoundly meaningful thing.

John tells us, **Then, when Mary came where Jesus was, and saw Him, she fell down at His feet, saying to Him, "Lord, if You had been here, my brother would not have died"** (v. 32). As with Martha's comment (v. 21), I hate to think that this was a rebuke. But there is a hint, a suggestion, that Mary's anguish over the loss of her brother was intensified by Jesus' failure to be there when she needed Him and when she expected Him. In a sense, Mary was saying, "Lord, You're too late."

We then come to verses that profoundly communicate the humanity of the Lord Jesus. We're told, **Therefore, when Jesus saw her weeping, and the Jews who came with her weeping, He groaned in the spirit and was troubled** (v. 33). The expressions of mourning that Jesus witnessed moved Him deeply. Frankly, however, I'm troubled by this verse, specifically the translation. I have to wonder whether the actual meaning of the original Greek bothered the translator, so that he didn't want to be exact in translating the term. I say this because the force of the verb here is much stronger than is indicated by the word *troubled*. A more accurate translation would be, "Jesus was irate." Jesus saw everybody around Him weeping and groaned in anger.

Why would Jesus have been angry? Some commentators suggest that maybe Jesus was angry at Mary and Martha and the crowd for their lack of faith.

Hadn't He just told Martha that He was the resurrection and the life? Maybe He was thinking, "What do I have to do to convince you people that I have power over life and death?"

Personally, I think that which caused the anger of the Son of God to boil up and overflow in His spirit was that He was in the presence of the ravaging destruction of the greatest enemy of mankind, death. This was His enemy. This was the foe that, in only a few days, He was going to confront head on in the throes of the agony He would experience on the cross, dying to conquer death. Sometimes when I go to a hospital and I see people suffering with cancer, I walk out and I say, "I hate cancer!" The affliction is so great and the pain is so enormous. I think this is the kind of visceral reaction Jesus had when He encountered the sorrow that death had provoked. Jesus entered into the affliction of His people so deeply that He was moved within Himself at the travesty of death.

From Anger to Grief

Then Jesus asked, **"Where have you laid him?" They said to him, "Lord, come and see." Jesus wept** (vv. 34–35). Jesus asked to see Lazarus' tomb, then, overcome, He wept. Verse 35 is the shortest verse in all of the Bible, but surely it is one of the most poignant. It does not tell us that Mary wept; we've already read that. It does not tell us that the Jews were weeping; we've already read that. It tells us that Jesus, the incarnate Son of God, the eternal Word of God, shed tears. Why did He weep? Had Jesus given in to despair? Did He not know what He was about to do? The Word of God teaches us, "Rejoice with those who rejoice, and weep with those who weep" (Rom. 12:15). Jesus was on the verge of perhaps His greatest miracle, but He entered into the feelings of grief and loss of those whom He loved. He wept with them at the tomb of Lazarus.

Jesus' tears did not go unnoticed: **Then the Jews said, "See how He loved him!" And some of them said, "Could not this Man, who opened the eyes of the blind, also have kept this man from dying?"** (vv. 36–37). The answer to this question is apparent—of course Jesus could have prevented Lazarus' death. But He did not, that the glory of God might be revealed (v. 4) and that His disciples' faith in Him might be strengthened (v. 15). It was good that those who asked this question trusted Jesus to heal. But they needed to know the full extent of His power.

Finally Jesus stood outside Lazarus' tomb. **Then Jesus, again groaning in Himself, came to the tomb. It was a cave, and a stone lay against it. Jesus said, "Take away the stone." Martha, the sister**

of him who was dead, said to Him, "Lord, by this time there is a stench, for he has been dead four days" (vv. 38–39). Martha was concerned about protocol—opening the tomb would release a foul odor. But at its root, this was an expression of unbelief. Therefore, Jesus said to Martha, **"Did I not say to you that if you would believe you would see the glory of God?"** (v. 40).

How do you feel when someone says to you, "I told you so"? How would you like to have Jesus say that to you? I can imagine that if God were to judge me for every trespass, I would probably hear Christ say to me, at least a hundred thousand times, "I told you this—why didn't you believe Me?" or "I said this would happen—why did you ignore Me?" It's so easy to believe in God; believing God is the test of the Christian life. It seems that Martha flunked the test here. In an instant, she forgot the promise of Christ for her, and Jesus had to remind her.

With that, **they took away the stone from the place where the dead man was lying. And Jesus lifted up His eyes, and said, "Father, I thank You that You have heard me. And I know that You always hear Me, but because of the people who are standing by I said this, that they may believe that You sent Me"** (vv. 41–42). In other words, Jesus said to His Father: "We've already had this conversation, Father, and I know You've heard Me. You know what I want; You know what I'm going to do. I know You've authorized Me; I have the assurance that You're going to heed what I request of You. I know that. But sometimes, Father, I have to pray for the benefit of other people, that they may know what's going on here."

Waking the Dead Man

John then writes, **Now when He had said these things, He cried with a loud voice, "Lazarus, come forth!"** (v. 43). Jesus didn't whisper an invitation to the corpse. He didn't use His regular tone of conversation. We are told that He cried with a loud voice; He shouted. This was a command given in power. The result was stupefying: **he who had died came out bound hand and foot with graveclothes, and his face was wrapped with a cloth** (v. 44a).

Sometimes exasperated parents facetiously tell their boisterous children, "You're so loud you could wake the dead." Jesus' command really was loud enough to wake the dead. His divine word of command echoed to the depths of Lazarus' tomb, penetrated the graveclothes, and brought life where there was death. The moment the voice of Christ called on Lazarus to come forth,

Lazarus' heart began to beat again, nerve impulses began to race throughout his body, and his rotting, putrefying flesh became whole and healed. Then Lazarus got up and walked out of the tomb with the graveclothes hanging from his body. He was alive again. **Jesus said to them, "Loose him, and let him go"** (v. 44b).

What would you do if you saw something like that? I'm sure some of the people stood paralyzed with fear or with astonishment, gasping at what their eyes had just beheld. This may have been the greatest of all Jesus' miracles during His incarnation, the climax to all the other signs He had performed earlier to corroborate who He was.

The raising of Lazarus is a glorious picture of what Jesus has done for us. We were "dead in trespasses and sins," Paul tells us in Ephesians 2:1. But the One who is "the resurrection and the life," the One who has the power of life and the power of death in His hand and in His Word, has called us from spiritual death and made us alive together with Him. We should stand in awe of such love and such power, then fall to our knees to confess that Jesus is the life-giving Savior and worthy of all glory.

31

EXPEDIENCY AND
EXTRAVAGANCE

John 11:45–12:8

Then many of the Jews who had come to Mary, and had seen the things Jesus did, believed in Him. But some of them went away to the Pharisees and told them the things Jesus did. Then the chief priests and the Pharisees gathered a council and said, "What shall we do? For this Man works many signs. If we let Him alone like this, everyone will believe in Him, and the Romans will come and take away both our place and nation." And one of them, Caiaphas, being high priest that year, said to them, "You know nothing at all, nor do you consider that it is expedient for us that one man should die for the people, and not that the whole nation should perish." Now this he did not say on his own authority; but being high priest that year he prophesied that Jesus would die for the nation, and not for that nation only, but also that He would gather together in one the children of God who were scattered abroad. Then, from that day on, they plotted to put Him to death. Therefore Jesus no longer walked openly among the Jews, but went from there into the country near the wilderness, to a city called Ephraim, and there remained with His disciples. And the Passover of the

Jews was near, and many went from the country up to Jerusalem before the
Passover, to purify themselves. Then they sought Jesus, and spoke among
themselves as they stood in the temple, "What do you think—that He will
not come to the feast?" Now both the chief priests and the Pharisees had
given a command, that if anyone knew where He was, he should report it,
that they might seize Him. Then, six days before the Passover, Jesus came
to Bethany, where Lazarus was who had been dead, whom He had raised
from the dead. There they made Him a supper; and Martha served, but
Lazarus was one of those who sat at the table with Him. Then Mary took
a pound of very costly oil of spikenard, anointed the feet of Jesus, and
wiped His feet with her hair. And the house was filled with the fragrance
of the oil. But one of His disciples, Judas Iscariot, Simon's son, who would
betray Him, said, "Why was this fragrant oil not sold for three hundred
denarii and given to the poor?" This he said, not that he cared for the
poor, but because he was a thief, and had the money box; and he used to
take what was put in it. But Jesus said, "Let her alone; she has kept this
for the day of My burial. For the poor you have with you always, but Me
you do not have always."

When I was in graduate school in the 1960s, a little book titled *The
Secular City* appeared. It troubled the theological world and put
the name of its author, Harvard Professor Harvey Cox, on the
map. In this book, Cox gave a sociological and theological analysis for the
decline of the United States into secularization. He also discussed the shape
of American culture, which he said was determined by pragmatism, America's
only indigenous philosophical system. Pragmatism, as a philosophical system,
is born out of skepticism as to our ability to understand ultimate truth. So
the pioneers of pragmatism, who, ironically, belonged to the Metaphysical
Club at Harvard, disowned any hope of discovering metaphysical truth and
addressed themselves to this question: "How do we live in a world where we
can't discern ultimate truth?" In this system, the good and the true is defined
as that which works.

Pragmatism is not really new. For instance, Socrates was provoked toward
his campaign for truth in Athens by the philosophy of sophism, which, in
that day, was a school of pragmatism that was skeptical of attaining ultimate
truth. This kind of skeptical philosophy has been around for ages. We even
encounter it here in the Gospel of John as we meet Caiaphas, the king of the
pragmatists of the first century.

The Reason for the Hostility

After Jesus raised Lazarus from the dead, the people were divided; many who had seen the miracle **believed in Him. But some of them went away to the Pharisees and told them the things Jesus did** (vv. 45b–46). With that, the authorities began to lay plans for the arrest and the elimination of Jesus. **The chief priests and the Pharisees gathered a council** (v. 47a), and at this council the question before them was stated this way: **"What shall we do? For this Man works many signs. If we let Him alone like this, everyone will believe in Him, and the Romans will come and take away both our place and nation"** (vv. 47b–48).

Here, at last, we discover the key motivation for the Jewish authorities' hatred of Jesus: they feared that Jesus' growing popularity might spark an uprising that the Romans would be forced to crush, and that in the imposition of order they might lose what little authority they had under the Roman yoke. The Romans allowed a certain measure of home rule to the nations they conquered; that meant that the Pharisees and the Sadducees enjoyed certain positions of authority on the council and a high degree of prestige. But Jesus threatened their situation.

Some years ago, I was asked to write an essay on the question of contemporary persecution in the Christian church. We have heard ghastly reports from various places around the world where Christians are being persecuted routinely. In my essay, I was asked to address this question: "Why don't we suffer the same level of persecution here in the United States?" There are many explanations for that. Part of it is the fact that this country was founded by refugees from religious persecution who tried to do everything in their power to structure our culture and our laws so as to guarantee religious freedom and the free exercise of religion. But we've seen a subtle shift away from toleration toward Christianity and a growing hostility from the secular world to the Christian faith in general and to Christians in particular.

However, that's not the whole story. Another part of the story is that we American Christians have become very artful in conflict avoidance. In the pages of the New Testament, we see the passion of the apostle Paul as he went on his missionary journeys and proclaimed the exclusivity of Jesus Christ as Savior and Lord. In the midst of paganism, he unabashedly declared monotheism. The response of people in some places was to throw Paul and his compatriots into jail, to beat them, or even to stone him. But we have learned to avoid that sort of thing; we say that it just isn't practical to be too bold in the proclamation of the gospel today. In other words, we have embraced expediency.

It has been said that the church in the United States of America has been placed on a reservation. We're still allowed to exist; we're still allowed to practice our faith; we're still allowed to pray in our churches. But we are tacitly forbidden from moving off the reservation and into the public square to make public proclamations of faith. For instance, if a Christian is asked to pray at a public event and then prays in Jesus' name, he is almost certain to be excoriated for having the audacity to pray publicly in the name of Christ. We're simply not allowed to do that today.

But I have noticed that it isn't just secularists who howl when a Christian wanders off the reservation and proclaims the gospel in the public square. Other Christians also make a fuss. Why? Because when some Christians draw the ire of secular society, everyone who enjoys peace on the reservation becomes frightened that they will become targets of the enemy. Many who claim the name of Christ would rather live peacefully on the reservation than disturb the world with the good news.

That's exactly what happened in Jerusalem. Those to whom God had entrusted the ministry of the truth of His Word compromised again and again so as not to upset the Romans and possibly endanger their positions of prestige. Thus, when Jesus attracted a following, the Jewish leaders said to themselves: "If we leave this man alone, He will stir up so much trouble that the Romans will take action. They'll come after us because they'll see that Jesus is a Jew, and we'll be held responsible for not controlling one of our own. Then our place and our whole nation will be lost. So what are we going to do?" In short, the Jews wanted to prevent Jesus from causing a stir among the people lest they lose their positions of power.

The Expedient Solution

At that point, one of their number proposed a solution: **And one of them, Caiaphas, being high priest that year, said to them, "You know nothing at all, nor do you consider that it is expedient for us that one man should die for the people, and not that the whole nation should perish"** (vv. 49–50).

Do you ever wonder why Pontius Pilate's name was included in the Apostles' Creed? The creed says in part, "I believe . . . in Jesus Christ, [the Father's] only Son, our Lord, who was conceived by the Holy Ghost, born of the Virgin Mary, suffered under Pontius Pilate, was crucified, dead, and buried. . . ." What was it about Pontius Pilate that made him so important as to be a part of this historic confession of faith? The Roman emperor didn't make it; Annas didn't make it; Caiaphas didn't make it. But Pontius Pilate did.

Historians say he made it because he passed judgment on Jesus, saying, "I find no fault in Him at all" (John 18:38) and "Behold the Man!" (John 19:5). The idea historically is that, in spite of himself, Pilate declared the truth of God in his judgment of Christ. God brings His Word to pass, even through unwilling spokesmen. In the end, however, Pilate was a pragmatist—he let Jesus be crucified to head off a "tumult" (Matt. 27:24). He refused to ask, "What's the right thing to do?" Instead, he asked, "What's the expedient thing to do?" The Jews, led by Caiaphas, did the same thing.

Several years ago, I was asked to serve on a presbytery commission charged with investigating a conflict that was threatening to split a local church. The chairman of the commission said, "Let's interview the pastor, the assistant pastor, the elders, and some people from the congregation." When we had done all that and had reviewed our notes, he said: "There's real conflict in this church. First, we need to come up with a solution that will protect the pastor, the assistant pastor, all the elders, and these members of the congregation. Is there anything else we're supposed to do?" I said, "Yes, our primary task is to administer justice according to truth and to grace, not just make a decision designed to keep everybody happy. That's not going to happen anyway." I believe we as a commission were in danger of falling prey to the spirit of pragmatism and expediency that has been in the heart of human beings from the beginning.

Do you realize how much like Caiaphas we are? We often make decisions out of fear. We don't want to be nonconformists; we don't want to have people think that we're marching to a different drumbeat; we don't want to provoke the hostility of the world. So we remain silent.

I once received a letter from an organization reporting that the leading distributor of pornography on cable television in the United States was a company owned by General Motors. The second largest purveyor of pornography was a subsidiary of AT&T. These companies are icons in our culture, yet according to this letter, they were making large sums of money with this filthy enterprise. We are confronted with issues like this all the time, but who wants to cry, "Foul"? It's not expedient to cry, "Foul." It's expedient to keep our mouths shut and remain safe.

Every time the gospel has been proclaimed boldly and accurately in church history, there has been persecution. Every time the church speaks out to confront ungodliness in the culture, there is a backlash. I have no desire to go looking for persecution and conflict, but the fact that I live so free of persecution makes me question my commitment to the things of God. I don't like conflict, but I hate to stand among people like Caiaphas.

John goes on to say, **Now this he did not say on his own authority; but being high priest that year he prophesied that Jesus would die for the nation, and not for that nation only, but also that He would gather together in one the children of God who were scattered abroad. Then, from that day on, they plotted to put Him to death** (vv. 51–53). Caiaphas was utterly expedient, but there was more going on here. John tells us that the high priest prophesied without knowing it. Jesus would die for the people, and not just those among the Jews but all His people. So, with the high priest's blessing, plans for Jesus' execution moved into high gear. As a result, Jesus left Jerusalem and **went from there into the country near the wilderness, to a city called Ephraim, and there remained with His disciples** (v. 54).

An Act of Extravagant Love

Immediately following this display of callous expediency on the part of Caiaphas, John gives us a much different picture. In the opening verses of Chapter 12, he shows us a manifestation of extravagant love and worship for Jesus. It happened sometime later, some six days before the Passover, when Jesus came back to Bethany and was invited to supper in the home of Mary, Martha, and Lazarus, whom He had raised from the dead. During the meal, **Mary took a pound of very costly oil of spikenard, anointed the feet of Jesus, and wiped His feet with her hair. And the house was filled with the fragrance of the oil** (v. 3).

This was an act of great devotion and humility. We have already seen that John the Baptist declared he was not worthy to untie Jesus' sandal strap (John 1:27). A rabbi's disciple was essentially a servant to his teacher, but he was never required to attend to his master's feet, for that was considered the lowest task of all. When John said he was not worthy to untie Jesus' sandal strap, he was saying he was lower than a disciple. Mary probably felt the same way, but she gladly cleansed Jesus' feet. She was happy to do for Him what a servant would be required to do.

This precious ointment was worth about one year's salary for people at that time, but Mary used it all in seconds. This was extravagant love. There are times for extravagance, and it is always time for an extravagant manifestation of adoration to Christ. What could you and I possibly do that would be too extravagant in honoring Jesus, too extravagant in praising Him, too extravagant in giving Him glory? Anyone who has ever been in love at some point has made an extravagant gift for the one that he or she loved, and the only justification for it was the love that he or she felt. If we love Christ, it is appropriate to love Him extravagantly, for He is worthy of extravagant love.

There was one at this supper who did not approve of such extravagance—Judas Iscariot. John writes: **But one of His disciples, Judas Iscariot, Simon's son, who would betray Him, said, "Why was this fragrant oil not sold for three hundred denarii and given to the poor?" This he said, not that he cared for the poor, but because he was a thief, and had the money box; and he used to take what was put in it** (vv. 4–6). Judas watched what Mary did and was upset. He objected, saying: "What are you doing? Don't you realize how much that ointment is worth? We should have sold it and given the money to the poor." He portrayed himself as driven by humanitarian concerns, but John tells us what was in his heart. He wanted that money to stay in the treasury because he had the key to the treasury. He was the keeper of the purse for Jesus and His disciples, and he sometimes helped himself to what was in it. When Mary anointed Jesus' feet, he saw a lot of potential profit for himself poured out on the floor.

Jesus defended Mary's action. He said, **"Let her alone; she has kept this for the day of My burial. For the poor you have with you always, but Me you do not have always"** (v. 7–8). Jesus' words here may sound callous, but He was not saying the poor should be ignored. Rather, He was saying that the opportunity to serve Him in a tangible way would not last long, while ministry to the poor would always be in demand.

I knew a minister who labored for decades in the inner city of Cleveland, Ohio. He worked among the poor, the oppressed, and those who were addicted to drugs and all kinds of violence. Oddly, he had one associate pastor after another; the average tenure of the ministers who came alongside to help him was two years. I asked him, "Why don't they last?" He said the problem was that they quickly became disillusioned. They came out of seminary and came to the ghetto because they wanted to labor for Christ where people were hurting. But soon they became depressed and left. I asked him, "Why have you been able to stay all this time?" He said, "Because of the words of Jesus, 'The poor you have with you always.'" I replied, "Every time I've ever heard anyone quote that, it was cited as an excuse to neglect the poor, not to minister to the poor." He said: "Well, what I understand Jesus to say is that I will never be able to eliminate poverty. Therefore, when I came here, I had no expectation that I was going to solve all these problems. I never thought I would eliminate poverty or get rid of the drug traffic or end unemployment among my parishioners. I realize that for every person that is brought out of the ghetto, more are brought in. If we get one person off of drugs, five more get hooked here. My mission isn't to get rid of the poor or to get rid of all these problems. My mission is to minister to people who are suffering from these things while they are here and while I'm here."

What a tremendous testimony my friend had. That's the way Mary was, too. Mary said: "I saved this for Jesus' burial, but I'm going to give this gift now. I can minister to the poor tomorrow and the day after tomorrow and the day after that, but I will not have every day to manifest my affection for Christ." After all, this was the man who had restored her brother to life. She was pouring this fragrance on the feet of Jesus while Lazarus sat the table, the same Lazarus who so recently had been rotting in the tomb.

Do you know who should have been at that feast with ten times the fragrance that Mary brought? Caiaphas should have been there saying: "We know who You are for we have seen Your signs. We don't care if the Romans come. We recognize You as our Lord, and we're going to pour out our love to You." Of course, it wasn't expedient for Caiaphas to do that, but it wasn't expedient for Mary to do what she did, either. But even today, two thousand years after that extravagant act of love, worship, exaltation, and glorification of Christ, Mary's devotion is still talked about because it has been memorialized in the Word of God forever.

Jesus Himself gave the deathblow to any philosophy of pragmatism and expediency when He told people that a philosophy of pragmatism ultimately is not practical. He said: "For what will it profit a man if he gains the whole world, and loses his own soul? Or what will a man give in exchange for his soul?" (Mark 8:36–37). How much is your soul worth? Your prestige? Your comfort? A year's wages? Safety? In Jesus' mind, there is nothing in this world, including the whole world itself, that can be given in exchange for the value of your soul to Him.

32

THE BLESSED KING

John 12:9–19

Now a great many of the Jews knew that He was there; and they came, not for Jesus' sake only, but that they might also see Lazarus, whom He had raised from the dead. But the chief priests plotted to put Lazarus to death also, because on account of him many of the Jews went away and believed in Jesus. The next day a great multitude that had come to the feast, when they heard that Jesus was coming to Jerusalem, took branches of palm trees and went out to meet Him, and cried out: "Hosanna! 'Blessed is He who comes in the name of the LORD!' The King of Israel!" Then Jesus, when He had found a young donkey, sat on it; as it is written: "Fear not, daughter of Zion; behold, your King is coming, sitting on a donkey's colt." His disciples did not understand these things at first; but when Jesus was glorified, then they remembered that these things were written about Him and that they had done these things to Him. Therefore the people, who were with Him when He called Lazarus out of his tomb and raised him from the dead, bore witness. For this reason the people also met Him, because they heard that He had done this sign. The Pharisees therefore said among themselves, "You see that you are accomplishing nothing. Look, the world has gone after Him!"

Yet another feast of the Jews was at hand and many people were gathering in Jerusalem. The stage was set for Jesus' triumphal entry. But even before that public event, word of Jesus' presence in the nearby village of Bethany leaked out, and many people came to the home of Mary, Martha, and Lazarus, **not for Jesus' sake only, but that they might also see Lazarus, whom He had raised from the dead** (v. 9b). This prompted the Jewish authorities to expand their plot against Jesus: **the chief priests plotted to put Lazarus to death also, because on account of him many of the Jews went away and believed in Jesus** (vv. 10–11). The news of Lazarus' resurrection was spreading across the land and adding fuel to the popular response to Jesus that the Sanhedrin so desperately feared. As they saw it, it would be to their advantage not only to get rid of Jesus but also to get rid of Lazarus, for if he were put to death it would be more difficult to proclaim his resurrection.

A Royal Greeting

John then writes, **The next day a great multitude that had come to the feast, when they heard that Jesus was coming to Jerusalem, took branches of palm trees and went out to meet Him** (vv. 12–13a). We're told that "a great multitude" had come to the feast. We aren't given exact numbers of how many people had come to Jerusalem, but attendance at the Passover was a solemn obligation for every Jew, and since the days of King Josiah people had not been permitted to celebrate Passover in their local communities but were called to travel up to the central sanctuary in Jerusalem to keep the feast. We also have the testimony of the Jewish historian Josephus, who estimated the attendance at the Passover in the years AD 64 and 65 to be some 2.7 million Jews. So it is reasonable to expect about two million visitors had come to the Holy City for the Passover mentioned in this passage.

When the people heard that Jesus was coming to Jerusalem, they took branches of palm trees and went out to meet him. The waving of palm branches in this narrative would seem to indicate that this event took place during the Feast of Tabernacles, when palm branches were customarily used as part of the celebration. But this is one of those few episodes in the life of Jesus that is recorded in all four of the Gospels, so we know that this event actually took place in conjunction with the celebration of the Passover. What, then, was the significance of the palm branches?

In the intertestamental period, something took place that would define the Jewish people in terms of their national identity for centuries to come. In the second century BC, the temple was desecrated by Antiochus IV Epiphanes, leader of the Seleucid Empire. In response, a Jewish man named Mattathias, who was committed to the ancient covenant of Israel, determined to rescue the temple and the nation from the invasion of the Seleucids. Mattathias became the leader of a guerrilla group that fought against the Seleucids. When he died, the leadership of this insurrectionist movement passed to his son Judas, who became known as Judas Maccabaeus, which means "the hammer." Judas Maccabaeus became a national hero, a Hebrew Robin Hood, who wreaked havoc among the troops of the Seleucids. He put so much pressure on the Seleucids that in 164 BC they released the temple for the Jews to practice their own faith. That event was met with so much celebration that a new feast was instituted called the Feast of Dedication or the Feast of Lights. We know it as Hanukkah, which is celebrated even to this day.

Later, Judas' brother Simon Maccabaeus actually drove the Seleucids out of Jerusalem altogether, and when that happened he was acclaimed a national hero and was celebrated with a parade, something like a ticker-tape parade in New York. In that parade, the Jews celebrated his victory with music and with the waving of palm branches. At that point in Jewish history, the palm branch became significant as a sign and symbol of a military victory, of a triumph. In fact, that symbolism became so deeply rooted in the Jewish consciousness that when the Jews revolted against the Romans in the decade of the sixties AD, they dared to mint their own coins with the image of a palm branch, because it is their national symbol of victory.

When the people waved their palm branches to welcome Jesus, they cried out: **"Hosanna! 'Blessed is He who comes in the name of the LORD!' The King of Israel!"** (v. 13b). Why did they say this? The word *hosanna* is derived from a Hebrew word that literally means "save now." Both this plea and "Blessed is He who comes in the name of the LORD" are found in the *hallel*, a series of psalms that were sung every morning at the Feast of Tabernacles. The series starts with Psalm 113 and goes through Psalm 118. In Psalm 118, we find these words:

> Open to me the gates of righteousness;
> I will go through them,
> And I will praise the LORD.
> This is the gate of the LORD,
> Through which the righteous shall enter.
> I will praise You,
> For You have answered me,

And have become my salvation.
The stone which the builders rejected
Has become the chief cornerstone.
This was the Lord's doing;
It is marvelous in our eyes.
This is the day the Lord has made;
We will rejoice and be glad in it.
Save now, I pray, O Lord;
O Lord, I pray, send now prosperity.
Blessed is he who comes in the name of the Lord!
We have blessed you from the house of the Lord. (vv. 19–26)

Every Jewish pilgrim was familiar with the words from the *hallel*, so when the crowds came out to see Jesus, they naturally used those words. The plea "Save now" near the end of the quoted passage is the English translation of the root word of *hosanna*. The words "Blessed is He who comes in the name of the Lord" and the additional description shouted by the people, "the King of Israel!" indicate that the people looked to Jesus for salvation, though most likely in a military sense.

A Lowly Donkey

Something very strange took place. John tells us that **Jesus, when He had found a young donkey, sat on it; as it is written, "Fear not, daughter of Zion; behold, your King is coming, sitting on a donkey's colt"** (vv. 14–15). The people welcomed Jesus as their victorious King. However, kings usually rode into their places of accession on royal steeds. Not Jesus. Knowing what was coming, He gave explicit directions to His disciples to go and bring a donkey that had never been ridden (Luke 19:29–30). The donkeys people ride in the Holy Land are nothing like the donkeys we breed in the United States. They're much smaller, so that grown men have to bend their knees as they ride so that their feet don't hit the ground. The donkey Jesus rode was of this small type, and it was young, too. So instead of riding the steed of a military victor or of a king, Jesus entered Jerusalem on this lowly donkey, self-consciously identifying with the messianic prophecy that we find in the book of Zechariah:

"Rejoice greatly, O daughter of Zion!
Shout, O daughter of Jerusalem!
Behold, your King is coming to you;

> He is just and having salvation,
> Lowly and riding on a donkey,
> A colt, the foal of a donkey.
> I will cut off the chariot from Ephraim
> And the horse from Jerusalem;
> The battle bow shall be cut off.
> He shall speak peace to the nations;
> His dominion shall be 'from sea to sea,
> And from the River to the ends of the earth.'" (9:9–10)

This is not the picture of the Messiah that the people had in mind. They wanted someone to ride into town on a mighty steed and drive the Romans out. But Jesus identified with God's Messiah, the Messiah who was to come in lowliness, meekness, and humility. Not surprisingly, the same people who cheered Him as He rode into Jerusalem screamed for His blood a few days later after He failed to give them what they wanted. This should be a lesson to all of us who come to Jesus with our agendas, making our demands of Him, only to become disappointed, angry, and sometimes bitter when He doesn't do things the way we want Him to do them.

It is important to note that when Jesus came into the city, He did not deny that He was the people's rightful King. However, by riding a donkey colt, He subtly informed them that He was the King God had appointed, not the King that they had conjured up in their expectations.

John then gives us an editorial comment, telling us that **His disciples did not understand these things at first; but when Jesus was glorified, then they remembered that these things were written about Him and that they had done these things to Him** (v. 16). Even the disciples missed the message Jesus was sending, but later, probably after the resurrection, they recalled the words of Zechariah and understood what God had intended.

John also notes: **Therefore the people, who were with Him when He called Lazarus out of his tomb and raised him from the dead, bore witness. For this reason the people also met Him, because they heard that He had done this sign** (vv. 17–18). Apparently the raising of Lazarus had been much talked about by the people who had been there to see it happen. It was this widespread discussion of the miracle that sparked the interest of the people to come out and welcome Jesus to Jerusalem.

Finally, John writes of the reaction of the Pharisees: **The Pharisees therefore said among themselves, "You see that you are accomplishing**

nothing. Look, the world has gone after Him!" (v. 19). The Jewish authorities saw that all their efforts to confront Jesus, to seize Him, and to warn the people to have nothing to do with Him had been useless; Jesus' following was growing by leaps and bounds. From their perspective, it seemed that the entire world was going after Jesus.

But if there is one thing this passage makes clear, it is that the people's interest in Jesus was based largely on curiosity and false expectations that would be dashed in no time. Jesus was God's King, and He had come to Jerusalem to fulfill a mission unlike what anyone, even those closest to him, could envision. All too soon the people would reject Him, but as Zechariah said, He would become the chief cornerstone.

33

THE HOUR HAS COME

John 12:20-34

Now there were certain Greeks among those who came up to worship at the feast. Then they came to Philip, who was from Bethsaida of Galilee, and asked him, saying, "Sir, we wish to see Jesus." Philip came and told Andrew, and in turn Andrew and Philip told Jesus. But Jesus answered them, saying, "The hour has come that the Son of Man should be glorified. Most assuredly, I say to you, unless a grain of wheat falls into the ground and dies, it remains alone; but if it dies, it produces much grain. He who loves his life will lose it, and he who hates his life in this world will keep it for eternal life. If anyone serves Me, let him follow Me; and where I am, there My servant will be also. If anyone serves Me, him My Father will honor. Now My soul is troubled, and what shall I say? 'Father, save Me from this hour'? But for this purpose I came to this hour. Father, glorify Your name." Then a voice came from heaven, saying, "I have both glorified it and will glorify it again." Therefore the people who stood by and heard it said that it had thundered. Others said, "An angel has spoken to Him." Jesus answered and said, "This voice did not come because of Me, but for your sake. Now is the judgment of this world; now the ruler of this world will be cast out. And I, if I am lifted up from the earth, will draw all peoples to Myself." This He said, signifying by what death He

would die. The people answered Him, "We have heard from the law that
the Christ remains forever; and how can You say, 'The Son of Man must
be lifted up'? Who is this Son of Man?"

Andrew is not among the best known of Jesus' apostles, but he had
a special gift. It seems that every time he appears in the biblical
record, he is bringing someone to Jesus. We saw earlier that Andrew
brought his brother, Peter, to Jesus (John 1:41–42). In the passage before us,
he is involved in bringing a group of Greeks to the Lord. This trait is one of
the reasons we chose to name the church where I serve St. Andrew's. Like
Andrew, we want to be busy bringing people to Jesus.

John tells us that **certain Greeks** (v. 20) were in Jerusalem for the Passover.
These may have been Greek-speaking Jews who lived outside Judea. However,
it is also possible that they were Gentile God-fearers, Gentiles who worshiped
the God of Israel, who were in Jerusalem for the feast. We know from Mark's
account of Holy Week that Jesus also cleansed the temple during this time
(Mark 11:15–17), and the part of the temple that He cleansed was the outer
court, the so-called "court of the Gentiles," which was where all the mer-
chandizing happened. Only the Jews could go into the temple courts; a wall
separated those areas from the court of the Gentiles. Gentiles, including the
God-fearers, could not pass this wall. Thus, these Greeks may have witnessed
Jesus' cleansing of the temple and desired to speak with Him.

These Greeks **came to Philip, who was from Bethsaida of Galilee,
and asked him, saying, "Sir, we wish to see Jesus"** (v. 21). It is not
clear why they approached Philip or why John felt it necessary to mention
that Philip was from Bethsaida in Galilee; perhaps the Greeks had some
relationship or affinity with Philip. In any case, these men did not say, "Can
we find out where Jesus is so we can take a look at Him?" No, they wanted
to have an audience with Jesus. They said, "We would like to meet with Him
personally; we have some things we'd like to discuss with Him."

So **Philip came and told Andrew, and in turn Andrew and Philip
told Jesus** (v. 22). Did Philip go to Andrew because he had doubts about
this request? Perhaps, but it does not seem that Andrew had any hesitations.
With Philip, he went straight to Jesus.

The Significance of the Moment

One of the oddities of this narrative is that John never tells us whether Jesus
acceded to the Greeks' request. We would expect him to say: "Of course.

Bring them over. I'm happy to meet with Gentiles. I didn't come simply to Israel; I have a mission beyond the borders of Israel. I have many sheep that are not of this fold." But we don't know whether He said any of these things. We aren't told.

Instead, Jesus immediately focused on the significance of the moment. He said, **"The hour has come that the Son of Man should be glorified"** (v. 23). Throughout John's Gospel to this point, we have seen several cryptic references to Jesus' "hour" (2:4; 7:30; 8:20). In the first instance, "hour" seemed to refer to the time of Jesus' exaltation, His hour of glorification, while the other occurrences seemed to point to the hour of His debasement, the time of His passion and humiliation. Always, however, we were told that this hour had not yet come.

In this passage, however, Jesus did not speak about the hour in a future way. He plainly said that the hour was no longer distant but was at hand. We also see in this statement that the distinction between the hour of shame and the hour of exaltation had disappeared; Jesus spoke here of the hour of His glorification, but we know that it was His passion that was about to begin. His following words confirm that He was speaking about His passion: **"Most assuredly, I say to you, unless a grain of wheat falls into the ground and dies, it remains alone; but if it dies, it produces much grain"** (v. 24). Thus, Jesus spoke in the same breath of the hour of His glorification and of the hour of His death.

We know that for Jesus, the way to glory was the *Via Dolorosa*, the way of suffering, the passion of the cross. Satan in the wilderness had offered him a different way, a way that would bypass the cross. All He had to do was genuflect for a moment where no one would see Him and all of the kingdoms of the world would be His—no cross, no suffering, no passion, no humiliation. But Jesus refused that way because it was not the Father's way.

However, Jesus was not stating that the only way He could be exalted was through His humiliation. He was not saying that the only way He could enter into glory was through the debasement of His trial and of His death. He was thinking about more than the consequences of that suffering. He said that His glory lay *in* the pain, the suffering, and the death. It wasn't that the passion was the pathway to glory. No, there was glory *in* the passion. How could this be? How could the cross be that moment in which the Son of Man was lifted up? Because in His death on the cross He was obeying the Father and glorifying the Father, and all who obey the Father and give glory to the Father are honored by the Father.

Earlier, we saw the pivotal importance of the bread of life discourse

(John 6) for this entire Gospel. We saw how radical Jesus' teaching was as He talked about being the new manna, as it were, the bread that had come down from heaven, the bread that satisfies our hunger forever. Now that His hour had come, He gave another lesson drawn from the agrarian environment of His day. Speaking as the bread of life, He said that unless a grain of wheat falls into the ground and dies, it remains alone. One grain plucked from the stalk, one seed of wheat, if it is put in a jar or placed on a shelf as a souvenir, is worthless. If anything is to come of that seed, anything to benefit anyone else, it has to fall into the earth and die. In dying, it will bring forth fruit in abundance.

How I love the promise that is given to the Servant of the Lord: "He shall see the labor of His soul, and be satisfied" (Isa. 53:11a). Away with the doctrine of the atonement that holds that Jesus died to make salvation *possible*—as if our Lord went to the cross, rose from the dead, returned to heaven, and there took a seat on the fifty-yard line to observe the consequences of His actions. The picture is of Jesus wringing His hands in anxiety and saying, "Oh, I hope somebody takes advantage of what I did and is saved." Jesus did not say that if a grain of wheat falls into the ground it *might* produce some fruit. Instead, He said that it *would* produce "much fruit." It is not possible, not even theoretically possible, that the atonement of Jesus could not bear fruit. The Father makes certain that the grain of wheat that dies bears fruit.

If you are in Christ and have tasted of the bread of heaven, you are that fruit. Indeed, the fruit encompasses the whole of Jesus' church, which includes these Greeks. No longer would they be kept on the fringes of the people of God; no longer would they be restricted to the outer court. The dividing wall between the Jew and the Gentile was demolished by the atonement of Christ.

Jesus went on to say: **"He who loves his life will lose it, and he who hates his life in this world will keep it for eternal life. If anyone serves Me, let him follow Me; and where I am, there My servant will be also. If anyone serves Me, him My Father will honor"** (vv. 25–26). Here we see the paradox of the Christian life that Jesus spoke about so often—we find life in dying to self and following Christ. In the next chapter of John, we will see that when Jesus spoke of going away, Peter asked, "Lord, where are You going?" Jesus replied, "Where I am going you cannot follow Me now, but you shall follow Me afterward" (13:36). Jesus warned Peter: "If you're going to be My disciple, you're going to have to follow Me, and that means you're going to walk in the shadow of the cross. You will participate in My humiliation." Our Lord, before He left this planet, gave the church her great commission to go into all the world, baptizing all people in the name of the Father, the Son, and the Holy Spirit (Matt. 28:18–20). If you are baptized, you have in your body the mark of your participation in the suffering of Christ, because we are buried with Him in baptism.

The apostle Paul warns that if we're not willing to participate with Christ in His humiliation, we will have no part in His exaltation. If you're ashamed of Him, He will be ashamed of you. A Christian must embrace Him not only in His exaltation, not only in His glory, but in His shame. Otherwise, you'll be numbered with those who are trying to save their own lives. They are the ultimate losers, Jesus said; but those who lose their lives for His sake participate in his Honor.

Feelings of Revulsion

Jesus then said, **"Now My soul is troubled"** (v. 27a). Let's pause and consider that brief statement. Too often we read these words but they fail to penetrate to our visceral parts. We don't really become engaged with them. But think about what we have seen as we have studied the life of Jesus so far. We have seen His power on display in His mighty miracles. We have heard His words as He taught with authority. Here He said, "My soul is troubled." The word that Jesus used here means "revulsion" or "horror." Our Lord said, "My soul is horrified by what I am facing." This is a side of Jesus we have never seen before.

He continued: **"And what shall I say? 'Father, save me from this hour'? But for this purpose I came to this hour"** (v. 27b). The construction of this sentence in the original language is difficult to follow. One interpretation holds that Jesus was saying, "Should I ask the Father to spare Me from the cross?" In other words, He was asking a rhetorical question. He was saying, "I'm troubled, but I won't ask the Father to spare Me from what lies ahead because that is what He sent Me to do." However, we know that Jesus, very soon after speaking these words, prayed in Gethsemane that the Father *would* take away the cup he had to drink, if it were His will.

However, there is another way to read this statement in the original language, and I prefer this interpretation. This view holds that Jesus expressed the horror that was gripping His soul, then said, "What can I say?" Then, directing His words to God, He said, "Father, save Me from this hour." In other words, Jesus was undergoing a crisis moment such as He would undergo in Gethsemane. But He quickly reminded Himself, "For this purpose I came to this hour. I know My Father cannot take this cup away. This is My destiny. This is why I'm here. It's horrible to Me now; I see it in all of its blackness, in all of its fullness as it awaits Me, and I wish I didn't have to endure it. But I know it is My Father's will for Me. This is why I'm here. This is why I came to this hour."

Then listen to what Jesus said: **"Father, glorify Your name"** (v. 28a). He didn't say, "Father, glorify *My* name." The Son would be glorified by what He was about to do, but the higher purpose of the cross was that the Father would be glorified by the satisfaction of His justice. When the Son paid the debt for sin, God would be glorified.

When Jesus uttered this prayer, there was a dramatic response. God spoke audibly from heaven and said, **"I have both glorified it and will glorify it again"** (v. 28b). This is one of only three occasions recorded in the Gospels when the Father spoke from heaven. He spoke at Jesus' baptism: "You are My beloved Son; in You I am well pleased" (Luke 3:22). He spoke at Jesus' transfiguration: "This is My beloved Son. Hear Him" (Luke 9:35). On this occasion, Jesus affirmed that **"This voice did not come because of Me, but for your sake"** (v. 30). The Father spoke to let the people there know that He would be glorified through the Son.

After the Father spoke, there was disagreement among the people as to what had occurred. Some said it had **thundered**, while others said, **"An angel has spoken to Him"** (v. 29). They didn't grasp what had happened. We don't know whether there was a difference in the degree of understanding among those who were there, but we know that some thought it was only thunder.

Is that what the Word of God sounds like to you—indistinguishable noise? Or has God, in His mercy, given you ears to hear when He speaks? I pray your ears have been opened and that God will give you a deeper understanding of His Word as we press ahead in this study of the Gospel of John—especially now as we approach Jesus' hour, the climax of His ministry on earth.

34

THE SENT ONE

John 12:35–50

Then Jesus said to them, "A little while longer the light is with you. Walk while you have the light, lest darkness overtake you; he who walks in darkness does not know where he is going. While you have the light, believe in the light, that you may become sons of light." These things Jesus spoke, and departed, and was hidden from them. But although He had done so many signs before them, they did not believe in Him, that the word of Isaiah the prophet might be fulfilled, which he spoke: "Lord, who has believed our report? And to whom has the arm of the LORD been revealed?" Therefore they could not believe, because Isaiah said again: "He has blinded their eyes and hardened their hearts, lest they should see with their eyes, lest they should understand with their hearts and turn, so that I should heal them." These things Isaiah said when he saw His glory and spoke of Him. Nevertheless even among the rulers many believed in Him, but because of the Pharisees they did not confess Him, lest they should be put out of the synagogue; for they loved the praise of men more than the praise of God. Then Jesus cried out and said, "He who believes in Me, believes not in Me but in Him who sent Me. And he who sees Me sees Him who sent Me. I have come as a light into the world, that whoever believes in Me should not abide in darkness. And if anyone hears My words and does not believe, I do not judge him; for I did not come to judge the world but to save the world. He who rejects Me, and does not receive My words, has that which judges him—the word that I have spoken will judge him in the last day. For I have not spoken on My own authority; but the Father who sent Me gave Me a command, what I should say and what I should speak. And I know that His command is everlasting life. Therefore, whatever I speak, just as the Father has told Me, so I speak."

The theological question I hear most often is this: "What happens to the innocent native in Africa who has never heard the gospel?" People want to know whether such people are taken to heaven or condemned to hell when they die. I always give the same answer: "The innocent native in Africa doesn't need to hear the gospel. Don't worry for another minute about the innocent native in Africa who's never heard of Christ. The innocent native in Africa, when he dies, goes straight to heaven because he is innocent."

But let's ask the question another way: "What happens to the *guilty* native in Africa who's never heard the gospel?" I don't worry about *innocent* natives in Africa or anywhere else in the world, because the Bible makes it clear there are no innocent natives anywhere. There is no one who is not guilty in God's sight. The whole world has rejected God's plain revelation of Himself in creation. God's light has shown into every nook and cranny of this universe, but every human being in his or her fallen condition suppresses that light of revelation and prefers darkness. This darkness pervades the whole world.

Into this darkness came the light of the world, Jesus Christ. He was the light in the sense that He brought the message of salvation from God the Father. He spent a mere three years preaching that message throughout the tiny Roman province of Judea. As the hour of His suffering approached, He was filled with a sense of urgency when He knew that He was about to be taken away. Therefore, He said: **"A little while longer the light is with you. Walk while you have the light, lest darkness overtake you; he who walks in darkness does not know where he is going. While you have the light, believe in the light, that you may become sons of light"** (vv. 35–36a). This was a warning. Jesus said: "The light is with you for only a little while longer. You need to hear My message, for you are in the darkness and do not know where you are going. You need to become sons of light." The window of opportunity was closing for the people to hear the gospel from Jesus Himself.

But Jesus did not remain for long to plead with the people. He gave His warning and then He **departed, and was hidden from them** (v. 36b). Sadly, few heeded the warning. John tells us, **But although he had done so many signs before them, they did not believe in Him** (v. 37).

The Reason for the Unbelief

John does not settle for reporting here; he goes on to editorializing, providing an explanation for why so many people rejected Jesus, despite His miracles, His authoritative teaching, even the audible testimony of the Father from heaven. The problem, according to his inspired evaluation, is that faith, in New Testament categories, is not something that rests, in the final analysis, simply on intellectual cognition or intellectual submission. All the signs that Jesus gave were not enough to persuade people of the truth of Christ, because what was required for faith then is the same thing that is required for faith now—namely, the ministry of the Holy Spirit, who accompanies the Word of God to remove the scales from our eyes and to unstop our ears that we might believe.

This brings us back once again to the relentless Calvinism of the apostle John. He tells us that the rejection of Jesus happened **that the word of Isaiah the prophet might be fulfilled, which he spoke:**

> **"Lord, who has believed our report?**
> **And to whom has the arm of the LORD been revealed?"**
>
> **Therefore they could not believe, because Isaiah said again:**
>
> **"He has blinded their eyes and hardened their hearts,**
> **Lest they should see with their eyes,**
> **Lest they should understand with their hearts and turn,**
> **So that I should heal them."**
>
> **These things Isaiah said when he saw His glory and spoke of**
> **Him** (vv. 37–41).

John here cites two passages from the book of Isaiah. He uses the first (Isa. 53:1) to show that Isaiah prophesied the widespread rejection of Jesus and His message. Then He goes on to make the point that the people were *not capable* of believing. To support this point, he cites Isaiah 6:9–10. This text is part of the famous passage that recounts Isaiah's great vision of God and his calling as a prophet. In giving Isaiah that commission, God warned him that his message would not be received, because God had made a judicial verdict against sinful Israel. He had blinded them spiritually and given them hard hearts to prevent them from believing.

God doesn't force people into sin and then refuse to rescue them from it. However, He sometimes turns a sinner over to his sin, which is the most ghastly judgment any person could ever receive from the hands of God. That is what happened to the people of Israel in Isaiah's day. God did the same thing in Jesus' day. Due to the rebelliousness of the people, God judged them with the inability to repent even though the message of salvation was being compellingly presented right before their eyes.

This is no new theme for John. As we saw when we looked at John 6, the apostle recorded some controversial words of Jesus, words that helped cause many of His disciples to cease following Him: "No one can come to Me unless the Father who sent Me draws him" (v. 44a). Jesus said that no one has the ability to believe in Him unless the Father acts upon his or her heart. The Holy Spirit must cause the sinner to be born again (John 3:3) and give him or her the gift of faith (Eph. 2:8). It was John's inspired conclusion that God refused to do this for the masses who heard Jesus and witnessed His miracles.

Verse 41 is a cryptic statement. It's not absolutely certain to whom John is referring when he says, "These things Isaiah said when he saw His glory and spoke of Him." However, the crux of the argument John makes concerns not God the Father but God the Son. There is much in this text to incline us to conclude that when Isaiah saw the Lord high and lifted up (Isa. 6:1), he was beholding the pre-incarnate *Logos*, the One whom God would send into the world to redeem us. He saw Christ on the throne in His glory before Christ was even born. I think that's what John is declaring here.

John tells us that God did give the gift of faith to some who heard Jesus. He writes, **Nevertheless, even among the rulers many believed in Him, but because of the Pharisees they did not confess Him, lest they should be put out of the synagogue; for they loved the praise of men more than the praise of God** (vv. 42–43). The group that seemed most opposed to Jesus, the religious leadership, was not the monolithic opposition bloc it seemed to be. Even among those vociferous opponents of Christ, there were some who believed in Him. However, they kept quiet about their belief because of the Sanhedrin's threat to expel anyone who confessed Christ from the synagogue (9:22). Among these were Joseph of Arimathea and apparently Nicodemus as well (19:38–39).

Jesus the Missionary

John goes on, **Then Jesus cried out and said, "He who believes in Me, believes not in Me but in Him who sent Me. And he who sees Me sees Him who sent Me. I have come as a light into the world, that whoever believes in Me should not abide in darkness"** (v. 44–46). As I stressed earlier, one cannot have the Son but reject the Father, and neither can one have the Father but reject the Son. The Father and Son are one, and They have the same goals and intentions. As Jesus said here, the Father "sent" the Son; He was sent to accomplish Their joint mission. The first missionary of the Christian church was Christ, and His mission was established not as an afterthought, after the fall of the human race, but in eternity, in what we call the "covenant of redemption." Before God made a covenant with Adam, before He made a covenant with Noah, before He made a covenant with Abraham, Isaac, Jacob, Moses, David, or anyone else, He made a covenant with Himself. It was among the three persons of the Godhead, the Father, the Son, and the Holy Spirit. From all eternity, it was the plan of God to create a world and to redeem that world by sending God the Son there as His appointed missionary.

Jesus continued: **"And if anyone hears My words and does not believe, I do not judge him; for I did not come to judge the world but to save the world. He who rejects Me, and does not receive My words, has that which judges him—the word that I have spoken will judge him in the last day"** (vv. 47–48). We know from the rest of Scripture that Jesus' purpose during His first coming was not to sit in judgment but to make atonement for His people. However, we know that when He comes again, He *will* judge (see John 5:22, 27–30; Matt. 25:31–32). At that time, those who have heard His message and have failed to respond to it will incur a harsher judgment (Luke 12:47–48).

Finally, Jesus said: **"For I have not spoken on My own authority; but the Father who sent Me gave Me a command, what I should say and what I should speak. And I know that His command is everlasting life. Therefore, whatever I speak, just as the Father has told Me, so I speak"** (vv. 49–50). Jesus spoke on the basis of His God-given authority, preaching a message that He had been commanded to preach, and relaying it exactly as He had been told to do. There is no doubt—Jesus was a divine missionary.

Later, of course, Jesus said to His disciples, "As the Father has sent Me, I also send you" (John 20:21). He gave them the same mission He Himself had been tasked to carry out. That's the basis for the missionary enterprise of the church. We live in a culture that embraces pluralism and relativism, and we are told every day that proselytizing people or trying to convert people to Christianity is taboo. But the Lord Himself was sent by the Father to seek and to save the lost (Luke 19:10), and He passed the baton to His disciples.

Some will ask, "If God has planned all things from the foundation of the world, including who will believe and who will not, why should we be engaged in this enterprise?" One of my professors asked that question in a seminary class. He went around the room, and every student said, "I don't know," or, "I've always wondered myself," or, "That beats me." Finally he came to me and I said, "Well, I know this isn't what you're looking for, but one small reason why we should be involved in evangelism and missionary activity is that Jesus commanded us to do it." The professor looked at me and laughed. He said, "Yes, Mr. Sproul, what could possibly be a more insignificant reason to be involved in missions and evangelism than that the Savior of your soul and the Lord God omnipotent should command you to do it?" So we have the command of God to compel us to this mission.

Also, we know that God ordains not only the ends but the means, and God, from all eternity, has chosen the foolishness of preaching as the means by which He brings His people to salvation. He doesn't need you or me, but He gives us the unspeakable privilege and opportunity of participating in this mission.

Oh, that the Lord God someday would look upon each of us and say: "Well done, good and faithful servant. You took seriously the mission that I gave you to go into all the world and to preach the gospel to every living creature, that people from every tongue, every tribe, and every nation might believe and be saved. Enter into the joy of your master." It should be our goal to please Him in the fulfillment of the task He has assigned to us—to walk in the footsteps of Christ the missionary.

35

THE FOOT WASHING

John 13:1–17

Now before the Feast of the Passover, when Jesus knew that His hour had come that He should depart from this world to the Father, having loved His own who were in the world, He loved them to the end. And supper being ended, the devil having already put it into the heart of Judas Iscariot, Simon's son, to betray Him, Jesus, knowing that the Father had given all things into His hands, and that He had come from God and was going to God, rose from supper and laid aside His garments, took a towel and girded Himself. After that, He poured water into a basin and began to wash the disciples' feet, and to wipe them with the towel with which He was girded. Then He came to Simon Peter. And Peter said to Him, "Lord, are You washing my feet?" Jesus answered and said to him, "What I am doing you do not understand now, but you will know after this." Peter said to Him, "You shall never wash my feet!" Jesus answered him, "If I do not wash you, you have no part with Me." Simon Peter said to Him, "Lord, not my feet only, but also my hands and my head!" Jesus said to him, "He who is bathed needs only to wash his feet, but is completely clean; and you are clean, but not all of you." For He knew who would betray Him; therefore He said, "You are not all clean." So when He had washed their feet, taken His garments, and sat down again, He said to them, "Do you know what I have done to you? You call Me Teacher and Lord, and you say well, for so I am. If I then, your Lord and Teacher, have washed your feet, you also ought to wash one another's feet. For I have given you an example, that you should do as I have done to you. Most assuredly, I say to you, a servant is not greater than his master; nor is he who is sent greater than he who sent him. If you know these things, blessed are you if you do them.

In 2003, when the United States invaded Iraq, I sat glued to my television set for days and watched the amazing footage that was broadcast. One scene that stands out in my mind from those days was the jubilant celebration of the Iraqi people as U.S. Marines pulled down a forty-foot statue of Saddam Hussein in Baghdad. The statue was torn from its pedestal and dragged through the streets, and children were shown riding on the head of the statue as if it were a sled. But I also remember the way in which the people of Iraq used their shoes or their sandals to pound against the statue and the posters of Saddam that were still being displayed in Baghdad. The commentators explained that among the Iraqi people, to beat a person or even a person's image with one's shoe is to show the deepest possible form of contempt for that person.

That incident came back to me as I dealt with the text that is before us in this chapter, in which we see our Lord Jesus washing the feet of His disciples. The Iraqi people's actions helped me understand the depth of lowliness to which Jesus stooped when He handled His disciples' filthy feet in this ritual of cleansing. We have already discussed the fact that in antiquity, when a rabbi had disciples, they typically acted as his servants. However, they were never required to wash the rabbi's feet; that task was reserved for slaves. But even some slaves were spared this task. Within Israel, if a Jewish person had a Jewish slave, the slave owner was not permitted to require that slave to wash his feet. Only a Gentile slave could be required to perform such a menial task. So the fact that Jesus Himself undertook this task, and that He did it during Holy Week, fills this narrative with theological and ethical significance for us.

The Shadow of the Cross

John tells us that this event took place **before the Feast of the Passover** (v. 1). Jesus and His disciples apparently had gathered for a **supper** (v. 2). One of the most difficult problems we face in biblical studies is trying to understand the relationship between John's Gospel and the Synoptic Gospels with respect to the timing of events during Holy Week. Sometimes it seems there were two different calendars in view. One of the questions is whether the meal that is referred to at the beginning of Chapter 13 was in fact a Passover celebration. I don't think that it was; I think it was an evening meal before the actual Passover meal. But all we can be sure about is that Jesus and His disciples were gathered around a table, having just eaten a meal.

We are told, **Jesus knew that His hour had come that He should depart from this world to the Father, [and] having loved His own who were in the world, He loved them to the end** (v. 1). It is important to understand that Jesus' washing of His disciples' feet was done in the shadow of the cross. We've seen that John frequently mentions Jesus' "hour," and now he tells us that Jesus knew the hour of His appointed death was at hand. We cannot properly understand the significance of the foot-washing episode apart from this proximity to the crucifixion, the ultimate act of love. But we need to notice that John says Jesus loved "*His own* who were in the world . . . to the end." In just a few more chapters, we will be eavesdropping on Jesus' High Priestly Prayer, in which He specifically said to the Father, "I do not pray for the world, but for those whom You have given Me" (John 17:9). As Jesus prepared to lay down His life, He was preparing to give an atonement not for the whole world but for His own, those whom the Father had given to Him. If the atonement were for the whole world, then everybody would be saved, but the Scriptures make it clear that this is not so. Jesus' love was for His sheep, and He manifested this love to the very end. That gives us a hint of the significance of what is about to take place.

John goes on, **And supper being ended, the devil having already put it into the heart of Judas Iscariot, Simon's son, to betray Him, Jesus, knowing that the Father had given all things into His hands, and that He had come from God and was going to God, rose from the supper and laid aside His garments, took a towel and girded Himself** (vv. 2–4). The stage was fully set. Satan had prepared Judas for his role as Jesus' betrayer. Meanwhile, Jesus was aware of who He was, the incarnate Son of God, and of what He was about to do. In this context, Jesus rose from the table and took off His garments. In the modern context, it would be as if a man took off his suit coat, his tie, his shirt, and his trousers. Then Jesus put on a loincloth. In short, He assumed the garb of a slave.

In Chapter 32, we looked at Jesus' triumphal entry to Jerusalem. We saw that He was a King riding to His accession, but whereas kings usually rode large, powerful horses on such occasions, Jesus chose a small donkey. He came humbly into Jerusalem. Here, as He prepared to wash His disciples' feet, Jesus behaved with great humility again. It seems He was consciously embracing symbols of humiliation as He strode toward the cross that was waiting for Him.

In these acts, Jesus embodied the picture Paul painted in the book of Philippians, where he wrote:

> Let this mind be in you which was also in Christ Jesus, who, being in the form of God, did not consider it robbery to be equal with God, but made Himself of no reputation, taking the form of a bondservant, and coming in the likeness of men. And being found in appearance as a man, He humbled Himself and became obedient to the point of death, even the death of the cross. Therefore God also has highly exalted Him and given Him the name which is above every name, that at the name of Jesus every knee should bow, of those in heaven, and of those on earth, and of those under the earth, and that every tongue should confess that Jesus Christ is Lord, to the glory of God the Father. (2:5–11)

Liberal theologians of the nineteenth century and the "death of God" theologians of the twentieth century looked at this passage and said it referred to Christ stripping Himself of His deity when He came to earth, setting aside His divine attributes. The great Princeton theologian B. B. Warfield opposed that view on the basis that God is immutable, so Jesus could not have laid aside His deity when He became incarnate. It was not His *deity* but His *dignity* that Jesus laid aside. He emptied Himself of the glory that He enjoyed with His Father from all eternity. He laid aside His prerogatives as the second person of the Trinity. For the sake of His people, He descended from glory to lay down His life.

The Centrality of Baptism

However, we must resist the tendency to see this narrative merely as a moral lesson of humility. It is certainly that; Jesus Himself later told His disciples He had given them an example (v. 15). But if we stop there and focus on that dimension of this action of Jesus, we will miss the central point.

There have been a handful of Christian communities throughout church history that have taken this text as the basis for the establishment of a sacrament called foot washing. Some of these communities regularly practice this ritual. In the Roman Catholic Church, in the annual Mass of the Lord's Supper, the priest typically washes the feet of twelve men. So there are these observances, but in the main throughout church history foot washing has not been considered a sacrament. That is proper, for Jesus was not instituting a sacrament that was to be repeated on a regular basis among the people of God, and we know that for this reason: the central significance of Jesus' washing of His disciples' feet has to do with baptism, which is the sacrament of the entrance into the new covenant. Baptism signifies many things, but at the very heart of the symbolism of baptism is the idea of cleansing.

My mentor, Dr. John Gerstner, once was invited to preach in a little country parish. When he got to the church, the elders met him at the door and said, "Dr. Gerstner, we forgot to tell you, we're having a celebration of infant baptism here this morning, and we wondered if you'd be willing to perform the sacrament." He said, "I'd be honored to do it." Then they said: "As part of the ritual we use here, we have the officiating minister pin a white rose to the gowns of the infants who are to be baptized. Would you please pin these white roses on the children before you baptize them?" Dr. Gerstner said: "Well, let me ask you a question first. What is the significance of the white rose?" The elders said, "It signifies the infant's innocence." Dr. Gerstner said: "Oh, I see. And what's the significance of the water?" The elders said, "Well, maybe we shouldn't be using the white rose." They had not realized that a child who is innocent would have no need of the cleansing that baptism symbolizes.

The water in baptism is a symbol of cleansing, and that symbolic cleansing directs our attention to the supreme act of cleansing by which we are made pure in the sight of God, a cleansing that is effected not by water but by the blood of Christ in the atonement. So our baptism, among other things, looks backward in time to the cross, to that event by which we are made clean in the presence of God, by which our sins are removed and remitted.

In Isaiah 1:18, we read, "'Come now, and let us reason together,' says the LORD, 'Though your sins are like scarlet, they shall be as white as snow; though they are red like crimson, they shall be as wool.'" That text marvelously captures the essence of what was accomplished by the Servant of Yahweh, the Suffering Servant of Israel, looking ahead to Christ, who took the crimson sin of our lives on Himself at Calvary. It was there that Christ performed the ultimate act of cleansing, and our baptism looks backward to that.

By contrast, the washing of the disciples' feet looked forward. Jesus clearly taught that it was tied to the cleansing that was about to take place. It was far more than just an example of humility for the disciples.

Complete Cleansing

John tells us that Jesus **poured water into a basin and began to wash the disciples' feet, and to wipe them with the towel with which He was girded. Then He came to Simon Peter. And Peter said to**

Him, "Lord, are You washing my feet?" Jesus answered and said to him, "What I am doing you do not understand now, but you will know after this." Peter said to Him, "You shall never wash my feet!" Jesus answered him, "If I do not wash you, you have no part with Me." Simon Peter said to Him, "Lord, not my feet only, but also my hands and my head!" Jesus said to him, "He who is bathed needs only to wash his feet, but is completely clean; and you are clean, but not all of you." For He knew who would betray Him; therefore He said, "You are not all clean" (vv. 5–11).

Peter was prone to speak first and think later. We remember the occasion when Jesus spoke of His coming suffering and death, and Peter took Him aside and rebuked Him, saying, "Far be it from You, Lord; this shall not happen to You!" (Matt. 16:21–22). Here he did the same thing: Jesus clearly intended and desired to wash Peter's feet, yet Peter exclaimed, "You shall never wash my feet!" Jesus did not reply, "Simon, you impetuous, rash person." He did not say, "Simon, you just watch Me—I'm going to wash your feet whether you like it or not." Instead, He replied by saying, "If I do not wash you, you have no part with Me." Oops! Suddenly Simon was saying: "My hands, my head—whatever it takes. Wash any part of me You want to wash."

We can transfer that warning to everyone reading this book. If you are reading this and have not been washed by Christ, you will have no part with Him in the Father's house. Jesus was preparing His disciples for that cleansing that would once and for all deliver them from their sin. He pointed them to the perfection of the cleansing that was to come, the atonement, which cleanses everyone who participates in the kingdom of Christ. Are you among them?

We've already seen Jesus making the point in the final weeks of His life, "Unless you're willing to participate in My humiliation, you have no part in My exaltation." Our very baptism is a sign not only of our being raised with Christ, but of our being buried with Christ. It is a sign that we join Him in His humiliation so that we may have a part in His glory.

Jesus told Simon, **"He who is bathed needs only to wash his feet, but is completely clean"** (v. 10a). In the ancient world, when a person took a bath, he was clean until he walked outside in the dust in his bare feet or in open sandals. He could keep the rest of his body relatively clean, but his feet got dirty quickly. That's why there was the ritual of the cleansing of the feet without having to take a complete bath. Jesus told Peter, "When I wash your feet, I make you clean all over." One touch of the cleansing power of Christ cleanses us from all sin.

Then Jesus warned that one was there who would betray Him. He said,

"You are clean, but not all of you" (v. 10b). He knew who would betray him, but He washed all their feet, even the feet of Judas, but not without the warning that the cleansing He spoke of would not apply to every one of them.

Thus our Lord showed forth His humility, pointing ahead to the spiritual cleansing He would bring, and set an example of servanthood. He said, **"If you know these things, blessed are you if you do them"** (v. 17). Those who give themselves in service to others find deep joy in it.

36

THE BETRAYAL

John 13:18–38

"I do not speak concerning all of you. I know whom I have chosen; but that the Scripture may be fulfilled, 'He who eats bread with Me has lifted up his heel against Me.' Now I tell you before it comes, that when it does come to pass, you may believe that I am He. Most assuredly, I say to you, he who receives whomever I send receives Me; and he who receives Me receives Him who sent Me." When Jesus had said these things, He was troubled in spirit, and testified and said, "Most assuredly, I say to you, one of you will betray Me." Then the disciples looked at one another, perplexed about whom He spoke. Now there was leaning on Jesus' bosom one of His disciples, whom Jesus loved. Simon Peter therefore motioned to him to ask who it was of whom He spoke. Then, leaning back on Jesus' breast, he said to Him, "Lord, who is it?" Jesus answered, "It is he to whom I shall give a piece of bread when I have dipped it." And having dipped the bread, He gave it to Judas Iscariot, the son of Simon. Now after the piece of bread, Satan entered him. Then Jesus said to him, "What you do, do quickly." But no one at the table knew for what reason He said this to him. For some thought, because Judas had the money box, that Jesus had said to him, "Buy those things we need for the feast," or that he should give something to the poor. Having received the piece of bread, he then went out immediately. And it was night. So, when he had gone out, Jesus said, "Now the Son of Man is glorified, and God is glorified in Him. If God is glorified in Him, God will also glorify Him in Himself, and glorify Him immediately. Little children, I shall be with you a little while longer. You will seek Me; and as I said to the Jews, 'Where I am going, you cannot come,' so now I say to you. A new commandment I give to you, that you love one another; as I have loved you, that you also love one another. By this all will know that you are My disciples, if you have love for one another." Simon Peter said to Him, "Lord, where are You going?" Jesus answered him, "Where I am going you cannot follow Me now, but you shall follow Me afterward." Peter said to Him, "Lord, why can I not follow You now? I will lay down my life for Your sake." Jesus answered him, "Will you lay down your life for My sake? Most assuredly, I say to you, the rooster shall not crow till you have denied Me three times."

I n the previous chapter, we focused on Jesus' washing of His disciples' feet. But the passage we studied in that chapter, John 13:1–17, contained some ominous hints about what lay ahead. Jesus told the disciples they were clean—with one exception. He said, "You are not all clean" (v. 11), and John tells us He was thinking of His betrayer, Judas Iscariot. This hideous betrayal comes into sharper focus as we move in the latter half of John 13.

Jesus said: **"I do not speak concerning all of you. I know whom I have chosen; but that the Scripture may be fulfilled, 'He who eats bread with Me has lifted up his heel against Me'"** (v. 18). As Jesus spoke on the subject of His betrayer, He made clear that there was a distinction among the disciples. Some of them were chosen; they had been marked for salvation from eternity past and brought to faith under Jesus' ministry. But there was one in their number who was not chosen. This one, who ate bread with the Lord, would "[lift] up his heel" against Him.

In this verse, Jesus quoted from Psalm 41, where David wrote:

> I said, "LORD, be merciful to me;
> Heal my soul, for I have sinned against You."
> My enemies speak evil of me:
> "When will he die, and his name perish?"

And if he comes to see me, he speaks lies;
His heart gathers iniquity to itself;
When he goes out, he tells it. (vv. 4–6)

Understand what David is saying. First of all, he confesses his sin. Secondarily, he cries out to God about an enemy who is spreading vicious lies about him. He goes on to describe the anguish this enemy is causing:

All who hate me whisper together against me;
Against me they devise my hurt.
"An evil disease," they say, "clings to him.
And now that he lies down, he will rise up no more."
Even my own familiar friend in whom I trusted,
Who ate my bread,
Has lifted up his heel against me. (vv. 7–9)

It is one thing to be hated by your enemy. However, to be betrayed by a friend is one of the darkest experiences that a human being can endure. That is what David was enduring; a friend had turned against him. David was a type of Christ, and so many of the things that took place in David's life were later recapitulated in the life of Christ. Of course, this whole psalm is not messianic in nature. At the beginning, as we saw, David confessed his sin, which has no relevance or application to Christ. But there is relevance in David's betrayal by a friend, and it is for that reason that Jesus quoted David's words in the upper room.

Yet the situation facing Jesus is even darker than this. In the ancient Near East, to betray a friend was considered a heinous crime, but far more heinous was to betray a friend with whom one had shared bread at the table. It appears that Jesus and His disciples were sharing bread at the moment when He spoke these words. Even as He and Judas shared this intimate meal, Judas was planning his treachery.

Even in the face of this coming betrayal, Jesus thought of His disciples' faith and looked to bring good out of the evil. He said, "**Now I tell you before it comes, that when it does come to pass, you may believe that I am He**" (v. 19). Throughout the Gospel of John, we have encountered the "I am" sayings of Jesus. We have seen that Jesus used the formula borrowed from the Old Testament, from the Greek Septuagint translation of the Hebrew, where the supreme name of God, "I AM WHO I AM," or *Yahweh* (Ex. 3:14), is rendered in the Greek by the words *ego eimi*. Here it is again. Jesus gave His disciples a prophecy of His betrayal so that when it was fulfilled they would believe that He was God incarnate.

"Lord, Who Is It?"

John then tells us: **When Jesus had said these things, He was troubled in spirit, and testified and said, "Most assuredly, I say to you, one of you will betray Me." Then the disciples looked at one another, perplexed about whom he spoke** (vv. 21–22). Jesus was troubled as He contemplated what Judas would do. Therefore, He spoke plainly of what was coming, using His standard formula, "Most assuredly, I say to you . . ." to reinforce His words. The disciples, in turn, were "perplexed"; they were startled, stunned, and confused.

I mentioned earlier that I tell my seminary students not to be satisfied to grasp the word meanings, the structure, the context, and so forth when they study a passage of Scripture. I encourage them to look for the drama. I want them to read the text in an existential way, not in the sense of existential philosophy, but in the sense of empathy. I encourage them to try to get in the skin of the people who were engaged in the drama of redemption— to try to imagine, to the best of their ability, what those people were thinking and feeling, and why they behaved as they did. Let's try to do that here.

Put yourself in the place of Jesus' disciples. They are in the upper room. They have been listening to Jesus talk for several weeks about the grim events that are in front of Him. He has told them that He is going to Jerusalem, and that He's going to suffer and die there. Now He tells them that the hour is at hand. He is saying that He is about to die. What do you think that means to the disciples? I cannot imagine that any of them does not ask himself some very hard questions: "Does this mean I will die with Him? Is it my hour, too? Were my hopes that Jesus was the One who would deliver Israel totally misplaced? Where did it all go wrong?" Then Jesus delivers another blow. He announces to those who are seated there, "One of you will betray me." This is stunning; it almost seems beyond belief that something so terrible could happen. Yet, the disciples know that every time Jesus has opened His mouth during the time they have been with Him, He has uttered nothing but the unvarnished truth. So each one of those assembled knows that there is absolutely no doubt that what Jesus has announced is true, and that someone in that room will betray Him.

I think there was a fleeting moment when each man there in the presence of our Lord thought: "Oh no! Please—don't let it be me!" In fact, in his Gospel, Mark tells us that "they began to be sorrowful, and to say to Him one by one, 'Is it I?'" (Mark 14:19). Most of them loved Jesus, and they all assumed that each of the others loved Him. Thus, none of them could be sure that he himself wasn't the betrayer. Each hoped it would not be him, but they couldn't be sure, as Jesus had not said who it would be.

There is one small detail about this scene that is important for our understanding of what happened next. When Jesus came to this meal, He "reclined at table, and the apostles with him" (Luke 22:14 ESV). That's a detail that the greatest artists in Western history have either overlooked or ignored when they have painted their depictions of this moment in the biblical record. Invariably when we see paintings of the Last Supper, from Leonardo da Vinci on down, we see people *seated* at a table. It's true that Jewish people normally had their meals that way, but it was not so on rare and special occasions.

Some of you may remember old Hollywood movies that depicted Roman feasts. The emperor and his guests would be shown reclining alongside low tables, leaning on their left arms while keeping their right arms free to eat and drink the food and wine that filled the tables. This depiction was fairly accurate historically. But when this custom of reclining at meals was first introduced to Palestine, it was rejected by the Jews as a sign of decadence because of its earlier association with the hedonistic cultures of the pagans. Over time, however, the practice of reclining at a meal found some acceptance among the Jews because it was seen as signifying a great occasion. So this practice gradually began to be adopted, and it came to be used in the celebration of the Passover.

Why do I go into this detail? John writes: **Now there was leaning on Jesus' bosom one of His disciples, whom Jesus loved. Simon Peter therefore motioned to him to ask who it was of whom He spoke** (vv. 23–24). John himself was the disciple whom Jesus loved, and he was reclining right next to Jesus and in such a way that all he had to do was lean backward and turn his head, and he would be head to head with Christ at the Last Supper. Peter prompted John to take advantage of this propitious position to find out the answer.

John goes on: **Then, leaning back on Jesus' breast, he said to Him, "Lord, who is it?" Jesus answered, "It is he to whom I shall give a piece of bread when I have dipped it"** (vv. 25–26a). John asked Jesus who the betrayer was, but it's obvious from the text that he didn't ask loudly; he whispered to Jesus, "Who is it?" Jesus said: "Watch, John. The man to whom I give the morsel of bread that I have dipped in wine, he's the one." Then we're told, **And having dipped the bread, He gave it to Judas Iscariot, the son of Simon** (v. 26b). With that simple action, Jesus revealed His betrayer, at least to John.

The story continues: **Now after the piece of bread, Satan entered him. Then Jesus said to him, "What you do, do quickly." But no one at the table knew for what reason He said this to him. For some thought, because Judas had the money box, that Jesus had said to him, "Buy those things we need for the feast," or that he should give something to the poor** (vv. 27–29). Something in Jesus' gesture of giving Judas the bread seemingly caused him to utterly reject the Savior, allowing Satan to take control of his heart. In a further sign of His submission to the Father's will, Jesus made no effort to dissuade Judas or even to reveal his intent. Instead, He appealed to Judas to do it quickly, to get it over with. The rest of the disciples, who were still in the dark about the identity of the betrayer and about Peter and John's effort to learn his identity, did not understand why Jesus said this to Judas. They simply concluded Jesus had sent Judas out on an errand. Then, Judas **went out immediately. And it was night** (v. 30).

A New Commandment

When Judas was gone, Jesus spoke to the remaining eleven disciples. He said: **"Now the Son of Man is glorified, and God is glorified in Him. If God is glorified in Him, God will also glorify Him in Himself, and glorify Him immediately"** (vv. 31–32). As we have already discussed, the cross would bring glory to Jesus, and through Him to the Father. He went on: **"Little children, I shall be with you a little while longer. You will seek Me; and as I said to the Jews, 'Where I am going, you cannot come,' so now I say to you"** (v. 33). He called His disciples "little children." Isn't that amazing? Jesus here adopted the role of *pater familia*, the head of the household, and addressed His disciples as His children.

Then we come to one of the most familiar passages in the Gospels. Jesus said: **"A new commandment I give to you, that you love one another; as I have loved you, that you also love one another. By this all will know that you are My disciples, if you have love for one another"** (vv. 34–35). Jesus here identified a sure sign of faith in Him and a test of one's salvation—love for the brethren. This is what Francis Schaeffer called "the mark of the Christian." However, there is irony in this statement, for there was nothing new about this commandment. The commandment to love one another was deeply rooted in the Old Testament law (Lev. 19:18). So what was new in Jesus' command? My best guess is that it had to do with the context of the betrayal. Perhaps Jesus was saying: "I'm going away. Where I am going you can't come yet, but you will come. In the meantime, I'm giving you a new commandment: that you love each other the way I have loved you; that is, that you not betray one another." In other words, Jesus asked His disciples to display steadfast love, love that stands up when push comes to shove. He drew attention to the betrayal by which He would actually be glorified, and in that context He demanded from His disciples and all who would follow Him a love that has no place for treason.

Peter's reaction is heart-wrenching; indeed, so is the entire ensuing conversation. John tells us: **Simon Peter said to Him, "Lord, where are You going?" Jesus answered him, "Where I am going you cannot follow Me now, but you shall follow Me afterward." Peter said to Him, "Lord, why can I not follow You now? I will lay down my life for Your sake." Jesus answered him, "Will you lay down your life for My sake? Most assuredly, I say to you, the rooster shall not crow till you have denied Me three times"** (vv. 36–38). Peter wanted to follow Jesus and be loyal to Him. But Jesus was forced to show him his inability, in his own strength, to remain faithful. So He predicted that Peter, before the sun rose, would prove himself much more Judas-like than he could wish.

There is a great deal of speculation among scholars about this conversation around the table. The discussion focuses on where the disciples were seated, especially John. Some argue that it's clear from the text that Jesus was seated and that John was at His right hand, for that is assumed to be the seat of honor, the logical place for the disciple Jesus loved. But in the ancient Near Eastern culture, the seat of honor at the dining table was not at the host's right but at his left, and we're not told who was on Jesus' left. Maybe it was Peter. Perhaps Peter leaned across and gave the signal to John and said, "Ask Him who it is." But if Peter was that close, he could have asked Jesus himself, and so most scholars conclude that Peter wasn't seated in the place of honor. The consensus is that the man who sat that night in the seat of honor, who was close enough for Jesus to simply reach over to him and give him a piece of bread, was Judas. If that is so, then the disciple who was honored that night was the disciple who proved most treacherous to Jesus.

We need to remember, however, that Peter was on the verge of denying Jesus, and all of the disciples, every one of them, would abandon Him in the night. Despite the best of intentions, they did not have the strength to stand firm for Jesus. We, too, are equally prone to fall. In fact, every time we sin, we commit cosmic treason against our Lord and Savior.

The failures of Judas, of Peter, and of their fellow disciples should cause us to fall to our knees in surrender, asking Christ to cause us to stand. Only by His power will we remain loyal to Him.

37

A PLACE FOR YOU

John 14:1–3

"Let not your heart be troubled; you believe in God, believe also in Me. In My Father's house are many mansions; if it were not so, I would have told you. I go to prepare a place for you. And if I go and prepare a place for you, I will come again and receive you to Myself; that where I am, there you may be also."

I occasionally see reports of polls that ask professing Christians which chapter of the Bible is their favorite. When I see these reports, two chapters seem to vie for the top spot. Sometimes one of them comes in first, sometimes the other. Both of the main contenders are from New Testament books. One is 1 Corinthians 13, the famous love chapter written by the apostle Paul. The other perennial favorite is the chapter we have now reached in our study of John's Gospel—John 14, which is beloved because it gives such profound comfort to people who read it or hear it.

One of the problems with understanding the content of John 14 is discerning its original context. As you know, when John penned his Gospel, he didn't divide it into chapters and verses. That came much later in church history, and sometimes we wonder why the chapters and verses were placed where they were. The beginning of Chapter 14 represents one of those curious decisions, because the material at the opening of this chapter must be understood in direct relationship to what comes immediately before it in Chapter 13. In fact, Chapter 14 begins in the middle of a speech of Jesus. Therefore, we need to try to connect it, if we can, to what went before.

This chapter begins with words that have been treasured by believers in Christian history: **"Let not your heart be troubled"** (v. 1a). Interestingly, the same word translated as "troubled" here also appeared in Chapter 13, where John wrote, "When Jesus had said these things, He was troubled in spirit" (13:21a). So our Lord seemingly was telling His disciples, "I'm troubled, but don't you be troubled." How are we to understand this apparent conflict between Jesus' example and His teaching?

First, we need to remember the reason for Jesus' troubled spirit. John tells us that Jesus was troubled just before he records Jesus' announcement that one of the disciples would turn against Him: "Most assuredly, I say to you, one of you will betray Me" (13:21b). So the immediate cause of Jesus' distress was His certain knowledge that one of those in the room with Him that night was about to betray Him.

Second, we need to keep in mind all the troubling factors that were before the disciples. When Jesus disclosed to His disciples that one of them would betray Him, they were gripped within by perplexity (13:22). In other words, like Jesus, they felt troubled by this horrible prospect of their Master's betrayal. Their distress was exacerbated when Jesus went on to say: "Little children, I shall be with you a little while longer. You will seek Me; and as I said to the Jews, 'Where I am going, you cannot come,' so now I say to you" (13:33). Peter revealed the distress this announcement caused him personally when he plaintively asked Jesus where He was going and why he could not follow (13:36–37). Peter said: "Lord, why can't I follow You now? I've been following You for three years. I've gone all over Galilee, all over Judea, with You. Wherever You're going now, take me with You. I'll lay down my life for Your sake." That heartfelt request only brought another horrible revelation from Jesus: "Most assuredly, I say to you, the rooster shall not crow till you have denied Me three times" (13:38b).

These words fell like a thunderbolt on the ears of those assembled in the upper room. In short order, they had been told that Judas was going to betray Jesus, that Jesus was about to leave them, and that Peter was going to deny Him. Can you imagine how these men felt upon hearing this series of dire announcements? Their hearts were troubled beyond description, and it was in that context that Jesus said to them, "Let not your heart be troubled."

Faith Banishes Distress

Jesus went on to say, **"you believe in God, believe also in Me"** (v. 1b). In the original Greek, the structure of the verbs in this phrase is somewhat ambiguous because they can be interpreted either in the indicative or the imperative. There are three ways we could read this statement. First, both verbs could be read in the indicative: "You believe in God and you believe in Me." Second, both verbs could be read in the imperative (that is, as commands): "Believe in God and believe in Me, too." Finally, the first verb could be read in the indicative and the second in the imperative: "You believe in God; therefore, believe in Me." This is the option chosen by the translators of the *New King James Version*, and rightly so, I believe.

When we looked at John 3, we saw that Nicodemus, a member of the Sanhedrin, a ruler of the Jews, came to Jesus by night and said to Him, "Rabbi, we know that You are a teacher come from God; for no one can do these signs that You do unless God is with him" (3:2). We don't know whether Nicodemus had seen Jesus change the water into wine or some of His other miracles, or whether he had simply heard about these signs. In any case, for one reason or another, he had become convinced that Jesus had performed actions that He could not do unless God Himself had empowered Him.

Imagine you are one of Jesus' disciples. You have seen much more than Nicodemus dreamed of seeing. You were there when Jesus changed the water into wine. You were there when He healed the paralytic at the pool of Bethesda. You were there when five thousand men, plus women and children, were hungry, and Jesus took five loaves and a couple of fish and multiplied them to feed all of those people. You were there in the boat that night on the Sea of Galilee when Jesus walked on the water. You were there when He gave sight to the man born blind. You were there when He raised Lazarus to life after he had been in his tomb for four days. If any group of men in human history ever had reason to believe that a man was sent by God, it was these disciples who were assembled there in the upper room that night. So the imperative should not really surprise us. Jesus was telling them to act on what they had seen: "Believe in Me." Faith in Jesus as the Son of God is the basis for preventing one's heart from being troubled.

Jesus continued on with his words of comfort for His friends: **"In My Father's house are many mansions" (v. 2a).** The *New King James Version* uses the word *mansions* here. That's not a very good translation. The NKJV provides a text note that tells us the Greek word literally means "dwellings," but even more precisely, the word calls attention to the idea of a suite.

Vesta and I were on a tour through Europe several years ago, and our tour group arrived in Grindelwald, a little village in Switzerland at the base of that huge, icy mountain that is known as the Eiger, or "the ogre." When we got to the hotel, there had been a problem with our reservations and the rooms we had booked for our tour group were not available. The manager of the hotel was filled with apologies and said, "I have a few other rooms available; they're more expensive than those you reserved, but because it was our mistake, we'll give you those rooms for the same price." Well, Vesta and I ended up in the royal suite. We've spent some time in hotels in our lives, but never have we experienced anything like the royal suite in that palatial hotel at the base of the Eiger.

That's something like the kind of accommodation Jesus promised. He said: "I'm going to prepare not a room, not a monk's cell, not a broom closet—I'm going to prepare for you a royal suite in My Father's house."

That suite is absolutely guaranteed. When I travel, all of my reservations are booked by my administrative assistant, Maureen. No one is more efficient at booking space than she, and once she has made a reservation, she calls several times to confirm it. Recently, when we were on our way to California, Maureen called our hotel while we were in the air and confirmed our reservation. However, when we got there, we were told that the hotel was overbooked and they had no rooms for us. So even Maureen's bookings can fail. But that suite in heaven has been booked by the King of kings. That reservation is backed by an ironclad guarantee.

The Assurance of New Life

Jesus also assured His disciples, **"if it were not so, I would have told you"** (v. 2b). The oldest theological question with which humanity has wrestled is that question that was voiced so poignantly by Job: "If a man dies, shall he live again?" (Job 14:14a). I'm sure that everyone reading this book has been touched by the death of a loved one. I have; by the mercy of God, both of my parents died at home in bed. My mother slipped away at night when I was asleep, but I was next to the bed, more than fifty years ago, when my father breathed his last. I watched death in front of my eyes, and in that moment I lost the person who meant more to me than any person on the face of the earth. When it happened, something stabbed my soul, causing me to say: "This is insane. This can't be real. He must merely be sleeping. O, God, will he live again?"

It's always interesting to ask people who they look forward to seeing in heaven. Some will single out biblical characters, such as Abraham, David, Jeremiah, and the apostle Paul. Others point to great figures from church history, such as Augustine, Martin Luther, John Calvin, and Jonathan Edwards. I desperately want to see my dad. I don't want to see him sick and dying. I want to see him alive, in his resurrected state. But, of course, more than anyone else, I want to see Jesus. I want to look into His face. I want to hear His voice. I want to behold His glory, the glory He had with the Father from the foundation of the earth.

If I had been one of Jesus' disciples, I would have pulled Him aside and said: "Lord, I can't believe what I have seen during your ministry, the things that You have done. I can't believe the insights that You have spoken that have meant so much to my soul. But Jesus, I have one burning question for You: Is it true that we will live again? Is it true or is it myth? Is the resurrection merely an opiate, a bromide for our troubled souls? Jesus, tell me the cold reality."

He would have said to me: "R. C., if this were not the truth, I would have told you. I would not have allowed you to go on committing yourself to a myth. I would not have allowed you to pursue devotion to a dream. If it were not so, I would have told you." That's exactly what He said here to His disciples, and I find this to be the most comforting text in sacred Scripture from the lips of Jesus.

Jesus also said, **"I go to prepare a place for you. And if I go and prepare a place for you, I will come again and receive you to Myself; that where I am, there you may be also"** (vv. 2c–3). The suite is ready. The reservation is guaranteed. But Jesus still has plans—He will come again to bring us home, so that we can be where He is.

In all honesty, there is in my heart and soul not the slightest fear of death. Death holds no fear for me because I know whom I have believed and I have His promises for what He will do for me when I die. I know that when I close my eyes in death, my soul will fly immediately to the bosom of Christ, which is far better than anything I can enjoy in this world. So I don't fear death, but if you ask me about *dying*, that's another matter. If I could just close my eyes and step across into heaven, that would be glory for me, but none of us knows the route we will take. It may be one that includes great affliction, pain, and suffering. But the travail will be for a moment compared with the other side. Though we may experience the pangs of terror as we consider the prospect of dying, death itself holds no fear for us because it is our entrance to that suite that Jesus has prepared for us in heaven, a suite in the house where He Himself dwells.

38

THE ONLY WAY

John 14:4–11

"And where I go you know, and the way you know." Thomas said to Him, "Lord, we do not know where You are going, and how can we know the way?" Jesus said to him, "I am the way, the truth, and the life. No one comes to the Father except through Me. If you had known Me, you would have known My Father also; and from now on you know Him and have seen Him." Philip said to Him, "Lord, show us the Father, and it is sufficient for us." Jesus said to him, "Have I been with you so long, and yet you have not known Me, Philip? He who has seen Me has seen the Father; so how can you say, 'Show us the Father'? Do you not believe that I am in the Father, and the Father in Me? The words that I speak to you I do not speak on My own authority; but the Father who dwells in Me does the works. Believe Me that I am in the Father and the Father in Me, or else believe Me for the sake of the works themselves."

The apostle Peter gave what has been called in church history "the great confession." It happened in Caesarea Philippi, when Jesus asked His disciples, "Who do men say that I, the Son of Man, am?" They gave Him a report of some of the rumors that were circulating among the people—He was suspected of being John the Baptist, Elijah, Jeremiah, or one of the other prophets. Jesus then personalized the question: "Who do you say that I am?" That prompted Peter to say, "You are the Christ, the Son of the living God." When Peter made this confession, Jesus congratulated him: "Blessed are you, Simon Bar-Jonah, for flesh and blood has not revealed this to you, but My Father who is in heaven" (Matt. 16:13–17).

I mention that account of the great confession to remind us, before we delve into our passage for this chapter, that the church Christ built and is building must always be a confessing church. When I speak of the church as a confessing church, I'm not simply speaking of the confession of sin that we utter before God, but rather the confession of our faith. Christ promises redemption to those who not only believe in His resurrection in their hearts but who confess Him with their mouths (Rom. 10:9).

The Unique Son of God

It is absolutely crucial that we see that we confess the uniqueness of Christ. Peter said, "You are *the* Christ, *the* Son of the living God." The Apostles' Creed echoes this confession of uniqueness when it proclaims, "I believe in God the Father Almighty, maker of heaven and earth; and in Jesus Christ, his *only* Son, our Lord . . . ." From the very beginning of the Christian church, the exclusive character of Christ, the uniqueness of the Son of God, has been at the heart of our confession. I stress that because, in this day, in this culture, and even in vast swaths of the modern church, there is nothing more politically incorrect, more repugnant to the relativists of this age, than claims of exclusivity given unto Jesus.

I once took a college class that was taught by a woman who was openly hostile to the Christian faith. She never missed an opportunity to attack Christianity in her classroom, so I tried to melt into the woodwork to escape the arrows of her wrath. One day, however, she called on me in front of the class. She said, "Mr. Sproul, do you believe that Jesus is the only way to God?" I knew how she felt about any exclusive claims to Jesus, so I knew I was caught between a rock and a hard place. If I said what I believed, I would experience an avalanche of wrath from the instructor. But if I didn't say what I believed, I would be guilty of nothing less than treason to the King of kings. I mumbled an answer, but she said, "What was that?" So I said: "Yes, ma'am. I do believe that Jesus is the only way to God." She went into a paroxysm of rage that spilled out on me. She said, "That is the most narrow-minded, arrogant, bigoted thing I've ever heard a student say." The rest of the class glared at me as she heaped her scorn on me.

After the class, as I was walking out the door, she stopped me and said: "I'm sorry. I didn't mean to be so hard on you. But I just can't understand how anybody could be that narrow-minded." I said to her: "Well, I hope you can understand my problem. I have been persuaded that Christ is the Son of God. I am a Christian. There is nothing more foundational to Christianity than the confession that Jesus is the Son of God. Now if I believed that Jesus was the only way to God because He happened to be *my* way, and the unspoken premise of my logic was that anything that R. C. Sproul believes must, by logical necessity, be the only true way to think, then I would agree with your assessment that that would be unspeakably arrogant, bigoted, and narrow-minded. But I hope you understand why I believe Jesus is the only way. It is because Jesus *said* that He was the only way, and if I deny that, I deny Him."

Let me just say parenthetically, if *you* deny that, *you* deny Him. There's probably no greater point of pressure in our society than that very point. Our friends, our community, and even many churches tell us that we must deny the uniqueness of Christ. But to do that, we must deny the church's confession of faith, and more importantly, we must deny Jesus' own confession about Himself.

Another Claim of Deity

In the text we have before us in this chapter, we find Jesus giving another of the "I am" sayings that are scattered throughout the Gospel of John. We have seen that Jesus called himself "the bread of life" (6:35, 48), "the light of the world" (8:12; 9:5), "the door of the sheep" (10:7, 9), "the good shepherd" (10:11, 14), and "the resurrection and the life" (11:25). As we have seen, in the Septuagint—the Greek translation of the Old Testament Scriptures—the sacred, ineffable name of God, the name *Yahweh*, which we translate as "I AM WHO I AM" (Ex. 3:14), is rendered by the phrase *ego eimi*, which literally means, "I am, I am." That phrase shows up in each of these "I am" sayings, indicating that Jesus makes a radical claim about His connection with God Himself. It shows up once again in John 14:6.

In the previous chapter, we saw that Jesus spoke comfort to His disciples (vv. 1–3) about a number of troubling things: one of the disciples was going to betray Him, He was about to go away, and Peter was going to deny Him. He then went on to say: **"And where I go you know, and the way you know"** (v. 4). By now, they should have understood that He was leaving earth to return to His Father in heaven. But Thomas professed ignorance: **"Lord, we do not know where You are going, and how can we know the**

way?" (v. 5). To this Jesus replied: **"I am the way, the truth, and the life. No one comes to the Father except through Me"** (v. 6).

The structure of this statement is such that Jesus was not giving a string of descriptive terms. He was not saying, "I am: A) the way, B) the truth, and C) the life." Rather, this statement is in an elliptical form, so that Jesus was saying: "I am the way *because* I am the truth and *because* I am the life. I am the way to the Father because I am the true manifestation or revelation of the Father. I am the way to the Father because I alone have the power of eternal life."

As I noted above, Jesus said: "I am the door. If anyone enters by Me, he will be saved" (10:9a). Elsewhere in the Scriptures we are told "there is no other name under heaven given among men by which we must be saved" (Acts 4:12). The apostle Paul tells us "there is one God and one Mediator between God and men, the Man Christ Jesus" (1 Tim. 2:5). Again, we read in the prologue of John's Gospel that Jesus is "the only begotten of the Father" (1:14). So John 14:6 is not giving us an exceptional statement from the lips of Jesus. What He said here is consistent with a theme that runs through the entire New Testament—that God has provided a road, a path, or a way of redemption, which was His plan from all eternity, and that the divine *Logos*, the second person of the Trinity, took on Himself a human nature to make that way.

When I explained all this to my college professor, she said: "But how could God be so narrow-minded? I thought God was a God of love." You see, she believed the widely accepted maxim in our culture that it doesn't really matter what you believe, just as long as you're sincere. If the Ephesians were sincere in their devotion to the goddess Diana, if the followers of Baal were sincere in their worship of Baal, or if the Muslims are sincere in their worship of Allah, that's all that matters. God doesn't care whether you worship idols just as long as you worship them sincerely. We remember that Satan appeared to Jesus in the wilderness and said: "All this authority I will give You, and their glory. . . . If You will worship before me, all will be Yours" (Luke 4:6–7). It was as if Satan was saying to Jesus: "It won't do any harm for You to bow to me for a moment. God won't mind. Don't be narrow-minded. There's room in the mercy of God for a little Satanism." But Jesus knew better. He said: "Get behind Me, Satan! For it is written, 'You shall worship the LORD your God, and Him only you shall serve'" (Luke 4:8).

I really cannot think of anything more antithetical to biblical Christianity than the idea that it doesn't matter what you believe, and yet it has been inculcated in us from the time we were in kindergarten. I think it is because, here in the United States, all religions are equally tolerated under the law, so we make a gratuitous leap from equality under the law to equal validity before God. That's a perilous place to stand because the Scriptures say there's a difference between truth and falsehood, between the true Messiah and false messiahs, and between Christ and Antichrist.

Father and Son Are One

Jesus then said to His disciples: **"If you had known Me, you would have known My Father also; and from now on you know Him and have seen Him"** (v. 7). Here again, as we have seen throughout this Gospel, Jesus affirmed the oneness between Himself and the Father. To know Him is to know the Father. In the disciples' case, to have seen Jesus in the flesh meant they had seen the Father. Once again, however, one of the disciples replied with perplexity: **Philip said to Him, "Lord, show us the Father, and it is sufficient for us"** (v. 8). It was as if Philip said: "Jesus, we've seen some fantastic things—You changed the water into wine, You fed the five thousand, You walked on the water. Old Testament people would have given their lives to see just one of these miracles You have performed. Angels would like to look into these things that we've been able to see. But now, please give us the big one, then we'll be satisfied. Do just one more miracle. Peel back the veil and let us see the face of God."

If ever we find Christ manifesting exasperation with His disciples, it is here. He said: **"Have I been with you so long, and yet you have not known Me, Philip? He who has seen Me has seen the Father; so how can you say, 'Show us the Father'? Do you not believe that I am in the Father, and the Father in Me? The words that I speak to you I do not speak on My own authority; but the Father who dwells in Me does the works. Believe Me that I am in the Father and the Father in Me, or else believe Me for the sake of the works themselves"** (vv. 9–11). Jesus had to go over the whole question of His oneness with the Father once again. He reiterated: to see Him is to see the Father. He is in the Father and the Father in Him. The words He taught were given Him by the Father, and the Father (who dwells in Jesus) gave miracles to corroborate Jesus' teaching. All these were implications the disciples should have drawn from the things they had heard Jesus say and seen Him do.

Jesus' last words here were a challenge to all the disciples, and, indeed, to us as well: "Believe Me that I am in the Father and the Father in Me, or else believe Me for the sake of the works themselves." It was time, Jesus said, for the disciples to understand in a life-changing way that He is the Son of

God, preferably because He said it, but if not then because His miracles proved it.

After the resurrection, when two disciples encountered Jesus on the road to Emmaus, they failed to recognize Him, a vivid example of their failure to grasp His true identity. When He stopped to take a meal with them, He said to them: "'O foolish ones, and slow of heart to believe in all that the prophets have spoken! Ought not the Christ to have suffered these things and to enter into His glory?' And beginning at Moses and all the Prophets, He expounded to them in all the Scriptures the things concerning Himself" (Luke 24:25–27). The disciples were "foolish . . . and slow of heart to believe." Does not that description apply to us as well? When we fail to grasp who Jesus is, we leave the door open to the pluralism our world insists on. We must understand that Jesus is *the* way and confess that truth joyfully before the watching world.

39

ANOTHER HELPER

John 14:12–17

"Most assuredly, I say to you, he who believes in Me, the works that I do he will do also; and greater works than these he will do, because I go to My Father. And whatever you ask in My name, that I will do, that the Father may be glorified in the Son. If you ask anything in My name, I will do it. If you love Me, keep My commandments. And I will pray the Father, and He will give you another Helper, that He may abide with you forever—the Spirit of truth, whom the world cannot receive, because it neither sees Him nor knows Him; but you know Him, for He dwells with you and will be in you."

I became a Christian in September 1957. At that time, I had a girlfriend with whom I had been "going steady" since 1952. She attended a different college, so I communicated to her by letter every day. As a result of my conversion, my letters were filled with spiritual matters and references to the newfound faith I was experiencing and to discoveries I was making from Scripture. Unfortunately, she was not a believer, and she thought I had taken leave of my senses. So a serious tension came into our relationship, and in the winter of 1958 I spent hours, literally, on my knees, praying for her redemption.

She decided to go home for a weekend, so we arranged that she would take a bus from her college to my campus, spend a day there, and then I would drive her home the following morning. The day that she came, I spent the entire morning on my knees, and when she arrived we went to a Bible study that I attended regularly on campus. In the midst of the Bible study, the ministry of Christ and the significance of the cross were presented to her in a way that caused the scales to fall from her eyes, and she came to a saving knowledge of Christ. The next day, my wife-to-be told me that she woke up every hour that night, asking herself: "Is it still there? Do I still have it?" Being assured that she did, she was able to go back to sleep. She said to me with great excitement, "R. C., now I know who the Holy Spirit is." We had been raised in the same church and had heard the liturgy, "In the name of the Father, Son, and Holy Ghost," but we had no idea about the person and the work of God the Holy Spirit until we were converted under His power.

If you have persevered with me to this point in John's Gospel, and if you can persevere with me for a few more chapters, you will be spared the kind of ignorance I suffered with respect to the Holy Spirit. That is because, beginning here in John 14 and extending through John 17, we encounter the longest discourse anywhere in Scripture concerning the ministry of God the Holy Spirit. As we study these chapters, it is my hope and purpose that we would deepen our understanding of who the Holy Spirit is, of why God sent Him to minister among us, and of what He does in our midst.

Greater Works Than Jesus Did?

As we pick up the discourse, we encounter a statement from Jesus that I have struggled all my life to fully understand. I think I know what He meant, but I'm not sure. He said, **"Most assuredly, I say to you, he who believes in Me, the works that I do he will do also; and greater works than these he will do, because I go to my Father"** (v. 12). I can hardly imagine that you or I would ever be capable of doing the works Jesus did, and it's unthinkable that we would do greater works than He did in His lifetime. But I think our Lord is getting at something that is extremely important for the church in every age to understand.

When Jesus performed miracles during His incarnation, He did so because He was endowed in a miraculous way by the Holy Spirit, which came upon Him at His baptism. The same was true for Moses, who also did many mighty works by the Spirit's power. We know of the Spirit's role in Moses' miracles because of the account in Numbers 11. Moses became overwhelmed with the burden of leading the Israelites, whereupon God commanded him to bring seventy elders of Israel to the tabernacle and said, "I will take of the Spirit that is upon you and will put the same upon them" (v. 17a). When God did that, the seventy elders were anointed and empowered by God for ministry. So we see the Spirit that was upon Moses, the mediator of the old covenant, distributed to those who were his followers.

On that occasion, two of the seventy elders designated to receive the Spirit that was upon Moses remained in the camp for an unexplained reason rather than coming to the tabernacle. But when God laid His Spirit on the other elders, these two also were anointed and began to prophesy in the camp. Joshua, jealous to protect Moses' unique authority, complained about that and said, "Moses my lord, forbid them!" (v. 28). But Moses rebuked him and said: "Are you zealous for my sake? Oh, that all the LORD's people were prophets and that the LORD would put His Spirit upon them" (v. 29).

That was only a wish expressed by Moses, a prayer at best. But later, in the Old Testament book of Joel, that wish became a prophecy. The prophet said, "And it shall come to pass afterward that I will pour out My Spirit on all flesh" (2:28). In other words, God said He would anoint the whole church, all believers, with His Spirit. That prophecy became a reality at Pentecost (Acts 2).

Therefore, I believe Jesus was preparing His disciples to understand that momentous event that was to take place in the near future. God would take the Spirit that was on Jesus, by Christ's own request, and distribute it to all who loved Him, so that the same power that was invested in Him would be invested in His church. I do not think He meant that we all would do miracles for all the ages, but that the church is empowered by the Holy Spirit to perform works that go far beyond the local community of Jerusalem or Judea. The church has been empowered for missionary and ministry work across the globe.

Sometimes we hear about the black eyes that the church has suffered in history because of the Crusades, religious persecution, and bigotry. People look at these events and say, "The track record of the Christian church is abysmal." Actually, if we look at the history of Western civilization, we see that the primary impetus for the abolition of slavery in the Western world came largely through the impact of the Christian church. Countless institutions of higher learning, universities and colleges, were founded by the ministry of Christians. It was the Christian community that moved across the globe building orphanages for children who were without hope. The hospital movement in Western history was driven largely by the Christian church. By the Spirit's endowment, the church extends the work of Jesus, the benefits of Jesus, indeed, the ministry of Jesus to the very ends of the earth. Jesus was preparing His disciples for this when He spoke these words in the upper room.

Note that Jesus said, "greater works than these he will do, *because* I go to My Father." There was no news that more deeply troubled the disciples of Christ than His announcement that He was leaving, and yet our Lord said to them, "It is to your advantage that I go away" (16:7). Why? Because Pentecost could not and would not happen until Christ had ascended to the right hand of the Father. It was only by His departure that the presence of the Spirit could come to the whole church. The disciples did not grasp this when they came to the upper room, but I believe they came to understand it largely through this discourse, so that when they watched Jesus ascend into heaven on the Mount of Ascension, they were able to return to the city rejoicing (Luke 24:52).

Praying in Jesus' Name

Jesus went on: **"And whatever you ask in My name, that I will do, that the Father may be glorified in the Son. If you ask anything in My name, I will do it"** (vv. 13–14). There are those in the church who have come to the conclusion that these statements are absolute. They think that a Christian may ask for anything he would like to have, and as long as he adds "in Jesus' name I pray" after his request, God will most certainly do what he asks Him to do. This interpretation of these verses is the basis for the "name it and claim it" movement throughout the church.

Another verse that similarly gets taken out of context is Matthew 18:19, where these words of Jesus are recorded: "Again I say to you that if two of you agree on earth concerning anything that they ask, it will be done for them by My Father in heaven." What could be clearer? All we have to do is find at least one other Christian who will agree with us about something, ask God for it, and wait for Him to do it. How many Christians would like to see the end of cancer? I would. In fact, I think we all would like to see cancer eradicated. According to the popular interpretation of this verse, I just need to find one other person who would like to see cancer ended. If I can find one person who will pray with me for God to eradicate cancer, that will be the end of cancer.

Obviously, it's not that simple. These statements of Jesus must be understood in the context of all that our Lord teaches regarding prayer. He never gave His people a blank check with the promise, "Anything you ask for I will do." The assumption behind these words is this: "I will do for you anything you ask that is within the parameters of what is legitimate, according to My teaching."

I believe the very next verse supports this interpretation. Jesus said, **"If you love Me, keep My commandments"** (v. 15). There are different ways that we can read this statement of Jesus. Some commentators take it this way: "If you love Me, then you are obligated to keep My commandments." That is, love is shown by obedience. Others believe Jesus was saying, "If you love Me, you will keep My commandments." In this view, obedience is a certain inevitable consequence of affection for Christ. The Reformers held to this view, and that is why they believed that while justification is not based on our works, true justification always generates a response of obedience. Sanctification always and ever flows automatically and necessarily out of justification. If we love Him, we will obey Him. If we do not obey Him, that's proof positive that no matter what we say, there is no love for Christ in our hearts.

Genuine love for Jesus manifests itself in obedience to His commandments. In other words, the one who loves Jesus subordinates his own desires to those of the Lord. That kind of love rules out treating Jesus as a celestial vending machine who exists to meet our wants and desires.

With His next statement, Jesus mentioned the Spirit for the first time: **"And I will pray the Father, and He will give you another Helper, that He may abide with you forever—the Spirit of truth, whom the world cannot receive, because it neither sees Him nor knows Him; but you know him, for He dwells with you and will be in you"** (vv. 16–17).

The Greek word that is translated as "Helper" here is *parakletos*, or, in this case, *parakleton*. This word gives us the English word *paraclete*. This word is translated in a number of different ways in the various Bible versions. Some say "Advocate," some say "Comforter," and others say "Counselor."

"Advocate" gives us a good idea of what a paraclete is. In antiquity, a paraclete was an attorney, basically a defense attorney. If you had problems with the law and you needed somebody to represent you, you called your paraclete. The prefix *para* means "alongside or beside" and the verb *kletos* means "to call." So the paraclete was someone you called to come alongside you and help you in your defense.

"Comforter," which is used in the King James Version, is a misleading word choice in our day. We know that the Holy Spirit does console us in times of pain and adversity. But the King James Version was written at a time when the English language was more closely connected with its Latin roots, and the word *comfort* came from two Latin words that meant "with strength." Thus, a comforter was someone who came to *strengthen* you. It wasn't the one who came to wipe your tears after the battle; it was the one who came to give you strength for the battle.

I also think "Counselor" can be misleading, because when we hear it we tend to think of a high school guidance counselor or a psychological therapist. However, a *parakleton* was more like an advocate, a counselor in a courtroom, someone who could defend your case during a trial.

The Original Paraclete

I used to play a game with my seminary students. I would ask them, "In the New Testament, who is the Paraclete?" They would all raise their hands and say: "Oh, we know that. That's easy. The Paraclete is the Holy Spirit." They said that because we sometimes refer to the Holy Spirit in theology as the Paraclete. But my question required a somewhat technical response. I would say: "That's right and it's not right. It's true that the Holy Spirit is a Paraclete, but Jesus did not call him *the* Paraclete. He called the Spirit "another Paraclete," and for there to be another Paraclete, there must be a prior Paraclete. So who is the Paraclete?

First John 2:1 clearly gives us the answer. It says: "My little children, these things I write to you, so that you may not sin. And if anyone sins, we have an Advocate with the Father, Jesus Christ the righteous." Christ is our Advocate, our Comforter, our Counselor, and our Helper. For this reason, Jesus spoke of the Spirit, the third person of the Trinity, as *another* Helper. Following Jesus' departure, the Spirit would come to perform the same ministry among the disciples of Christ. Jesus was saying: "I'm not going to leave you helpless. I'm praying to the Father that He will send you One who comes with strength to help you when you're called before magistrates and when death is threatening you. He will help you stand by the power of God."

Jesus used a marvelous title for the Spirit here—the Spirit of truth. It is the Holy Spirit who inspired the Bible. It is the Holy Spirit who illumines the Bible. It is the Holy Spirit who applies the truth of the Word of God with power, so that it cuts between bone and marrow (see Heb. 4:12). It is the Holy Spirit who exposes falsehood.

Jesus also noted that the world—that is, those who are not believers—could not receive the Spirit. Why? Because they did not see Him or know Him. By contrast, Jesus said, the disciples did know Him, for He dwelled in them. The context here is clearly saving knowledge, for the Spirit is given to all who are born again.

There is a theory as to why Jesus gave so much attention to the Holy Spirit in this upper room discourse. It holds that what happened in the upper room was a kind of dynastic succession celebration. The concept of dynasties is sprinkled throughout the Old Testament—the patriarchal blessing was handed down from father to son, Moses passed the leadership of the people of Israel and his authority into the hands of Joshua, and kings routinely passed their crowns to their sons. In a similar manner, Jesus was about to leave, so He turned the leadership of the earthly church over to the Holy Spirit, who would now be the Paraclete.

40

THE LEGACY

John 14:18–31

"I will not leave you orphans; I will come to you. A little while longer and the world will see Me no more, but you will see Me. Because I live, you will live also. At that day you will know that I am in My Father, and you in Me, and I in you. He who has My commandments and keeps them, it is he who loves Me. And he who loves Me will be loved by My Father, and I will love him and manifest Myself to him." Judas (not Iscariot) said to Him, "Lord, how is it that You will manifest Yourself to us, and not to the world?" Jesus answered and said to him, "If anyone loves Me, he will keep My word; and My Father will love him, and We will come to him and make Our home with him. He who does not love Me does not keep My words; and the word which you hear is not Mine but the Father's who sent Me. These things I have spoken to you while being present with you. But the Helper, the Holy Spirit, whom the Father will send in My name, He will teach you all things, and bring to your remembrance all things that I said to you. Peace I leave with you, My peace I give to you; not as the world gives do I give to you. Let not your heart be troubled, neither let it be afraid. You have heard Me say to you, 'I am going away and coming back to you.' If you loved Me, you would rejoice because I said, 'I am going to the Father,' for My Father is greater than I. And now

I have told you before it comes, that when it does come to pass, you may believe. I will no longer talk much with you, for the ruler of this world is coming, and he has nothing in Me. But that the world may know that I love the Father, and as the Father gave Me commandment, so I do. Arise, let us go from here."

Thanks to the apostle John's inspired record, we have the unspeakable privilege of eavesdropping on Jesus and His disciples as Jesus spoke to them in the upper room. As we saw in the previous chapter, Jesus spoke of His coming departure and of His plans to send the Holy Spirit to carry on His ministry as His disciples' Paraclete, or Advocate. He continued to address these subjects and their implications in the section of John's Gospel that is before us in this chapter.

This portion of Jesus' discourse begins with a poignant statement. Jesus said, **"I will not leave you orphans; I will come to you"** (v. 18). A few chapters ago, I wrote about my desire to be reunited with my father when I reach heaven. I remember the pangs I felt, as a teenage boy, when I lost my father's strength and guidance. My mother died just a few years later, and even though I was in my twenties and was a grown man, as it were, I really felt the pain of being alone in the world. There was no one I could go to in times of need for counsel, comfort, and support. Jesus anticipated that His disciples would feel this way when He left them, so He promised them: "I'm not going to leave you in that condition. I'm not going to leave you without support or counsel."

The Coming of Christ

But notice the words Jesus appended to the end of this statement: "I will come to you." It is somewhat unclear what Jesus meant by this. Since this statement is bracketed by discussion about the coming of the Holy Spirit as Jesus' representative, we might think He was referring to Pentecost, when the Holy Spirit would come on His church in power. Jesus promised, just before He ascended, "I am with you always, even to the end of the age" (Matt. 28:20b). He said that, by virtue of the Spirit's ministry, He would still be with His disciples. We know that in terms of Jesus' human nature, He's no longer present with us. However, with respect to His divine nature, He's never absent from us. So it may be that when Jesus said, "I will come to you," He was referring to Pentecost, when the Spirit descended.

Another alternative that many commentators suggest is that Jesus was referring to His final coming at the end of the age, when He will return to gather His church. That is the least likely of the alternatives in this immediate context, I think.

Yet another possibility is that Jesus was referring to His resurrection. On two occasions in the New Testament, accounts of Jesus' resurrection appearances to His disciples speak of Him "coming" to them (see Matt. 28:18; John 20:26). When He rose from the grave, He did not go to downtown Jerusalem and manifest Himself miraculously to all of the pagans in the community, but He concentrated His appearances to His disciples, His followers. These "comings" may have been what our Lord had in mind. The next verse reinforces that theory. Jesus said, **"A little while longer and the world will see Me no more, but you will see Me"** (v. 19a). Jesus would die and would drop out of sight of most people. But since He would focus on the disciples in His post-resurrection appearances, they *would* see Him.

Jesus' next words also seem to have the resurrection in view: **"Because I live, you will live also. At that day you will know that I am in My Father, and you in Me, and I in you"** (v. 19b–20). Jesus overcame death and so became "the firstfruits of those who have fallen asleep" (1 Cor. 15:20b), that is, the first of many to be raised to new life. When the disciples saw Him in His resurrected glory, they knew that certain things were undeniably true. All doubts were removed. They were convinced that Jesus was God, just as He had claimed all along.

When Paul went to Athens and debated the philosophers on Mars Hill, He told them that God "commands all men everywhere to repent, because He has appointed a day on which He will judge the world in righteousness by the Man whom He has ordained. He has given assurance of this to all by raising Him from the dead" (Acts 17:30b–31).

In other words, God showed who His appointed Judge would be by raising Him from the grave. The resurrection was God the Father's way of authenticating all of the truths that were declared by Jesus; thus, the resurrection became Jesus' ultimate credential (cf. Rom. 1:4).

I don't want to hasten past verse 20 because it contains a profound statement that has great consequences for our lives and our behavior. Jesus said, "At that day you will know that I am in My Father, and you in Me, and I in you." In the epistles, Paul talks frequently about not just believing *about* Jesus but believing *in* Jesus. The Greek word he uses, which is often translated "in," is *eis*, which literally means "into." Paul says we are to believe *into* Jesus, and every person who believes into Jesus is *en Christo*—that is, in Christ Jesus. The New Testament emphasizes the mystical union of the believer with Christ, and just as Christ is in the Father, so the believer is in Christ and He is in the believer. For the church, this means that if you are a Christian, you are in Christ; and if I'm a Christian, I am in Christ. As a result, we have a mystical union not only with Christ but with each other, and that union transcends all other human relationships.

This has staggering implications. If I hate someone who is in Christ, I'm not only sinning against that person, I'm sinning against Christ Himself. How can I despise one in whom Christ resides? That's why we are called to have an extraordinary love for one another. If we cannot love another person for his or her own sake, we must do it for Christ's sake, loving the person because Christ indwells him or her. This mystical union is the foundation for a special love and communion in the body of Christ.

Jesus went on to say: **"He who has My commandments and keeps them, it is he who loves Me. And he who loves Me will be loved by My Father, and I will love him and manifest Myself to him"** (v. 21). Jesus was saying, "If you love Me, you will obey Me." This was the second time in this discourse He had said that (see v. 15). A person shows by obedience that he is truly a disciple of Christ, that he truly loves the Lord.

Keeping the Word of Christ

At this point in Jesus' discourse, Judas (not Judas Iscariot, who had already left; see 13:30) raised a question: **"Lord, how is it that You will manifest Yourself to us, and not to the world?"** (v. 22). Jesus did not really answer the question. Instead, He said, **"If anyone loves Me, he will keep My word"** (v. 23a). This was similar to the point Jesus had made earlier, but with a subtle shift in language. Earlier, Jesus said that those who loved Him would obey Him. Here He said that those who loved Him would keep His Word.

I don't know how many people I've talked to in my academic life who don't hesitate to debate the authority of the Scriptures while professing to be followers of Christ. They say, "I don't believe the Bible is the Word of God, but I love Jesus." I try to be polite when someone says that to me, but I can't help thinking, "You're just kidding yourself about loving Jesus because you can't love Jesus and not love His Word." You may find this book pointless. You may think Sunday morning sermons are boring beyond words. However, the one thing that never should bore you is the reading of the Word. You can discount what I say or what a preacher might say, but you cannot discount what the Word says. I have been in churches many times when I got nothing from the sermon, but at least I heard the Word of God read to me. There is an inseparable relationship between your affection for Christ and your affection for the Scriptures.

Many years ago, I engaged in a discussion with the faculty at a seminary on the West Coast over the doctrine of Scripture, and the dean of that institution said to me: "R. C., what are you so exercised about the authority of the Bible? What difference does it make to you?" I said: "Are you kidding? If you take away the Word, you take away my life. I have nothing left, because this is the Word of Christ. If you take away the Word, you take Him away."

So Jesus said, "If anyone loves Me, He will keep My word," then He added, **"and My Father will love him, and We will come to him and make Our home with him"** (v. 23). He said, "If you love Me and you love My Word, then My Father is going to love you because He loves Me and He loves My Word." He continued, showing that the opposite was also true: **"He who does not love Me does not keep My words"** (v. 24a). Just as one must love Christ in order to keep His Word, those who do not love Him cannot keep His Word. They have no desire to please Him; indeed, they hate Him. Therefore, the last thing they want to do is obey Him. Finally Jesus said, **"and the word which you hear is not Mine but the Father's who sent Me"** (v. 24b). The Word of Christ that He expected His followers to obey had His Father's full authority behind it. The Father gave it to the Son to communicate it to men. Therefore, obedience was all the more required.

The Spirit Who Reminds

Jesus then shifted gears and returned to the subject of the Holy Spirit. He said: **"These things I have spoken to you while being present with you. But the Helper, the Holy Spirit, whom the Father will send in My name, He will teach you all things, and bring to your remembrance all things that I said to you"** (vv. 25–26). This passage has been central to one of the fiercest theological debates in the history of the church—the question, "Is the Holy Spirit sent strictly by the Father or by both the Father and the Son?" In the Nicene Creed, we confess that the Spirit is sent by both the Father and the Son. Someone might object that verse 26 says that "the Father will send" the Spirit. That is true, but notice *how* the Father was going to send the Spirit—Jesus said He would do it "in My name." To the ancient Jew, the words "in my name" meant "as my emissary." Jesus did not say, "The Father is going to send the Spirit as My substitute." Instead, He said, "The Father is going to send the Spirit as My ambassador." Therefore, the Spirit is sent by both Father and Son.

The sending of the Spirit took place in agreement between the Father and the Son.

Jesus said the Spirit would both teach the disciples new things and remind them of things Jesus had said. Jesus was a rabbi, which means "teacher," and His followers were disciples, which means they were "students" or "learners" in Jesus' school. That school was a mobile school. When Jesus chose His disciples, He said to them, "Follow me," and He meant that literally. He was a peripatetic teacher; that is, He walked around and lectured while He walked. His students could not take notes or record His words; they had to engrave what He said in their minds. That's why Jesus spoke so frequently in parables and short, pithy aphorisms that were easy to remember. He aimed to make His words and His lessons easy for His students to recall.

But even the best students were not capable of memorizing everything Jesus said during His lifetime. Humanly speaking, we forget things; important facts and such slip from our minds. But Jesus said, "I'm going to take care of that—one of the first tasks that the Holy Spirit is going to take care of when He comes is to bring all of these things to your remembrance." That's part of the reason we have so much confidence in the accuracy of the Gospels. These accounts do not rest simply on the natural ability of the disciples to recall perfectly what Jesus taught them. Rather, their record was super-intended by the Holy Spirit Himself, the Spirit of truth, whom Jesus sent to represent Him.

Jesus' Legacy of Peace

Verse 27 is Jesus' legacy, His last will and testament. The only thing that we know Jesus owned was His robe, and that was taken by the soldiers who gambled for it at the foot of the cross (John 19:23–24). He didn't have an IRA, a trust fund, real estate, or a fat bank account to pass on to His disciples. Nevertheless, as He was about to leave, He bequeathed to His disciples a monumental legacy.

Jesus said, **"Peace I leave with you, My peace I give to you"** (v. 27a). Jesus' peace was His legacy to His followers. That may not seem significant, but this was no ordinary peace. Jesus told them, **"not as the world gives do I give to you"** (v. 27b). The peace of the world is temporary and tentative. But the peace that Christ gave His disciples was far more valuable than the richest earthly inheritance. Why? We find the answer when we read about the great drama of the gospel and our justification by faith alone. After Paul expands on these truths in his epistle to the Romans, he proclaims, "Therefore, having been justified by faith, we have peace with God through our Lord Jesus Christ" (Rom. 5:1).

O sinner, you are in the most perilous situation any human being could ever be. You are at war with God, estranged from Him. It is a war you cannot win. I urge you as strongly as I can to flee to the cross that you might have peace with God; that your name might be in this last will and testament. Christ gave Himself on your behalf and took upon Himself the just wrath of the Father against you. If you trust Jesus for this substitutionary work, you will have the unspeakable inheritance of peace with God.

O Christian, you know what it means to sin, to displease Christ, to feel a wedge in your relationship with Him. We all go through that when we are brought under conviction. Christ chastens us, but at no point after our redemption is He ever at war with us again. When we are reconciled to the Father through Christ, the war is over.

I do not believe there could be a greater legacy from Christ than His peace—not a peace such as the world gives, a fragile truce that can be ended any moment by new acts of hostility, but an eternal peace that never can be disrupted.

Because such peace was His legacy to His beloved disciples, Jesus could say to them again, **"Let not your heart be troubled, neither let it be afraid"** (v. 27b). He then added: **"You have heard Me say to you, 'I am going away and coming back to you.' If you loved Me, you would rejoice because I said, 'I am going to the Father,' for My Father is greater than I"** (v. 28). The Father is greater than the Son, not in substance, but greater in the economy of redemption. Thus, the Father sent the Son, not the other way around. Jesus told His disciples they should rejoice because He was going back to His place of glory, His place at the right hand of the Father.

Jesus concluded by saying: **"And now I have told you before it comes, that when it does come to pass, you may believe. I will no longer talk much with you, for the ruler of this world is coming, and he has nothing in Me. But that the world may know that I love the Father, and as the Father gave Me commandment, so I do. Arise, let us go from here"** (vv. 29–31). Once again, Jesus stressed that He was prophesying His departure to bolster the disciples' faith in Him as the divine Son of God. But His words here were bleak, as He revealed that Satan was coming for what he believed would be his hour of triumph. Nevertheless, Jesus was determined to follow through with the Father's plan as a witness to His love for the Father.

Jesus' final words are an exhortation: "Go from here, gentlemen, girded about with the truth of the Holy Spirit, armed with the Word of My Father, and blessed with the peace of God." What a great legacy that is, a legacy that has come down to all who bear the name of Jesus Christ.

41

"I AM THE VINE"

John 15:1–8

"I am the true vine, and My Father is the vinedresser. Every branch in Me that does not bear fruit He takes away; and every branch that bears fruit He prunes, that it may bear more fruit. You are already clean because of the word which I have spoken to you. Abide in Me, and I in you. As the branch cannot bear fruit of itself, unless it abides in the vine, neither can you, unless you abide in Me. I am the vine, you are the branches. He who abides in Me, and I in him, bears much fruit; for without Me you can do nothing. If anyone does not abide in Me, he is cast out as a branch and is withered; and they gather them and throw them into the fire, and they are burned. If you abide in Me, and My words abide in you, you will ask what you desire, and it shall be done for you. By this My Father is glorified, that you bear much fruit; so you will be My disciples."

Throughout this study of the Gospel of John, we have taken note of Jesus' "I am" sayings. We have seen that He called Himself "the bread of life" (6:35, 48), "the light of the world" (8:12; 9:5), "the door of the sheep" (10:7, 9), "the good shepherd" (10:11, 14), "the resurrection and the life" (11:25), and "the way, the truth, and the life" (14:6). In the passage before us, we come to the last of these sayings, but this one contains a new element. This is the only one of the "I am" sayings that has a second aspect to it. Jesus said, **"I am the true vine, and my Father is the vinedresser"** (v. 1). With these words, Jesus distinguished between His role and the role of His Father.

Jesus' words carry great significance in light of Old Testament imagery. Ancient Israel was an agrarian society, and one of its key crops was grapes. As a result, there are many metaphors and allusions in the pages of the Old Testament that have to do with vines. In fact, the vine was used as a metaphor for Israel as a nation. We see that God called the nation of Israel His vine. He planted and tended it, and He expected it to bear fruit to all nations (see Ps. 80; Isa. 5; Jer. 2:21).

The Gospels show that much of the teaching of the Old Testament with respect to Israel was fulfilled in Christ, and the vine imagery is no exception. In this bold declaration in the upper room, Jesus said, in effect, "I am the true Israel of God."

Much of the evangelical Christian world today is given over to a novelty theology that arose in the nineteenth century and is committed to the idea that God has had two distinct plans of redemption—one for the Jews of the Old Testament and another one for the New Testament church. This school of theology categorically rejects the idea that the church of Jesus Christ is the fulfillment of Old Testament Israel. This is an unfortunate departure from orthodox Christianity, and its sheer popularity does not make it sound. In fact, this verse undercuts it, for here our Lord clearly identifies Himself with the Israel of God. He declared that He fulfilled all that was required of the nation of Israel in the Old Testament.

In Psalm 80, one of the Old Testament passages that uses the vine metaphor, God calls the people of Israel to repent of their sins and to return to fidelity to His covenant relationship with them. The psalmist writes:

> Return, we beseech You, O God of hosts;
> Look down from heaven and see,
> And visit this vine
> And the vineyard which Your right hand has planted,
> And the branch that You made strong for Yourself.
> It is burned with fire, it is cut down;
> They perish at the rebuke of Your countenance.
> Let Your hand be upon the man of Your right hand,
> Upon the son of man whom You made strong for Yourself.

Then we will not turn back from You;
Revive us, and we will call upon Your name. (vv. 14–18)

The psalmist first calls for God to return to the people, for He has departed from them; in this context, he speaks of Israel as the vine (v. 14) and as the vineyard God Himself planted (v. 15). The vineyard is in poor condition (v. 16). So the psalmist pleads that God would restore His grace upon Israel, and that He would do it through the Son of Man (v. 17). In this we see a prefigurement of Christ. When He came in the fullness of time, He announced that He was the true vine, and that God the Father was the vinedresser. The Father owned the vineyard and was responsible for its care, its nurture, and ultimately its productivity. Christ was the vine because He was the fulfillment of Israel.

Saved to Be Fruitful

Jesus went on, **"Every branch in Me that does not bear fruit He takes away; and every branch that bears fruit He prunes, that it may bear more fruit"** (v. 2). This verse sets forth a major emphasis on the relationship of the believer to Christ. Jesus' exhortation throughout this portion of His discourse is that, as Christians, as His disciples, we are to be fruitful. That is, we are to be productive.

This theme is declared so often in the pages of the New Testament, you would think it would be almost a cliché among Christians, but that is not the case. I frequently encounter the idea in the Christian world, and particularly in academic circles, that if you are a Christian, you do not really have to do very much. The idea is that since we are justified by grace through faith alone, works are utterly inconsequential, so we can kick back, take our ease in Zion, rest on the grace of God, and be utterly worthless for His kingdom. It seems that our proper emphasis on the monergistic saving work of God causes us to give no heed to the Bible's calls to good works. We must see that while we are justified by faith *apart from* works, we are justified by faith *unto* works.

I don't know how many times, when giving exams to college students, I have seen something like this written in response to an essay question: "Dear Professor, I didn't prepare adequately for this examination. I'm so sorry. I won't let it happen again. Please be merciful to me because I really do love Jesus." These students made the argument that I should not require responsible behavior from them because of their professions of faith in Christ. When I saw a plea like that, I jotted a note on the exam page, saying, "I am delighted to hear of the state of your soul, and I hope you've grasped the doctrine of justification by faith alone, but when grading my students, I practice justification by works alone."

I see it in Christian ministries—we think that because we're in Christian ministry, we do not have to be concerned about productivity. On the contrary, our calling as Christians is the highest calling there is, and the idea of being productive is not the invention of capitalism, it is the mandate of Christ. He saves us in our futility and calls us to be fruitful. He makes it clear that if He were to leave us to ourselves, we would be completely impotent. We would produce nothing worthwhile, because, as our Lord says in this passage, **"without Me you can do nothing"** (v. 5).

What is the fruit Jesus is concerned to see in our lives? There has been much debate about that. Some believe that the only fruit Jesus is concerned about is people coming to saving faith in Him. In other words, "bearing fruit" means leading people to Christ. Others argue that the fruit is obedience to the law of God. Certainly both of these aspects are important, and both are involved in bearing fruit, but the central emphasis on fruit in the New Testament has to do with the fruit of the Holy Spirit. This is the fruit of a changed life, a changed character, a character that is strengthened and nurtured by the source of holiness, Christ Himself.

We must not neglect the warning Jesus gives in this passage: "Every branch in Me that does not bear fruit He takes away; and every branch that bears fruit He prunes, that it may bear more fruit" (v. 2). Frankly, I don't like the translation here. This translation is an attempt to render into English something that simply cannot be communicated in the exact way it comes across in the Greek. In the Greek, there is a play on words, and that's probably the most difficult thing to translate from one language to another. Jesus said that those who do not bear fruit receive from God *ario*, which means "to be cut off," and everyone who bears fruit receives *kathario*, which is translated here as "to prune." There is *ario* and *kathario*, two words that sound alike. *Kathario* is the word from which we get the term *catharsis*, which means "a cleansing." So Jesus said, "Those who are in Me and do not bear fruit are cut off; those who do bear fruit are cleansed, purified, nurtured, and pruned, so that they may become even more productive."

The Work of the Vinedresser

Keep in mind that this metaphor is based on the production of grapes through the cultivation of grapevines. To make the vineyard rich in its productivity, the husbandman went along the rows of vines, and when he saw branches that were producing no fruit but were taking sap and strength away from the vine, he cut them off. Then the husbandman gathered those dead sticks and threw them in the fire to get rid of them. But the ones that were bearing fruit he cut back, clipped, and pruned so that their fruit would increase.

Isn't that a wonderful metaphor for the Christian life? Once we're converted, God does not say: "I have now put My stamp of approval on you, so 'Let go and let God.' I'll take care of the rest of your life. You don't have to worry about anything." No, He loves us so much that He cleanses us. In other words, He chastens us. He brings his hand on us heavily from time to time. That is part of the process we must go through to be made pure.

I hasten to note that when dealing with a metaphor, it is exceedingly dangerous to push each element of it absolutely. One of the problems that immediately comes up when we analyze this metaphor of the vine and the vinedresser is that it seems to indicate that people who are truly Christian can lose their salvation. Can you become a branch of the vine, only to be cut off later and thrown into the fire?

Before I respond to this question, let me say that I believe John, more than the other Gospels, strongly proclaims the doctrine of God's gracious election and all its implications, including the perseverance of the saints. If we have any question here in Chapter 15 about God preserving His elect forever, we need only to flip over to Chapter 17. As we will see when we consider that chapter, John makes it clear that Jesus taught that He will not let His people go.

We need to keep this truth in mind as we consider Jesus' warning against apostasy here in John 15:2. We tend to think that no one can be in the vine unless he or she is truly converted. That is true—if being in the vine represents being in a state of salvation. However, it may have reference to being in the visible church. A person can have a relationship with Christ that is merely external. I believe this was the kind of relationship Jesus had in mind in His parable of the sower, when He spoke of the seed that fell on the rock. It sprouted up quickly but soon withered. Jesus said this seed represented "those who, when they hear, receive the word with joy; and these have no root, who believe for a while and in time of temptation fall away" (Luke 8:13). Such people may seem to be truly saved, but they are not in Christ and ultimately fall away.

I once received a letter from a person who wrote: "I prayed the sinner's prayer. Does that mean that I can never be lost?" I answered this way: "No, that doesn't mean you can never be lost because nobody is saved by saying the sinner's prayer." If you say the sinner's prayer in faith, in true faith, then Christ not only will redeem you, but He will never let you go. But no one is saved by a profession of faith.

Likewise, no one is saved by joining a church. However, by joining a Christian church, a person is brought into that earthly sanctuary where the means of divine grace are most heavily concentrated. It is a tremendous advantage to be where the Word of God is preached and where the people of God are gathered in prayer. But being in the midst of these blessings is no guarantee that you are, in fact, in a state of grace or in Christ permanently.

Abiding in Christ

Jesus went on to say: **"You are already clean because of the word which I have spoken to you. Abide in Me, and I in you. And as the branch cannot bear fruit of itself, unless it abides in the vine, neither can you, unless you abide in Me"** (vv. 3–4). Here Jesus introduced that rich word *abide*, which has to do with remaining close to Him. Jesus declared that our productivity, our fruitfulness, is directly linked to our abiding in Him. As Christians, we *will* bear fruit, but it will vary in degree. The closer we stay to Christ, the more fruit we will bear. The more we wander out from the center and neglect the means of grace that He has given to us, the less fruit we will produce.

I remember the story of a man who joined a church but never attended worship services. However, he came to the church picnic, and the minister spoke to him. He said, "I haven't seen you in church lately." The fellow said: "That's true. I have learned that I don't need to go to church to be a Christian. I can commune with God in my own way. I don't need to be a part of the worshiping community on Sunday morning." The pastor said, "I understand what you're saying." Then he casually walked over to a nearby charcoal grill, where hamburgers were sizzling. Using tongs, he moved one of the white-hot coals over to the side of the grill. He continued to chat with his wayward parishioner for a few minutes, then said: "Look at this coal. A few moments ago, this coal was radiant in its heat and warmth, and was useful for grilling these burgers. But what has happened since I removed it from the fire and set it apart by itself? It has grown cool and has become worthless for the task it was created to do."

This is what happens to us when we move away from Christ. That's why Jesus told His disciples: "Abide in Me. Stay close to Me. Take hold of Me and hold on tightly. Don't think that you can make it on your own, because without Me you can do nothing." This is an exhortation that we, Christ's disciples in the twenty-first century, must take to heart.

42

THE COST
OF DISCIPLESHIP

John 15:9–27

⟨⟨⟨⟨⟩⟩⟩⟩

"As the Father loved Me, I also have loved you; abide in My love. If you keep My commandments, you will abide in My love, just as I have kept My Father's commandments and abide in His love. These things I have spoken to you, that My joy may remain in you, and that your joy may be full. This is My commandment, that you love one another as I have loved you. Greater love has no one than this, than to lay down one's life for his friends. You are My friends if you do whatever I command you. No longer do I call you servants, for a servant does not know what his master is doing; but I have called you friends, for all things that I heard from My Father I have made known to you. You did not choose Me, but I chose you and appointed you that you should go and bear fruit, and that your fruit should remain, that whatever you ask the Father in My name He may give you. These things I command you, that you love one another. If the world hates you, you know that it hated Me before it hated you. If you were of the world, the world would love its own. Yet because you are not of the world, but I chose you out of the world, therefore the world hates you. Remember the word that I said to you, 'A servant is not greater than his master.' If they persecuted Me, they will also persecute you. If they kept My word, they will keep yours also. But all these things they will do to you for My name's sake, because they do not know Him who sent Me. If I had not come and spoken to them, they would have no sin, but now they have no excuse for their sin. He who hates Me hates My Father also. If I had not done among them the works which no one else did, they would have no sin; but now they have seen and also hated both Me and My Father. But this happened that the word might be fulfilled which is written in their law, 'They hated Me without a cause.' But when the Helper comes, whom I shall send to you from the Father, the Spirit of truth who proceeds from the Father, He will testify of Me. And you also will bear witness, because you have been with Me from the beginning."

When we looked at John 14:18–31 (see Chapter 40), we discussed the inheritance Jesus was leaving behind for His disciples—His peace. In the passage we are considering in this chapter, Jesus expanded on that legacy. In addition to peace, He announced that He was leaving them three other things—His love, His joy, and the enmity of the world. All of these gifts are connected. The peace that Jesus gives is inseparably connected to the love that He sheds abroad in the hearts of those who are His, and that love and peace are the basis for our participation in His joy (cf. Rom. 5:1–5). His peace, love, and joy persist through all the world's hatred and sustain the Christian as he endures it.

The Savior's Love

Jesus said, **"As the Father loved Me, I also have loved you"** (v. 9a). If you ever wonder how much Christ loves you, or whether He loves you at all, whether you are His, think for a moment of the incredible comparison that He made here. Jesus was not simply saying that the Father loved Him, He loved His disciples, and the disciples loved each other. No, He was saying, "I love you the same way that My Father loves Me." Who of us can possibly plumb the depths of the love that God the Father has for God the Son, the One whom the Father called "My beloved Son" (Matt. 3:17; 17:5)? So our Lord was saying, "I'm loving you the same way that My Father loves Me."

Then He went on to say: **"Abide in my love. If you keep My commandments, you will abide in My love, just as I have kept My Father's commandments and abide in His love"** (vv. 9b–10). The English translation of this portion of the passage is a bit awkward, and that awkwardness can easily mislead us from Jesus' intended meaning. I fear that the language here, "*If* you keep My commandments, you *will* abide in My love," makes abiding in Christ seem conditional. It seems as if Jesus was telling His disciples, "I'll love you as long as you're obedient, but the moment you're disobedient, you can kiss My love goodbye." That is not the thrust of what Jesus was saying. He gave a weighty mandate to His disciples to persevere in their faith, to stay close to Him, to be fruitful, and to be obedient. He actually was saying, "If you stay in My love, you will be obedient." His love is not a result of our obedience; rather, our obedience is the result of our love for Him. That's why He said, "If you love Me, keep My commandments" (John 14:15). Here He deepened that by saying: "Because I love you and have chosen you out of the world and brought you to Myself, you will be fruitful. You will be obedient."

I'll never forget my professor in graduate school in the Netherlands saying in one of his lectures, "Gentlemen, the essence of Christian theology is grace, and the essence of Christian ethics is gratitude." We are not driven to obey Christ in order to get in good with Him; we are driven to obey Christ by a heart that is filled with gratitude for the way He plucked us out of this world and poured His love out on us.

The Fullness of Joy

Jesus then took up the subject of joy. He said, **"These things I have spoken to you, that My joy may remain in you, and that your joy may be full"** (v. 11). As we know, Jesus was "a Man of sorrows and acquainted with grief" (Isa. 53:3). He knew pain beyond any measure that we have experienced. Yet beyond the pain, the sorrow, the afflictions, and the humiliation stood One whose life was marked by joy. This, too, was His legacy to His disciples. We may weep, we may endure pain, we may be crushed by the exigencies of life and the afflictions that we experience in this world, but in the depths of our hearts and souls there should be a spirit of joy. Nothing more clearly marks the Christian than the joy he or she manifests apart from circumstances. It was Jesus' purpose that His joy would "remain" in His disciples and that their joy would be "full." Jesus experienced the fullness of joy when He sat down at the right hand of His Father and had His glory restored, the glory He had enjoyed with the Father from eternity. That is the joy He shares with us.

Jesus then said, **"This is My commandment, that you love one another as I have loved you"** (v. 12). I liked it when Jesus said, "As the Father loved Me, I also have loved you" (v. 9), but I don't like this statement in verse 12. I can try to love you, but to love you as much as Jesus has loved me is beyond my natural ability. He loved us when we were unlovely, and we are called to model that kind of love. No wonder Jesus talked so much about sending the Holy Spirit to help us.

Continuing, Jesus said, **"Greater love has no one than this, than to lay down one's life for his friends"** (v. 13). Paul reminds us that Jesus demonstrated the greatest love by dying for His people while they were still in a state of enmity with Him (Rom. 5:7–8). Here, Jesus spoke about the nature of friendship. He said that the greatest love that one can show a friend is to lay down one's life for that person, to sacrifice everything on that person's behalf.

Shortly after Charles Colson was released from prison, he gave a speech at an Ivy League school. As he began his address, a group of students began heckling him and interrupted his speech. They shouted, "How could you have defended Richard Nixon?" Finally, Colson stopped his speech, looked at the hecklers, and said, "I defended him because he was my friend." Instantly the students were on their feet, applauding, because Colson struck a nerve with that comment. He understood that in this wasteland of broken relationships in which we live today, every one of those students was longing to have at least one friend who would sacrifice on his or her behalf.

From Teacher to Friend

Jesus gave further exposition of His meaning when He said, **"You are My friends if you do whatever I command you"** (v. 14). Again, He was not making a conditional statement. He was saying, "You are My friends, and you will do whatever I command you." He continued, **"No longer do I call you servants, for a servant does not know what his master is doing; but I have called you friends, for all things that I heard from My Father I have made known to you"** (v. 15). He didn't tell the disciples that He was about to cease being their Lord. Rather, He was saying: "I have related to you as a master relates to his students. You have been My disciples; you have enrolled in My school. I have been your professor; you have been My subordinates. But today is graduation day, and from now on I want you to look at Me as your friend."

After I came back from graduate school in Europe, I went to dinner with Dr. Gerstner, one of my professors from seminary. I said, "It's good to see you, Dr. Gerstner." He said, "No, no, no, call me Jack." However, I always found it impossible to do that. I had a friend who worked with me, and every time he saw Dr. Gerstner he would call him Jack. I said to him one night, "How can you call him Jack?" He said, "Well, he wants us to call him Jack." I said, "He might *want* me to call him Jack, but I'll never call him Jack." To this day, except in this illustration, I have never, ever referred to him as anything but Dr. Gerstner. That's what happens when a student is deeply impacted by a teacher or a professor. That esteem can last for a lifetime, and it leads you to want to show your affection and your respect by using titles of honor.

Jesus showed His friendship for His disciples by confiding to them the deepest things His Father had confided to Him. A master does not confide in a servant, He said. However, He had told them *all things* His Father had commissioned Him to make known. This is the way of a friend.

An Inheritance from the World

As Jesus' disciples and friends, we receive His peace, His love, and His joy, but we must also participate in the inheritance that He receives from this world. The legacy of the world to Christ is its enmity, scorn, rejection, and hatred. He said: **"If the world hates you, you know that it hated Me before it hated you. If you were of the world, the world would love its own. Yet because you are not of the world, but I chose you out of the world, therefore the world hates you"** (vv. 18–19).

One of the most embarrassing experiences of enlightenment that I ever had happened in the first month after I became a Christian. I was in college when I was converted, and shortly thereafter I went home for a weekend visit. When I got back to my hometown, I went to the drugstore where my friends always gathered on Friday nights. All through high school, I had been their unofficial leader, and when I came back home I wanted to share with my friends the greatest thing that ever happened to me, the cause of my highest happiness, my discovery of Christ as my Savior. So I told my buddies about Christ, and I fully expected every one of them to get in line and say, "Way to go, R. C., we're right with you." Instead, they were unanimous in their rejection of everything I said, and not only did they reject what I said, they manifestly rejected me. I was hurt, because they were my friends, and I loved them, and I wanted them to meet my new friend, Jesus.

Has there ever been a Christian who was converted by the grace of God who did not want to share that experience with all of his friends and loved ones? Yet, after a while, even the most enthusiastic new believers learn to be more discreet because of the often low-key but nevertheless real hostility to Christ that is deeply imbedded in this world. This world hates the things of God. This world hates Christ. Unbelievers can tolerate Christ only as long as He is stripped of His real identity. But if Jesus' followers proclaim the real

Christ, the biblical Christ, and demonstrate their allegiance to Him, they are despised by this world. That's why Jesus warned, "Woe to you when all men speak well of you" (Luke 6:26a). If you've made friends with the world, you must have done it by compromising Christ.

That does not mean we should go out into the world and do everything we can to be as obnoxious as possible in order to prove that we are truly Jesus' disciples. We are not supposed to go looking for persecution or hostility, but if we never experience it, that should be a wake-up call to tell us we may not be as committed to Christ as we say we are.

Jesus said: **"Remember the word that I said to you, 'A servant is not greater than his master.' If they persecuted Me, they will also persecute you. If they kept My word, they will keep yours also"** (v. 20). Jesus came to a world that was against Him. God gave Him some out of that world, and it is for that reason we still plead with our friends. We still bear witness to our friends in the world. We still give them love in the hope that some of them will come and participate in the joy that is the legacy of Christ. But we must expect that some will reject all that and reject us for offering it. They rejected Jesus, and a servant must expect no better treatment than his master receives.

No Plea of Ignorance

Jesus went on: **"But all these things they will do to you for My name's sake, because they do not know Him who sent Me. If I had not come and spoken to them, they would have no sin, but now they have no excuse for their sin"** (vv. 21–22). Jesus reminded the disciples that the Father had demonstrated categorically that He was God's Son. He did not just say it, He demonstrated it by the power that was entrusted to Him, by the miracles that He performed in the presence of eyewitnesses all over Israel. No one in that generation could claim ignorance as an excuse for rejecting Him. No one could say, as the Pharisees did, "We embrace the Father, but we reject this crazy lunatic running around calling himself the Messiah." Jesus said that no one could have it both ways. If you believe the Father, if you love the Father, you must submit to the Son, and if you do not submit to the Son, that's manifest evidence that you are an enemy of the Father.

Jesus continued, saying: **"He who hates Me hates My Father also. If I had not done among them the works which no one else did, they would have no sin; but now they have seen and also hated both Me and My Father. But this happened that the word might**

be fulfilled which is written in their law, 'They hated Me without a cause'" (vv. 23–25). Building on what He said above, Jesus here declared that by refusing to accept the Son, those who claimed to love the Father were actually showing hatred for the Father. They should have bowed to the Son. But instead they hated Him without reason, simply because their sinful hearts could not tolerate His rule.

Finally, Jesus touched on the Holy Spirit once more: **"But when the Helper comes, whom I shall send to you from the Father, the Spirit of truth who proceeds from the Father, He will testify of Me. And you also will bear witness, because you have been with Me from the beginning"** (vv. 26–27). The Holy Spirit would both testify of Jesus and empower the disciples to testify of Him in the face of the world's hatred, hostility, and persecution. This promise has been fulfilled for two thousand years, and it continues to be fulfilled as Christians around the globe bear witness to Christ even unto death.

43

REDEMPTION APPLIED

John 16:1–15

"These things I have spoken to you, that you should not be made to stumble. They will put you out of the synagogues; yes, the time is coming that whoever kills you will think that he offers God service. And these things they will do to you because they have not known the Father nor Me. But these things I have told you, that when the time comes, you may remember that I told you of them. And these things I did not say to you at the beginning, because I was with you. But now I go away to Him who sent Me, and none of you asks Me, 'Where are You going?' But because I have said these things to you, sorrow has filled your heart. Nevertheless I tell you the truth. It is to your advantage that I go away; for if I do not go away, the Helper will not come to you; but if I depart, I will send Him to you. And when He has come, He will convict the world of sin, and of righteousness, and of judgment: of sin, because they do not believe in Me; of righteousness, because I go to My Father and you see Me no more; of judgment, because the ruler of this world is judged. I still have many things to say to you, but you cannot bear them now. However, when He, the Spirit of truth, has come, He will guide you into all truth; for He will not speak on His own authority, but whatever He hears He will speak; and He will tell you things to come. He will glorify

Me, for He will take of what is Mine and declare it to you. All things
that the Father has are Mine. Therefore I said that He will take of Mine
and declare it to you."

Virtually every Christian church throughout the ages has included
in its confessional statements some affirmation of the doctrine of
the Trinity, the teaching that God is three in one. Yet, in every generation, there are assaults against this biblical concept. In our own day, we
have a theoretical Trinitarianism, but in many instances we have a practical
Unitarianism.

For instance, there are many churches where the person and work of
Christ are given such focus that all thought of the Father and the Holy Spirit
is removed. These churches seem to have as their creed, "Jesus is all that I
need." Of course, these churches affirm that they believe in the Father and
the Spirit, but for all practical purposes, they are Unitarian in their religious
behavior. Theirs is a Unitarianism of the second person. At the same time, in
the past century, there probably have been more books written on the person
and work of the Holy Spirit than were written in the first nineteen centuries
of the Christian church. This is a direct result of the charismatic movement
and Pentecostalism, which give so much attention to the Holy Spirit. Please
don't misunderstand—I think it is a wonderful thing that the church has been
awakened to the power and the presence of the Holy Spirit. We need that.
But we need to be careful that we don't slip into a practical Unitarianism of
the third person, because Scripture shows that the work of God is Trinitarian
in every dimension.

When we look at the Trinitarian work of redemption, we make a distinction between its design and its accomplishment. Our redemption is designed
and mandated by the Father (in conjunction with the other members of
the Godhead), and the Father sends the Son into the world. This is why,
throughout the Gospel of John, we repeatedly have heard Jesus say, both to
His disciples and to His adversaries, that He came to do the will of the Father.
The work of the Son of God was to accomplish the task of redemption that
the Father intended.

The first question of the Heidelberg Catechism asks, "What is your only
comfort in life and in death?" The answer beautifully describes the work of
Christ: "That I am not my own, but belong—body and soul, in life and in
death—to my faithful Savior, Jesus Christ, who with his precious blood has
fully satisfied for all my sins, delivered me from all the power of the devil, and

preserves me so much that without the will of my heavenly Father, not a hair can fall from my head." This is a description of what Christ did to accomplish our redemption. He lived His life of perfect obedience for our righteousness and He died on the cross for our guilt. In living and dying, Christ objectively accomplished all that was necessary for human redemption. He satisfied the law and the Father's justice.

So far, we have an objective reality that has been accomplished by the Son. But the big question theologically is, how does what Christ has accomplished impact our lives? How does the objective redemption become a subjective reality for each of us? At this point in theology, we make a distinction between the accomplishment of redemption and its application. It is the task of the Holy Spirit, who is sent by the Father and the Son, to apply the work of Christ to our lives. The Spirit never brings attention to Himself, but always drives attention to Christ and to His accomplishment, and Christ in turn drives us to the Father. So the whole of redemption, from beginning to end, is Trinitarian, and we see this powerfully in the passage from Jesus' upper room discourse that we are studying in this chapter.

The Form of Persecution

In the previous chapter, we saw that Jesus promised the disciples that "If they persecuted Me, they will also persecute you" (15:20). In the opening verses of our passage for this chapter, John tells us that Jesus offered some specifics as to the form that persecution would take: **"These things I have spoken to you, that you should not be made to stumble. They will put you out of the synagogues; yes, the time is coming that whoever kills you will think that he offers God service. And these things they will do to you because they have not known the Father nor Me. But these things I have told you, that when the time comes, you may remember that I told you of them"** (vv. 1–4a). The disciples, Jesus said, could expect to be expelled from the synagogues and even killed for their testimony. He also told the disciples that He was telling them these things so they would not be surprised and so that their faith would be strengthened when they saw His prophetic Word come to pass.

Jesus went on to say: **"And these things I did not say to you at the beginning, because I was with you. But now I go away to Him who sent Me, and none of you asks Me, 'Where are You going?'"** (vv. 4b–5). Jesus knew what was in store for Him from the start of His ministry, but there was no need for Him to tell His disciples; until His "hour" came, He could not be silenced or harmed. But the opposition was soon to have its way with Him, and since He was about to depart, His followers also would be exposed to persecution.

Jesus' curious statement, "None of you asks Me, 'Where are You going?'" may seem like a blatant contradiction, because when Jesus talked earlier about His departure, Peter asked, "Lord, where are You going?" (13:36a). Jesus had not forgotten Peter's earlier question. When He said, "None of you asks Me, 'Where are You going?'" He was saying: "The time has come. I am leaving. But you're still not really concerned about where I'm going." He knew this because He could see that they were overcome by grief. He said, **"But because I have said these things to you, sorrow has filled your heart"** (v. 6). This meant that they didn't understand. They were just like the contemporary church—they had no sense of the importance of the ascension. They were focused only on their loss—their Master and Teacher was going away. They had not yet grasped the glory and grandeur of what was about to happen to Jesus, and the implications of that for the church. That prompted Jesus to make the astounding statement recorded for us in verse 7: **"Nevertheless I tell you the truth. It is to your advantage that I go away; for if I do not go away, the Helper will not come to you; but if I depart, I will send Him to you."**

The first time I really grasped the implications of this text, I literally began to dance in the street and jump over fire hydrants. I said: "Eureka! I can't believe it! All this time I have felt like Abraham, living in the Old Testament, looking forward to the time of Christ's coming, or wishing that I could have been alive during Jesus' earthly ministry, because those people heard and saw Him and His miracles. If only I could have been an earthly eyewitness disciple of Jesus, my Christian life would be so much better than it now is." Yet our Lord said our situation now is better than that of His disciples when He was walking on the earth. I think that is one of the most difficult statements of Christ to embrace. Certainly the disciples struggled with it, but between the time when Jesus announced his departure and the day He actually ascended to heaven, they took it to heart, for they were able to return to Jerusalem with joy (Luke 24:52). They saw that when Jesus left them, He was going to His coronation. He was going to enter into the heavenly sanctuary to sit down at the right hand of the Father and to be their Great High Priest.

I'm sure you've seen the victory celebrations that happen every time there is a presidential election. The candidate's supporters gather together on Election Night, waiting for the voting results to come in. Gradually excitement builds as it appears the candidate is winning. Finally, when the outcome is certain, the opponent gives his concession speech, and when that happens, the winning candidate's supporters all throw their hats in the air, confetti spills down, the champagne is uncorked, and the candidate steps up to make his victory speech. Just imagine if he were to say: "Hey, this is great. Let's stay here. This celebration is so much fun, I don't think I'll ever go to Washington." The candidate's supporters would be sure to say: "Oh, yes, you will. That's why we elected you. We want you in Washington to work for us."

Jesus was going to a much more important place than Washington. He was going to the right hand of God. It was far better for Him to go there than to stay in Jerusalem. There He would be in a position of power, and one of His first acts would be to send the Holy Spirit to minister to the disciples.

The Conviction of the Spirit

That brings us to yet another comment from Jesus about the Holy Spirit in this upper room discourse. Jesus said: **"And when He has come, He will convict the world of sin, and of righteousness, and of judgment: of sin, because they do not believe in Me; of righteousness, because I go to My Father and you see Me no more; of judgment, because the ruler of this world is judged"** (vv. 8–11).

I have to tell you frankly that I am not certain what this passage means. That uncertainty frustrates me, because this passage is so crucial to this discussion. But Jesus' words here haven't stumped only me; biblical scholars have struggled with this statement for centuries. What was Jesus saying?

There are two main views that war against each other when it comes to interpreting this passage. The first holds that Jesus was talking about certain events that would follow from His resurrection. According to this view, the Spirit's conviction of the world would happen like this:

Conviction of sin. Paul tells us later that Christ was raised by the power of the Holy Spirit (Rom. 8:11) and that the resurrection vindicated Jesus' claims (Rom. 1:4; 1 Tim. 3:16). This proved that Jesus' enemies were in the wrong and that Jesus was in the right, and so it can be said that it was by the resurrection that the Spirit convicted Jesus' enemies—this world—of their sin by exposing their guilt.

Conviction of righteousness. The New Testament tells us that Christ was raised for our justification (Rom. 4:25). So we are justified and made righteous through the resurrection, and the Greek work translated as "righteousness" throughout the New Testament is *dikaiosune*, which is the same word used here by John.

Conviction of judgment. Paul says that by the cross, Christ "disarmed principalities and powers . . . [and] made a public spectacle of them, triumphing over them in it" (Col. 2:15). He defeated Satan, "the ruler of this world," when He died and rose again. Thus, Satan was effectively judged by the resurrection.

The second main interpretation of this passage, which is the one I favor, holds that Jesus was referring to the work of the Holy Spirit in His ministry of applying the work of Christ to people in the world who sin without any real contrition. What drives the behavior of the world is the morality of the world. The word *morality* comes from the concept of the mores of a social group, their behavioral patterns, and morality describes how people behave, what they do, their societal conventions, and so on. People aren't concerned about doing what is objectively right. Instead, that which is deemed to be right is whatever is acceptable to the culture. As far as these people are concerned, it doesn't matter what God says.

All of us, even the most pious Christians among us, are overwhelmingly influenced by the cultural customs and conventions of the societies in which we live. It starts in school, where popularity means "being with it," that is, being in line with the morality of the society, even if that morality includes things of which God does not approve. That's what our innate struggle with sin is all about. We listen every day to the voices of the culture around us that tell us what's politically correct and what isn't, what is socially acceptable and what isn't. Then, for a few minutes on Sunday morning, we hear the law of God. We know they don't match up, but unless or until the Holy Spirit takes the law and pierces our souls with it and convicts us of sin, we don't really pay attention to it.

Real conversion is an experience of repentance and forgiveness before God. It is not merely praying a prayer, joining a Christian church, or receiving a sacrament. It is being brought to our knees by the conviction of God the Holy Spirit. The Spirit then convinces us of what true righteousness is and shows us we do not have it, so that we understand we need an alien *dikaiosune*, a righteousness that is not our own. The Spirit exposes us; He strips us of our self-righteousness. He shows us the utter inadequacy of our own behavior to satisfy the demands of God and drives us to that redemption that was accomplished by Jesus. Then He brings us to a state of judgment. The Spirit forces us to face what societal conventions would have us avoid.

The Source of Real Power

The Protestant Reformation of the sixteenth century was a major recovery of the light of the gospel. Martin Luther played a huge role in that recovery, but by the end of his life, Luther was very concerned that the gospel would be lost again within one generation and replaced by superstition. In February 1546, just a few days before he died, Luther preached his last sermon in his hometown of Eisleben. In that sermon, he said:

> In times past, we would have run to the ends of the world if we had known of a place where we could have heard God speak. But now that we hear this every day in sermons . . . we do not see this happening. You hear at home in your house, father and mother and children sing and speak it; the preacher speaks it in the parish church—you ought to lift up your hands and rejoice that we have been given the honor of hearing God speak to us through the Word. Oh, people say, what is that? After all, there is preaching every day, often many times every day, so that we soon grow weary of it. What do we get out of it? All right, go ahead, dear brother, if you don't want God to speak to you every day at home in your house and in your parish church, then be clever and look for something else: in Traer is our Lord God's coat, in Aachen are Joseph's britches and our blessed Lady's chemise; go there and squander your money, buy indulgence and the pope's secondhand junk."[1]

What was Luther referring to when he spoke of "our Lord's coat," "Joseph's britches," and so on? He was talking about the practice in his time of going on lengthy pilgrimages to see the so-called relics of the church. One could find a hair from the beard of John the Baptist, a vial of milk from the breast of Mary, pieces of the cross, and many other objects that supposedly came from biblical times. Luther's own benefactor, Frederick the Wise, had nearly eighteen thousand of these dubious objects. People would go over land and sea to search for the indulgences that would be granted by making a pilgrimage to these relics.

Why did this happen? Why did pilgrims flock to various places to view these relics? The answer is simple: the people were suffering from impotency in their spiritual lives, and they believed there was wonder-working power in the relics of the church. They wanted the heavens to open with miracles and showers of divine demonstrative power, and they looked for it in the bones and possessions of the dead.

We're far too sophisticated for that now, aren't we? I'm not so sure. Turn on your television. Watch the televangelists slay people in the Spirit, knock them to the floor. Likewise, people travel here and there to engage

---

[1] Cited in Gordon W. Lathrop and Timothy J. Wengert, *Christian Assembly: Marks of the Church in a Pluralistic Age* (Minneapolis: Augsburg Fortress, 2004), 129.

in hysterical laughter or other odd practices. What are they looking for? They seek the power of God.

The true power, the power that will change your life, is the power, the *dunamis*, of God the Holy Spirit, and God promises to attend the preaching of His Word with that power. Preaching has no power unless God the Holy Spirit takes His Word and penetrates hearts with it. That's where the power is—if you believe the Word of God.

44

OVERCOMING THE WORLD

John 16:16–33

"A little while, and you will not see Me; and again a little while, and you will see Me, because I go to the Father." Then some of His disciples said among themselves, "What is this that He says to us, 'A little while, and you will not see Me; and again a little while, and you will see Me'; and, 'because I go to the Father'?" They said therefore, "What is this that He says, 'A little while'? We do not know what He is saying." Now Jesus knew that they desired to ask Him, and He said to them, "Are you inquiring among yourselves about what I said, 'A little while, and you will not see Me; and again a little while, and you will see Me'? Most assuredly, I say to you that you will weep and lament, but the world will rejoice; and you will be sorrowful, but your sorrow will be turned into joy. A woman, when she is in labor, has sorrow because her hour has come; but as soon as she has given birth to the child, she no longer remembers the anguish, for joy that a human being has been born into the world. Therefore you now have sorrow; but I will see you again and your heart will rejoice, and your joy no one will take from you. And in that day you will ask Me nothing. Most assuredly, I say to you, whatever you ask the Father in My name He will give you. Until now you have asked nothing in My name. Ask, and you will receive, that your joy may be full. These things I have spoken to you in figurative language; but the time is coming when I will no longer speak to you in figurative language, but I will tell you plainly about the Father. In that day you will ask in My name, and I do not say to you that I shall pray the Father for you; for the Father Himself loves you, because you have loved Me, and have believed that I came forth from God. I came forth from the Father and have come into the world. Again, I leave the world and go to the Father." His disciples said to Him, "See, now You are speaking plainly, and using no figure of speech! Now we are sure that You know all things, and have no need that anyone should question You. By this we believe that You came forth from God." Jesus answered them, "Do you now believe? Indeed the hour is coming, yes, has now come, that you will be scattered, each to his own, and will leave Me alone. And yet I am not alone, because the Father is with Me. These things I have spoken to you, that in Me you may have peace. In the world you will have tribulation; but be of good cheer, I have overcome the world."

Throughout the upper room discourse (John 14–17), Jesus provided small details about coming events. In the opening verse of the passage we are considering in this chapter, He did this again, sharing a very basic time frame for things that were about to happen. This statement left His disciples completely befuddled. He said, **"A little while, and you will not see Me; and again a little while, and you will see Me, because I go to the Father"** (v. 16).

There has been extensive scholarly debate about what Jesus meant in this statement. Was He talking about going to heaven and then being made manifest in power and glory on the Day of Pentecost? Was He saying, "In just a few weeks, I'm going to leave this planet, and you won't see Me again until I come at the end of the age"? Those are possible options, but I don't think they're good ones. I think His meaning was much simpler. I think that our Lord was talking about His coming death, burial, and resurrection.

This discourse is one of the most intimate, searching, revealing conversations Christ ever had with His disciples, but in less than twenty-four hours Jesus would be completely unavailable to them because He would be dead. Furthermore, they would not be able to view His body because it would be consigned to a cave, a sepulcher, closed with a massive stone. But then, a few days later, would come the resurrection, when they would see Him again.

A Striking Contrast

Given that scholars have debated Jesus' meaning, it is not surprising that the disciples themselves were confused. **Then some of His disciples said among themselves, "What is this that He says to us, 'A little while, and you will not see Me; and again a little while, and you will see Me'; and, 'because I go to the Father'?" They said therefore, "What is this that He says, 'A little while'? We do not know what He is saying"** (vv. 17–18). They asked these questions of one another and did not put them directly to Jesus. But John tells us, **Now Jesus knew that they desired to ask Him, and He said to them, "Are you inquiring among yourselves about what I said, 'A little while, and you will not see Me; and again a little while, and you will see Me'? Most assuredly, I say to you that you will weep and lament, but the world will rejoice"** (vv. 19–20a).

Notice the contrast Jesus made. He said the disciples "will weep and lament, but the world will rejoice." He told them: "When I go, you will be sobbing. You'll be torn apart with lamentation. You'll tear your garments. You'll cry, 'Woe is me.' But meanwhile, all around you, the world will rejoice because I am gone."

We used to have a saying on the golf course that every shot makes somebody happy. If it is a good shot, the one who made it is happy. If it is a bad shot, the opponent is happy. So it is when there's conflict and competition, and Jesus was talking about the supreme conflict, the conflict that pitted Him against the world, the flesh, and the Devil, who couldn't wait for Jesus' blood to be spilled on the cross and for His corpse to be put into the tomb. His crucifixion and death would unleash a flood of jubilation for those who had hated and plotted against Jesus for three years. Jesus said, "The world is going to be throwing their hats into the air tomorrow, but for you there will be grief, lamentation, and tears."

However, note that Jesus said they would see Him again in "a little while." That little phrase is used often in Scripture to describe the interval of pain, sorrow, and grief we're called to endure in this life. Still, it may not seem like a little while when we are enduring something difficult. Ten minutes in an ice cream parlor is a little while; ten minutes in a dentist's chair is an eternity. So these little whiles can seem quite long when we are enduring them.

I once talked with a dear Christian woman and ministered to her just days before her death after a ten-year battle with cancer. She looked at me with tears running down her cheeks and said, "R. C., I just can't take it anymore." Have you been there? It's one thing to hurt for a day, but when the pain lasts for a month or a year, and then that year turns into ten years, all of a person's reserves of strength seem to drain away. This woman had trusted God through that whole time, and she finally said, "I can't take it anymore." Within a few days, the Lord took her home, took her away from the pain and the lament to unspeakable joy.

This kind of change was what Jesus promised His disciples, and He reinforced it with a simple analogy, one that's found throughout the pages of the Old Testament, about the pain and the anguish that goes with childbirth (Est. 9:22; Isa. 35:10; Jer. 31:13). He said: **"You will be sorrowful, but your sorrow will be turned into joy. A woman, when she is in labor, has sorrow because her hour has come; but as soon as she has given birth to the child, she no longer remembers the anguish, for joy that a human being has been born into the world. Therefore you now have sorrow; but I will see you again and your heart will rejoice, and your joy no one will take from you"** (vv. 20b–22). Jesus assured them "I will see you again," and He promised that their sorrow would turn to joy, a joy no one would be able to take away.

Jesus then said: **"And in that day you will ask Me nothing. Most assuredly, I say to you, whatever you ask the Father in My name He will give you. Until now you have asked nothing in My name. Ask, and you will receive, that your joy may be full"** (vv. 23–24). Christ spoke of a day when the disciples would have no more questions for Him. In a very real sense, seminary ends the day one sees the resurrected Christ. There is nothing more to ask. It is enough to marvel and worship. But Jesus gave the disciples license to make requests of the Father, assuring them that anything requested in His name would be granted. The result of such a proper relationship with the Father is overflowing joy.

Failing to Follow the Master

He went on: **"These things I have spoken to you in figurative language; but the time is coming when I will no longer speak to you in figurative language, but I will tell you plainly about the Father. In that day you will ask in My name, and I do not say to you that I shall pray the Father for you; for the Father Himself loves you, because you have loved Me, and have believed that I came forth from God. I came forth from the Father and have come into the world. Again, I leave the world and go to the Father"** (vv. 25–28). Much of what Jesus said here was a recapitulation of earlier comments, but the disciples seemed to understand Him more clearly at this point. They said: **"See, now You are**

speaking plainly, and using no figure of speech! Now we are sure that You know all things, and have no need that anyone should question You. By this we believe that You came forth from God" (vv. 29–30). The disciples got excited because Jesus seemed to be speaking plainly, and in their excitement they expressed a new depth of trust in Him.

Jesus' response to this outburst was one of righteous indignation: **Jesus answered them, "Do you now believe?"** (v. 31). It's almost as if He were saying: "Oh, *now* you believe? Where have you been for the past three years? Where were you when I told you that the Son of Man had to go forth to die?" He said to them: **"Indeed the hour is coming, yes, has now come, that you will be scattered, each to his own, and will leave Me alone"** (v. 32a). This was a dire prediction. He said: "You may be full of belief and trust now, but it isn't going to last. You all are going to leave. When you see the guards coming through the Garden of Gethsemane, led by Judas, when you see the swords of the Roman soldiers being brandished in the moonlight, you're going to run for your lives, and you're going to leave Me alone."

In the first year I was a Christian, I attended a weekly prayer meeting, and we sang a number of old hymns. One of them was "Where He Leads Me," and the first stanza and refrain went like this:

I can hear my Savior calling,
I can hear my Savior calling,
I can hear my Savior calling,
"Take thy cross and follow, follow Me."

Where He leads me I will follow,
Where He leads me I will follow,
Where He leads me I will follow;
I'll go with Him, with Him, all the way.

When I sang that hymn, my soul was filled with joy and I thought: "Yes, Lord. I'm yours. Wherever You want me to go, I'll go." I look back on the zeal that filled my heart in those days and I can't help but think of all the places He has gone that I didn't go, all the times that He beckoned me to follow and I went the other direction and left Him alone.

Jesus said this was what His closest friends were about to do to Him— leave Him alone. Yet, He said, **"I am not alone, because the Father is with Me"** (v. 32b).

Paul was alone at the end of his life, when he wrote his second letter to Timothy. He wrote: "Demas has forsaken me, having loved this present world" (2 Tim. 4:10). Others of his friends had left on various mission trips. Only Luke was with him. The upshot of it was that "at my first defense no one stood with me, but all forsook me" (v. 16a). But then he adds, "But the Lord stood with me and strengthened me" (v. 17a). Jesus faced this same situation, and He had the same assurance that One would be with Him. He told His disciples: "You're going to run, but the Father is going to stay with me, so I will not be alone."

Good Cheer in Tribulation

Jesus continued: **"These things I have spoken to you, that in Me you may have peace. In the world you will have tribulation; but be of good cheer, I have overcome the world"** (v. 33). A few years ago, I had the experience of standing on top of the Acropolis in Athens, right next to the Parthenon, and gazing out over that amazing vista. I could see the ruins of the ancient Agora, where Paul preached the gospel every day when he was in Athens. Nearby was a big, bare rock that once was the site of a temple to the god Aries, the Greek god of war, equivalent to the Roman god Mars. It was there on Mars Hill where Paul stood and confronted the philosophers of Athens, saying: "Men of Athens, I perceive that in all things you are very religious; for as I was passing through and considering the objects of your worship, I even found an altar with this inscription: TO THE UNKNOWN GOD. Therefore, the One whom you worship without knowing, Him I proclaim to you" (Acts 17:22–23).

The philosophers who debated with Paul were the Stoics and the Epicureans. The Stoics said: "Everything is a result of natural causes. We have no control over anything that takes place. The only thing we can control is how we react to what happens. We can choose to let circumstances defeat us or to keep a stiff upper lip." So the Stoics aimed to endure all life's vagaries because they did not believe they could change their circumstances. The Epicureans were famous for their creed of hedonism. They said: "Eat, drink, and be merry, for tomorrow you will die. We might as well have a good time tonight." They were the precursors of Friedrich Nietzsche, who said life is meaningless.

Well, Jesus was not a Stoic or an Epicurean, and He certainly had nothing to do with Nietzsche. He told His disciples, "You will have a difficult time in the world, but be of good cheer." He then gave them a completely rational reason to be of good cheer: Jesus said, "I have overcome the world." In other words, Jesus said: "I have overcome the world. I have taken everything it could throw at Me, and I have come forth victorious." He crushed His enemies under His feet by His blood.

The world threatens to crush you and me every minute of our lives. It hurls insults, tribulations, pain, death—all sorts of things that take away the joy that should be ours in Christ. But Jesus overcame the world. That's why the apostle Paul could say we are more than conquerors through Christ who loved us (Rom. 8:37). It isn't because we have the power to beat the world. We don't. It is because He overcame the world for us.

45

THE GLORY OF CHRIST

John 17:1–5

Jesus spoke these words, lifted up His eyes to heaven, and said: "Father, the hour has come. Glorify Your Son, that Your Son also may glorify You, as You have given Him authority over all flesh, that He should give eternal life to as many as You have given Him. And this is eternal life, that they may know You, the only true God, and Jesus Christ whom You have sent. I have glorified You on the earth. I have finished the work which You have given Me to do. And now, O Father, glorify Me together with Yourself, with the glory which I had with You before the world was."

One winter night in 1969, a snowstorm blanketed downtown Philadelphia as I prepared to drive home after teaching an evening class at the Conwell School of Theology on the campus of Temple University. As I left the building, I encountered a man who, like me, was about to venture out into the snow in his overcoat and galoshes. I had seen him around the building occasionally, but I didn't know him, so I asked his name. He introduced himself as Henry Barraclough and told me that he had retired many years earlier, but he was spending his retirement volunteering his help a couple of nights a week in the accounting office of the seminary.

When he said his name, a light bulb of recognition went on in my mind. I stopped and said something silly like, "Not *the* Henry Barraclough?" He clearly wasn't used to people fawning over him, so I asked, "Are you the man who wrote the famous hymn, 'Ivory Palaces'?" That is one of my favorite hymns. The refrain goes:

> Out of the ivory palaces,
> Into a world of woe.
> Only His great eternal love
> Made my Savior go.

This man allowed that he was indeed that Henry Barraclough, then he told me the inspiration for the hymn. He said he had been attending a series of Lenten addresses in a church in downtown Philadelphia when the minister preached one evening from Philippians 2, where the apostle Paul writes:

> Let this mind be in you which was also in Christ Jesus, who, being in the form of God, did not consider it robbery to be equal with God, but made Himself of no reputation, taking the form of a bondservant, and coming in the likeness of men. And being found in appearance as a man, He humbled Himself and became obedient to the point of death, even the death of the cross. Therefore God also has highly exalted Him and given Him the name which is above every name, that at the name of Jesus every knee should bow, of those in heaven, and of those on earth, and of those under the earth, and that every tongue should confess that Jesus Christ is Lord, to the glory of God the Father." (Phil. 2:5–11)

Mr. Barraclough said that as he listened to the sermon, he was overwhelmed by a sense of the sacrifice that the second member of the Trinity had accepted. Jesus put aside the eternal glory that He had with the Father and made Himself of no reputation by taking on the form of a man and becoming a slave, obedient even unto death. There was no emptying of any divine attributes, but an emptying of prerogatives, an emptying of status, of exaltation, of glory, for the sake of redemption and for the sake of the ultimate glory of the Father. For these purposes, our Lord put aside His own glory for a season.

Focused on the Joy before Him

In our study of John's Gospel, we have come to the seventeenth chapter, which contains Jesus' High Priestly Prayer, in which He prayed for Himself, for His disciples, and for His church. In the passage before us in this chapter, we see that He prayed for Himself, and it is clear that He was focused on "the joy that was set before Him" (Heb. 12:2). He asked the Father to glorify Him "with the glory which I had with You before the world was" (v. 5). His mission in this "world of woe" nearly complete, He looked forward to returning to the "ivory palaces" of heaven.

Jesus began His prayer with decisive words: **"Father, the hour has come"** (v. 1b). Over and over throughout John's Gospel we have heard Jesus speak about His "hour." As I mentioned previously, "hour" had reference both to the hour of Jesus' abject humiliation and the hour of His exaltation, because His glory was to come through His shame. Here, in the upper room, on the night of His betrayal, Jesus was staring at the cross. The hour was no longer remote; it was looming right in front of Him. The moment planned by the Trinity from all eternity was at hand. Therefore, Jesus needed to say certain things to God, so He went to prayer.

As I noted above, Jesus' first petitions were for Himself. He first asked, **"Glorify your Son, that your Son also may glorify You"** (v. 1c). When we seek glory, we do so at the expense of the glory of God. But when Jesus asked the Father to glorify Him, it was not at the expense of the Father because the glorification of the Son *is* the glorification of the Father. We saw that Paul declares that every knee will bow and every tongue confess that Jesus Christ is Lord "to the glory of God the Father" (Phil. 2:11b). When the Son is exalted and honored, the Father is honored as well, because the Father and the Son are one. When Jesus asked for His glory back, He was not asking selfishly; He had the completion of His mission in view. He knew that He must be lifted up on the cross in order to be lifted up in the sight of the angels. So He prayed, "Father, glorify Me, and in doing that, glorify Yourself."

Continuing His thought, Jesus went on to say, **"as You have given Him authority over all flesh, that He should give eternal life to as many as You have given Him"** (v. 2). Again, throughout this study, we have heard Jesus talk frequently about those whom the Father had given to Him. This comment harkens back to some statements that Jesus made early in His ministry, statements that quite a few of His disciples found distasteful and which caused them to cease from following Him (see John 6). These statements focused on the Father's sovereign role in salvation.

Many rival theologies coexist in the Christian world in the twenty-first century. Even among so-called evangelical Christians, there are various diverse and competing theologies. One of these is Reformed theology, which holds to the teachings of the Protestant Reformers of the sixteenth century. The key theological beliefs of Reformed Christians are sometimes summed up by the five points of Calvinism, which are crystallized by the famous acrostic T-U-L-I-P. This acrostic is derived from the doctrines of total depravity, unconditional election, limited atonement, irresistible grace, and the perseverance of the saints. Reformed theology is a minority report in the evangelical church today.

By contrast, probably the overwhelming majority theology in evangelicalism is one that was developed in the nineteenth century and spread dramatically across this land. This school of theology is known as dispensationalism. There are many differences between Reformed theology and dispensationalism, but one key difference prompts some dispensationalists to call themselves "four-point Calvinists." In other words, they have a problem with one of the five points of Calvinism. Specifically, they want to get the "L" out of the TULIP. The doctrine of limited atonement is controversial. I happen to believe that part of the reason it is so controversial is because it is so widely misunderstood. I cannot understand how anyone can hold to the other four points and deny the "L," but dispensationalists insist that they can.

The Purpose of the Cross

The doctrine of limited atonement (also known as "definite atonement" or "particular redemption") says that the atonement of Christ was limited (in its scope and aim) to the elect; Jesus did not atone for the sins of everybody in the world. In my denomination, we examine young men going into the ministry, and invariably somebody will ask a student, "Do you believe in limited atonement?" The student will respond by saying, "Yes, I believe that the atonement of Christ is sufficient for all and efficient for some," meaning the value of Christ's death on the cross was great enough to cover all of the sins of every person that ever lived, but that it applies only to those who put their faith in Christ. However, that statement doesn't get at the real heart of the controversy, which has to do with God's *purpose* in the cross.

There are basically two ways in which to understand God's eternal plan. One understanding is that, from all eternity, God had a desire to save as many people as possible out of the fallen human race, so He conceived a plan of redemption by which He would send His Son into the world as the sin-bearer for fallen people. Jesus would go to the cross and die for all who would at some point put their trust in him. So the plan was provisional—God provided atonement for all who take advantage of it, for all who believe. The idea is that Jesus died potentially for everybody, but that it is theoretically possible that the whole thing was in vain because every last person in the world might reject the work of Jesus and choose to remain dead in their trespasses and sins. Thus, God's plan could be frustrated because nobody might take advantage of it. This is the prevailing view in the church today—that Jesus died for everybody provisionally. In the final analysis, whether salvation happens depends on each individual person.

The Reformed view understands God's plan differently. It says that God, from all eternity, devised a plan that was not provisional. It was a plan "A" with no plan "B" to follow if it didn't work. Under this plan, God decreed that He would save a certain number of people out of fallen humanity, people whom the Bible calls the elect. In order for that plan of election to work out in history, He sent His Son into the world with the specific aim and design to accomplish redemption for the elect. This was accomplished perfectly, without a drop of the blood of Christ being wasted. Everyone whom the Father chose for salvation will be saved through the atonement.

The implication of the non-Reformed view is that God doesn't know in advance who is going to be saved. For this reason, there are theologians today saying, "God saves as many people as He possibly can." How many people can God save? How many people does He have the power to save? If He is really God, He has the power to save all of them. How many people does He have the authority to save? Cannot God intervene in anyone's life, just as He did in Moses' life, Abraham's life, or the apostle Paul's life, to bring them into a saving relationship with Him? He certainly has the right to do that.

We cannot deny that the Bible speaks about Jesus dying for "the world." John 3:16 is the premier example of a verse that uses this language. But there is a counterbalancing perspective in the New Testament, including John's Gospel, that tells us Jesus laid down His life not for everyone but for His sheep. Here in John's Gospel, Jesus speaks about His sheep as those whom the Father has given Him.

In John 6, we saw that Jesus said, "No one can come to Me unless the Father who sent Me draws him" (v. 44a), and the word translated as "draws" properly means "compels." Jesus also said in that chapter, "All that the Father gives Me will come to Me" (v. 37a). His point was that everyone whom the Father designed to come to His Son would come, and no one else. Thus, your salvation, from start to finish, rests on the sovereign decree of God, who decided, in His grace, to have mercy on you, not because of anything He saw in you that demanded it, but for the love of the Son. The only reason I can give under heaven why I'm a Christian is because I'm a gift of the Father to the Son, not because of anything I've ever done or could do.

Ensuring the Salvation of the Elect

Let's go back to our original question: What was God's purpose in the cross? It was to ensure the salvation of those whom He had given to His Son. That's why our election must always be understood biblically to be in Christ. I'm not elected as an isolated American preacher. I'm elected in Christ Jesus, as one whom the Father gave to Him.

Jesus made this clearer a little later when He prayed for those whom the Father had given Him (v. 9). Clearly He was not praying for everyone. But such a limited prayer runs counter to the all-inclusive spirit and mentality of American Christianity. We say, "It's not fair that God doesn't include everyone in His plan." Suppose that Christ did, in fact, make atonement for all people and every sin that has ever been committed. Would that cover the sin of unbelief? Yes. Therefore, a person could remain an unbeliever all his life, never submit to Christ, and die in sin, but God could not condemn that person because his sins had been covered by the atonement of Christ.

Here's where the rubber meets the road. If you say to me, "R. C., did Jesus die for me?" I'm going to tell you that I don't know. Then I will ask whether you are a believer. If you reply, "Yes, I'm a believer," I'll say, "Well, then, He died for you." However, if you say, "No, I'm not a believer," I'll say: "I still don't know that He didn't die for you because you may become a believer tomorrow. But I know this—He died only for those who put their trust in Him." The bottom-line question is this: "Do you, or do you not, trust in Christ alone for salvation from the just punishment that is due to you for your sins?" If you can say yes to that, then you can sleep easy tonight, knowing that Christ died for you, and that the atonement He made was perfect, complete, and absolute in that it covered every single sin you have committed or ever will commit in this world. That's the benefit of having been given to Jesus by the Father.

It is only when we understand that we have done nothing to earn our way into heaven, that even the faith that we exercise is the gift of God, that it is all by grace alone, that we can say, "*Soli Deo gloria*"—"Glory to God alone." Those who have received the unspeakable grace of God should be the first to pray with Jesus that the Father might be glorified.

Jesus went on to say: **"And this is eternal life, that they may know You, the only true God, and Jesus Christ whom You have sent. I have glorified You on the earth. I have finished the work which You have given Me to do"** (vv. 3–4). It is interesting that Jesus prayed this way the night *before* His passion. The cross had not even happened yet, but Jesus spoke of His mission as completed. He said: "Father, it's all over and

I've come to the end of the road. I'm not going to quit between now and Golgotha. I'll go to that cross."

With this understanding, He raised His final petition for Himself: **"O Father, glorify Me together with Yourself, with the glory which I had with You before the world was"** (v. 5). He said, in effect: "I'm ready to come home. I'm ready to return to the ivory palaces from whence I came."

46

THE INTERCESSION

John 17:6–19

"I have manifested Your name to the men whom You have given Me out of the world. They were Yours, You gave them to Me, and they have kept Your word. Now they have known that all things which You have given Me are from You. For I have given to them the words which You have given Me; and they have received them, and have known surely that I came forth from You; and they have believed that You sent Me. I pray for them. I do not pray for the world but for those whom You have given Me, for they are Yours. And all Mine are Yours, and Yours are Mine, and I am glorified in them. Now I am no longer in the world, but these are in the world, and I come to You. Holy Father, keep through Your name those whom You have given Me, that they may be one as We are. While I was with them in the world, I kept them in Your name. Those whom You gave Me I have kept; and none of them is lost except the son of perdition, that the Scripture might be fulfilled. But now I come to You, and these things I speak in the world, that they may have My joy fulfilled in themselves. I have given them Your word; and the world has hated them because they are not of the world, just as I am not of the world. I do not pray that You should take them out of the world, but that You should keep them from the evil one. They are not of the world, just as I am not of the world.

Sanctify them by Your truth. Your word is truth. As You sent Me into the world, I also have sent them into the world. And for their sakes I sanctify Myself, that they also may be sanctified by the truth.

T he passage before us in this chapter constitutes the second of three sections in Jesus' High Priestly Prayer. After praying for Himself (vv. 1–5), He made petitions for others. However, as I mentioned in the previous chapter, Jesus was restrictive in this portion of His prayer. He did not pray for everyone in the world indiscriminately; rather, He prayed specifically on behalf of those whom the Father has given to Him out of the world during His incarnation—His disciples.

It is important to understand that when Jesus spoke of "the world" throughout this prayer, He was referring not primarily to this planet but to the fallen world, that population of people who are lost in sin and in an adversarial relationship with the Creator. Jesus was from outside the physical world—He left the position of glory He had enjoyed from all eternity as the second person of the Godhead to walk the earth as a man. Likewise, He was outside the world of sin, but God gave to Him a number of followers who had been part of that world, whom God had rescued from that world and given to the Son.

Adherents of the Gospel

Jesus said to the Father, **"I have manifested Your name to the men whom You have given me out of the world"** (v. 6a). In other words, Jesus had made God's name—that is, the sum total of His perfections—obvious and clear. To whom did He manifest God's name? It was to those the Father had given Him, the disciples. **"They were Yours, You gave them to Me, and they have kept Your word"** (v. 6b). The disciples were God's by virtue of His creation and election of them, and He had given them to Jesus.

What did Jesus mean when He said "they have kept Your word"? The following words of Jesus' prayer help explain it. He said: **"Now they have known that all things which You have given Me are from You. For I have given to them the words which You have given Me; and they have received them, and have known surely that I came forth from You; and they have believed that You sent Me"** (vv. 7–8). I believe Jesus used "Your word" as a shorthand expression for the gospel. He was not saying that the disciples had obeyed every jot and tittle of the Mosaic Law or that they had kept all of the commandments that Jesus had given to them.

However, they had embraced the essential truths. They had come to see Him as the Messiah sent from God, and they had put their faith in Him.

That is no different, in the final analysis, from what God does with us. If I am in Christ, it is because God took me out of the world and gave me to Christ, who manifested His Word to me, with the result that the gospel is now in my heart.

As Jesus continued His prayer, He asked that what had taken place in His disciples would not be aborted. He said: **"I pray for them. I do not pray for the world but for those whom You have given Me, for they are Yours. And all Mine are Yours, and Yours are Mine, and I am glorified in them. Now I am no longer in the world, but these are in the world, and I come to You. Holy Father, keep through Your name those whom You have given Me, that they may be one as We are"** (vv. 9–11). That final request, that God would "keep" the disciples through His name, was the essence of what Jesus prayed for.

In the previous chapter, I discussed one of the disagreements over the so-called five points of Calvinism, which are summed up by the acrostic T-U-L-I-P. In that discussion, we dealt with the controversy over the "L," which designates the doctrine of limited atonement. No less controversial is the "P," the doctrine of the perseverance of the saints (a poor name because we do not persevere, we are preserved). Reformed theology stands vehemently in favor of the perseverance of the saints. Nevertheless, some Christians who accept the doctrines of total depravity, unconditional election, limited atonement, and irresistible grace believe that those who come to faith in Christ through the sovereign grace of God can lose that salvation and fall away in the end.

The Reformed position is this: If you have salvation—if you are truly reborn and have saving faith in your soul—you will have it forever, because if you have it, you never can lose it, and if you seemingly lose it, you never really had it. In his first epistle, John writes about a group that left the church, saying, "They went out from us, but they were not of us; for if they had been of us, they would have continued with us" (1 John 2:19a). Those who went out are a good illustration of people who were in the church and seemed to be saved, but were not.

The Reformed confidence regarding the preservation of believers rests on the mercies of God and especially on the High Priesthood of Christ, who went into the heavenly places to be our Intercessor (Rom. 8:34) and who prays for our preservation. We rest on confidence in the efficacy of the prayers of Jesus, not our own consistency as Christians. In addition we have marvelous promises such as the one we saw earlier in John's Gospel: "I give them eternal life, and they shall never perish; neither shall anyone snatch them out of My hand" (10:28).

Kept by Father and Son

Of course, we never find the phrase "the perseverance of the saints" in the Bible. Instead, we find the idea of "keeping." To be kept is to be protected, to be preserved. The great priestly blessing of the Old Testament began with these words: "The LORD bless you and *keep* you" (Num. 6:24). Those who are saved are kept, not just today, but forever; not by their own resources, but by the power of God Himself. Thus, it is not surprising that we find Jesus praying, "Holy Father, *keep* through Your name those whom You have given Me" (v. 11).

This petition can be read in a couple of ways. Jesus might have been saying, "Keep them *through the power of* Your name." He may have been appealing to the instrument by which believers are preserved. On the other hand, Jesus might have been saying, "Keep them *in* Your name." I prefer this interpretation. If I am "in God's name," I am numbered among the redeemed. That's how the disciples were on that night before the death of Jesus, before they were to face their supreme crisis. So Jesus prayed for them, asking God: "Keep them. Don't release them. Don't let them go. Hold on to them."

In an earlier chapter, I used an illustration of this concept that is worth repeating here. Imagine a father walking beside a railroad track with his three-year-old son. There is danger at hand, so the father holds the child's hand. If the boy's safety depends on the strength of his grasp on his father's hand, he is in grave danger—he could lose his grip and wander into the path of a train. What keeps the child from destruction is not the boy's grip on his father's hand but the father's grip on the child's hand. That is what Jesus was asking the Father to do—to keep His grip on the disciples.

Jesus also expressed the desire that the disciples "may be one as We are." I think this is one of the most misinterpreted verses in the entire Bible. It is used as the key proof text by those who are committed to the ecumenical movement. They say that Jesus' prayer will not be answered until every church is united as one, with no divisions in the body of Christ. I am sure that God is grieved by all of our disunity, but I don't think that we are still waiting for this request Jesus made to the Father to come to pass two thousand years later. In actuality, this prayer *was* answered, because everyone who is in Christ Jesus is in union with Him, and therefore in union with one another. The communion of saints that is spoken of in the Apostles' Creed is real, and it transcends every conceivable boundary—denominational, geographic, racial, cultural, and socioeconomic. There already is a spiritual unity of all the saints; we are one with each other as the Father is with the Son—not by virtue of our activities or of our practices but by the spiritual unity that is wrought by the Holy Spirit in our salvation.

Jesus went on: **"While I was with them in the world, I kept them in Your name. Those whom You gave Me I have kept; and none of them is lost except the son of perdition, that the Scripture might be fulfilled"** (v. 12). Jesus had just asked the Father to "keep" His disciples, but here He revealed that He had been keeping them while He was with them in the world. Not all of the disciples were kept—one of them was lost, the "son of perdition," Judas. Can the experience of Judas be used as evidence that someone can come to faith and later make shipwreck of his faith and end up in destruction? No. Judas was never born again; much earlier in His ministry, Jesus referred to Judas as "a devil" (John 6:70). He was numbered among the Twelve only to fulfill a role that was prophesied for him (Ps. 41:9).

I once heard a speaker say that since the Bible doesn't use harsh language with respect to Judas, we ought not take too dim a view of him. I can't think of any more harsh description of a human being than "son of perdition." Perdition refers to the final eschatological damnation that comes at the hands of God in His righteous wrath, and Jesus Himself attached that term to the name of Judas.

In the World but Not of It

Jesus then said: **"But now I come to You, and these things I speak in the world, that they may have My joy fulfilled in themselves. I have given them Your word; and the world has hated them because they are not of the world, just as I am not of the world"** (vv. 13–14). Jesus was never of the world. Every one of us was of the world at one time, but we're no longer of the world. We are *in* the world (we still live here) but not *of* the world (we are not part of the godless world system). This mixed citizenship engenders the world's hatred toward us, but nevertheless it was Jesus' prayer that we would have His joy.

Continuing along those lines, He said: **"I do not pray that You should take them out of the world, but that You should keep them from the evil one"** (v. 15). Jesus did not pray that the Father would give His disciples the safety of isolation, that He would remove them entirely from the theater of operations. Martin Luther said that Christianity has to be a "profane faith." The word *profane* literally means "out of the temple." Luther meant that the church is not to spend all of its time gathered together in a "holy huddle," basking in the glory of God. Yes, there are to be times of worship and fellowship, but then we are to go back into the world, where we are to bear witness to the glory of Christ. Jesus prayed that the Father would protect His disciples as they went forth, especially from the wiles of the Evil One, Satan.

He went on: **"They are not of the world, just as I am not of the world. Sanctify them by Your truth. Your word is truth"** (vv. 16–17). Just a few moments earlier, Jesus referred to the Father as "Holy Father," for God is inherently holy. It was Jesus' desire that His disciples would become holy, for this is the purpose of redemption. Paul writes, "For this is the will of God, your sanctification" (1 Thess. 4:3a). How does this take place? It happens through the Word of God. Paul put it this way: "Do not be conformed to this world, but be transformed by the renewing of your mind, that you may prove what is that good and acceptable and perfect will of God" (Rom. 12:2). In other words, we are brought to greater holiness, greater godliness, by doctrine renewing our minds.

Hardly a day goes by that I don't hear someone say, "Doctrine doesn't matter. What matters is relationships." If doctrine doesn't matter, then truth doesn't matter, and if truth doesn't matter, our sanctification doesn't matter, because sanctification doesn't come through relationships. Our sanctification comes from the Word of God and from the truth that is poured into our souls, truth that renews our minds, renews our thinking, and renews our lives. That truth, in turn, defines godly relationships. You can't have a godly relationship without being in the truth. You can't even know what a godly relationship looks like without understanding the content of the gospel. Doctrine *does* matter.

Jesus concluded His prayer for His disciples with these words: **"As You sent Me into the world, I also have sent them into the world. And for their sakes I sanctify Myself, that they also may be sanctified by the truth"** (vv. 18–19). When we think about sanctification, we think about that process that follows conversion by which we become more Christlike. Although we must work diligently to advance in holiness, we understand that sanctification is wrought in us by the power of the Holy Spirit, and without His aid we will not see progress (cf. Phil. 2:12–13). It would be very strange to hear a Christian say, "I am sanctifying myself." Jesus, however, made that comment in His High Priestly Prayer. What did He mean?

I think the only way we can understand this is to remember that Jesus was preparing to finish His God-given mission to redeem His people. The language here harkens back to the Old Testament, to the Day of Atonement.

The priests had to go through a ritual cleansing before they could offer the sacrifice. Likewise, the animals used in that sacrifice had to be consecrated before they could be slain and offered to God. In other words, they had to be set apart.

The New Testament shows us that Christ is the Great High Priest, but He differed from all other priests in Israel in this manner: not only did He, as the priest, offer the sacrifice that was necessary for atonement, but the sacrifice He offered was Himself. So Christ was both the subject and the object of His priestly work. In the upper room, our Great High Priest was sanctifying Himself, consecrating Himself, setting Himself apart, for the task that lay ahead of him on the morrow.

Finally, Jesus prayed that the disciples would be "sanctified by the truth." Falsehood corrupts us. The fall of the human race began with a lie, with a distortion of the truth. It began with a false doctrine that came through the message of a Serpent from hell, and since that day, every time the truth is negotiated, compromised, denied, and weakened, our corruption gets worse and worse. The only thing that rescues you from yourself or me from myself is a true understanding of God, a true understanding of Christ, a true understanding of our hopeless condition, and a true understanding of grace. The truth redeems. The truth preserves. The truth makes us free. The truth makes us holy. Jesus understood that, and in the agony of His intercession, He prayed that His disciples might be people of the truth.

47

PRAYER
FOR THE CHURCH

John 17:20–26

"I do not pray for these alone, but also for those who will believe in Me through their word; that they all may be one, as You, Father, are in Me, and I in You; that they also may be one in Us, that the world may believe that You sent Me. And the glory which You gave Me I have given them, that they may be one just as We are one: I in them, and You in Me; that they may be made perfect in one, and that the world may know that You have sent Me, and have loved them as You have loved Me. Father, I desire that they also whom You gave Me may be with Me where I am, that they may behold My glory which You have given Me; for You loved Me before the foundation of the world. O righteous Father! The world has not known You, but I have known You; and these have known that You sent Me. And I have declared to them Your name, and will declare it, that the love with which You loved Me may be in them, and I in them."

Ith the words **"I do not pray for these alone"** (v. 20a), Jesus transitioned to a new focus in His High Priestly Prayer. As we have seen in the previous two chapters, Jesus prayed first for Himself (vv. 1–6), then turned His attention to His disciples (vv. 7–19). In that second section, Jesus restricted His intercession to praying specifically for His disciples, for those whom the Father had given Him during His earthly ministry. Then the broadening of His focus continued and He prayed for others—not the entire world, but believers besides His disciples.

This is a special text, one that should be treasured by every Christian. I sometimes ask my students, "Where in the Bible does Jesus pray for you?" The answer is right here (if you are a believer). In this final section of the High Priestly Prayer, Jesus did not pray only for those who were gathered with Him in the upper room, He prayed for all who would be brought to faith by the ministry and the testimony of His apostolic band, which He was about to send into the world. Anyone who is a Christian today is in that state of grace because of the fidelity of the apostolic community in broadcasting the teaching of Christ and bringing it to the world so that it has been faithfully passed down to our own generation. In a very real sense, we, as believers, were in the mind of Jesus on that night He prayed this prayer of intercession. His words give us an idea of what He does in His ongoing ministry of intercession at the right hand of the Father, where He intercedes for us daily.

We can be rather superficial with each other. Someone may tell me he has a problem, and I say, "I'll pray for you," but then I forget. Or I may ask someone to pray for me, and he says, "I will," but then he forgets. We are not as diligent as we should be in our intercession for others. But we also know people who are true prayer warriors. When I was in college, I met two of them.

Shortly after my conversion, a friend took me to visit a dear woman who lived in a mobile home by herself. She was known simply as "Sister Deeder." When she learned I had been a Christian for only a few weeks, she said, "Young man, you need to plant a spiritual stake in the ground and let that stake always remind you of what Christ has done in the saving of your soul." I remember that admonition even now, decades later. Then she began to pray like I had never heard anyone pray in my life, and how much I appreciated that she prayed for me.

In the town where I went to college, there was a doctor who had been a medical missionary for more than forty years. When I met Dr. Jameson, he was in his eighties, and was retired and infirm. He couldn't practice medicine or do anything strenuous, but he still went to work every morning and worked for eight hours. His labor was prayer. He got on his knees and prayed every single day for eight hours. He said, "I can't do anything else, but I can still pray." We students would go to him with our concerns because we believed what Scripture says: "The effective, fervent prayer of a righteous man avails much" (James 5:16b). Knowing that I was in this godly man's prayers was one of the greatest comforts and encouragements I experienced as a young student.

But the comfort, consolation, and encouragement that the prayers of Sister Deeder and of Dr. Jameson had in my life pale into insignificance when I think of the intercession of our Lord Himself. If He had prayed for us only on the one occasion recorded for us in Scripture, it would be good and right for us to praise Him for the rest of our lives. But He didn't pray for us only once. Since He ascended to the right hand of the Father, He has continued to pray on your behalf and my behalf. I don't think we could bear life in the trenches of the kingdom without that intercession.

We have a vivid example of the efficacy of Jesus' prayers in the New Testament. We've already seen how Jesus revealed to the disciples that one of them would betray Him. He then gave a piece of bread to Judas and said, "What you do, do quickly." At that moment, Satan entered into Judas (13:27). Likewise, Satan wanted to get his hands on Peter. Jesus said to him: "Simon, Simon! Indeed, Satan has asked for you, that he may sift you as wheat. But I have prayed for you, that your faith should not fail; and when you have returned to Me, strengthen your brethren" (Luke 22:31–32). That prompted Peter to declare that he was ready to go with Jesus to prison and death, but Jesus said, "I tell you, Peter, the rooster shall not crow this day before you will deny three times that you know Me" (v. 34). As we know, events unfolded as Jesus said they would. Judas betrayed Him and Peter denied Him. But these two men's stories have very different endings. Judas proved himself to be the "son of perdition" (John 17:12) and eventually hung himself. Peter came back and became a pillar of the early church. Why? I'm sure there are many reasons, but I think the most significant one is the intercessory prayer of Christ. Jesus had prayed that Peter's faith would not fail in the face of Satan's onslaughts, and that prayer was answered.

The Testimony of Unity

As Jesus began to pray for His church, He said: **"I do not pray for these alone, but also for those who will believe in Me through their word; that they all may be one, as You, Father, are in Me and I in You; that they also may be one in Us, that the world may believe that You sent Me. And the glory which You gave Me I have given**

them, that they may be one just as We are one: I in them, and You in me; that they may be made perfect in one, and that the world may know that You have sent Me, and have loved them as You have loved Me" (vv. 20–23).

This section of Jesus' prayer is loaded, but a key petition concerned a matter about which He had already prayed for the disciples—the unity of His people. As I pointed out earlier, there's a very real sense in which this petition already has been fulfilled. Every person who is a Christian is in Christ, so if you are in Christ and I am in Christ, there is a real unity between us by virtue of our common union with Him. This is true for all genuine believers. Even though we may differ on this point or that point, there is a real unity that binds us together—and that unity should be evident to the world.

In his introduction to the English translation of Athanasius' *On the Incarnation*, C. S. Lewis tells of perusing the writings of great Christians from history during his student days. He read Thomas Aquinas, Martin Luther, Thomas à Kempis, and others, and while he recognized that all of these people had certain nuances of differences between them, he couldn't get over the oneness that kept coming through their testimony as to the truth of the gospel.

Jesus prayed that those who would believe on Him would have a unity that unbelievers could see, that they might learn various things. He asked the Father that believers would be "made perfect in one . . . that the world may know that You have sent Me, and have loved them as You have loved Me." The love, concern, and compassion that we have one for another should be so atypical of the world that they serve as definitive proof that Jesus was not merely a great moral teacher but the second person of the Trinity, sent by God. This unity should also testify to the world that God loves believers just as He loves Christ. The clear demonstration of a supernatural work going on in the midst of the people of God shows the love, favor, and grace of God.

Incidentally, believers themselves need a deeper grasp of the love of God for them. In His tender mercies, God has an incredible capacity to love the unlovely. How do I know that? He knows every ugly part of my soul and of my life, yet He loves me. How can that be? We always have to understand that the love He has for us is not because we are inherently lovable. He loves us in the Son, and the same love that He pours out to His Son, He pours out to those who are in the Son. This love that He has for the Son is the only reason I can give as to why God chose to save me.

A Place in His Presence

Jesus then prayed, **"Father, I desire that they also whom You gave Me may be with Me where I am"** (v. 24a). Jesus desired not only that we would be *in* Him, but that we would be *with* Him. There is no place in the universe I would rather be than in the presence of Christ. There is no more marvelous presence than His. Incredibly, He also wants me to be with Him. Remember, He prayed here not just for the disciples but for you and for me. He was asking the Father that *we* might be with Him. The greatest benefit of Christianity is not the forgiveness of sins; that's simply a means to an end. The greatest benefit that we have is access to the presence of God and His Son. That's where Jesus wants us to be.

Jesus had a specific reason for wanting His people to be with Him: **". . . that they may behold My glory which You have given Me; for You loved Me before the foundation of the world"** (v. 24b). Of all the books I have written, I don't think I enjoyed writing one more than *The Glory of Christ*. In that book, I worked through the life of Christ, showing that while His glory was hidden for most of His earthly ministry, there were moments when His glory broke through and shone on those who were present. The clearest example of that was on the Mount of Transfiguration, where, in the presence of Peter, James, and John, He was transfigured, so that His face shone like the sun (Matt. 17:1–8). Later, they wrote of having "beheld His glory" (John 1:14; see also 2 Peter 1:16–18). What a glorious experience it was for me to focus on those vignettes of the shining of Jesus' glory during His earthly sojourn. Yet those were only brief foretastes of the glory that awaits us in the consummation of the kingdom, when we will enter the new heaven and behold the glory of Christ in its fullness.

Jonathan Edwards is often criticized as a dour hellfire-and-brimstone preacher, but scholars have found that the two words that occur most frequently in Edwards' writings are *sweetness* and *excellence*. Edwards was consumed by the sweetness of the glory of Christ. When he wrote so earnestly about the religious affections, the inclinations of the soul and the heart to the things of Christ, he was describing the supernatural response of the believer to Christ.

When the Holy Spirit transforms us and fills our hearts with love for Jesus, nothing will satisfy us more than to behold the unveiled glory of Christ. There can be nothing sweeter or more excellent than that. That is the end for which we were made. People will save money to go to a rock concert or a professional sports contest so that they can see some celebrities for an hour or two. But we are going to see the King of kings one day in all of His glory. That joyous moment is as good as guaranteed because of our Lord's intercession.

Finally, Jesus prayed: **"O righteous Father! The world has not known You, but I have known You; and these have known that You sent Me. And I have declared to them Your name, and will declare it, that the love with which You loved Me may be in them, and I in them"** (vv. 25–26). We are called to participate in the death of Christ, in the afflictions of Christ, in the humiliation of Christ, for if we do not, we never will share in His glory. But in order to be faithful disciples in this world, to fulfill the mission that He has given to His church, we need to be encouraged by the knowledge of His love that He has shed abroad in our hearts. The knowledge of His everlasting love for us gives us the strength we need to fulfill the mission that He has given to us.

48

THE ARREST OF JESUS

John 18:1–14

When Jesus had spoken these words, He went out with His disciples over the Brook Kidron, where there was a garden, which He and His disciples entered. And Judas, who betrayed Him, also knew the place; for Jesus often met there with His disciples. Then Judas, having received a detachment of troops, and officers from the chief priests and Pharisees, came there with lanterns, torches, and weapons. Jesus therefore, knowing all things that would come upon Him, went forward and said to them, "Whom are you seeking?" They answered Him, "Jesus of Nazareth." Jesus said to them, "I am He." And Judas, who betrayed Him, also stood with them. Now when He said to them, "I am He," they drew back and fell to the ground. Then He asked them again, "Whom are you seeking?" And they said, "Jesus of Nazareth." Jesus answered, "I have told you that I am He. Therefore, if you seek Me, let these go their way," that the saying might be fulfilled which He spoke, "Of those whom You gave Me I have lost none." Then Simon Peter, having a sword, drew it and struck the high priest's servant, and cut off his right ear. The servant's name was Malchus. So Jesus said to Peter, "Put your sword into the sheath. Shall I not drink the cup which My Father has given Me?" Then the detachment of troops and the captain and the officers of the Jews arrested Jesus and bound Him. And they led

Him away to Annas first, for he was the father-in-law of Caiaphas who was high priest that year. Now it was Caiaphas who advised the Jews that it was expedient that one man should die for the people.

I have vivid memories of Nick Green's orchard. I remember it as a place that boasted many rows of grapevines, apple trees, pear trees, and peach trees. The length of the orchard, to the best of my recollection, was about two hundred yards, though my memory may be exaggerating the size of it. Meandering through this orchard was a path that led from the end of McClellan Drive, the street on which I lived, to the back of Harold Wiegel's grocery store and butcher shop. Every day I would be sent to Harold's store to buy a loaf of bread, a sack of potatoes, or whatever was needed, and I always took the path through Nick Green's orchard.

I liked the orchard, except at night, especially winter nights, because right behind Harold's store, at the entrance to the path into the orchard, stood a huge tree with gnarled limbs. When there were no leaves on the tree, it looked like a specter, and it scared me. A full moon made it worse, because instead of diminishing my fear, the moon heightened the terror of those long boughs that came from the mammoth tree. As a result, when I had to follow the path at night, I would set out from Harold's store and run as fast as I could the entire two hundred yards until I got to the safety of McClellan Drive.

I cannot help but remember that experience when I read the biblical account of the arrest of Jesus. The arrest took place at night. Because it was the night before the Passover, there was a full moon. The arrest apparently took place on the slopes of the Mount of Olives, near the Garden of Gethsemane. In Jesus' day, the Mount of Olives was covered with ancient olive trees, and they were even more gnarled than that tree behind Harold Wiegel's grocery store. All those trees were cut down for firewood when the Romans besieged Jerusalem some three decades later, but they were still standing when Jesus and His disciples went there, casting their weird shadows in the moonlight to set the stage for the arrest of the Lord.

The Arrest of the Messiah

John does not give us an account of Christ's agony in Gethsemane. The other Gospel writers tell us that He became so sorrowful that His sweat was like great drops of blood falling down, and that He begged the Father to let the cup of His suffering pass from Him. John focuses instead on the arrest of Jesus there in the garden.

John begins by noting, **When Jesus had spoken these words, He went out with His disciples over the Brook Kidron, where there was a garden, which He and His disciples entered** (v. 1). When we think of "the Brook Kidron," we may envision a beautifully flowing stream that separated the Mount of Olives from the city of Jerusalem. In actuality, it was a *wadi*, a dry gulch; the only time water flowed in it was during the two rainy seasons. When the rains came, water would pour down the Kidron and it would become a rushing waterway, a dangerous torrent to cross. But most of the time, the creek bed was dry and people could walk across it without any difficulty.

Why did Jesus go to this garden? When pilgrims came to Jerusalem for the feast of the Passover, they were required to spend the night before the feast within the broader vicinity of Jerusalem. This section where Jesus went with His disciples was considered within the limits. That is why He did not go to Bethany, site of the home of Mary, Martha, and Lazarus, where He often stayed—their home was outside the visitation limits.

John then tells us, **And Judas, who betrayed Him, also knew the place; for Jesus often met there with His disciples** (v. 2). This little detail is significant. In the upper room, Jesus had said that Judas was going to betray Him; He then dismissed him to that diabolical task and said, "What you do, do quickly" (13:27). Jesus knew that Judas was headed for the authorities to commit his act of betrayal. Therefore, we might expect that Jesus, in order to escape arrest, would have gone anywhere other than a place where He regularly met with His disciples, a place Judas knew about. It was only natural that Judas would lead the arresting officers to the garden. But Jesus was not seeking to avoid arrest. It almost seems that He went out of His way to be apprehended. That is significant, as we will see.

John's account continues, **Then Judas, having received a detachment of troops, and officers from the chief priests and Pharisees, came there with lanterns, torches, and weapons** (v. 3). Notice that John tells us that two groups of people came with Judas for the purpose of arresting Jesus. The first group is called simply "a detachment"; the second group was composed of temple police sent by the Jewish authorities. This was a joint operation between the Romans and the temple police. Normally, the Romans didn't have a large garrison of troops in Jerusalem; Roman soldiers were stationed in Caesarea. But during the Passover, when hundreds of thousands of Jews from around the region flooded into Jerusalem, the Roman authorities sent a detachment of troops to Jerusalem to handle riot control and protect against a local insurrection, housing them in the Antonia Fortress right next to the quarters of Pontius Pilate.

On paper, a detachment of Roman soldiers numbered one thousand men. Usually, however, units did not have their full complement of soldiers, so it is estimated that the troops who came out to arrest Jesus were between six hundred and seven hundred in number. When we add in the temple police, we can guess that almost a thousand men were sent out to capture one man. With a crowd that large, and with many of them carrying torches and lanterns, it was no doubt easy for Jesus and the disciples to hear and see them coming.

Protecting the Disciples

John writes, **Jesus therefore, knowing all things that would come upon Him, went forward and said to them, "Whom are you seeking?" They answered Him, "Jesus of Nazareth." Jesus said to them, "I am He." And Judas, who betrayed Him, also stood with them** (vv. 4–5). Jesus didn't fall back into the shadows. He didn't hide behind His disciples. He took the initiative, stepped up to the front, greeted the soldiers as they came, and said, "Whom are you seeking?" They said, "Jesus of Nazareth," to which Jesus replied, "I am He."

Throughout John's Gospel, we have looked at the "I am" sayings of Jesus: "I am the bread of life," "I am the light of the world," and so forth. Each time Jesus gave one of these sayings, He used a unique phrase, rendered in the Greek as *ego eimi*. Both of these words mean "I am," so if you put them together, *ego eimi* literally means "I am, I am." As we saw earlier, the Greek translation of the Old Testament rendered the ineffable name of God, Yahweh, by this same strange construction, *ego eimi*, which can be translated "I AM WHO I AM" (Ex. 3:14). Thus, when Jesus used this construction, He was claiming deity for Himself. That is the phrase Jesus used here, when He addressed those who had come to arrest Him.

As soon as Jesus said these words, there was a remarkable reaction. John writes: **Now when He said to them, "I am He," they drew back and fell to the ground"** (v. 6). This mass of soldiers, many of them battle-hardened, confronted Jesus, and when they heard Him say "I am He," they fell to the ground; they retreated.

There were two groups of people that night who were terrified. The first group was the disciples. You can imagine the fear that enveloped them when they heard the swords clanging, saw the lanterns moving, and saw the torches burning. They knew that Jesus' arrest, and probably theirs as well, was imminent. But the group that was more afraid than the disciples was the soldiers. They may have had Jesus outnumbered a thousand to one, but they were scared nonetheless.

Doesn't this situation remind you of Moses and the people of Israel, trapped between Migdol and the Red Sea as the chariots of Pharaoh moved in (Ex. 14)? Doesn't it remind you of Elisha, who found himself in Dothan, surrounded by the soldiers of Syria (2 Kings 6)? To the naked eye, Moses' situation was hopeless. There was a sea of water in front of him and a sea of chariots behind. But God made a way through the sea for Moses and the Israelites. Elisha's situation seemed equally hopeless. His servant said, "Alas, my master! What shall we do?" Elisha replied, "LORD, I pray, open his eyes that he may see" (2 Kings 6:15–17). God opened the eyes of Elisha's servant so that he saw chariots of fire surrounding the city to protect God's prophet.

Like Elisha, Jesus knew that He was surrounded at that moment by a host of angels. In biblical terms, a "host" is not a master of ceremonies at a banquet; rather, it is an army. Jesus knew the promise of the Word of God, that the Father would give His angels charge over Him, to protect Him (Ps. 91:11). He also knew that if He asked, legions of angels would come to His aid (Matt. 26:53). It almost seems that the soldiers understood that, too, because they never had encountered anyone like Jesus before. So when He said, "I am He," they fell back, asking themselves, "What is He going to do?"

He didn't call on the angels. Instead, **Then He asked them again, Whom are you seeking?" And they said, "Jesus of Nazareth." Jesus answered, "I have told you that I am He. Therefore, if you seek Me, let these go their way," that the saying might be fulfilled which He spoke, "Of those whom You gave Me I have lost none"** (vv. 7–9). Jesus was not concerned for His own safety, but for the safety of His disciples.

Jesus Allows No Resistance

But Peter was not prepared to go even if the soldiers would let him: **Then Simon Peter, having a sword, drew it and struck the high priest's servant, and cut off his right ear. The servant's name was Malchus. So Jesus said to Peter, "Put your sword into the sheath. Shall I not drink the cup which My Father has given Me?"** (vv. 10–11). Peter, ever the impetuous one, took out a sword, which was probably more of a dagger, took a wild swing at one of those in the crowd, and cut off the man's ear. Although all four Gospel writers report this event, John is the only one who tells us that Peter was the one who wielded the sword. Luke adds that Jesus healed the man's ear (Luke 22:51). He then rebuked Peter: **"Put your sword into the sheath. Shall I not drink the cup which My Father has given Me?"** (v. 11).

In theology, when we talk about the work of Jesus by which we are redeemed, we make a very important distinction, one that's often overlooked, between what we call the active obedience of Christ and the passive obedience of Christ. Both are necessary; if Jesus had come from heaven on a parachute, gone straight to Golgotha, gone to the cross, and died, that would not have been enough to save us. God also requires true righteousness in those He accepts. Therefore, Jesus was born and lived thirty-three years under the law of God, a life of perfect obedience, for our justification. He earned the righteousness that we need but that we don't have in and of ourselves. He actively obeyed every law that God had ever given. This was His active obedience. By contrast, Jesus' passive obedience was that obedience by which He passively allowed Himself to suffer the penalty for our guilt.

Jesus' passive surrender to this punishment did not start at the cross. It started the minute He got off His knees in the Garden of Gethsemane. It was then that He took the cup and completely acquiesced to the vocation the Father had set before Him. He assented in obedience to the Father to be our substitute in His death. So He told the crowd: "Here I am. I am the One you're looking for." He made no attempt to flee. He would not allow His disciples to fight. Like a lamb led to the slaughter, He opened not His mouth, but went passively to His death (cf. Isa. 53:7).

Even when we understand that Jesus was being heroically obedient, the facts of what happened next are difficult to read: **Then the detachment of troops and the captain and the officers of the Jews arrested Jesus and bound Him. And they led Him away to Annas first, for he was the father-in-law of Caiaphas who was high priest that year. Now it was Caiaphas who advised the Jews that it was expedient that one man should die for the people** (vv. 12–14). He was arrested. He was bound. Then He was led away to stand before the Jewish authorities. Thus the stage was set for the completely illegal kangaroo-court trial to which Jesus was subjected.

49

PETER'S DENIAL

John 18:15–27

And Simon Peter followed Jesus, and so did another disciple. Now that disciple was known to the high priest, and went with Jesus into the courtyard of the high priest. But Peter stood at the door outside. Then the other disciple, who was known to the high priest, went out and spoke to her who kept the door, and brought Peter in. Then the servant girl who kept the door said to Peter, "You are not also one of this Man's disciples, are you?" He said, "I am not." Now the servants and officers who had made a fire of coals stood there, for it was cold, and they warmed themselves. And Peter stood with them and warmed himself. The high priest then asked Jesus about His disciples and His doctrine. Jesus answered him, "I spoke openly to the world. I always taught in synagogues and in the temple, where the Jews always meet, and in secret I have said nothing. Why do you ask Me? Ask those who have heard Me what I said to them. Indeed they know what I said." And when He had said these things, one of the officers who stood by struck Jesus with the palm of his hand, saying, "Do You answer the high priest like that?" Jesus answered him, "If I have spoken evil, bear witness of the evil; but if well, why do you strike Me?" Then Annas sent Him bound to Caiaphas the high priest. Now Simon Peter stood and warmed himself. Therefore they said to him, "You are not also

one of His disciples, are you?" He denied it and said, "I am not!" One
of the servants of the high priest, a relative of him whose ear Peter cut
off, said, "Did I not see you in the garden with Him?" Peter then denied
again; and immediately a rooster crowed.

There is a word in the English language that drips with pain. It is a word
that sends shivers up our spines whenever we hear it or contemplate it,
and most especially whenever we experience it. That word is *betrayal*.
When I hear that word, I get an empty feeling in the pit of my stomach, because
betrayal is one of the most devastating experiences any human being can
endure. I am sure that everyone who reads this book has had the experience
of being betrayed. This is our lot as people, to be betrayed by our friends and
family, those we love and trust the most, because none of us is so flawless in
our behavior as to be able to give total loyalty. The prevalence of betrayal is
understandable in light of the prevalence of sin.

Still, I confess that I struggle to understand how anyone could have betrayed
the Lord Jesus Christ. The biblical record of what happened on the night
before Jesus' crucifixion focuses precisely on that problem of betrayal, not
only at the hands of Judas, but also by the lips of Peter.

I find it fascinating that when the apostle Paul gives the words of institution for the Lord's Supper (1 Cor. 11:23–26), he does not speak about "the
night in which our Lord broke bread with His disciples," "the night in which
our Lord was arrested," or "the night in which our Lord was put on trial for
His life." Instead, he references "the same night in which He was betrayed."
The hideous betrayal of Jesus by those closest to Him was a major event in
redemptive history.

Peter's Fickle Devotion

John does not record the story of Jesus' transfiguration, but the other three
Gospels make clear that it was a highlight of the disciples' experience with
Jesus during His earthly ministry (Matt. 17:1–7; Mark 9:1–8; Luke 9:28–36).
Jesus took three of His disciples—the inner circle, Peter, James, and John—
and went up on a mountain. There, He was transfigured before their eyes,
and His face began to glow as bright as the sun, and His clothes began to
gleam as white as the light. Then Moses and Elijah appeared and spoke with
Him. When Peter saw these things, he said, "Lord, it is good for us to be here;
if You wish, let us make here three tabernacles: one for You, one for Moses,
and one for Elijah" (Matt. 17:4). He said: "Let's pitch our tents right here,

right now. Forget about going to Jerusalem. Let's just bask in Your glory on the mountaintop." You see, at that moment, more than anything else in the world, Peter wanted to be as close to Jesus as he possibly could get, and he wanted to stay there forever.

We are like Peter. In the flesh, we are all groupies. We love to get close to the rich and famous, to those who are in positions of power and of adulation. However, we are like Peter in another way. When those we idolize fall, we run for cover; when our heroes come under criticism, we no longer want to be identified with them at all. Just a few days after the transfiguration, when Jesus was betrayed by Judas and arrested, Peter could not bring himself to acknowledge his Lord.

It was to the home of Annas that Jesus was taken after his arrest (v. 13). Annas was the father-in-law of Caiaphas, who was high priest that year. Why did the troops do this? Why didn't they take Him directly to the high priest? If the Jewish leaders wanted to have Jesus judged and condemned, they would have to go through Pontius Pilate, the Roman governor, and the steppingstone to Pilate in the legal system was Caiaphas, not Annas. However, in the eyes of the Jews, Annas *was* the high priest. The Romans had deposed Annas as high priest, but in Israel, the high priest was appointed for life and could not be deposed. So these pious, orthodox Jews took Jesus to Annas first because they saw him as the true high priest, despite what the Romans said.

John writes, **And Simon Peter followed Jesus, and so did another disciple** (v. 15a). The disciple who was with Peter is not named, and there has been much debate as to who it was. Usually, when John refers obliquely to himself in his Gospel, he speaks of "the disciple whom Jesus loved." However, I am persuaded that he is referring to himself here, too, because there is much evidence to suggest that John was a member of a priestly group within the Sanhedrin, so if any of the disciples had access into the priestly environs, it would have been John. In any case, **Now that disciple was known to the high priest, and went with Jesus into the courtyard of the high priest. But Peter stood at the door outside. Then the other disciple, who was known to the high priest, went out and spoke to her who kept the door, and brought Peter in** (vv. 15b–16). The disciple who was known to the high priest was able to vouch for Peter, so that he, too, could come into the high priest's courtyard.

Then it happened: **Then the servant girl who kept the door said to Peter, "You are not also one of this Man's disciples, are you?" He said, "I am not"** (v. 17). Something about Peter caught the eye of the servant girl who was tending the gate and caused her to associate him with

Jesus. Notice how she worded her question. She did not say, "Are you a member of this Man's entourage?" or "Are you one of this Nazarene's disciples?" Rather, she phrased it this way: "You are not one of His disciples, are you?" Peter could have said, "Well, actually, yes, I am," but he chose to agree with the direction of her question and murmured, "No, I'm not."

An Improper Trial

John then interrupts his account of Peter's denials to report on some of the events that were happening in the courtyard and in Jesus' trial: **Now the servants and officers who had made a fire of coal stood there, for it was cold, and they warmed themselves. And Peter stood with them and warmed himself** (v. 18). Peter, trying to be anonymous, hid in the shadows, but he didn't want to run out of the courtyard altogether. Eventually, in the cold, he went to the fire, where some other servants and soldiers were standing, to get warm in front of the flames. This little detail is significant for John's account of the trial of Jesus because it points out that these events took place at night. This calls attention again to the illegality of this trial, which should not have been held in the middle of the night.

When the trial commenced, **the high priest then asked Jesus about His disciples and His doctrine** (v. 19). We don't know for sure how these sorts of trials were conducted, but there is abundant Jewish testimony that the prisoner who was on trial was never required to testify or answer questions. Instead, witnesses were called to speak at the trial—witnesses against the accused and witnesses on behalf of the accused. The procedure was this: first the witnesses on behalf of the accused were called to testify to the integrity of the one who was on trial, then witnesses against the accused spoke. But all of these procedures seem to have been dispensed with as Annas proceeded to interrogate Jesus, asking Him about His disciples and His doctrine. It is interesting that when Jesus was delivered into the hands of Pilate, the charge against him was political, not theological; the Jews said, "We found this fellow perverting the nation, and forbidding to pay taxes to Caesar, saying that He Himself is Christ, a King" (Luke 23:2). But at this stage, the Jewish leadership asked about His theology.

Jesus responded with these words: **"I spoke openly to the world. I always taught in synagogues and in the temple, where the Jews always meet, and in secret I have said nothing. Why do you ask Me? Ask those who have heard Me what I said to them. Indeed they know what I said"** (vv. 20–21). Do you see what Jesus was doing? He challenged Annas to follow the proper protocol for a Jewish trial. He said: "If you want to know what I teach, ask anybody, because what I teach openly is no different from what I teach in private. I don't have a double agenda. What I say in the public square, I say in the cloakroom, so if you want to know what I teach, ask My disciples, or the people, or even My opponents, because I have been teaching openly and publicly." He suggested that Annas should call witnesses, as was proper.

John then writes: **And when He had said these things, one of the officers who stood by struck Jesus with the palm of his hand, saying, "Do You answer the high priest like that?" Jesus answered him, "If I have spoken evil, bear witness of the evil; but if well, why do you strike Me?"** (vv. 22–23). One of the officers thought that Jesus' reply to the high priest was disrespectful, so he slapped Jesus in the face. He said, in effect, "Who do You think You are?" Jesus' reply again called for a return to proper procedure. He challenged the officer to point out the wrong in His words or, if there was no wrong, to refrain from slapping Him.

Finally, **Annas sent Him bound to Caiaphas the high priest** (v. 24). It was Caiaphas who had authority to deliver Jesus to the Romans. By sending Jesus to his son-in-law, Annas declared that he wanted to see Jesus destroyed.

The Dark Human Heart

John's account is like a novel, in which the plot shifts from one character to another, and he now reverts to Peter's story. He writes: **Now Simon Peter stood and warmed himself. Therefore they said to him, "You are not also one of His disciples, are you?" He denied it and said, "I am not!" One of the servants of the high priest, a relative of him whose ear Peter cut off, said, "Did I not see you in the garden with Him?" Peter then denied again; and immediately a rooster crowed** (vv. 25–27). Two more questions about Peter's relationship with Jesus were fired at him, apparently in quick succession. Matthew tells us that, in his growing desperation and irritation, Peter issued his second denial "with an oath" (Matt. 26:72), and when he was questioned the third time, he "began to curse and swear" (Matt. 26:74). In the face of questions from lowly servants, not from the Roman governor or the Jewish authorities, Peter vehemently denied that he had anything to do with Jesus. He betrayed his Lord with curses. And as soon as the third denial was out of his mouth, the rooster crowed, fulfilling the prediction of Christ.

What does this teach us? I think it teaches us something hideous, something we don't want to see—the darkness of the human heart. This shows us what people are capable of doing. Even after making a glorious confession, even after swearing allegiance to Jesus—"I will lay down my life for Your sake" (13:37b)—Peter failed at the moment of truth. Such is the fallen human nature.

The passage also teaches us, especially in light of Peter's later restoration, what kind of people Jesus died to save. He had no need to die for people who are sinless, for there are no such people. He gave Himself for people who have it in them to betray Him, people like you and me. However, He will never betray those on whom He sets His love, but will love them faithfully for all time.

50

JESUS AND PILATE

John 18:28–38

Then they led Jesus from Caiaphas to the Praetorium, and it was early morning. But they themselves did not go into the Praetorium, lest they should be defiled, but that they might eat the Passover. Pilate then went out to them and said, "What accusation do you bring against this Man?" They answered and said to him, "If He were not an evildoer, we would not have delivered Him up to you." Then Pilate said to them, "You take Him and judge Him according to your law." Therefore the Jews said to him, "It is not lawful for us to put anyone to death," that the saying of Jesus might be fulfilled which He spoke, signifying by what death He would die. Then Pilate entered the Praetorium again, called Jesus, and said to Him, "Are You the King of the Jews?" Jesus answered him, "Are you speaking for yourself about this, or did others tell you this concerning Me?" Pilate answered, "Am I a Jew? Your own nation and the chief priests have delivered You to me. What have You done?" Jesus answered, "My kingdom is not of this world. If My kingdom were of this world, My servants would fight, so that I should not be delivered to the Jews; but now My kingdom is not from here." Pilate therefore said to Him, "Are You a king then?" Jesus answered, "You say rightly that I am a king. For this cause I was born, and for this cause I have come into the world, that I should bear witness

to the truth. Everyone who is of the truth hears My voice." Pilate said to
Him, "What is truth?" And when he had said this, he went out again to
the Jews, and said to them, "I find no fault in Him at all."

The Apostles' Creed reads, in part: "[Jesus] was conceived by the Holy
Ghost, born of the Virgin Mary, suffered under Pontius Pilate, was
crucified, dead, and buried." Through the centuries, theologians and
historians have puzzled over this section of the creed, asking why it is that of
all the historic personages who surround the life of Jesus, it is Pontius Pilate
who is mentioned every time the creed is confessed. Why not the Roman
emperor? Why not Caiaphas or Annas, the high priests mentioned in John's
Gospel? Why Pontius Pilate?

The answer that has been given by the theologians of the church is that
Pilate is mentioned in the creed because of the role he played in the history
of redemption. In the drama of the death of Christ, Pilate functioned as the
persona publica, that public authority who was in the position of judgment. It
is significant that the judgment he rendered after his interrogation of Jesus
was this: "I find no fault in Him at all." The Roman governor found Jesus
innocent of the charges brought against Him.

Yet Pilate turned Jesus over to the mob and sentenced him to death.
Why?

Governor of a Restive Province

The Gospels tell us little about Pilate other than his role in the trial of Jesus
and in the sacrilegious murder of Jews who offered sacrifices (Luke 13:1).
But there are other references to Pontius Pilate in extra-biblical sources that
have survived through the ages. We have portraits of Pilate and records of
his activity from the Jewish historian Josephus and the Jewish theologian
Philo of Alexandria.

We know Pilate was appointed governor of Judea in AD 26 by the Emperor
Tiberius and that he served in that post till AD 37. During that time, Judea was
considered one of the least desirable outposts for a Roman official because the
Jews were notorious for not being acquiescent to Roman rule. Thus, Pilate's
assignment to rule over the Jews was not considered a plum appointment.
He indicated his hostility to the Jewish people very early in his rule. When
he came to Jerusalem, he brought the Roman standards with the image of
the emperor into the city, which incensed the Jews. To see the image of the
emperor set up in the Holy City was outrageous to the populace of Jerusalem,

and Josephus tells us that they responded by coming into the city and staging a literal sit-down strike. They surrounded the house of Pilate, then sat down in the street and refused to move for five days. Finally, Pilate called in his troops and warned the Jews that if they did not leave, the soldiers would cut off their heads. The Jews then laid back and stretched out their necks, awaiting execution. Pilate finally backed down and removed the standards from the city.

Later, Pilate tried again. He brought the votive shields of the emperor into the Holy Place, which was another sacrilege in the sight of the Jews, and once again the people gathered in protest. The four sons of Herod sent a protest to the emperor, and the emperor commanded Pilate to respect the Jews' religious freedom and to remove the shields from the Holy Place. Once again, Pilate was frustrated by the insurgent Jews.

Pilate again stirred protests when he took the sacred treasure from the Jewish temple to build an aqueduct in the province. This sparked another protest by Jews. This time, Pilate sent his soldiers into the crowd, and they clubbed people to death. That created even more trouble for Pilate.

One other incident bears mentioning. A Roman governor had the privilege of striking coins with any image he so desired. Pilate made copper coins bearing images of pagan religion. That was another outrage in the eyes of the Jews.

I give you this background because it helps explain why Pilate was so weak and pliable that he bowed to the clamoring of a multitude to crucify a man he had declared to be faultless. It is important to understand the political pressure that he was under; with all Jerusalem crying for the blood of Jesus, Pilate probably thought, "If I don't give them what they want and word gets back to Rome, this might end my career." We need to keep that in mind as we look at Pilate's interactions with Jesus.

Delivering the Lamb to the Slaughter

John writes: **Then they led Jesus from Caiaphas to the Praetorium, and it was early morning. But they themselves did not go into the Praetorium, lest they should be defiled, but that they might eat the Passover** (v. 28). The Praetorium was the headquarters of the Roman governor when he was in Jerusalem. He normally stayed in Caesarea and came to Jerusalem only when there were massive gatherings of Jewish pilgrims for the annual feasts. It was early morning when the Jews brought Jesus there after he had appeared before Caiaphas (a hearing which John does not record).

Note that the Jews who brought Jesus to Pilate did not go into the Praetorium lest they should be defiled and thus be prevented from eating the Passover. This verse raises a question. It is possible that Jesus had eaten the Passover the night before. So why were these Jews worrying about eating the Passover? The Passover feast lasted seven days, and in order to participate in the entire feast, the priests and the officials had to maintain complete cleanliness from all forms of defilement. To enter the pagan residence of Pilate would have brought them into defilement, preventing them from participating in the whole feast. So they turned Jesus over to the Praetorium guard and stayed outside. These men were scrupulous to avoid any ritual defilement even while they were carrying out the most vile act of human history. As they delivered the Lamb of God to the slaughter, they made sure their hands were ceremonially clean.

What does this tell us? Here were people who paid attention to the minute details of religion while their hearts were far from God. When we read the Scriptures, especially the Old Testament prophets, we are told over and over again that God sometimes hates religion. When does He hate it? When it is offered from hearts that are faithless. These Jews went through all the motions, maintained all the rituals, and kept themselves totally clean while they crucified the Son of God. Of course, we can look back from our vantage point in the twenty-first century and say what hypocrites these people were, but we need to look at ourselves, because we crucify the Son of God afresh every time we honor Him with our lips while our hearts are far from Him. Instead of looking disdainfully at these people who betrayed Jesus, we have to see ourselves in that crowd, because this is what fallen humanity is like. This is what fallen humanity does. Religion without faith is a deadly thing.

John continues: **Pilate then went out to them and said, "What accusation do you bring against this Man?" They answered and said to him, "If He were not an evildoer, we would not have delivered Him up to you." Then Pilate said to them, "You take Him and judge Him according to your law." Therefore the Jews said to him, "It is not lawful for us to put anyone to death," that the saying of Jesus might be fulfilled which He spoke, signifying by what death He would die** (vv. 29–32). Because the Jews could not come into the Praetorium, Pilate came out to them, and he asked them what Jesus had done wrong. Pilate was following the rules. He was saying: "You have to level charges against Him. You can't just turn Him over to me. I want to know what the charges are." Reading these words, I sense a hint of disgust in Pilate. Remember, he didn't like these people in the first place, and he no doubt was wondering why they had brought a man to him so early in the morning in an apparent dispute over theology.

The Jews answered Pilate arrogantly. Their response was something along these lines: "Why do you *think* we brought Him to you, Pilate? Do you think we brought Him to you because we think He's a saint? We brought him to you because He's an evildoer, and it's your job to get rid of evildoers around here. If He weren't an evildoer, we wouldn't be bothering you so early in the morning." They didn't want to give Pilate a charge against Jesus; they simply wanted him to accept their word that Jesus was a troublemaker. Pilate's response shows that he didn't like their attitude. He said, "You take Him and judge Him according to your law." He wanted to wash his hands of it.

Then the Jews revealed why they had brought Jesus to Pilate: "It is not lawful for us to put anyone to death." At last Pilate could see their game— they wanted the death penalty imposed. So Pilate, as it were, agreed to hear the case.

Interrogating the King

John writes: **Then Pilate entered the Praetorium again, called Jesus, and said to Him, "Are You the King of the Jews?"** (v. 33). This question indicates that Jesus' accusers did give Pilate some specific charges against Jesus. Clearly their trumped-up case was political, not theological. They said to Pilate: "He's calling himself a king, and you Romans can't put up with that sort of thing. That's insurrection." So Pilate summoned Jesus and cut right to the chase: "Are You the King of the Jews? Is it true what they say?"

Jesus' reply is very interesting: **"Are you speaking for yourself about this, or did others tell you this concerning Me?"** (v. 34). Now who was the interrogator? Suddenly, Pilate was on trial before the Judge of heaven and earth as Jesus asked, "Did you come up with this question on your own or are you asking on the basis of hearsay?" Jesus understood the rules of evidence, and He knew hearsay convictions were prohibited. But Pilate responded like a seasoned, cynical politician: **"Am I a Jew? Your own nation and the chief priests have delivered You to me. What have You done?"** (v. 35). Pilate said: "Do You really think *I* would bring this up? What do I care about what the Jews are doing? I'm not a Jew, so I'm not interested in who the King of the Jews may be. Your own priests have delivered You to me and told me what You claim to be. So what is it You have done?"

Jesus' response was rather cryptic: **Jesus answered, "My kingdom is not of this world. If My kingdom were of this world, My servants**

would fight, so that I should not be delivered to the Jews; but now My kingdom is not from here" (v. 36). He did not say that His dominion and authority did not include this world or that His realm was a transcendent spiritual Neverland. This was the same Jesus who affirmed, "All authority has been given to Me in heaven and on earth" (Matt. 28:18). He told Pilate: "My kingdom is not like your kingdom. My kingdom is not built on violence, on blood, on war. That's the way the kingdoms of this world function. My kingdom is not a world-like kingdom." In other words, Jesus said that He did not plan to establish a kingdom by force. He had no intention of leading a rebellion against the Romans, no matter what the Jews might say.

Pilate did not take time to deal with the substance of Jesus' reply; he simply wanted to know whether Jesus was a king. John writes: **Pilate therefore said to Him, "Are You a king then?" Jesus answered, "You say rightly that I am a king. For this cause I was born, and for this cause I have come into the world, that I should bear witness to the truth. Everyone who is of the truth hears My voice"** (v. 37). What did this response mean? Jesus acknowledged His royal mission, but He declared that He had not come to subjugate the world but to bear witness to the truth. He said, "I came here to make plain the truth of God."

Pilate's reply is full of sarcasm: **Pilate said to Him, "What is truth?" And when he had said this, he went out again to the Jews, and said to them, "I find no fault in Him at all"** (v. 38). It is impossible for me to believe that Pilate was asking Jesus to teach him the truth because he didn't even wait for Jesus' reply. Pilate's question was the response of someone who had given up hope of finding truth in a world of skepticism. In this cynicism, he was like so many people today, for ours is an age when truth is slain in the streets, and people say truth is whatever you want it to be, that what you believe is "true for you" and what I believe is "true for me," even if the two "truths" are polar opposites. In short, truth is no longer objective.

I noted earlier that Francis Schaeffer talked about "true truth," because he understood that the issue in our day in regard to truth is whether there is an objective reality that is true for everyone, no matter who we are, where we live, or what we do. The same issue was on the front burner in Jesus' day, and Jesus said He was a witness of that "true truth"; in fact, He had declared earlier that He was the "true truth" (14:6).

Pilate went out and told the crowd, "I find no fault in Him at all" (v. 38). He had evaluated the accusation, he had interrogated the prisoner, he had listened to Jesus' responses, and his mind was made up. He *saw* no fault in Jesus because there *was* no fault in Him. In an indirect way, this judge of the earth, this public person, Pontius Pilate, acknowledged the sinlessness of Christ. The Man who stood before Pilate that day was truth incarnate and a Lamb without blemish.

51

THE JUDGMENT
OF PILATE

John 18:39–19:16

"But you have a custom that I should release someone to you at the Passover. Do you therefore want me to release to you the King of the Jews?"
Then they all cried again, saying, "Not this Man, but Barabbas!" Now
Barabbas was a robber. So then Pilate took Jesus and scourged Him. And
the soldiers twisted a crown of thorns and put it on His head, and they
put on Him a purple robe. Then they said, "Hail, King of the Jews!"
And they struck Him with their hands. Pilate then went out again, and
said to them, "Behold, I am bringing Him out to you, that you may know
that I find no fault in Him." Then Jesus came out, wearing the crown of
thorns and the purple robe. And Pilate said to them, "Behold the Man!"
Therefore, when the chief priests and officers saw Him, they cried out,
saying, "Crucify Him, crucify Him!" Pilate said to them, "You take Him
and crucify Him, for I find no fault in Him." The Jews answered him,
"We have a law, and according to our law He ought to die, because He
made Himself the Son of God." Therefore, when Pilate heard that saying,
he was the more afraid, and went again into the Praetorium, and said to
Jesus, "Where are You from?" But Jesus gave him no answer. Then Pilate

said to Him, "Are You not speaking to me? Do You not know that I have
power to crucify You, and power to release You?" Jesus answered, "You
could have no power at all against Me unless it had been given you from
above. Therefore the one who delivered Me to you has the greater sin."
From then on Pilate sought to release Him, but the Jews cried out, saying, "If you let this Man go, you are not Caesar's friend. Whoever makes
himself a king speaks against Caesar." When Pilate therefore heard that
saying, he brought Jesus out and sat down in the judgment seat in a place
that is called The Pavement, but in Hebrew, Gabbatha. Now it was the
Preparation Day of the Passover, and about the sixth hour. And he said
to the Jews, "Behold your King!" But they cried out, "Away with Him,
away with Him! Crucify Him!" Pilate said to them, "Shall I crucify your
King?" The chief priests answered, "We have no king but Caesar!" Then
he delivered Him to them to be crucified. Then they took Jesus and led
Him away.

The Jewish people were given a stark choice. They could spare the life
of their Messiah, the spotless Lamb of God, or they could win the
release of a notorious terrorist. It was the custom during the Passover
Feast for the Roman governor of Judea to release a prisoner. So Pilate said to
the people: **"But you have a custom that I should release someone
to you at the Passover. Do you therefore want me to release to you
the King of the Jews?"** (v. 39). Pilate gave the people the opportunity to do
the right thing, but they would have none of it. John writes: **Then they all
cried again, saying, "Not this Man, but Barabbas!"** (v. 40a). They
chose an evil man and condemned the innocent one.

John tells us that **Barabbas was a robber** (v. 40b), but the other Gospels
show us that his crimes were more extensive. He had committed robbery
and murder in the course of a rebellion against Rome (Mark 15:7; Luke
23:18–19). Basically, he was a terrorist. The chief priests and scribes had
nothing but contempt for terrorists from among their own people, and yet,
when they were presented with a choice between Jesus and this notorious
terrorist, their hostility toward Christ was so profound that they clamored
for the release of Barabbas. According to tradition, Barabbas' full name
was Jesus Barabbas, and the name *Barabbas* can mean and probably did
mean "son of the father." Thus, the people cried for the freedom of this
Jesus, "son of the father," rather than the Jesus who was ultimately the Son
of the Father.

Scourging and Mocking

As Chapter 19 opens, John writes, **So then Pilate took Jesus and scourged Him** (v. 1). The scourgings that the Roman government administered as part of its penal system were of three types. The first type was a kind of whipping that was painful but not debilitating. People who committed minor crimes were whipped. There was a second level that was more severe and then a third level that was the most severe of all, but that type of scourging was not used until a prisoner was sentenced to execution. That third type was administered with a leather thong embedded with pieces of metal, and victims were scourged until their bones were laid bare and their entrails were exposed. The idea was to beat them half to death in order to hasten their expiration on the cross.

John tell us that the scourging that Jesus underwent happened before Pilate sentenced Him to execution, but Matthew and Mark speak of the scourging happening much later in the process, just before Pilate delivered Jesus to the soldiers to be crucified. In all probability, there were two scourgings, the first being the lightest type. Perhaps this was a last-ditch effort by Pilate to satisfy the blood lust of the crowd so that he could avoid having to condemn a man he had publicly declared to be innocent.

John tells us: **And the soldiers twisted a crown of thorns and put it on His head, and they put on Him a purple robe. Then they said, "Hail, King of the Jews!" And they struck Him with their hands** (vv. 2–3). Depictions of this event have been rendered by the greatest artists of the ages in an effort to capture something of the physical agony caused by this crown of thorns. Few, if any, of them are accurate. The thorns that were woven together to make this crown were spikes that reached a length of twelve inches. Then the whole mass of thorns was shoved down on Jesus' head so that the thorns were driven into His temples, all for the sport of the soldiers. Mocking Him further, they threw across His back a garment of the color of royalty, purple. Then they gave obeisance to Him in their mockery, saying, "Hail, King of the Jews," and took turns slapping Him. The whole idea was to make Jesus look not like a king but a court jester.

After Jesus had endured this mockery and mistreatment, He was taken back to Pilate. John writes: **Pilate then went out again, and said to them, "Behold, I am bringing Him out to you, that you may know that I find no fault in Him." Then Jesus came out, wearing the crown of thorns and the purple robe. And Pilate said to them, "Behold the Man!"** (vv. 4–5). Jesus was taken before the crowd with all the trappings of the soldiers' mockery still in place, and Pilate proclaimed that phrase that has come down through church history loaded with such weighty theological import: "*Ecce Homo*," which means, "Behold the Man!" Obviously we can't pry into Pilate's mind and extract the precise intent of that famous phrase. It may be that Pilate was saying to those who were watching this spectacle: "Look at His humiliation. How can anyone perceive this Man as a threat? He looks like a clown. Isn't that enough? Let's be done with this." But even if that is what Pilate had in mind, he could not escape the invisible hand of Providence that was working in that moment. In a supreme irony, the One who was standing in the costume of a fool was not only the incarnation of God but a portrait of perfect humanity. This was what man was created to be. This was the second Adam standing in front of this crowd. When Pilate said, "Behold the Man," the people in the crowd should have looked on Him and said, "Yes, here is man as God intended him to be, as God designed him to be, man with no fault in him."

Whatever Pilate's intent, it had little impact on the hate-filled crowd. Pilate said to them: "Behold the Man! Look at Him." John notes, **Therefore, when the chief priests and officers saw Him, they cried out, saying, "Crucify Him, crucify Him!"** (v. 6a). The people in the crowd did what Pilate suggested—they looked at Jesus. But the sight of Him in abject humiliation did not satisfy them. Instead, they cried out for His death.

By this time, Pilate was beside himself with frustration, and he finally said, obviously in a sardonic manner, **"You take Him and crucify Him, for I find no fault in Him"** (v. 6b). Pilate knew very well that the Jews did not have the authority to crucify Jesus, so he couldn't hand Him over to them. But he was frustrated by his inability to stem the tide of hatred against Jesus. So he said, "All right, then, you do it. I'm not going to do it because I can't find anything wrong with Him." Pilate tried to stand against the demands of the mob at this point.

True Intentions Revealed

John tells us that the Jewish authorities replied, **"We have a law, and according to our law He ought to die, because He made Himself the Son of God"** (v. 7). They were trying to strengthen their argument for Jesus' execution. We saw earlier that Jesus was taken to the Romans on the charge of sedition, setting Himself up as a king in opposition to Caesar. In other words, the Jews claimed that Jesus' crime was political, but we know that what really bothered them was not the political overtones of Jesus' ministry but the theological overtones of His identity. It wasn't Jesus' politics that made them hate Him; it was His theology they couldn't stand.

But they knew they wouldn't get the time of day from a Roman magistrate if they brought a theological issue to him, so they trumped up the charge of sedition. However, that charge didn't work with Pilate, so they said, in effect: "Pilate, we want you to kill Him because our law prohibits people from making themselves equal with God, so He ought to die. We want you to do our work for us."

John's next statement is strange indeed: **Therefore, when Pilate heard that saying, he was the more afraid** (v. 8). Pilate was afraid? What did he fear? Maybe John is saying that when Pilate heard the Jews changing gears, coming up with a different charge, and refusing to back off from their blood lust, he became more uneasy about the power of this multitude. But perhaps it was more than that. Perhaps he realized he had never encountered a prisoner like Jesus. Then he heard the Jews say that Jesus claimed to be the Son of God. I wonder whether Pilate thought, "If this man is the Son of God, I'm in real trouble."

To buy time, Pilate **went again into the Praetorium, and said to Jesus, "Where are You from?" But Jesus gave him no answer** (v. 9). This question indicates to me that Pilate was terrified by the suggestion that Jesus might be more than a man. When Jesus said nothing, Pilate's frustration seemed to boil over and he said: **"Are You not speaking to me? Do you not know that I have power to crucify You, and power to release You?"** (v. 10). He basically asked Jesus, "Do you understand who I am and the power I hold over you?" His words were coercive, offering both the threat of execution ("power to crucify") and the offer of assistance ("power to release"). Here we see Pilate in his role as the *persona publica*, that public authority who was in the position of judgment.

When Pilate spoke these words about authority, Jesus responded with a magnificent statement about the true source of authority in the world. **Jesus answered, "You could have no power at all against Me unless it had been given you from above. Therefore the one who delivered Me to you has the greater sin"** (v. 11). God had ordained Pontius Pilate to be the actor in this drama. Yes, Pilate had real authority, but it was delegated authority. God had placed Jesus at Pilate's mercy so that His will might be done. It was as if Jesus were saying to Pilate: "Pilate, you're like clay in My Father's hands. It has been ordained from the foundation of the world that you would do what you are about to do. Still, you're doing it of your own free will because you have a wicked heart and you are a slave to public opinion. So go ahead, do what you have to do, because you're doing what My Father has ordained for you to do."

We see here a hint of the biblical doctrine of concurrence, the truth that God works in and through even the evil actions of sinful men to accomplish His purposes. Remember, these events happened on that day we celebrate as "Good Friday." Pilate's intent was wicked, but in condemning Jesus he did a great service for the people of God. When Joseph's brothers sold him into slavery in Egypt, their actions were contemptible, but God used Joseph in Egypt to make preparations for a massive famine, preparations that ultimately saved his own evil brothers. For that reason, Joseph told his brothers, "You meant evil against me; but God meant it for good" (Gen. 50:20a).

What did Jesus mean when He told Pilate, "The one who delivered Me to you has the greater sin"? We cannot be sure who Jesus had in mind here. Was it Caiaphas? Annas? Judas? All of these had a role in Jesus' deliverance to Pilate.

I don't want us to miss the underlying assumption in this statement from Jesus—there are degrees of wickedness. Not all sin is equally heinous, and in this case there was a greater and a lesser sin. The Jews' betrayal of the precious blood of their Messiah into the hands of the Gentiles was a gross and heinous crime. The lack of justice displayed by Pontius Pilate was also a sin, but to a lesser degree than the betrayal of Jesus by own people. Jesus did not declare Pilate guiltless, but He did say Pilate's sin was not as heinous as that of those who had delivered Him to Pilate.

No Friend of Caesar?

Something changed at that moment, and Pilate decided he wanted to set Jesus free. John writes: **From then on Pilate sought to release Him, but the Jews cried out, saying, "If you let this Man go, you are not Caesar's friend. Whoever makes himself a king speaks against Caesar"** (v. 12). Presumably Pilate mentioned his intention to the crowd, but they still howled for Jesus' blood, and they charged that failure to condemn Jesus would show that Pilate was no friend of Caesar. They didn't just say that Pilate would be a poor servant of the emperor by letting Jesus go. There was more to these words than that.

By AD 75, "friend of Caesar" was a formal title well established in Roman politics and protocol. To be a friend of Caesar was to be accorded a certain status in the empire. We do not know at what point it became an official title, though it may have been as early as the trial of Jesus. The Jews may have been telling Pilate that he would lose or would never gain this status if he did not bow to their wishes. Given his already shaky political standing, the Jews probably could undermine Pilate by promoting public disorder.

There is another possibility. We know from Philo and Josephus that Pilate was tutored by a certain Sejanus, who was very high in the elite inner circle of the Emperor Tiberius in Rome. Sejanus was a true friend of Caesar. It was by Sejanus' recommendation that Pilate was given the position of governor of Judea. We also know that in AD 31, Sejanus got in trouble with Tiberius, and the emperor had Sejanus and his most intimate cohorts executed in Rome. We do not know exactly when Jesus was condemned; many think it was in AD 30, but some place it as late as AD 33. Let's imagine that this conversation between Pilate and the Jews took place after AD 31, after the execution of Sejanus, the friend of Caesar. It may be that the Jewish officials were saying: "Remember your friend Sejanus, Pilate. If you don't do what we want you to do, you will be next."

Events moved quickly from that point. John tells us: **When Pilate therefore heard that saying, he brought Jesus out and sat down in the judgment seat in a place that is called The Pavement, but in Hebrew, Gabbatha. Now it was the Preparation Day of the Passover, and about the sixth hour. And he said to the Jews, "Behold your King!" But they cried out, "Away with Him, away with Him! Crucify Him!" Pilate said to them, "Shall I crucify your King?" The chief priests answered, "We have no king but Caesar!" Then he delivered Him to them to be crucified. Then they took Jesus and led Him away** (vv. 13–16).

This was the ultimate betrayal of the kingdom of God by the ruling class of the Jews. Pilate presented Jesus to the Jews as their King. When they demanded His death once again, Pilate said, "Shall I crucify *your King?*" He was asking, "Do you want to take the chance of executing this Man who claims to be your King?" They cried, "We have no king but Caesar." How could they forget that their nation had been established as a theocracy? God was their King, but they denied Him. As a result, Pilate turned Jesus over to be crucified.

Depending on which generation you belong to, you remember where you were when you heard of the assassination of President Kennedy or of the terrorist attacks on Sept. 11, 2001. But memories of President Kennedy have faded over the decades, and the number of flags that adorn our homes and cars has diminished since the first week after 9/11. But even today, two thousand years later, we remember the trial of our Lord and the unjust Roman governor who condemned Him. Christ "suffered under Pontius Pilate," but because He suffered in submission to the command of His Father, we can celebrate Good Friday until He comes again.

52

THE CRUCIFIXION
OF CHRIST

John 19:17–37

And He, bearing His cross, went out to a place called the Place of a Skull, which is called in Hebrew, Golgotha, where they crucified Him, and two others with Him, one on either side, and Jesus in the center. Now Pilate wrote a title and put it on the cross. And the writing was: JESUS OF NAZARETH, THE KING OF THE JEWS. Then many of the Jews read this title, for the place where Jesus was crucified was near the city; and it was written in Hebrew, Greek, and Latin. Therefore the chief priests of the Jews said to Pilate, "Do not write, 'The King of the Jews,' but, 'He said, "I am the King of the Jews."'" Pilate answered, "What I have written, I have written." Then the soldiers, when they had crucified Jesus, took His garments and made four parts, to each soldier a part, and also the tunic. Now the tunic was without seam, woven from the top in one piece. They said therefore among themselves, "Let us not tear it, but cast lots for it, whose it shall be," that the Scripture might be fulfilled which says: "They divided My garments among them, and for My clothing they cast lots." Therefore the soldiers did these things. Now there stood by the cross of Jesus His mother, and His mother's sister, Mary the wife of Clopas, and

Mary Magdalene. When Jesus therefore saw His mother, and the disciple whom He loved standing by, He said to His mother, "Woman, behold your son!" Then He said to the disciple, "Behold your mother!" And from that hour that disciple took her to his own home. After this, Jesus, knowing that all things were now accomplished, that the Scripture might be fulfilled, said, "I thirst!" Now a vessel full of sour wine was sitting there; and they filled a sponge with sour wine, put it on hyssop, and put it to His mouth. So when Jesus had received the sour wine, He said, "It is finished!" And bowing His head, He gave up His spirit. Therefore, because it was the Preparation Day, that the bodies should not remain on the cross on the Sabbath (for that Sabbath was a high day), the Jews asked Pilate that their legs might be broken, and that they might be taken away. Then the soldiers came and broke the legs of the first and of the other who was crucified with Him. But when they came to Jesus and saw that He was already dead, they did not break His legs. But one of the soldiers pierced His side with a spear, and immediately blood and water came out. And he who has seen has testified, and his testimony is true; and he knows that he is telling the truth, so that you may believe. For these things were done that the Scripture should be fulfilled, "Not one of His bones shall be broken." And again another Scripture says, "They shall look on Him whom they pierced."

We have come, in our study of John's Gospel, to the apostle's record of the crucifixion of Jesus. The twenty-one verses we will cover in this chapter give us a very sparse account of this pivotal event in redemptive history. The other Gospel writers provide some additional details, but none of them gives us a comprehensive portrait of all that transpired on that Friday afternoon. We know, for example, that Jesus uttered seven so-called words or statements from the cross, but John includes only three. Thus, we are dealing, as it were, with just one person's eyewitness report in the limited account the Bible provides. Nevertheless, I will confine myself to John's Gospel, though I encourage you to spend time reading and studying the other Gospel accounts for your edification and understanding.

The Facts about Crucifixion
John begins by saying, **And He, bearing His cross, went out to a place called the Place of a Skull, which is called in Hebrew, Golgotha, where they crucified Him, and two others with Him, one on either**

side, and Jesus in the center (vv. 17–18). When John says that Christ bore His cross, we might visualize, as some artists have in the past, Jesus struggling down the road bearing the complete cross on His shoulders. That's not the way it happened. It was customary for the Romans, when executing prisoners, to prepare the vertical beam of the cross at the crucifixion site before the actual execution. The prisoner was then given the crosspiece, the horizontal beam, and required to hoist it on his shoulders and carry it to the place of execution. So before Jesus made His way from the Praetorium to the Place of a Skull, or Golgotha, outside the gates of Jerusalem, the vertical piece had already been planted in the ground, and Jesus was forced to carry the crossbeam.

On many occasions, prisoners were not able to accomplish the task, depending on the severity of the scourgings they had received immediately before going out to the execution site. We know from the other Gospels that Jesus was not able to carry His crossbeam the entire way, and that a passerby, Simon of Cyrene, was commanded by the soldiers to pick up the crossbeam for Jesus and take it to the hill of execution (Matt. 27:32; Mark 15:21; Luke 23:26).

Once at the execution site, the prisoner was placed flat on the ground and his arms were either nailed or tied to the crossbeam. In the case of Jesus, nails were used. We don't know whether He was pierced through the hands or through the wrists; that remains a questionable point in the historical record.

Then the prisoner was hoisted up and the crossbeam was attached to the vertical beam, usually by nails. A tiny platform was affixed toward the bottom of the vertical beam as a place for the feet of the prisoner to be secured, and then the feet were nailed or tied to the vertical beam. That small platform was provided so that the prisoner could push his body up, raising his diaphragm so that he could breathe during the agony of crucifixion. At first glance, that may seem to be a drop of mercy for the condemned prisoner. On the contrary, it was done to extend the torture, because prisoners dying by this method involuntarily gasped for breath, and if they could not draw air, they would die much more quickly, usually by asphyxiation. By allowing the prisoner to push himself up, an almost involuntary action, the executioners prolonged the agony.

John tells us that two criminals were crucified with Jesus, one on either side. Matthew and Mark tell us these men were robbers, but Luke tells us that one of the men repented on the cross and Jesus promised him, "Today you will be with Me in Paradise" (Luke 23:43). Jesus' crucifixion alongside criminals happened in fulfillment of prophecy (Isa. 53:12).

John goes on: **Now Pilate wrote a title and put it on the cross. And**

the writing was: JESUS OF NAZARETH, THE KING OF THE JEWS. Then many of the Jews read this title, for the place where Jesus was crucified was near the city; and it was written in Hebrew, Greek, and Latin. Therefore the chief priests of the Jews said to Pilate, "Do not write, 'The King of the Jews,' but, 'He said, "I am the King of the Jews.""'" Pilate answered, "What I have written, I have written" (vv. 19–22).

It was customary for a placard to be tacked to a condemned man's cross stating the reason for his execution. Pilate himself wrote the placard for Jesus' cross, and he wrote the message of the placard in three languages: Hebrew, which was the language of the Jews; Koine Greek, the common language of the day due to the conquests of Alexander the Great and his process of Hellenization; and Latin, which was the language of the soldiers, the Romans. But Pilate's placard did not state a common charge; it simply said, "Jesus of Nazareth, the King of the Jews," as if Jesus' kingship was an established fact. That greatly upset the Jewish authorities, who did not believe that He was the King of the Jews. They protested to Pilate and asked him to change the placard to say that "King of the Jews" was only Jesus' claim about Himself, implying that it had no basis in fact. But Pilate by this time had had enough of the Jewish authorities, so he simply dismissed their protest with the imperious words, "What I have written, I have written."

A Series of Indignities

John's account of these horrifying events continues: **Then the soldiers, when they had crucified Jesus, took His garments and made four parts, to each soldier a part, and also the tunic. Now the tunic was without seam, woven from the top in one piece. They said therefore among themselves, "Let us not tear it, but cast lots for it, whose it shall be," that the Scripture might be fulfilled which says: "They divided My garments among them, and for My clothing they cast lots." Therefore the soldiers did these things** (vv. 23–24).

This passage is full of indignities. Notice first of all that the soldiers divided Jesus' clothes among themselves. They were able to do this because Jesus had been stripped. Prisoners were crucified naked. This practice stemmed from the ancient notion that the worst form of humiliation that could be imposed on an enemy was to strip him of his clothing. Frequently, when the Romans were victorious in battle, they paraded the officers of the conquered army through the streets bare naked to reduce them to total shame. If you can bear it, in all probability the Son of God was made a public spectacle in the shame of nakedness, following the ancient custom.

A prisoner who was executed normally had five articles of clothing. The tunic, which was a seamless garment, was the undergarment. The four soldiers divided Jesus' other articles of clothing among themselves, but the tunic presented a problem for them. Because the tunic had been made with no seam, it was significantly valuable, and they didn't want to lessen its value by cutting it into four pieces. Therefore, they decided to cast lots for it, winner take all.

This indignity also was prophesied (Ps. 22:18). John does not say that the Roman soldiers got together and said, "We should gamble for His garments because it says in the Jewish Scriptures that someone is going to cast lots for His clothes and we want to make sure that the Scriptures are fulfilled down to the last detail." No, this is John's editorial comment, pointing out that the soldiers, when they went through this act of gambling for the garments of Christ, unknowingly and involuntarily were fulfilling the precise details of the Old Testament prophesies concerning the death of the Messiah. John is zealous to help his reader understand that what happened on the cross was not an accident of history, but it came to pass through the invisible hand of a sovereign Providence.

John then tells us of some of the people who came to Golgotha to witness Jesus' crucifixion: **Now there stood by the cross of Jesus His mother, and His mother's sister, Mary the wife of Clopas, and Mary Magdalene** (v. 25). We do not know from this sentence exactly how many people John is talking about. Specifically, we do not know whether Jesus' mother's sister was Mary, the wife of Clopas, or whether Mary, the wife of Clopas, was an unrelated friend. Even the structure of the Greek is uncertain. In any case, there were three or four women standing at the cross watching the execution, including Jesus' own mother. This was that which Simeon had prophesied so many years earlier on the day the baby Jesus was presented in the temple. Simeon had said, "Yes, a sword will pierce through you own soul also" (Luke 2:35a). As Jesus suffered, Mary was enduring her own agony.

Jesus' Tender Concern for His Mother

John then relates one of the seven sayings of Jesus from the cross: **When Jesus therefore saw His mother, and the disciple whom He loved standing by, He said to His mother, "Woman, behold your son!"**

Then He said to the disciple, "Behold your mother!" And from that hour that disciple took her to his own home (vv. 26–27). We learn here that John himself, "the disciple whom He loved," was there at the cross. Seeing His mother and His beloved disciple there, Jesus said to Mary, "Woman, behold your son!" He then said to John, "Behold your mother!" Jesus did not say to His mother, "Mother, look at Me"; rather, He said to her, "I want you to consider John as your son now." To John He said, "I want you to care for My mother." Presumably Mary's husband, Joseph, had died and Jesus' brothers were not present in Jerusalem at this time, so He commended His mother to the care of John, and John tells us that he faithfully carried out that commission.

There is something in the original Greek here that I find very special, very touching. Jesus addressed His mother as "Woman," and that sounds somewhat impersonal and disrespectful to our ears. But the word Jesus used in the Greek is *gune*, from which we get our word *gynecology*. This was the universal term for "woman," but it also was used frequently as an honorific, a title of endearment. When Jesus addressed His mother as "Woman," He was using a term of tenderness. He used this same term when He spoke to His mother at the wedding feast in Cana (2:4), and He also used it to address the woman caught in adultery (8:10); in the midst of her shame and embarrassment, He spoke to her with tenderness. This is a side of our Savior we need to see—He was tender and respectful toward His mother and other women.

John then writes: **After this, Jesus, knowing that all things were now accomplished, that the Scripture might be fulfilled, said, "I thirst!" Now a vessel full of sour wine was sitting there; and they filled a sponge with sour wine, put it on hyssop, and put it to His mouth** (vv. 28–29). John writes, under the Spirit's inspiration, that Jesus knew at this point that "all things were now accomplished." Most commentators believe this statement means that Jesus' substitutionary bearing of God's wrath against sin, which was accompanied by darkness and caused Jesus to cry out, "My God, My God, why have You forsaken Me?" (Matt. 27:46), was now behind Him.

At this point, Jesus had been on the cross for hours in the middle of the hot Judean day, going through physical agony and spiritual torment. Not surprisingly, Jesus expressed the fact that He was thirsty. This, too, fulfilled prophecy (Ps. 22:15). A vessel of sour wine was there, probably for the soldiers' use. The soldiers therefore filled a sponge with the wine, put it on a hyssop stick, and put it to Jesus' mouth to assuage His thirst.

A Work Finished, a Debt Paid in Full

Then came the death of the Son of God: **So when Jesus had received the sour wine, He said, "It is finished!" And bowing His head, He gave up His spirit** (v. 30). When Jesus received the sour wine, His thirst had been assuaged, and He said, "It is finished." The Greek word translated as "finished" here is *tetelestai*. It is in a form of the Greek that indicates an action that has been totally completed. It comes from the verb form of the Greek word *telos*, which is a very important word in the history of Greek thought. It is the word that means "end" or "goal."

When I read this word, I think of an experience I had as a senior in college. That year, I took a course called "bonehead biology," Biology 101. This course was normally taken in one's freshman year, but I hadn't been able to take it my first year because I had a conflict with another course. So I was a senior in a class full of freshmen. Our biology teacher was a dear woman. On the first day of class, she made this comment: "We're going to study biology together, and since this is a scientific enterprise, we won't be concerned with teleological matters. Rather, we're going to confine our study to descriptive matters, trying to learn how it is that things operate in the biological realm, and not ask questions about purpose." I was a senior philosophy major, and I almost jumped out of my chair. I couldn't believe what she had said. I went up to her after class and said: "Mrs. Fine, how can we rule teleology out of scientific inquiry? How can we study anything and not be interested in its purpose or its significance?" She said, "We leave that to the philosophers." I still haven't gotten over that stance she took.

Jesus was concerned about purpose. The significance of His entire life came down to this moment. When He said, "It is finished," He was saying not just that His life was over but that His mission had been fulfilled. His purpose in coming to earth and going to the cross was accomplished.

Tetelestai was also sometimes used in the commercial arena in the Greek world. It was stamped on a purchase or written on a receipt, because it meant "paid in full." Jesus said: "I've done it all. I've drunk the cup to its dregs. The sin debt of My people has been paid in full."

With nothing left to do, Jesus "gave up His spirit." He had said, "I lay down My life that I may take it again" (10:17b). When His mission was accomplished, when the atonement was complete, Jesus made the decision to die.

More Prophecies Fulfilled

What happened in the aftermath of Jesus' death? John tells us: **Therefore, because it was the Preparation Day, that the bodies should not**

remain on the cross on the Sabbath (for that Sabbath was a high day), the Jews asked Pilate that their legs might be broken, and that they might be taken away. Then the soldiers came and broke the legs of the first and of the other who was crucified with Him. But when they came to Jesus and saw that He was already dead, they did not break His legs. But one of the soldiers pierced His side with a spear, and immediately blood and water came out (vv. 31–34). The Jews were concerned because it was a preparation day for the Sabbath, and the next day was a high Sabbath. If the bodies of the condemned men hung on their crosses overnight, the land would be defiled (Deut. 21:23), and that would have major repercussions for the Sabbath observances. So the Jews asked Pilate to order the soldiers to break the men's legs. With their legs broken, the crucified men would not be able to elevate their chests and gain any breath, so they would die quickly from asphyxiation. The Jews were not concerned with putting Jesus out of His misery; they were concerned about the purity of their feast. They had just killed the One for whom the feasts were established in the first place, but they did not want to be guilty of violating the Old Testament law against bodies hanging on crosses overnight on the preparation day.

Pilate granted the Jews' request in this instance, so the soldiers broke the legs of one of the robbers, then broke the legs of the other. But when they came to Jesus, they found He was already dead, having died much sooner than was normal in a crucifixion. Thus, they did not break His legs, but one of the soldiers jammed his spear into Jesus' side, perhaps to ensure that He was dead, and blood and water poured out. Some Bible commentators see symbolic significance in the blood and water, but I think they read too much into the text. John finds much more significance in the fact that both of these incidents fulfilled Old Testament prophecies: **For these things were done that the Scripture should be fulfilled, "Not one of His bones shall be broken." And again another Scripture says, "They shall look on Him whom they pierced"** (vv. 36–37). These prophecies are found in Psalm 34:20 and Zechariah 12:10, respectively.

In the midst of these historical notes, John inserts a personal comment: **And he who has seen has testified, and his testimony is true; and he knows that he is telling the truth, so that you may believe** (v. 35). Why does John choose to make this comment? This statement is a form of an oath. It's as if John considers himself to be on trial. He takes a sacred vow before God as to the accuracy of what he is reporting. He wants his readers' trust for one reason—that they might believe. You see, faith is not supposed to be based on a leap into the dark through a mindless act of credulity; instead, faith should be an acquiescence to the truth. That which is not true is never worthy of our trust or our belief. John pleads with us here, declaring by a vow that his testimony is sober, unvarnished truth. He says that we can build our lives on it. I urge you, if you do not already believe, to accept the truth of the sacrifice of the Lamb of God.

53

THE BURIAL OF JESUS

John 19:38–42

᠕᠕᠕᠕

After this, Joseph of Arimathea, being a disciple of Jesus, but secretly, for fear of the Jews, asked Pilate that he might take away the body of Jesus; and Pilate gave him permission. So he came and took the body of Jesus. And Nicodemus, who at first came to Jesus by night, also came, bringing a mixture of myrrh and aloes, about a hundred pounds. Then they took the body of Jesus, and bound it in strips of linen with the spices, as the custom of the Jews is to bury. Now in the place where He was crucified there was a garden, and in the garden a new tomb in which no one had yet been laid. So there they laid Jesus, because of the Jews' Preparation Day, for the tomb was nearby.

When we recite the Apostles' Creed, we affirm, among other things, that Jesus "suffered under Pontius Pilate, was crucified, dead, and buried." It is easy to grasp the significance of the Lord's crucifixion and His death, but why was such a seemingly minor incident as His burial enshrined as an article of faith in the Apostles' Creed?

One reason is that the burial of Jesus marked an important turning point in Jesus' mission. We normally understand the life of Jesus as a progression from humiliation to exaltation. The nadir of His humiliation was His crucifixion on the cross, but that was soon followed by exaltation in His resurrection and His ascension to the right hand of God. We can easily see the strong contrast between humiliation and exaltation, but we often overlook the fact that the transition from humiliation to exaltation did not begin at His resurrection but rather at His burial.

As we begin to consider Jesus' burial, it is helpful to review a crucial passage in the Old Testament:

> He was oppressed and He was afflicted,
> Yet He opened not His mouth;
> He was led as a lamb to the slaughter,
> And as a sheep before its shearers is silent,
> So He opened not His mouth.
> He was taken from prison and from judgment,
> And who will declare His generation?
> For He was cut off from the land of the living;
> For the transgressions of My people He was stricken.
> And they made His grave with the wicked—
> But with the rich at His death,
> Because He had done no violence,
> Nor was any deceit in His mouth. (Isa. 53:7–9)

This is a portion of Isaiah's prophecy concerning the Suffering Servant of Israel. Did you catch the subtle change of tone here? Everything is negative, calling attention to humiliation, until Isaiah mentions a seemingly minor detail—that the Servant made His bed with the rich in His death because He had done no evil thing. This is a picture of the circumstances that surrounded the life and death of Jesus, and just as the prophecy indicated, there was a remarkable change in Jesus' circumstances between His death and His burial.

Jesus Spared from Indignities

The circumstances of Jesus' burial were very different from that of most prisoners executed by the Romans. When a Jew was executed, his family had the right to request the body. Their relative could not be buried inside the city of Jerusalem lest the sacred places be defiled, but the family could see that he received a proper burial elsewhere. Unclaimed bodies were thrown unceremoniously on the garbage dump outside Jerusalem, where the trash from the city was burned night and day. That burning dump was called Gehenna, and it became the chief metaphor for hell, where the flames of divine wrath never go out. However, when someone was executed for sedition, his body was usually left on the cross, often for days, until the vultures finished it off. Since Jesus was crucified for sedition, His body might have met this fate, but He was spared this indignity.

John writes: **After this, Joseph of Arimathea, being a disciple of Jesus, but secretly, for fear of the Jews, asked Pilate that he might take away the body of Jesus; and Pilate gave him permission. So he came and took the body of Jesus** (v. 38). Joseph of Arimathea was a man of significant status and wealth, and probably a member of the Sanhedrin. He was a believer in Christ, but he was not vocal about it. John has already told us that "even among the rulers many believed in Him, but because of the Pharisees they did not confess Him, lest they should be put out of the synagogue" (12:42). Joseph apparently was in this group. However, his faith compelled him to do something to spare Jesus' body from more indignities. So he went to Pilate, even though he was not a relative of Jesus, and requested the authority to take care of the body of Christ in an appropriate manner. Pilate, perhaps to infuriate the Jews all the more, or perhaps out of a sense of guilt, gave his approval for Joseph to dispose of the body of Jesus.

John then notes, **And Nicodemus, who at first came to Jesus by night, also came, bringing a mixture of myrrh and aloes, about a hundred pounds** (v. 39). Nicodemus, the Sanhedrin member who came to Jesus by night early in His ministry (John 3), came with Joseph to help prepare Jesus' body for burial. It seems Nicodemus also was among those rulers of the Jews who were secret followers of Jesus, but he, like Joseph, was willing to take a stand for the burial of Jesus.

What was the purpose of the fragrances Nicodemus brought? The Jewish people did not embalm their dead as the Egyptians did, but they did wrap them in a shroud of linen, and they covered the linen with precious ointments and fragrances in the burial process for the simple purpose of disguising the stench of decomposing flesh. With the extraordinary amount of myrrh and aloes Nicodemus had brought, Jesus' body was prepared for burial: **Then they took the body of Jesus, and bound it in strips of linen with the spices, as the custom of the Jews is to bury** (v. 40).

John continues: **Now in the place where He was crucified there was a garden, and in the garden a new tomb in which no one had yet been laid. So there they laid Jesus, because of the Jews' Preparation Day, for the tomb was nearby** (vv. 41–42). There was a need for haste—Jesus' body had to be buried quickly because the high Sabbath was at hand. Providentially, there was a new and unused tomb in a garden quite near to Golgotha. The other Gospels tell us that this tomb was owned by Joseph of Arimathea himself. So Jesus was laid in a brand-new tomb owned by this wealthy man, a tomb probably prepared for Joseph's own burial. It is highly unlikely that Jesus' family could have provided such a burial. Thus, we see the beginning of the transition from Jesus' humiliation to His exaltation.

Where Did Jesus Go?

There is great debate as to what happened to Jesus between His death and His resurrection. Where was He? We know where His body was—lying in Joseph's tomb. But where was His soul? There are many in the history of the church who believe that in the interim between His death and resurrection, Jesus visited hell. In fact, the Apostles' Creed states that Jesus "suffered under Pontius Pilate, was crucified, dead, and buried: *he descended into hell*; the third day he arose again from the dead" (emphasis added). However, it is important to note that this phrase does not appear in the earliest versions that we have of the Apostles' Creed. It did not appear until the middle of the third century, so the phrase itself is textually questionable, not to mention theologically suspect.

Why would Jesus have gone to hell during the time He lay in the grave? One theory is that in order to pay fully for our sins, He had to experience some time in hell. Thus, the belief is that He went to hell as part of His atoning work of satisfaction for His people.

Others, such as the Roman Catholic Church, believe Jesus went to hell to release captives who had been held in limbo from Old Testament days. He went there not to punish or to be punished, but to continue His work of redemption, to set the captives in hell free from their condition. The text that is most frequently cited to support this theory is 1 Peter 3:18–20: "For Christ also suffered once for sins, the just for the unjust, that He might bring us to God, being put to death in the flesh but made alive by the Spirit, by whom also He went and preached to the spirits in prison, who formerly were disobedient, when once the Divine longsuffering waited in the days of Noah, while the ark was being prepared, in which a few, that is, eight souls, were saved through water." Peter refers to a mission of Jesus to the spirits in prison. Many commentators understand the spirits in prison to be Old Testament saints who were still being held, waiting for the day of rescue. The prison mentioned here is assumed to be hell.

John Calvin had a different view. He believed that Jesus *did* descend into hell and thought that Christians should recite this article in the Apostles' Creed, but he believed the creed's wording should be changed to say, ". . . suffered under Pontius Pilate, crucified, descended into hell, dead, and buried." It was Calvin's view that Jesus' experience of hell took place while He was on the cross. That's what the atonement was all about—He received the full measure of punishment for sin, enduring the wrath of God as it is experienced by those in hell.

The question of where Jesus went during His time in the grave raises the issue of the relationship of the divine nature and the human nature in Christ. On the cross, the divine nature did not die, because the divine nature is immutable. If God had been dead for three days, that would have been the end of all things. If God dies for two seconds, everything else goes. In short, God did not stop being God on the cross. Jesus suffered and died in His human nature.

But what was the relationship between Christ's divine and human natures in that three days? His divine nature had been perfectly united with a human nature in a healthy body. After the crucifixion, the divine nature was perfectly united with a human corpse. The union of the two natures still existed, but the living soul of Christ was absent from the body. Where was it? It was in heaven. How do we know that? We know it because Jesus said to the thief on the cross who made a profession of faith, "Assuredly, I say to you, today you will be with Me in Paradise" (Luke 23:43). It is theoretically possible that Jesus died, made a quick trip to hell, and went to heaven that same day, but that scenario requires us to really torture the text.

Even that statement by Jesus isn't accepted by everyone. Some point out that there is no punctuation in the original Greek, so Jesus may have said, "I say to you today, you will be with Me in Paradise." In other words, the "today" may have been referring not to when Jesus was going to be with the man in paradise, but to the moment when Jesus was making this promise. We could put it like this: "I'm telling you today that sometime in the distant future, you and I are going to be together in paradise." However, I cannot believe that the Son of God, gasping for breath in His dying moments, would have added unnecessary verbiage in His words to the robber. I think it is clear what Jesus said. He made a promise to this man: "This very day, you will be with Me," and it wasn't going to be in hell but in paradise.

We also know that at the end of His experience on the cross, He said, "Father, 'into Your hands I commit My spirit'" (Luke 23:46). So we have every reason to believe that at the moment Jesus died, the divine nature remained united to His soul, which was in heaven, and to his body, which was in the tomb, waiting to be reunited at the moment of resurrection.

Preaching in Resurrection Power

What, then, are we to do with the text in 1 Peter? In the final analysis, I don't know. If we consulted ten commentaries on this portion of 1 Peter, chances are we would get ten different opinions about it. We will look at it closely, and I will tell you what I believe it means, but I cannot state definitively what Peter had in mind.

Peter writes that Jesus was "put to death in the flesh but made alive by the Spirit, by whom also He went and preached to the spirits in prison" (3:18b–19). If we apply basic principle of biblical interpretation, seeing how phrases are used elsewhere in the New Testament, we find that the phrase "made alive by the Spirit" almost certainly refers to His resurrection. So Jesus died bodily and then was made alive again by the Spirit. Also, He went and preached to the spirits in prison by the Spirit.

Notice that Peter speaks of Jesus preaching to the spirits in prison *after* he apparently speaks about the resurrection. There is an order here—death, resurrection, then this visit to the spirits in prison. If we follow this sequence, we must say that Jesus' visit to the spirits in prison took place not between His death and resurrection, but after the resurrection. On the other hand, the fact that these events are mentioned in a particular order does not necessitate a temporal sequence. We have to be careful that we don't read a temporal sequence into this passage, because Peter doesn't say, "*After* He was raised by the Spirit, *then* He went and preached to the spirits in prison." He simply says that it was by the same Spirit who raised Jesus from the dead that He ministered to the spirits in prison.

The assumptions that many bring to this text are that the word *spirits* refers to dead people and that *prison* refers to hell. That may be what Peter has in mind here. On the other hand, the term *spirit* is used in biblical language many times for living people. Genesis 2:7 says that God "formed man of the dust of the ground, and breathed into his nostrils the breath of life; and man became a living soul" (KJV). We use the same speech patterns in our own vocabulary. If you were to ask me, "How many people were in church last Thursday night?" I might say, "There wasn't a soul there." I wouldn't be saying that there were no ghosts there; I would mean that there weren't any people there. So the fact that Peter refers to spirits does not necessarily mean he was thinking of departed spirits.

What about the prison? It is possible Peter was referring to hell. On the other hand, the condition in which Israel found herself during the period of Jesus' incarnation was one of bondage to sin. It was the mission of the Messiah to "proclaim liberty to the captives, and the opening of the prison to those who are bound" (Isa. 61:1b). So Peter may be reminding us that the same power by which Jesus was raised from the dead accompanied His earthly ministry of releasing the captives from the prison house of sin.

As I said, I am not certain as to what Peter is saying. But I am confident about what John is telling us in His Gospel. He wants us to see that God was not willing to allow the humiliation of His Son to continue one second longer than was necessary for Him to pay our debt. His body was treated tenderly and given an honorable burial in a rich man's tomb that had never been used before. This was like getting a burial with full military honors at Arlington National Cemetery rather than being thrown into the garbage heap or being left to the vultures.

Our Lord was exalted in the manner of His burial, but that was simply a hint of what was to come—the resurrection. The Scriptures say "it was impossible for death to keep its hold on him" (Acts 2:24b NIV). So as honoring as the linen and the precious spices and ointments were to Jesus, they were absolutely unnecessary, a waste of good linen and good fragrance.

54

THE RESURRECTION

John 20:1–18

Now the first day of the week Mary Magdalene went to the tomb early, while it was still dark, and saw that the stone had been taken away from the tomb. Then she ran and came to Simon Peter, and to the other disciple, whom Jesus loved, and said to them, "They have taken away the Lord out of the tomb, and we do not know where they have laid Him." Peter therefore went out, and the other disciple, and were going to the tomb. So they both ran together, and the other disciple outran Peter and came to the tomb first. And he, stooping down and looking in, saw the linen cloths lying there; yet he did not go in. Then Simon Peter came, following him, and went into the tomb; and he saw the linen cloths lying there, and the handkerchief that had been around His head, not lying with the linen cloths, but folded together in a place by itself. Then the other disciple, who came to the tomb first, went in also; and he saw and believed. For as yet they did not know the Scripture, that He must rise again from the dead. Then the disciples went away again to their own homes. But Mary stood outside by the tomb weeping, and as she wept she stooped down and looked into the tomb. And she saw two angels in white sitting, one at the head and the other at the feet, where the body of Jesus had lain. Then they said to her, "Woman, why are you weeping?" She said to them,

"Because they have taken away my Lord, and I do not know where they have laid Him." Now when she had said this, she turned around and saw Jesus standing there, and did not know that it was Jesus. Jesus said to her, "Woman, why are you weeping? Whom are you seeking?" She, supposing Him to be the gardener, said to Him, "Sir, if You have carried Him away, tell me where You have laid Him, and I will take Him away." Jesus said to her, "Mary!" She turned and said to Him, "Rabboni!" (which is to say, Teacher). Jesus said to her, "Do not cling to Me, for I have not yet ascended to My Father; but go to My brethren and say to them, 'I am ascending to My Father and your Father, and to My God and your God.'" Mary Magdalene came and told the disciples that she had seen the Lord, and that He had spoken these things to her.

The passage before us in this chapter is one of my favorite texts in sacred Scripture. It is a text that is filled not only with wonder and delight, but with a certain poignancy. It is sad that we usually look at this text, and the parallel texts in the other Gospels, only on Easter Sunday. For the Christian, every Lord's Day is to be a celebration of the resurrection of Christ, so this text should be one we come back to again and again.

John writes: **Now the first day of the week Mary Magdalene went to the tomb early, while it was still dark, and saw that the stone had been taken away from the tomb** (v. 1). John, in agreement with the writers of the other Gospels, tells us that these events occurred on the first day of the week, Sunday. We know from the book of Acts that because the resurrection of Christ took place on the first day of the week, the Christian community began the practice of gathering on that day each week for apostolic teaching, prayer, and the breaking of bread. So it has continued throughout the Christian era—the Sabbath has been celebrated by the vast majority of Christians on the first day of the week rather than the seventh. Nevertheless, that choice remains a point of dispute among some Christians to this day.

An Empty Tomb

The Synoptic Gospels speak of multiple women going to the tomb for the purpose of giving attention to the body of Jesus with fragrant spices. John, however, mentions only Mary Magdalene. But it is customary in Scripture to identify a group simply by reference to one member of the group, particularly the one who is in the position of leadership. Since this chapter in John's Gospel focuses attention on the intimate encounter between Mary

Magdalene and Jesus, it is not strange that he should mention only Mary Magdalene. Notice, too, that when Mary reported the empty tomb to the disciples, she said, "*We* do not know where they have laid Him" (v. 2). So it appears she was not alone when she went to the tomb.

John tells us that when Mary Magdalene came to the tomb, she found the stone that had been placed over the entrance rolled away. Initially, this may have seemed to be good news. The women were coming in grief to express their devotion to Jesus with more spices and fragrances, but they didn't know whether they would be able to gain access to Jesus' body: "They said among themselves, 'Who will roll away the stone from the door of the tomb for us?'" (Mark 16:3). None of the Gospel writers tells us what reaction the sight of the open tomb provoked in the women, but their emotions may have ranged from surprise to fear to relief that the tomb was open. We know from the other Gospels (though John does not mention it) that the women looked into the tomb, and because Mary did not see Jesus' body, she was filled with grief. Therefore, John writes, **she ran and came to Simon Peter, and to the other disciple, whom Jesus loved, and said to them, "They have taken away the Lord out of the tomb, and we do not know where they have laid Him"** (v. 2).

It's not hard to understand why Mary Magdalene reacted this way. The faith of the Christian church in the resurrection of Christ does not rest on an inference drawn from an empty tomb, because an empty tomb could have indicated many things, and the option that would have been last on the list would have been a resurrection. Just as today, when people died, they almost always stayed dead. But grave robbery was common, and robbers especially liked to invade the tombs of the wealthy in the hope of finding valuables. Sometimes the bodies themselves were stolen for more ghoulish enterprises. Mary may well have feared something like this had happened to Jesus' body.

When Peter and John heard Mary's story, they went to investigate. John writes: **Peter therefore went out, and the other disciple, and were going to the tomb. So they both ran together, and the other disciple outran Peter and came to the tomb first. And he, stooping down and looking in, saw the linen cloths lying there; yet he did not go in. Then Simon Peter came, following him, and went into the tomb; and he saw the linen cloths lying there, and the handkerchief that had been around His head, not lying with the linen cloths, but folded together in a place by itself** (vv. 3–7). The disciples discovered something strange—Jesus' body was gone, but His graveclothes were still there, and they did not appear to have been disturbed. If someone had stolen the body, it is unlikely the linen strips would have been left as they were wrapped around Jesus' body.

This reference to the graveclothes that had not been unraveled raises questions about the nature of the glorified body of Christ. I've had to grade term papers by young theologians who speculated beyond measure about the nature of Jesus' resurrected body, and they appealed primarily to texts like this one and a couple of others. One of these is in Luke 24, where we find the story of the two disciples walking to Emmaus. Jesus fell in step with them, but their eyes were prevented from recognizing Him. In the course of the conversation, the disciples confessed their grief over the crucifixion and their confusion over the reports that Jesus was alive. Jesus then began to teach them about Himself from the Old Testament Scriptures. When they reached Emmaus, they invited Him to eat with them. When He blessed and broke the bread, they recognized Him, but "He vanished from their sight" (Luke 24:31b).

Another oft-quoted text is found later in John 20. We are told there that the disciples were huddled in the upper room and that the door was shut (or locked, depending on how the Greek is translated) because of their fear of the Jews. Suddenly, Jesus appeared in their midst. Some who read this text draw the inference that Jesus was able to enter the room without opening the door.

When I receive papers that quote these texts to bolster speculative conclusions about Jesus' resurrected body, I caution my students that these texts don't prove that Jesus had an ability to vanish into thin air or to walk through doors. There are other ways to read these texts. When Luke says that Jesus vanished, he may mean that in the moment when the two disciples recognized Him and were startled and dumbfounded, Jesus quietly excused Himself. When John tells us of Jesus appearing in a room where the door was shut or locked, his purpose may have simply been to show how frightened the disciples were by the Jewish authorities. Jesus may have opened the door and slipped in.

I think I can explain those two incidents. However, I cannot explain how Jesus' graveclothes were not disturbed. I think this incident does give credence to the idea that the resurrected body of Christ was in another dimension of reality. It was still a physical body—Jesus could eat and be touched—but it appears it had properties it did not have before His death and resurrection.

This sparse information should restrain us from speculating about what our bodies will be like after the resurrection. We know that our spirits will be rejoined to our glorified bodies, for Paul writes: "So also is the resurrection of the dead. The body is sown in corruption, it is raised in incorruption. It is sown in dishonor, it is raised in glory. It is sown in weakness, it is raised in power.

It is sown a natural body, it is raised a spiritual body. There is a natural body, and there is a spiritual body" (1 Cor. 15:42–44). We cannot be sure exactly what those bodies will be like; as John tells us "it has not yet been revealed what we shall be" (1 John 3:2b). However, we know our resurrected bodies will be patterned after the resurrected body of Christ: "we know that when He is revealed, we shall be like Him, for we shall see Him as He is" (1 John 3:2c). We can be sure that the bodies we will have will be far better than we currently have. Beyond that, we cannot be sure.

John tells us: **Then the other disciple, who came to the tomb first, went in also; and he saw and believed. For as yet they did not know the Scripture, that He must rise again from the dead. Then the disciples went away again to their own homes** (vv. 8–10). John is almost certainly speaking of himself here. He writes that he reached the tomb first, but did not go in (vv. 4–5). After Peter went in (vv. 6–7), John followed. John testifies that when he saw the empty tomb and the graveclothes, he believed that Jesus was alive again. He also notes that he and the other disciples did not yet understand the scriptural teaching that the Messiah *had* to rise from the dead, but he had heard Jesus say that He would come back from the grave, and he now believed that it had happened.

A Moving Exchange

The portion of this narrative that I find most moving is the exchange between Jesus and Mary Magdalene. John begins his account this way: **But Mary stood outside by the tomb weeping, and as she wept she stooped down and looked into the tomb. And she saw two angels in white sitting, one at the head and the other at the feet, where the body of Jesus had lain. Then they said to her, "Woman, why are you weeping?" She said to them, "Because they have taken away my Lord, and I do not know where they have laid Him"** (vv. 11–13). After John and Peter went to their homes, Mary stood outside the tomb, weeping. There is speculation that she came back to the tomb with Peter and John after she told them that Jesus' body was missing. Now she was alone in the garden, still in a state of grief. As she wept, she stooped and looked into the tomb, and she saw two angels in white sitting where Jesus body had been. John again does not give us Mary's reaction to this new surprise. Instead, he tells us that the angels asked the reason for Mary's tears, implying that this was not an occasion for grief, and she explained that it was because she could not locate Jesus' body.

Then came the most unexpected encounter Mary could have imagined.

John tells us: **Now when she had said this, she turned around and saw Jesus standing there, and did not know that it was Jesus** (v. 14). As I mentioned above, when the two disciples traveling to Emmaus encountered Jesus, their eyes were prevented from recognizing Him (Luke 24:16). John gives no explanation for why Mary did not recognize Jesus. It may be that she was supernaturally prevented from recognizing Him. It may have been that her eyes were so full of tears that she didn't recognize the One who was standing outside the tomb. Or it may have been that she was expecting the gardener or some other person, but not Jesus.

John goes on: **Jesus said to her, "Woman, why are you weeping? Whom are you seeking?" She, supposing Him to be the gardener, said to Him, "Sir, if You have carried Him away, tell me where You have laid Him, and I will take Him away." Jesus said to her, "Mary!" She turned and said to Him, "Rabboni!" (which is to say, Teacher)** (vv. 15–16). I noted in an earlier chapter that the greeting Jesus used here, "Woman," was an honorific, a term of respect and tenderness. Jesus spoke tenderly to Mary in her grief and asked why she was weeping. John tells us that she surmised that He was the gardener, and hoping that He was the One responsible for the missing body, she asked Him to tell her where the body had been taken, saying she would take it elsewhere if necessary. At this point, Mary Magdalene was desperate. She wasn't seeing or thinking coherently. Her grief had gone to a whole new level.

But Jesus put an end to her grief, her confusion, her entire devastation with one simple word—her name. It seems that when Jesus said her name, "Mary!" that the scales fell from her eyes and she recognized Him. Something in His voice revealed Him to her. When Jesus spoke of Himself as the Good Shepherd, He said, "When he brings out his own sheep, he goes before them; and the sheep follow him, for they know his voice" (John 10:4). This was a typical characteristic of sheep in relation to their shepherd, and the same is true for Jesus' sheep. Because of her love for Jesus and her faith in Him, Mary knew His voice. She turned back to Him and cried, "Rabboni," a lengthened form of the word *rabbi*, which means "teacher."

Not long ago, I watched an episode of the old television drama *The Lone Ranger*. As always, the Lone Ranger wore his mask; his face was partly hidden. But as I watched and listened, something did not seem right. It was the usual actor, Clayton Moore, playing the Lone Ranger, as far as my eyes could tell, but his voice sounded different. When the credits rolled across the screen at the end, I saw that another actor, not Moore, had played the Lone Ranger in the episode. I wasn't surprised; I had seen enough *Lone Ranger* episodes to know Clayton Moore's voice, and all the masks in the world wouldn't have fooled me. I knew I was seeing another actor in that particular episode. The voice gave him away. Likewise, it was the voice of Jesus that revealed Him to Mary.

John writes: **Jesus said to her, "Do not cling to Me, for I have not yet ascended to My Father; but go to My brethren and say to them, 'I am ascending to My Father and your Father, and to My God and your God.'" Mary Magdalene came and told the disciples that she had seen the Lord, and that He had spoken these things to her** (vv. 17–18). We can only guess, but it appears that when Mary recognized Jesus, she fell on her face, grabbed Him about the ankles, and held on tenaciously. But the words of Jesus that followed, as He urged her not to cling to Him and then apparently gave a reason why she should not, constitute one of the most difficult texts in all of Scripture to unpack. You would not believe the speculation that has come out of this text, from the sublime to the ridiculous, and not only ridiculous, but blasphemous. Why did Jesus say these things, especially given that, a few hours later, He invited Thomas to touch His hands and side (20:27)?

Some have argued that Jesus' body was metamorphosing to its glorified state and that the process was still in transition. Therefore, He told her, "Don't touch Me, because it's not finished yet; I haven't ascended into heaven." But He hadn't ascended into heaven when He invited Thomas to touch him, so that theory does not seem correct. I could cite other speculative theories, but I think the answer is simple. She was hanging on to Him for dear life because she thought she had lost Him, but now she had Him back. So He said: "It's OK, I'm not leaving yet. We still have some more time. I'm going to come and be with the disciples. I'm going to be with you for forty days or so. You don't have to hold Me captive."

Jesus then gave Mary a task—to go to His disciples with the news that He was alive and soon to ascend to the Father's right hand. Matthew, relating a similar incident, writes that Jesus told a group of women to let the disciples know He was going to Galilee and they would see Him there (Matt. 28:9–10). In any case, Mary Magdalene was sent with the glorious news of the resurrection, and she went faithfully and did as Jesus commanded.

We, too, are sent as messengers of the incredible news that Jesus who died is alive again. He has overcome death and triumphed on behalf of His people. Will you hear the Savior's voice and take this glorious good news to a world that is lost and dead in sin?

55

DOUBTING THOMAS

John 20:19–31

Then, the same day at evening, being the first day of the week, when the doors were shut where the disciples were assembled, for fear of the Jews, Jesus came and stood in the midst, and said to them, "Peace be with you." When He had said this, He showed them His hands and His side. Then the disciples were glad when they saw the Lord. So Jesus said to them again, "Peace to you! As the Father has sent Me, I also send you." And when He had said this, He breathed on them, and said to them, "Receive the Holy Spirit. If you forgive the sins of any, they are forgiven them; if you retain the sins of any, they are retained." Now Thomas, called the Twin, one of the twelve, was not with them when Jesus came. The other disciples therefore said to him, "We have seen the Lord." So he said to them, "Unless I see in His hands the print of the nails, and put my finger into the print of the nails, and put my hand into His side, I will not believe." And after eight days His disciples were again inside, and Thomas with them. Jesus came, the doors being shut, and stood in the midst, and said, "Peace to you!" Then He said to Thomas, "Reach your finger here, and look at My hands; and reach your hand here, and put it into My side. Do not be unbelieving, but believing." And Thomas answered and said to Him, "My Lord and my God!" Jesus said to him, "Thomas, because you have seen Me, you have believed. Blessed are those who have not seen and yet have believed." And truly Jesus did many other signs in the presence of His disciples, which are not written in this book; but these are written that you may believe that Jesus is the Christ, the Son of God, and that believing you may have life in His name.

Jesus' disciples had seen the empty tomb and heard Mary Magdalene's report that Jesus was alive, but they had difficulty coming to terms with the full significance of what had happened. We know this because John tells us, **The same day at evening, being the first day of the week, . . . the doors were shut where the disciples were assembled, for fear of the Jews** (v. 19a). It was Sunday evening, the same day in which Mary had seen the risen Lord and reported it to the disciples, but they were huddled in the upper room with the doors locked because they were frightened the Jewish authorities might be looking for those who had been with Jesus. One would think that the possibility that their Lord was alive again from the dead would have dispelled all their fears, but that was not the case. They were a bit slow to grasp what was taking place.

John then writes, **Jesus came and stood in the midst, and said to them, "Peace be with you." When He had said this, He showed them His hands and His side. Then the disciples were glad when they saw the Lord. So Jesus said to them again, "Peace to you!"** (vv. 19b–21a). "Peace be with you" or "Peace to you" was the standard greeting of one Jew to another; even to this day, one Jew will say to his friend, "Shalom aleichem," or "Peace be upon you," and the other will respond, "Aleichem shalom," or "Upon you be peace." It is interesting to note that Jesus extended this greeting to His disciples not once but twice. This repetition is a signal for most of the scholars who look closely at the text of John that Jesus was telling His disciples something. These greetings are very reminiscent of words Jesus spoke to His disciples in the upper room on the night before His execution, when He pronounced His last will and testament. He said: "Peace I leave with you, My peace I give to you; not as the world gives do I give to you. Let not your heart be troubled, neither let it be afraid" (14:27). Before His death, He promised the full reality of the bequest of His peace on these people. Now, having been raised from the dead, He entered their midst and said, "Peace be with you." Then He showed them His hands and His side, as if to say, "I did what I said I was going to do, and I have won that peace for you." Finally, He said a second time, "Peace to you!"

Then Jesus said, **"As the Father has sent Me, I also send you"** (v. 21b). This is John's version of Jesus' giving of the Great Commission (see Matt. 28:19-20; Mark 16:15; Luke 24:47), in which the risen Christ commissioned His disciples to go into all of the earth, to every tribe, to every tongue, to every nation, proclaiming the work of Jesus. In John's account, Jesus gave the disciples their commission in the context of His own mission. He said, "I remind you, the Father sent Me here. And just as the Father has sent Me, so I send you. Carry on My mission!"

An Object Lesson on the Spirit

When Jesus said this, He did something unusual, something that is difficult to understand. John tells us: **And when He had said this, He breathed on them, and said to them, "Receive the Holy Spirit"** (v. 22). Jesus had told the disciples that the Spirit would not fall on them until He left them; that is, the Spirit would come after His ascension to His Father in heaven (16:7). We know that the Spirit did indeed come at Pentecost, weeks after Jesus returned to heaven (Acts 2). But now, well before His ascension, Jesus told the disciples, "Receive the Holy Spirit." What is this about?

There have been numerous attempts to explain how this incident fits with Pentecost. Rather than rehearsing all of the alternatives, let me say what I think Jesus had in mind. The prophets of the Old Testament not only preached with their mouths the word they were given, they also communicated through object lessons, acting out certain dimensions of the promises of God that were yet to be fulfilled. I believe Jesus was doing that here. This was not a surprise Pentecost; rather, it was an object lesson to the disciples about what was going to take place in the very near future on the Day of Pentecost.

It is significant that Jesus depicted the disciples' reception of the Holy Spirit by the gesture of exhaling. When Nicodemus came to Jesus by night, Jesus told him: "Unless one is born of water and the Spirit, he cannot enter the kingdom of God. . . . The wind blows where it wishes, and you hear the sound of it, but cannot tell where it comes from and where it goes. So is everyone who is born of the Spirit" (3:5-8). In that statement, Jesus played with the language, because the Greek word translated as "wind" is the same word translated as "Spirit." Jesus said to Nicodemus: "The *pneuma* blows where it wishes. . . . So is everyone who is born of the *pneuma*." Furthermore, *pneuma* also can be translated as "breath," so when Jesus breathed on the disciples, He was equating His breath with the giving of the Holy Spirit. Jesus had already promised that He would send the Spirit (16:7), and now He dramatized that promise. This object lesson that Jesus gave is one of the reasons why the church says that the Holy Spirit proceeds not only from the Father but from the Son. So in this symbolic action, He gave the disciples a foretaste of what would take place at Pentecost, when He would pour the Holy Spirit upon them.

Jesus added, **"If you forgive the sins of any, they are forgiven them; if you retain the sins of any, they are retained"** (v. 23). Jesus was speaking here to the apostolic authority the disciples were about to take on. Under the power of the Spirit, they would have authority to declare God's condemnation of sin and His offer of forgiveness.

The Unbelieving Disciple

We now come to the story of Doubting Thomas. John writes: **Now Thomas, called the Twin, one of the twelve, was not with them when Jesus came. The other disciples therefore said to him, "We have seen the Lord." So he said to them, "Unless I see in His hands the print of the nails, and put my finger into the print of the nails, and put my hand into His side, I will not believe"** (vv. 24–25). Thomas had missed the incredible first appearance of Jesus to the disciples in the upper room. When they told him about it, he was skeptical. He said: "Thanks for your testimony. I can see you're excited with what you think you've seen, but I must see for myself. The only thing that will satisfy me is irrefutable, empirical evidence. Unless I see Him, hear Him, and touch Him, I will not believe."

Thomas got the chance he wanted. John writes: **And after eight days His disciples were again inside, and Thomas with them. Jesus came, the doors being shut, and stood in the midst, and said, "Peace to you!" Then He said to Thomas, "Reach your finger here, and look at My hands; and reach your hand here, and put it into My side. Do not be unbelieving, but believing"** (vv. 26–27). We don't know what elapsed in the eight days between the time when Thomas vocalized his unbelief and Christ's appearance recorded here. Maybe the other disciples spoke with Jesus in the interim and said: "Jesus, we're all with you, except Thomas. He's not going to believe unless he sees with his own eyes." On the other hand, maybe Jesus didn't need to hear a report from the rest of them. Knowing men's hearts, perhaps He already knew the state of Thomas's unbelief, just as He knows this very moment the state of our faith or lack of it.

This second appearance presumably was exclusively for the benefit of Thomas. Jesus said to him: "Thomas, here's what you want. Go ahead and put your finger into My wounds. Put your hand into the side where I was pierced by the spear." John doesn't say whether Thomas accepted Jesus' offer and touched the wounds. Apparently he didn't have to do that after all. When he saw the living Christ standing there, challenging him to touch His wounds, Thomas gave the highest confession of faith in Jesus that we read anywhere in Scripture. In a posture of worship, reverence, and adoration, **Thomas answered and said to Him, "My Lord and My God!"** (v. 28). He did not call Jesus "Teacher," "Master," or even "Messiah." The word translated as "Lord" here is the same word used in the Greek translation of the Old Testament for God's high name, Yahweh. Thomas confessed that Jesus was Yahweh, His God, standing before him in the flesh.

Maybe Thomas got carried away, as people were wont to do in biblical days. We remember on the occasion when Paul and Barnabas healed a crippled man in the city of Lystra, those who saw the miracle began to hail them as Zeus and Hermes, and made preparations to sacrifice to them. But Paul sternly rebuked them and said: "Men, why are you doing these things? We also are men with the same nature as you" (Acts 14:15). They stopped the people's attempt to worship them. Likewise, it is not uncommon in Scripture, when angels appear, for those who see them to be so awed by their supernatural endowments that they fall down and worship. In all such cases, the angels rebuke the people for committing an act of idolatry in worshiping anything or anyone less than God.

But when Thomas confessed the deity of Christ, there was no hint of rebuke from the lips of Jesus. Jesus did not say, like Paul did, "Stop that, I'm just a creature." Not only did He receive worship from Thomas, He pronounced His benediction on it. He said: **"Thomas, because you have seen Me, you have believed. Blessed are those who have not seen and yet have believed"** (v. 29). With these words, Jesus put His benediction on all who receive Him as Lord and as God, and He even gave an added benediction to those who believe without the benefit of being eyewitnesses.

The Favor of God

In order to fully understand what Jesus meant when He made these remarks to Thomas, we have to understand the concept of blessedness as it comes to us through the pages of Scripture. Some modern translations depict blessedness simply as a degree of joy or happiness that we experience. So if God says, "Blessed are you," we take that to mean that we're going to experience great happiness. Blessedness has that element in it, but that's not the primary sense of it. The primary meaning of blessedness is to be looked on favorably by God. It has more to do with the disposition of God than with our feelings. When Jesus said, "Blessed are those who have not seen and yet have believed," He was saying that God is pleased that there are people who believe in Christ who have never seen Him.

Why would that be? Having been a professor of philosophy most of my adult life, I've been deeply concerned about the question of epistemology. How do we know what we know? How can we know anything for sure? There are various ways by which we know truth—rational deduction, which gives us formal truth; empirical investigation, which gives us the physical evidence by which science makes decisions about reality; and other means. Then there is testimony, which includes the record of the past, the witness that is given to us from the pages of history. I believe that George Washington was the first president of the United States, even though I've never met him, I've never even seen a photograph of him, and I've never seen him on television. I believe that the historical record is reliable enough that I can accept the information that he was the first president of the United States.

What is the highest method of knowing something? I submit to you that the highest source of truth we can possibly have is the Word of God. The testimony of the Word of God is higher than rational deduction, higher than empirical evidence, and higher than historical testimony. That is what Jesus was saying. He did not say that hearsay is better evidence than eyewitness testimony. Remember how Jesus rebuked the two disciples on the road to Emmaus. He said to them, "O foolish ones, and slow of heart to believe in all that the prophets have spoken!" (Luke 24:25). Then He began to teach them about Himself from "all the Scriptures" (24:27). Thus, He showed them that God had prepared history for that moment.

If you believe in Christ today, one way or the other, you believe because of the testimony of sacred Scripture. The Bible is better than any epistemological source known to human science or investigation, and the Author of the Bible is pleased when men receive the testimony of sacred Scripture, get on their knees, and say, "My Lord and My God."

The last two verses of this chapter are usually seen as the climactic verses of the entire Gospel. John writes: **And truly Jesus did many other signs in the presence of His disciples, which are not written in this book; but these are written that you may believe that Jesus is the Christ, the Son of God, and that believing you may have life in His name** (vv. 30–31). John is saying: "I have provided this record for a reason—that my readers may believe that Jesus is the Christ, the Son of God." But he doesn't finish there. He doesn't say that these are written that people might believe the right things, that they might be orthodox, or that their theology might be sound. There is an added purpose beyond coming to the knowledge of the truth of Christ: "that believing you may have life in His name." John is echoing Jesus' own words: "I have come that they may have life" (John 10:10b). People who don't have Christ don't have life, and they don't even know it. To have the life that God created us to have, we must find it in the Son of God.

56

BREAKFAST
ON THE SEASHORE

John 21:1–14

After these things Jesus showed Himself again to the disciples at the Sea of Tiberias, and in this way He showed Himself: Simon Peter, Thomas called the Twin, Nathanael of Cana in Galilee, the sons of Zebedee, and two others of His disciples were together. Simon Peter said to them, "I am going fishing." They said to him, "We are going with you also." They went out and immediately got into the boat, and that night they caught nothing. But when the morning had now come, Jesus stood on the shore; yet the disciples did not know that it was Jesus. Then Jesus said to them, "Children, have you any food?" They answered Him, "No." And He said to them, "Cast the net on the right side of the boat, and you will find some." So they cast, and now they were not able to draw it in because of the multitude of fish. Therefore that disciple whom Jesus loved said to Peter, "It is the Lord!" Now when Simon Peter heard that it was the Lord, he put on his outer garment (for he had removed it), and plunged into the sea. But the other disciples came in the little boat (for they were not far from land, but about two hundred cubits), dragging the net with fish. Then, as soon as they had come to land, they saw a fire of coals there, and fish laid on it, and bread. Jesus said to them, "Bring some of the fish which you have just caught." Simon Peter went up and dragged the net to land, full of large fish, one hundred and fifty-three; and although there were so many, the net was not broken. Jesus said to them, "Come and eat breakfast." Yet none of the disciples dared ask Him, "Who are You?"—knowing that it was the Lord. Jesus then came and took the bread and gave it to them, and likewise the fish. This is now the third time Jesus showed Himself to His disciples after He was raised from the dead.

Many critical scholars believe that John 21 does not belong in the canon of Scripture. They cannot understand why John would have taken the trouble to add this lengthy account of another manifestation of the risen Christ when the climax of the book was reached at the end of Chapter 20, when John explained why he wrote the Gospel in the first place. But anyone who does serious reading of literature, particularly history and fiction, knows that it is customary to include some kind of epilogue to tie up the loose ends. One of the big loose ends in the Gospel of John is the status of Peter, who so dismally betrayed Jesus in his public denial.

We know Peter rushed to the tomb after Mary Magdalene brought word that Jesus' body was missing, and we know he was present in the upper room when Jesus twice appeared to the disciples there. But what about their relationship? We know that Jesus looked at Peter in the high priest's courtyard right after Peter had uttered his third denial with curses, and their eyes met (Luke 22:61). I cannot imagine any deeper level of shame a human being could experience than that which Peter must have felt when he saw Christ looking at him. I think John understood that and decided not to leave that loose end hanging. Thus, he wrote about the restoration of Peter in the second part of the incident that begins in this chapter.

An Unsuccessful Fishing Trip

John begins with these words: **After these things Jesus showed Himself again to the disciples at the Sea of Tiberias** (v. 1a). John immediately tells us he is reporting a showing, an unveiling, a manifestation, a visible revelation of Jesus in His resurrected state. This one takes place not in Jerusalem, the site of Jesus' first two appearances to the disciples, but in Galilee, on the shores of the Sea of Tiberias, or the Sea of Galilee. Jesus had sent word by the women who first went to His tomb that the disciples would see Him in Galilee (Matt. 28:10), and a number of the disciples made the trek north. John tells us who some of them were: **and in this way He showed Himself: Simon Peter, Thomas called the Twin, Nathanael of Cana in Galilee, the sons of Zebedee, and two others of His disciples were together** (vv. 1b–2). John mentions seven of the eleven disciples here. Three are named, but we know that the sons of Zebedee were James and John. Two other disciples are not identified.

We are told, **Simon Peter said to them, "I am going fishing." They said to him, "We are going with you also." They went out and immediately got into the boat, and that night they caught nothing** (v. 3). The disciples were waiting for Jesus to appear, so we should not conclude that Peter abandoned his mission in order to return to the profession of fishing. Neither was Peter wasting his time. Fishing was his business, his profession. He had been called from his nets to follow Jesus, to be a fisher of men (Matt. 4:18-20), but now, as he waited for the next summons of Christ, he said, "I'm going to go fishing." The others said, "We'll go along."

Their fishing trip was not successful. They fished all night but caught nothing. This part of the text is very reminiscent of a passage in Luke 5, which tells us that Jesus borrowed Peter's boat one day as a teaching platform, then suggested he row out into deeper water and let down his nets. Peter complained that he had fished all night with no success, but he nevertheless obeyed Jesus, and he subsequently caught a great number of fish. But there are striking dissimilarities between the two events, as we shall see. In fact, the only common elements are the disciples, the Sea of Galilee, the unsuccessful night of fishing, and Jesus' help. So it appears these were two separate incidents.

Peter Swims to Jesus

John continues: **But when the morning had now come, Jesus stood on the shore; yet the disciples did not know that it was Jesus. Then Jesus said to them, "Children, have you any food?" They answered Him, "No." And He said to them, "Cast the net on the right side of the boat, and you will find some." So they cast, and now they were not able to draw it in because of the multitude of fish** (vv. 4–6). Jesus appeared on the shore. He was about a hundred yards away (v. 8), and they did not recognize him at that distance. He called out to them, addressing them as "Children," which could be loosely translated as "fellows," "lads," or "boys," and asked whether they had any food. On this occasion, they apparently did not recognize His voice. When they told Him they had no food, He suggested they drop their net on the other side of the boat. Consider—the disciples did not know who was coaching them from the shore. They were professional fishermen. They had had their net out all night. Yet, they accepted the suggestion of this unknown person. The result was a huge catch of fish, so big they could not pull in the net.

Something about this incident tipped John off. He writes, **Therefore that disciple whom Jesus loved said to Peter, "It is the Lord!" Now when Simon Peter heard that it was the Lord, he put on his outer garment (for he had removed it), and plunged into the sea** (v. 7). Do you notice something strange about Peter's actions in this verse? When people spontaneously decide to go swimming, what do they do? They take their clothes *off*; they don't put them *on*. The Greek text indicates that Peter was naked, or close to it. He may have had his outer cloak draped over his body while the disciples were fishing, but when he decided to go to Jesus, he covered himself—but not to keep out the cold. In the Garden of Eden, after Adam and Eve sinned, they tried to cover their nakedness because of their shame under the gaze of the holy God. Now Peter was going to face the Savior he had denied and betrayed, so he covered himself and plunged into the water.

The fact that Peter *wanted* to go to Jesus marks a major difference between this incident and the other great catch of fish recorded in Luke 5. On that occasion, when Jesus told Peter where the fish were, he and his partners caught so many fish they filled two boats to the point of sinking. I have to say, if I had been in Peter's shoes, being a professional fisherman and now seeing the greatest catch of fish I had ever witnessed, I believe I would have said to Jesus: "Let's make a deal. Just one day a week, You come down here and do this little trick again, and I'll give You fifty percent of the business, because we are going to make a killing." However, that is not what Peter did.

When Peter saw the great catch of fish, he had a very strange response. He looked at Jesus and said, "Depart from me, for I am a sinful man, O Lord!" (Luke 5:8b). This is the universal response of people when they recognize the character of Jesus. It is the universal response of the creature who beholds the unveiled glory of the holy. Our basic nature is to put as much space between Christ and ourselves as we can. When Peter realized the One with whom he was dealing, he was overwhelmed with a sense of his guilt. He wanted relief from that guilt more than anything else, and that meant he wanted space between Jesus and himself. So he said, "Jesus, please leave, I can't stand it."

That was how Peter reacted early on in the ministry of Jesus. But that was not what he did when Jesus gave this second great catch of fish. This time, even though he had so much more to be ashamed of, so much more to be embarrassed about, instead of trying to put distance between himself and his Savior, he dove in the water and swam as quickly as he could. He couldn't wait to get to the shore, where Jesus stood.

When I was in college, I worked as a counselor at a Jewish boys' camp in Ohio. There was a big lake there and I was in charge of the waterfront. One afternoon, a tremendous storm came through Ohio; there were sightings of tornados, and the day turned almost as dark as night. It was such a violent storm that we sounded the alarm at the camp, which was the signal that every camper, every counselor, and every staff member had to come right away to the dining hall for safety. When it seemed everyone had arrived at the dining hall, we made a count. We found that two campers were missing, so some of us went out to look for them. I headed toward the waterfront, and I clearly saw at the end of the lake, about four hundred or five hundred yards out, these two campers in a canoe, fighting as hard as they could against the wind and the waves to get back to safety.

There was an empty canoe on the shore, so I jumped into it and went down the lake as fast as I could; I had a tailwind, so it took me about five minutes to get to there. When I got to them, they were terrified because lightning was flashing and they were in an aluminum canoe. I got them turned around so that they could paddle into the wind and got them on a course to safety. Then I had to get myself in. Against the current and the wind, it took me forty-five minutes to travel that four hundred or five hundred yards back to shore. If I could have abandoned the canoe and jumped in the water, that's what I would have done. I felt like Peter at that point—I couldn't wait to get to the shore.

Jesus Serves His Disciples (Again)

So Peter swam to shore. John then tells us: **But the other disciples came in the little boat (for they were not far from land, but about two hundred cubits), dragging the net with fish. Then, as soon as they had come to land, they saw a fire of coals there, and fish laid on it, and bread** (vv. 8–9). The other disciples followed in the little boat, dragging the net with the fish. When they reached the shore, they saw a fire of coals. That's an odd detail. Why did John mention the fire? What is its significance? It may have no significance at all. But remember, this narrative is heavily concerned with Peter. Two times in the Gospel of John we find mention of fires made of coals—here and in 18:18, where John recounts the events in the high priest's courtyard after Jesus' arrest, when Peter stood warming his hands beside a fire of coals as various people asked him whether he was with Jesus. But this time, instead of servant girls and soldiers tending the fire, it was Jesus.

John writes: **Jesus said to them, "Bring some of the fish which you have just caught." Simon Peter went up and dragged the net to land, full of large fish, one hundred and fifty-three; and although there were so many, the net was not broken** (vv. 10–11). Hearing Jesus' command, Peter went and dragged the net to the land by himself. His attitude seems to have been, "Whatever you say, Lord."

John provides another odd detail here—there were one hundred and fifty-three fish in the net. I'm not sure why John tells us this and I'm less sure it is important, but some giants of church history have given somewhat bizarre interpretations of this fact. Jerome pointed out that the naturalists of his era argued that there were a hundred and fifty-three known species of fish at that time, so he believed John was saying that in their work as fishers of men, the disciples would be catching people from every tribe, every nation and every tongue. It was a nice theory. Unfortunately, the naturalists Jerome cited had actually enumerated a hundred and fifty-seven varieties of fish, not a hundred and fifty-three. Others have looked to obscure references, such as the image of the river of life in Ezekiel 47, where we find mention of "a...multitude of fish" (v. 9). Still others hold that the disciples wanted to divide the fish, so they had to count them to make a fair distribution. Unfortunately, the number wasn't divisible by seven. Another view is that the disciples counted the fish simply because it was a record-breaking catch, and they wanted to see how many they had landed. In the end, we don't really know whether there was any significance to the number or not.

John then writes: **Jesus said to them, "Come and eat breakfast." Yet none of the disciples dared ask Him, "Who are You?"—knowing that it was the Lord. Jesus then came and took the bread and gave it to them, and likewise the fish** (vv. 12–13). This was a poignant moment, as Jesus invited His disciples to have breakfast after their night of labor. Then He Himself gave them bread and fish to eat. This was the same Jesus who had washed their feet in the upper room, who had taken their places on the cross, and who had assumed their sin in His person at Golgotha. Jesus still served them, providing their daily bread there on the seashore. And so He provides for you and for me, His disciples in the present day.

57

"FEED MY SHEEP"

John 21:15–25

So when they had eaten breakfast, Jesus said to Simon Peter, "Simon, son of Jonah, do you love Me more than these?" He said to Him, "Yes, Lord; You know that I love You." He said to him, "Feed My lambs." He said to him again a second time, "Simon, son of Jonah, do you love Me?" He said to Him, "Yes, Lord; You know that I love You." He said to him, "Tend My sheep." He said to him the third time, "Simon, son of Jonah, do you love Me?" Peter was grieved because He said to him the third time, "Do you love Me?" And he said to Him, "Lord, You know all things; You know that I love You." Jesus said to him, "Feed My sheep. Most assuredly, I say to you, when you were younger, you girded yourself and walked where you wished; but when you are old, you will stretch out your hands, and another will gird you and carry you where you do not wish." This He spoke, signifying by what death he would glorify God. And when He had spoken this, He said to him, "Follow Me." Then Peter, turning around, saw the disciple whom Jesus loved following, who also had leaned on His breast at the supper, and said, "Lord, who is the one who betrays You?" Peter, seeing him, said to Jesus, "But Lord, what about this man?" Jesus said to him, "If I will that he remain till I come, what is that to you? You follow Me." Then this saying went out among the brethren that this disciple would not die. Yet Jesus did not say to him that he would not die, but, "If I will that he remain till I come, what is that to you?" This is the disciple who testifies of these things, and wrote these things; and we know that his testimony is true. And there are also many other things that Jesus did, which if they were written one by one, I suppose that even the world itself could not contain the books that would be written. Amen.

The previous chapter and this one form something of a two-part "concluding episode" to our study of the Gospel of John, as both deal with the final chapter of the book, which is entirely concerned with the final appearance of Christ to His disciples that John records. Our story so far: Jesus appeared on the shore of the Sea of Galilee as several of His disciples were fishing, and He granted them a miraculous catch of fish. Peter then swam to shore out of a strong desire to be in the presence of Christ while the disciples followed in the boat, dragging the overflowing net. Jesus then served breakfast to the disciples on the beach. In this final passage, the focus is squarely on Jesus and Peter, and we read here the final recorded interchange between the big fisherman and his Lord. It is not without significance that the interrogation proceeds in the manner it does.

A Higher Degree of the Highest Love?

John writes, **So when they had eaten breakfast, Jesus said to Simon Peter, "Simon, son of Jonah, do you love Me more than these?"** (v. 15a). A couple of the words in this question deserve comment. The first is *love*. As I'm sure you know, there are three words in Greek that can be translated into the English language as "love." The first is *eros*, which refers to sexual love. The second is *phileo*, which generally refers to brotherly love. That's why Philadelphia is known as "The City of Brotherly Love." The third is *agape*, which is the highest expression of love mentioned in the New Testament. It is that spiritual love that is rooted and grounded in the power of God. In this question, Jesus used the verb form of *agape*. He was asking whether Peter had the highest form of love for Him.

The second word I'd like to comment on is *these*. This word is ambiguous. What or who are "these?" One possibility is that Jesus was asking: "Do you love Me more than these things that have been such an integral part of your life: your nets, the boat, the fishing equipment? Do I take precedence over your career, over your vocation?" A second option is that He was asking, "Do you love Me more than you love your fellow disciples?" A third possible meaning is that Jesus was asking, "Do you love Me more than these other men love Me?" We do not know conclusively what our Lord meant.

My educated guess is that He was asking Peter, "Do you love Me more than the rest of the disciples love Me?" This is why I think that: Jesus taught that "to whom little is forgiven, the same loves little" (Luke 7:47b). The corollary is true: he who is forgiven much, loves much. There is a sense in which the depth of our affection for Christ is inseparably related to the depth of our understanding of that which we have been forgiven. Peter understood that of all of those surviving, he had betrayed Christ more deeply than the rest. Therefore, in being forgiven, restored, and invited back, not only into the fellowship of Christ, but into the ministry of Christ—rather than being dismissed from ministry for the rest of his life for his scandalous transgression—he saw the grace of God more fully than the rest. I believe that was what Jesus was driving at with His question.

John continues, **He [Peter] said to Him, "Yes, Lord; You know that I love You"** (v. 15b). There is irony in this answer. When Jesus predicted Peter's denial, Peter replied, "Even if I have to die with You, I will not deny You!" (Matt. 26:35a). Essentially he was saying: "No, Lord, you don't know what I'm going to do. You don't know what's in my heart. I would never deny You." Here on the shore of the Sea of Galilee, it appears Peter had learned not to dispute Jesus' knowledge of what was going on inside of him.

All commentators notice that when Peter said, "Yes, Lord; You know that I love You," he used the Greek word *phileo*. Jesus used the Greek *agape* in His question, but Peter responded with *phileo*. Many commentators believe the different words indicate Jesus was challenging Peter to a higher love than Peter had been able to demonstrate to this point. But other commentators point out that throughout his writings, John uses the words *phileo* and *agape* interchangeably, so there is no reason to assume that the change in words here is due to anything more than stylistic preferences without any profound theological significance. I'm convinced of that. I don't think Peter was saying, "I love You, but not to the degree You want me to love You." After all, Peter said, "You know the answer to this question."

The Requirement of Love

What is more important to me in this text is what Jesus said love for Him requires. John writes, **He [Jesus] said to him, "Feed My lambs"** (v. 15c). If Peter was going to be restored, if he was going to be a pastor, a shepherd to the flock of Christ, loving Jesus meant feeding Christ's lambs. Let's quickly run ahead: **He said to him again a second time, "Simon, son of**

Jonah, do you love Me?" He said to Him, "Yes, Lord; You know that I love You." He said to him, "Tend My sheep." He said to him the third time, "Simon, son of Jonah, do you love Me?" Peter was grieved because He said to him the third time, "Do you love Me?" And he said to Him, "Lord, You know all things; You know that I love You." Jesus said to him, "Feed My sheep" (vv. 16–17). Some have made much out of the variation in the terms here—"Feed My lambs," "Tend My sheep," and "Feed My sheep." Some believe the lambs are the new converts and the sheep are the old ones, and that there's a difference between tending and feeding. I don't think Jesus' words had any such meaning. I think He was simply saying, "If you want to be a pastor, a shepherd, then feed My sheep; don't starve them. Make them your highest concern."

We are witnessing a great tragedy in the revolution of worship in the United States. Following the model of "seeker-sensitive" worship is harming the church. The idea is that if you want your church to grow, you must design worship to meet the desires and the interests of non-Christians. I believe in seeker-sensitive worship, but not in the way most modern worship theorists define it. The Bible says in our natural state, no one seeks after God. It is only when a person's heart is regenerated by the Spirit of God so that he is born again that he begins to seek God. That is why Jonathan Edwards said that seeking after God should be the main business of the life of the Christian.

On the night of my conversion, I went to the dorm parking lot with my best friend in college. We got in my car and I turned the engine over, then hit myself in the shirt pocket. I said to my buddy, "I'm out of cigarettes; I need to go back in the dorm." So I went in, down the stairs to the cigarette machine, and got a pack of Luckies for a quarter. When I turned to go back upstairs, there was a fellow there who said, "Sit down." So I did and he told me about Jesus. I wasn't seeking Jesus; I was seeking cigarettes, but I found Jesus. Seeking after God starts at conversion; it doesn't end there. That's why a truly seeker-sensitive worship service is designed for Christians.

The saints, the holy ones, those called out from the world assemble together on Sunday mornings to be fed. We are to do evangelism, engage in outreach, and be involved in ministries of mercy, but Sunday morning belongs to the sheep. It is the task of the pastor and of the church to feed the sheep. If someone who is not a sheep comes in, that's fine, but we're not going to change the menu and give the sheep goats' food. Worship is for the sheep.

Why did Jesus put so much emphasis on feeding the sheep? When the sheep of Christ are fed, nurtured, and filled with the strength of Christ and of His word, they become a mighty army turned loose on the world. Babies have almost no influence in a culture. Before they can turn the world upside down, they have to grow up, they have to become mature, and that happens as they are fed the Word of God. Nothing less will do.

Notice that when Jesus spoke to Peter, He did not say, "Peter, if you love Me, feed the *goats*." Neither did He say, "Peter, take care of *your* flock; feed *your* sheep." He said, "Feed *My* sheep, feed *My* lambs, tend *My* sheep." He said, "If you love Me, if I make you a pastor, whatever else you do, take care of *My* sheep—feed them, tend them, strengthen them." Those who are called as pastors are undershepherds, given the task of tending Jesus' sheep.

John tells us that when Jesus asked Peter the same question for a third time, Peter was grieved. It doesn't require a rocket scientist to figure out why Jesus asked the question three times. Peter had denied Him three times, so in his restoration, Jesus required Peter to profess his faith in triplicate, too.

A Look into the Future

Jesus then changed direction and said: **"Most assuredly, I say to you, when you were younger, you girded yourself and walked where you wished; but when you are old, you will stretch out your hands, and another will gird you and carry you where you do not wish."** **This He spoke, signifying by what death he would glorify God. And when He had spoken this, He said to him, "Follow Me"** (vv. 18–19). This conversation took place a little more than thirty years before Peter met his death at the hands of Nero in Rome. Tradition says that Peter was crucified upside down. John says these cryptic words of Jesus here—"you will stretch out your hands, and another will gird you"—were Jesus' prophetic forecast for how Peter's life would end. Nevertheless, Jesus said to Peter, "Follow Me," and despite this Sword of Damocles hanging over his head for thirty years, Peter did just that. He followed Jesus and he fed the Lord's sheep.

John then writes: **Then Peter, turning around, saw the disciple whom Jesus loved following, who also had leaned on His breast at the supper, and said, "Lord, who is the one who betrays You?" Peter, seeing him, said to Jesus, "But Lord, what about this man?"** (vv. 20–21). The disciple whom Jesus loved, John himself, apparently heard the exchange between Jesus and Peter. He seems to have been nearby, and Peter, seeing him, said, "Lord, what about him?" It's not clear what Peter was asking, but let's assume Peter asked, "You have told me what's going to become of me; what's going to happen to John?" History tells us that John was the only one of the apostles who was not martyred for the faith, though he did not escape persecution, for he was exiled to the island of Patmos.

How did Jesus reply to Peter? He said: **"If I will that he remain till I come, what is that to you? You follow Me"** (v. 22). John then tells us that this answer came to be widely misinterpreted among the Christians: **Then this saying went out among the brethren that this disciple would not die. Yet Jesus did not say to him that he would not die, but, "If I will that he remain till I come, what is that to you?"** (v. 23). In other words, many thought Jesus had said that John would still be alive at the second coming, but John denies that was what Jesus meant. Jesus was simply telling Peter: "What happens to John is none of your concern. I'm not going to give a prophecy about each of you. Just follow Me and do what I require you to do."

As is so often the case, Peter was a picture of us when he asked this question. If the Lord gives me one thing, I think everybody should get it, or if you get something I don't get, I say, "What's the matter with me? Why didn't I get it?" The Lord has jobs for each of us to do, and what others do is ultimately none of our business. Each of us must do what God has given him or her to do, and fulfill the mandate of Christ.

John goes on: **This is the disciple who testifies of these things, and wrote these things; and we know that his testimony is true** (v. 24). Why did John feel the need to attest to his own credibility here? As a Jew, he knew the sanctity of an oath before God and the severity of the punishment for false witness; he understood the danger to his soul if he vowed and did not pay. So here, at the very end of his Gospel, John takes an oath, and he says of his testimony, "We know that this testimony is true." John is apparently using the editorial "we" here, declaring that, in the sight of God, what he has written is true.

Finally, John adds this footnote: **And there are also many other things that Jesus did, which if they were written one by one, I suppose that even the world itself could not contain the books that would be written. Amen** (v. 25). He is saying: "I've given you just the tip of the iceberg. Time doesn't permit me to record everything that Jesus did during His earthly ministry." There could be many Gospels testifying to the person and work of Christ, so many that the whole world could not contain them. But we have enough. I can't contain the Gospel of John; can you? The record that we have is enough to sate our appetites and call us back to this testimony again and again and again. Amen.

FOR FURTHER STUDY

Borchert, Gerald L. *John 1–11* and *John 12–21*. The New American Commentary. Nashville: B&H, 1996, 2002.

Carson, D. A. *The Gospel According to John*. Pillar New Testament Commentary. Leicester: Apollos, 1991.

Hendriksen, William. *Exposition of the Gospel According to John: Two Volumes Complete in One*. New Testament Commentary. Grand Rapids: Baker Academic, 2002.

Keener, Craig S. *The Gospel of John*. Peabody, Mass.: Hendrickson, 2003.

Kostenberger, Andreas J. *John*. Baker Exegetical Commentary on the New Testament. Grand Rapids: Baker Academic, 2004.

Morris, Leon. *The Gospel According to John*. New International Commentary on the New Testament. Grand Rapids: Eerdmans, 1971.

Ridderbos, Herman. *The Gospel of John*. Grand Rapids: Eerdmans, 1997.

INDEX OF NAMES

ABOUT THE AUTHOR

Dr. R.C. Sproul is the founder and chairman of Ligonier Ministries, an international multimedia ministry based in Sanford, Florida. He also serves as copastor at Saint Andrew's Chapel in Sanford and as chancellor of Reformation Bible College, and his teaching can be heard around the world on the daily radio program *Renewing Your Mind*.

During his distinguished academic career, Dr. Sproul helped train men for the ministry as a professor at several theological seminaries.

He is the author of more than one hundred books, including *The Holiness of God*, *Chosen by God*, *The Invisible Hand*, *Faith Alone*, *Everyone's a Theologian*, *Truths We Confess*, *The Truth of the Cross*, and *The Prayer of the Lord*. He also served as general editor of the *Reformation Study Bible* and has written several children's books, including *The Knight's Map*.

ABOUT LIGONIER MINISTRIES

Ligonier Ministries, founded in 1971 by Dr. R. C. Sproul, is an international teaching ministry that strives to help people grow in their knowledge of God and His holiness.

"We believe that when the Bible is taught clearly, God is seen in all of His majesty and holiness—hearts are conquered, minds are renewed, and communities are transformed," Dr. Sproul says.

From its base near Orlando, Florida, Ligonier carries out its mission in various ways:

- By producing and broadcasting solid, in-depth teaching resources.
- By publishing and promoting books true to the historic Christian faith.
- By publishing *Tabletalk*, a monthly theological/devotional magazine.
- By publishing the *Reformation Study Bible*.
- By training and equipping young adults, laypeople, and pastors through Reformation Bible College and the Ligonier Academy of Biblical and Theological Studies.
- By producing and promoting conferences.

For more information, please visit Ligonier.org